ACTION!

The Action Movie A-Z

ACTION!

The Action Movie A-Z

by Marshall Julius

Indiana University Press
Bloomington and Indianapolis

'You want results? You have to go to the Schwarzeneggers,
the Stallones, and, to a lesser extent, the Van Dammes.'

- Bart Simpson

Dedication

For all those cheerful, laid-back Saturday afternoons spent watching the classics on TV. For sitting through a decade of rubbery monster movies with me at the cinema. For braving *RoboCop*, and getting it, and loving it... This book's for you, Mum.

Acknowledgements

Since they threatened to kill me if I didn't mention them first, I'd just like to thank Paul MacGechan, Michael Kaufman, Ronald Fogelman, Justin Kaye and 'Sensei' Steve DeCaro for letting me live. Laura Zackon, Jo Ware, Lisa MacGechan and Lyndsey Conway have also been pretty cool lately. My mother's the greatest, and both she and my brother Anthony (a serious Arnie fan) have been very supportive. Thanks also to Martina Stansbie, James Cameron-Wilson, David Clark, Jeremy Clarke, Lise Colyer, Michael Darvell, Karen Price, Howard Maxford, Mark Fitzpatrick, Howard Posner, Brian Robinson, Robert Sims, Dal Uppal and Peter Ware. Finally, I would like to reveal to the world that my editor, Richard Reynolds, is, in fact, Superman.

Introduction

Where do you turn for a fair review of an action movie? Most critics have such a problem with ultra-violent mayhem that they can't tell the good from the bad. And the next time somebody accuses an action film of provoking copycat violence, they're cruising for a bunch of fives. The honest, uncomplicated truth of the matter is that these fine flicks are not here to corrupt, but to entertain. They do not exist to prompt weak-minded individuals into random acts of madness. They're escapist, not instructional, and if you need proof of their popularity, box-office figures suggest that there are one or two billion people out there who kinda like a dose of sex and violence before bedtime. I'm not advocating real-life violence. I just want to see it up on the screen, where it belongs.

Vengeful cops and car chases, lunatic villains and martial arts masters, male-bonding, gun fights and super secret agents, swords and sorcerers, wartime Nazi-bashing, boys' own adventures, casual destruction and general death-defiance... this is what we want to see, and if you feel the same way, *Action!* is for you, a fan's guide to the wackiest genre of 'em all, with 250 key movies rated and reviewed, star biographies (**Death Becomes Them**), quotation favourites (**Verbal Assaults**), a vast amount of trivia (**Trivialists**) and a quiz (**Brainstorms**) designed to keep you on your toes.

The scoring system is pretty straightforward, from a pitiful mini gun (for hopelessly boring rubbish) to a fabulous five guns (for all-time action classics), with the best of the worst, the funniest and trashiest ranking somewhere in between.

You're travelling through another dimension, a dimension not only of sight and sound but of mind; a journey into a wondrous land whose boundaries are that of imagination. That's the signpost up ahead – your next stop, the Action Zone. You've got your guide, now it's time to explore. Good luck, and may the Force be with you.

Marshall Julius

Above the Law (aka Nico)

USA 1988 99 mins

Steven Seagal piles the bodies high and wide as he guns for cardboard psycho Henry Silva in this unremarkable thriller, a cop movie with a taste for blood and a blunt political edge. Bones snap and bullets fly as single-minded Chicago cop Nico Toscani (Stevie) hunts a well-connected gang of ruthless CIA assassins on the streets of Chicago, swaggering from one violent confrontation to the next, hampered only by a screenplay which takes itself too seriously, a feeble supporting cast and a director intent on adding depth to a plot which doesn't deserve the effort.

Seagal made his screen debut with this one, stumbling over the acting segments, but cracking skulls with the ruthless efficiency of a martial arts master. Sorely lacking in the charisma department, Seagal puts on a brave face and delivers attitude a-plenty, a Dirty Harry wannabe with some deadly moves and the shortest of fuses.

'You guys think you're above the law', he hisses, 'well you ain't above mine.' He's tough, that's for sure, and extremely Italian. Who else would come up with a threat like, 'If I find out you're lying I'll come back and kill you in your own kitchen'?

Henry Silva, meanwhile, is as coolly certifiable as ever, a 2-D TV villain with a vicious streak no wider, in fact, than Nico's own. After all, they're both trained killers who take pleasure in tormenting and exterminating their enemies, and if you're up for their particular brand of violence, there's a great deal of mayhem here to enjoy. Just nothing to get your blood boiling.

Director: Andrew Davis; **Producers:** Steven Seagal, Andrew Davis; **Screenplay:** Steven Pressfield, Ronald Shusett, Andrew Davis, based on a story by Steven Seagal, Andrew Davis; **Production Design:** Maher Ahmad; **Editor:** Michael Brown; **Photography:** Robert Steadman; **Music:** David M. Frank; **Cast:** Steven Seagal, Pam Grier, Henry Silva, Daniel Faraldo, Sharon Stone, Nicholas Kusenko.

A.W.O.L. (aka Lionheart, Wrong Bet)

USA 1990 108 mins

Kicking off with the savage flame-grilling of a hapless LA drug dealer, A.W.O.L. leaps to North Africa where we meet the victim's brother, a French Legionnaire named Lyon (Jean-Claude Van Damme, wooden but agile) who promptly busts out of camp, absent without a brain, and heads for the States to be with his sibling. Predictably enough, by the time Lyon makes it to the US his brother is toast, but rather than seek revenge, as any respectable action hero would, Lyon decides that it's more important to bond with his niece and widowed sister-in-law, and earn enough cash to be able to take them to safety, far away from the city.

Now, this might not sound like much of an action movie yet, but when you take on board the fact that Lyon earns his pocket money as underworld street-fighter 'Lionheart', guided by ruthless promoter Cynthia (Deborah Rennard) and hustler sidekick Joshua (Harrison Page), it suddenly becomes clear that violence is at the top of this movie's agenda. Pursued by a couple of chunky legionnaires intent on bringing him to justice, Lyon keeps his head down and his fists flying as he takes on an increasingly challenging range of fighters (all of them trained by *Bloodsport*'s Frank Dux), from *Only the Strong*'s Paco Christian Prieto to man mountain Atilla (Abdel Qissi), a posturing killer with freaky sideburns and a taste for ripping people in half.

Elsewhere, be prepared for a deluge of ham-handed sentiment, a desperate *Pretty Woman*-style shopping scene and, yes, another trademark Jean-Claude Van Damme butt shot. Although *A.W.O.L.* suffers from a chronic lack of direction and general shortage of imagination, the good news is that no matter where you are in the movie, the next no-holds-barred, one-on-one fight scene is never very far away, but you'd best be prepared for one encounter to look much the same as the next because variety is a spice this film makes do without.

Director: Sheldon Lettich; **Producers:** Ash R. Shah, Eric Karson; **Screenplay:** Sheldon Lettich, Jean-Claude Van Damme, based on a screenplay by S.N. Warren, story by Jean-Claude Van Damme; **Production Design:** Gregory Pickrell; **Editor:** Mark Conte; **Photography:** Robert C. New; **Music:** John Scott; **Cast:** Jean-Claude Van Damme, Harrison Page, Deborah Rennard, Lisa Pelikan, Ashley Johnson, Brian Thompson, Abdel Qissi.

Action Jackson

USA 1988 95 mins

Carl Weathers gives Craig T. Nelson a face full o' bicep in *Action Jackson*.

Long before RoboCop patrolled the streets of Detroit, an earlier breed of law enforcer tore off his shirt, pumped up his pecs, oiled down his bod and played the hero game. Jericho Jackson was his name, excessive force his only game, a mighty, macho superman capable of apocalyptic destruction and breathtaking feats of obnoxious behaviour. Villains quake and ladies swoon as 'Action' struts his stuff in this lunatic blaxploitation picture from producer Joel Silver. Impossible action, outrageous (and often unintentional) humour, a liberal sprinkling of nudity (Sharon Stone before *Basic Instinct*, Vanity after Prince) and a jazzy, funky soundtrack combine to create the perfect showcase for tough guy Carl Weathers, a leading man at last, if only for this one film.

A respected pillar of the community, businessman Peter Dellaplane (Craig T. Nelson) is, of course, a complete scumbag. Only Action knows the truth, and only he can do what's right, namely kill a bunch of people and wreck half of Detroit in the name of justice. Befriending Dellaplane's wife Patrice (Stone) and teaming up with junkie singer Sydney (Vanity), Jackson jumps through windows, pounds gigantic henchmen, outruns speeding cabs and proves just how sensitive he is when, shortly after a man is blown apart in a huge explosion, comments that 'there wasn't enough of him left to spread on a pizza'.

If you're on the prowl for some good, dumb, chaotic fun, you've found the perfect B-movie.

 Joel Silver often uses the same actors and stunt players over and over, and why not? In this movie alone, *Predator*'s Carl Weathers leads the way, *Commando*'s Bill Duke plays his Captain, *Die Hard*'s Robert Davi plays a freaky informant and *Lethal Weapon*'s Al Leong pops up as Dellaplane's chauffeur.

Director: Craig R. Baxley; **Producer:** Joel Silver; **Screenplay:** Robert Reneau; **Production Design:** Virginia Randolph; **Editor:** Mark Helfrich; **Photography:** Matthew F. Leonetti; **Music:** Herbie Hancock, Michael Kamen; **Cast:** Carl Weathers, Craig T. Nelson, Vanity, Sharon Stone, Tomas F. Wilson, Bill Duke, Robert Davi.

The Adventures of Don Juan

USA 1948 110 mins

'I have loved you since the beginning of time', vows Don Juan. 'But', replies the lovely maiden, 'you only met me yesterday.' 'Why', he declares, 'that was when time began!' Oh yes, we could all learn a lot from Don Juan, legendary lover, practised swordsman, charming rogue. And who better to play him than Hollywood's favourite scoundrel, Errol Flynn, a man whose appetites matched that of the seventeenth-century Lothario?

A grand swashbuckling spectacular with laughs, thrills and a hell of a lot of romance (usually, we don't go in for this sort of thing, but it's fun - and instructional - to see Flynn in action), *The Adventures of Don Juan* follows the dashing one as he returns to Spain, wows the ladies, earns the trust of a Queen (Viveca Lindfors, quite a babe in her day) and battles the evil forces of the dastardly Duke de Lorca (Robert Douglas), a 'boo-hiss' type of villain with designs on the throne.

Assisted by perennial sidekick Alan Hale, Flynn and company engage in brief bursts of lively, light-hearted action throughout, building to a glorious staircase duel as Don and the Duke settle their differences man-to-menace. Enjoy!

Director: Vincent Sherman; **Producer:** Jerry Wald; **Screenplay:** George Oppenheimer, Harry Kurnitz, based on a story by Herbert Dalmas; **Production Design:** Edward Carrere; **Editor:** Alan Crossland Jr; **Photography:** Elwood Bredell; **Music:** Max Steiner; **Cast:** Errol Flynn, Viveca Lindfors, Robert Douglas, Alan Hale, Romney Brent, Ann Rutherford, Raymond Burr. **Academy Award:** Best Costumes.

The Adventures of Robin Hood
USA 1938 102 mins 🔫 🔫 🔫 🔫 🔫

Errol Flynn has the time of his life robbing from the rich, giving to the poor, romancing fair Maid Marion (Olivia de Havilland) and battling vile Prince John (Claude Rains, the original Invisible Man) while modelling the snuggest green tights in creation (not many people realize that nylon was available in medieval England) in what is undoubtedly the greatest Hollywood swashbuckler of 'em all.

The gang's all here, from Friar Tuck (Eugene Pallette) to Little John (Alan Hale), as brave, bold Sir Robin (Flynn), consummate archer, good-hearted outlaw and leader of men, struggles to free England from the clutches of absent King Richard's greedy younger brother, John.

With a record-breaking budget of $2 million (at the time, it was the most Warner Bros. had ever spent on a movie), directors William Keighley and Michael Curtiz (whose job was to pump up the action) do a grand, glossy job, bringing the legend to life with a collection of show-stopping rescues, escapes, ambushes, assaults and, best of all, a classic one-on-one encounter between Sherwood Forest's favourite hero and the despicable Sir Guy of Gibson, a truly magnificent henchman with no time for small talk, a master stroke of malice from the great Basil Rathbone, whose swordfighting skills were considered beyond compare in Hollywood, although, since he played mostly villains, he rarely got to win on-screen (other examples of his art can be found in *Captain Blood* and *The Mark of Zorro*).

Add to this a rousing, Oscar-winning soundtrack from the incomparable Erich Wolfgang Korngold, and you have yourselves one hell of an entertaining movie.

Directors: Michael Curtiz, William Keighley; **Producer:** Hal B. Wallis; **Screenplay:** Norman Reilly Raine, Seton I. Miller; **Production Design:** Carl Jules Weyl; **Editor:** Ralph Dawson; **Photography:** Tony Gaudio; **Music:** Erich Wolfgang Korngold; **Cast:** Errol Flynn, Olivia de Havilland, Basil Rathbone, Claude Rains, Alan Hale, Eugene Pallette, Patric Knowles, Melville Cooper, Ian Hunter. **Academy Awards:** Best... Score, Art Direction, Editing.

Aliens
USA 1986 137 mins 🔫 🔫 🔫 🔫

Director James Cameron takes us to the edge and boots us over in this epic sequel to Ridley Scott's claustrophobic monster movie, *Alien*. As dark and scary as the original, but on a much larger scale, *Aliens* is as much an action picture as it is a horror flick, epic, atmospheric, exciting and intense, with big, bad guns, buckets of gore and the ugliest bug-eyed beasties of all time.

Discovered and revived after 57 years of space-bound hypersleep, Ripley (Sigourney Weaver) travels back to the aliens' home planet with a squad of marines intent on blasting those suckers to kingdom come. Surprises in store include a ruined human colony, a wild child survivor (Carrie Henn), a mighty, acid-spewing army, and the biggest, baddest mother of 'em all, the Alien Queen.

A leisurely first hour serves to set up the story and introduce us to the film's leading players: Ripley, our heroine, smart and gutsy; strong, silent Corporal Hicks (Cameron regular Michael Biehn); 'artificial person' Bishop (Lance Henriksen); scheming company man Burke (Paul Reiser); 'Tank Girl' Private Vasquez (Jenette Goldstein); freaked-out wise-ass Hudson (Bill Paxton) and the dangerously inexperienced Lieutenant Gorman (William Hope). Once we know who everyone is and what the hell is going on, Cameron takes his foot off the brake and all of a sudden we're up to our eyeballs in face-hugging, chest-bursting, nail-biting alien terror, and if you think that's exciting, wait till you get a load of the grand finale, as Ripley straps on a loader exoskeleton for a dazzling confrontation with the Queen bitch herself.

 James Cameron's original cut, running 17 minutes longer than the theatrical release, includes background information on Ripley and the ill-fated colonists of planet L.V.426. Available on video as a Special Edition, it is highly recommended.

Sequel: *Alien 3*.

Director: James Cameron; **Producer:** Gale Anne Hurd; **Screenplay:** James Cameron, story by James Cameron, David Giler, Walter Hill, based on characters created by Dan O'Bannon and Ronald Schusett; **Production Design:** Peter Lamont; **Editor:** Ray Lovejoy; **Photography:** Adrian Biddle; **Music:** James Horner; **Cast:** Sigourney Weaver, Carrie Henn, Michael Biehn, Paul Reiser, Lance Henriksen, Bill Paxton, William Hope, Jenette Goldstein. **Academy Awards:** Best... Visual Effects, Sound Effects Editing..

American Cyborg: Steel Warrior

USA 1992 91 mins

Beyond the meaning of life, the existence of God, and the purpose of infomercials, there is a fourth, all-important question which boggles the mind when seriously considered: if a tree falls in a forest and there's no-one around to hear it, how come it takes five grown men to write a single *Terminator* knock-off? Stealing good ideas from better movies and trashing them for the purpose of cheap exploitation rarely requires more than half a brain, yet here we are, looking at ten times that amount, a surplus of effort and shortage of ability which can only mean one thing: the end of the world is nigh, particularly for those of you tempted by this post-apocalyptic foolishness.

A spiritless adventure which makes Van Damme's like-minded *Cyborg* seem like Oscar material in comparison, *American Cyborg: Steel Warrior* coughs up a bloody gob of violence and destruction, two of our favourite elements, to be sure, but ruined when combined with a witless plot, dumb-ass dialogue, pedestrian performances and plasticine make-up effects.

Down, out and infertile to boot, mankind is an endangered species, dominated by an evil super computer and massacred to the brink of extinction by hordes of bloodthirsty cyborgs (aka Terminators). The future seems bleaker than a life without Twinkies when, all of a sudden, this chick turns up, a platinum bimbo with womb for one more inside, a pregnant plot device with a foetal backpack and a plan to escape the wilds of America for the science and civilization of Europe, where, it is believed, propagation is a way of life.

And so, with a sticky bun in the last working oven, Mary (Nicole Hansen, our heroine - yes, we are in trouble) hits the road, hooks up with anti-hero for hire Austin (Joe Lara, long-haired caveman) and comes to blows (over and over) with unstoppable, regenerative cyborg John Ryan (black leather gear, cropped blond hair and 'tache, bit of a Nazi), our villain.

Additional dangers include roving transvestite gangs, searing acid rain, radioactive cannibals, sloppy film-making and a shocker of a plot twist which manages to surprise Austin and Mary (if no-one else), while poor old Mr Ryan, throughout his murderous rampage, has to suffer the indignity of being stabbed in the throat, shot in the face, blown up, impaled, dismembered and forced to impersonate Arnold Schwarzenegger.

For drunks, junkies and desperadoes only.

Director: Boaz Davidson; **Producer:** Mati Raz; **Screenplay:** Brent Friedman, Bill Crounse, Don Peqingnot, story by Boaz Davidson, Christopher Pearce; **Production Design:** Kuly Sander; **Editor:** Alain Jakubowicz; **Photography:** Avi Karpick; **Music:** Blake Leyh; **Cast:** Joe Lara, Nicole Hansen, John Ryan, Yoseph Shiloa, Uri Gavriel, Hellen Lesnick.

American Ninja (aka American Warrior)

USA 1986 95 mins

Back in the real world, violence rarely solves anything, but there's another place, an alternate reality we know as Actionland, where excessive force can always be relied upon to take care of business. This is where *American Ninja*, and most of the other movies in this book, live bloody, contented lives, secure in the knowledge that chaos cures.

A prime example of positive brutality can be found in the tale of Joe and Steve. Joe's an 18-year-old army private stationed in the Philippines, an amnesiac martial artist who keeps to himself and makes enemies fast. Steve's a lot less complicated and a lot more popular, a wise-cracking, muscle-bound GI who challenges Joe to a fight because he doesn't like his attitude. Anyway, five minutes later they're the best of friends and Joe's the big man on campus, and all because every time Steve got anywhere near him, Joe knocked him down, spun him around and sent him packing.

You see, Joe could have tried to express his feelings verbally, he might have attempted to win the hearts of his fellow men through hard work and sacrifice, but at the end of the day, all he really needed to do to prove himself was to beat someone up. Ultimately, Steve respects this and pledges allegiance to Joe. Scientific bods explain this phenomena as Macho Bullshit + Mortal Combat = Male Bonding. Here endeth the lesson.

As for the movie, well, it's probably one of the most efficient comic book actioners ever churned out by producers Golan and Globus, a relentlessly exciting, endearingly shallow tale of heroes and the men they must slaughter.

Michael Dudikoff leads the carnage as Joe, who, besides falling in love with the Colonel's daughter and obsessing over his forgotten past, thrills us to bits with his Ninja moves as he takes on an entire army of terrorists trained in Ninjitsu, the secret art of assassination. As an actor and general screen presence, Dudikoff's a bit of a baby-faced lightweight, but boy, he sure knows how to move. Strong, agile and quick as a flash, Dudikoff leads Joe through an hour-and-a-half of well-choreographed, non-stop action, bumping off a never-ending supply of bad guys using everything from his bare hands to an assortment of machine guns, Samurai swords and even the occasional screwdriver.

Tadashi Yamashita gives our young star a run for his money as the monstrous Black Star Ninja, a Japanese killing machine decked out with smoke bombs, poison darts and, because it's better to be safe than sorry, a laser gun. Jackson (Steve James), meanwhile, pops up from time to time in his capacity as action man's best friend, but on the whole it's up to Joe to single handedly save the day, a gung-ho hero giving 'em hell in a classic kick ass movie.

Sequels: American Ninja 2: The Confrontation, American Ninja 3: Blood Hunt, American Ninja 4: The Annihilation, American Ninja 5.

Director: Sam Firstenberg; **Producers:** Menahem Golan, Yoram Globus; **Screenplay:** Paul De Mielche, story by Avi Kleinberger and Gideon Amir; **Production Design:** Adrian H. Gorton; **Editor:** Michael J. Duthie; **Photography:** Hanania Baer; **Music:** Michael Linn; **Cast:** Michael Dudikoff, Steve James, Judie Aronson, Guich Koock, Tadashi Yamashita.

American Ninja 2: The Confrontation

USA 1987 89 mins

Army Rangers Joe Armstrong (marauding Michael Dudikoff) and Curtis Jackson (stormy Steve James) return to our screens in fine, butt-kicking form, doing what they do best, namely killing folk, on the Caribbean island of St Thomas, a tropical, bimbo-encrusted paradise where there's no end of bad guys scrapping for a fight. They'll get one too, from our dynamite duo. A Ninja hiding in a boy's body, mild-mannered Joe takes 'em on ten at a time, which hardly seems fair, since he could take on twice that many without even breaking a sweat. As for Curtis, a muscle-bound amalgam of Shaft, Bruce Lee and Action Man with a PhD in Macho, well, they say that man's a mean mother - *shut your mouth* - but I'm talking about Jackson - *and we can dig it.*

Together, the guys crash through a pulp comic book plot, searching for missing Marines on the mysterious Blackbeard Island, home of billionaire drug lord Leo 'The Lion' Burke (Gary Conway), a run-of-the-mill evil type with his very own kidnapped professor and a (Dick) dastardly scheme to genetically engineer a race of Super Ninjas, 'the ultimate fighting machine - strong, obedient, heartless'. Hey, it could happen...

Director Sam Firstenberg chucks in an additional army of regular Ninjas to keep us happy, offering a familiar but no less welcome bombardment of non-stop, ultra-violent action as Joe and Curtis give the movie all they've got, throwing fists and knives, shooting up a storm, and even jumping off a cliff into a waiting speedboat. Best of all, though, is a high-speed battle between Joe and a particularly stubborn Ninja, who clings to our hero's truck like cheese on a pizza and absolutely refuses to let him escape.

It's a heady, bloody brew, that's for sure, as broad as an elephant's backside and dumber than an underachieving ox, but spirited and hilarious just the same, with tons of well-orchestrated action and enthusiastic performances from a couple of tough guys who don't know the meaning of restraint. Go-go power rangers!

 Believe it or not, the screenplay for *American Ninja 2: The Confrontation* was co-written by 'Lion' man Gary Conway and actor James Booth, best known for playing self-centred Private Henry Hook in *Zulu*.

Director: Sam Firstenberg; **Producers:** Menahem Golan, Yoram Globus; **Screenplay:** Gary Conway, James Booth; **Production Design:** Holger Gross; **Editor:** Michael J. Duthie; **Photography:** Gideon Porath; **Music:** George S. Clinton; **Cast:** Michael Dudikoff, Steve James, Larry Poindexter, Gary Conway, Jeff Weston, Michelle Bates, Ralph Draper.

The Armour of God

Hong Kong 1987 90 mins

Indiana Jones braves an eastern makeover and emerges looking like Jackie Chan in this blockbusting comedy adventure, a frantic and unusually expensive excuse for wild action set-pieces and dangerous stunt work. The screenplay is pure Hong Kong shlock, the performances as subtle as foghorns, but, armed with a huge budget, director Chan goes wild with those production values: exotic, international locations; gadgets worthy of 007; a vast and varied supporting cast of bad guys and their lackeys; several maniacally well-choreographed rescues and getaways; and finally, Chan, the man himself, as likeable and irrepressible as ever, probably the greatest single commodity an action flick could hope for.

The armour of the title is a five-piece outfit scattered around the world. Blessed with the power to ward off evil, its destruction would open the doors to the forces of darkness (totally plausible so far...). The race is on, then, to collect and protect the armour before it falls into the dastardly clutches of a gang of drug-dealing monks up to no good.

Leading the way we have indestructible obtainer of rare antiquities, Asian Hawk (Chan), no relation to Hudson, and boy, what a relief that is. Comedy ham Alan Tam offers his services as Hawk's hopeless sidekick, while female support comes from Euro-babe Lola Forner (occasional combat duties, light romantic interest) and Rosamund Kwan as Hawk's kidnapped ex-girlfriend (motivation).

Forget the plot, the talk, the vain attempts to act. Focus on the mayhem and you'll be just fine: Hawk's greatest hits include hurtling down a mountain on a makeshift sled, taking on four wild 'catwomen' single handed, dishing out dozens of martial arts beatings during an extended monastery showdown and, best of all, an outrageous, climactic stunt which sees Chan diving from a mountain on to a hot air balloon.

It's not quite *Raiders of the Lost Ark*, but it'll do.

 Don't forget to catch the closing credit footage of one of Chan's most horrific accidents, as he leaps from a castle wall on to a tree, slips, lands on the rocks below and ends up with a fractured skull and ruptured inner ear. This is why most other movie heroes use stunt men.

 The castle featured in the picture is, in fact, the very same Yugoslavian stronghold featured in the 1975 Hammer horror chiller, *To The Devil a Daughter*.

Sequel: *Armour of God II: Operation Condor*.

Director: Jackie Chan; **Producers:** Leonard K. C. Ho, Chua Lam; **Screenplay:** Edward Tang, Barry Wong; **Production Design:** William Cheung; **Editor:** Cheung Yiu Chung; **Photography:** Bob Thompson; **Music:** Michael Rai; **Cast:** Jackie Chan, Alan Tam, Rosamund Kwan, Lola Forner.

Brainstorms 1

PEOPLE ARE STRANGE
Name the movie in which...

1. Charles Bronson uses a rocket launcher indoors.
2. Sean Connery apologises to a rat.
3. Tim Curry pretends to be a girl scout.
4. Michael Douglas wrestles a crocodile.
5. Clint Eastwood harpoons a weirdo.
6. Miguel Ferrer learns to kill again.
7. Mel Gibson develops a taste for dog biscuits.
8. Chuck Norris kills a couple of Ninjas without even getting out of bed.
9. Lori Petty does the wild thing with a mutant kangaroo.
10. Cynthia Rothrock swears 'I'll never touch a gun again'.
11. Arnold Schwarzenegger punches a camel right in the kisser.
12. Steven Seagal blows up a microwave oven.
13. Charlie Sheen describes himself as a 'flying penis'.
14. Marc Singer befriends a panther, an eagle and a pair of wacky ferrets.
15. Sylvester Stallone eats a ratburger.
16. Patrick Stewart is buried alive.

17. Patrick Swayze rips a man's throat out with his bare hands.
18. Denzel Washington strips down to his boxers to put a lunatic at ease.
19. Jean-Claude Van Damme kicks down a palm tree.
20. Bruce Willis runs barefoot over broken glass.

Army of Darkness: The Medieval Dead

USA 1992 86 mins

Sam Raimi takes us back in time for the third and final chapter of his high-camp horror series, *The Evil Dead*, a twisted trilogy for warped young minds from the director who invented the rapist tree.

Continually plagued by the forces of evil, ghoulbuster Ash (Bruce Campbell) is thrown back in time to medieval England, a perilous land of black magic and bug-ugly monsters where our reluctant hero must fight for his life, first against the armies of the living, and later against the re-animated forces of the dead. All Ash really wants is to go back home, but in return for the privilege, he's expected to nab the all-powerful *Book of the Dead* before the Deadites can lay their bony hands on it. And then there's this girl...

Fans of the earlier movies are already well acquainted with director Raimi's exaggerated visuals and sick sense of humour, although this third chapter opens the story much wider than before, and is more of a tongue-in-cheek, fantasy adventure than a ferocious, rollercoaster horror ride. Still, you'd have to be sedated not to jump at least a couple of times.

Bruce Campbell makes the most of his larger-than-life role, further establishing Ash as probably the coolest shotgun-toting, chainsaw-wielding B-movie horror hero of all time. Armed with enough hardware and technical know-how to baffle a small army (conveniently, Ash's '73 Sedan travels back in time too, a powerful automobile with a trunk full of technical manuals and useful raw materials), not to mention some of the most delinquent one-liners ever spoken on film ('Give me some sugar baby', whispers Ash as he pulls medieval babe Embeth Davidtz towards him), Ash is a living anachronism, a twentieth-century boy who stands out in medieval England as obviously and as awkwardly as a liberal sentiment in a Steven Seagal movie.

The gang's all here: soul-sucking demons, kings and wizards, a posse of miniature Ash clones and a cast of thousands who never say die. Smart, silly and born to be wild, this imaginative mixture of gothic pop and creature feature is a serious scream.

Army of Darkness comes complete with either of two different endings, a cheesy convenience store showdown and a mind-bendingly apocalyptic climax which came first, works better, and is available to see on video. And while we're on the trivia trail, it's cameo time, so keep an eye out for Hollywood cheesecake Bridget Fonda.

Director: Sam Raimi; **Producer:** Robert Tapert; **Screenplay:** Sam Raimi, Ivan Raimi; **Production Design:** Tony Tremblay; **Editors:** Bob Murawski, R.O.C. Sandstorm; **Photography:** Bill Pope; **Music:** Joseph Loduca, 'March of the Dead' theme by Danny Elfman; **Cast:** Bruce Campbell, Embeth Davidtz, Marcus Gilbert, Ian Abercrombie, Richard Grove.

Assassins

USA 1995 132 mins

Rath (Sylvester Stallone) is an assassin, the best in the business, but he wants out. Bain (Antonio Banderas), meanwhile, is a rising young psychopath who wants to prove himself by wasting you-know-who. Then there's Electra (Julianne Moore), a surveillance expert who helps pad out the story with a computer disk loaded with top secret information. Put 'em together with the *Lethal Weapon* team (director Donner, producer Silver) and what have you got? A pretty lifeless thriller, actually, intended, it seems, for the same 'mature' audience which avoided *The Specialist*.

Drawn out, dull and way too serious, *Assassins* aims for smart and stylish but falls way short of the mark. There are a couple of passable action sequences, a cemetery gunfight, a clever bit of business in a taxi cab, but on the whole it's talk first, shoot later, and it'll send you straight to sleep.

As the older, wiser killer, Sly's a weary bore in this one, and though Banderas fares better with a showier role, even he fails to overcome the hurdles presented by a screenplay you wouldn't wrap fish and chips in. Worst of all is a tedious Mexican finale offering 5% action and 95% sitting around. Ultimately, *Assassins* is a whole lot deadlier than both Rath and Bain combined. Run for your lives.

Director: Richard Donner; **Producers:** Richard Donner, Joel Silver, Bruce Evans, Raynold Gideon, Andrew Lazar, Jim Van Wyck; **Screenplay:** Andy Wachowski, Larry Wachowski, Brian Helgeland; **Production Design:** Tom Sanders; **Editor:** Richard Marks; **Photography:** Vilmos Zsigmond; **Music:** Mark Mancina; **Cast:** Sylvester Stallone, Antonio Banderas, Julianne Moore.

Bad Boys

USA 1995 126 mins

TV comedy stars Martin Lawrence (*Martin*) and Will Smith (*The Fresh Prince of Bel Air*) join forces in this glossy blaxploitation from pop video director Michael Bay, an all-action cop thriller played mostly for laughs, both deeply moronic and enthusiastically destructive, an ultra-violent slaughter-fest with a foul mouth and some slick visuals. We're talking seriously enjoyable trash, people, relentlessly over-produced by Don Simpson and Jerry Bruckheimer, whose commitment to mindless entertainment knows no bounds.

Miami detectives Marcus Burnett (Lawrence) and Mike Lowrey (Smith) are an odd couple indeed. Marcus is a family man, as desperate for cash as he is for sex, while Mike lives the good life, a fast-talking rich kid with a need for speed and babes a-plenty. At first glance they might not seem compatible, truth is though, they share a common love of killing which bonds them on a daily basis.

The carnage kicks off when Mike and Marcus are given 72 hours to track down a hundred million dollars worth of heroin after it vanishes from their department's evidence room. With the FDA and DEA breathing down their necks, our heroes get to work, favouring shoot-outs and car chases over solid investigation as they hurtle towards an outrageous showdown with arch-villain Fouchet (*Nikita*'s Tcheky Karyo).

Brace yourselves for a desperate and tiresome sitcom-style subplot which calls for the guys to switch identities, and don't be surprised when Lawrence and Smith's quick-fire routine starts to wear itself thin after a while. And, whatever you do, don't expect any nudity, even though the movie teases us with a production line of beautiful women. In fact, the only nipples you're destined to see here belong to Will Smith, running through the streets with his shirt wide open, a study in slow motion, ridiculous at best.

Take your laughs where you can, be they intentional or otherwise, enjoy the chaos for its own sake and, for heaven's sake, try not to think too much. That way, you might just get along with the *Bad Boys*.

Director: Michael Bay; **Producers:** Don Simpson, Jerry Bruckheimer; **Screenplay:** Michael Barrie, Jim Mulholland, Doug Richardson, story by George Gallo; **Production Design:** John Vallone; **Editor:** Christian Wagner; **Photography:** Howard Atherton; **Music:** Mark Mancina; **Cast:** Martin Lawrence, Will Smith, Téa Leoni, Tcheky Karyo, Theresa Randle, Marg Helgenberger, Joe Pantoliano.

Batman

USA 1989 126 mins

Bigger than The Beatles. Bigger than Jesus. Back in 1989, Batman ruled the planet. Months before Tim Burton's blockbuster made it to the cinema, the mighty wheels of publicity and promotion began to turn, cranking out shiploads of cheesy merchandise to millions of eager Batfans, plastering the Dark Knight's trademark symbol on to every billboard, T-shirt, badge, toy and lunchbox in existence. Shortly before the movie's release, psychologists confirmed that every man, woman, child, dog, cat, parrot and slug had been brainwashed into coughing up their dough for a seat in the dark with Bats and co. And still, the Hollywood bandwagon rolled on...

Only true fans were nervous: the guys 'n' dolls whose knowledge of Bruce Wayne extended beyond Frank Miller's best-selling 'Batman: The Dark Knight Returns'; the shiny, happy people who paid their dues at comic conventions long before collecting 'graphic novels' became fashionable; the cuddly couch potatoes who thrilled to the adventures of Adam West's '60s incarnation - pot belly and all - years before nostalgia became the Next Big Thing.

When the film finally hit the screens, things went pretty much as expected. Cinemas played to capacity crowds, merchandising flew off the shelves, and the world was a better place for all but a chosen few who knew Bob Kane's creation too well to be palmed off with Burton's flashy re-interpretation which, though it looked the part, managed to trash the entire Batman myth.

The story was simple enough: haunted by the murder of his parents, millionaire Bruce Wayne (Michael Keaton) fights crime as athletic genius the Batman, protecting Gotham City from the likes of the Joker (Jack Nicholson), clown prince of crime. Meanwhile, Bruce gets it on with gorgeous photographer Vicki Vale (Kim Basinger, window dressing), who, as it happens, plans on taking the first-ever shots of the mysterious Caped Crusader.

Time to play 'What's right with this movie? What's wrong with this movie?'. First, the down side: Keaton, miscast and awkward, lumbers around in a cumbersome suit, weakening the character almost as much as the screenplay; origins are changed (for convenience, Burton has the Joker killing Bruce Wayne's parents); long-established characters are needlessly revised (for the sake of the plot, trusty butler Alfred makes errors in judgement and doesn't seem anywhere near as handy as his comic book counterpart); some of the special effects are none too special, particularly Derek Meddings' Batwing, an expensive plastic miniature which looks, on screen, like a cheap plastic miniature.

Now for the up side: Nicholson, charismatic ham, having fun and stealing the show as the fiendishly comical and ever-homicidal Joker; Anton Furst's production design, a masterpiece of gothic engineering with an art deco twist; the Batmobile, loaded with gadgets, sleek, black, beautiful and cooler than a ice cube wearing Ray-Bans; and finally, the music, from Prince's funky contributions ('Partyman' is a real show-stopper) to a typically spirited orchestral work from Burton's long-time collaborator Danny Elfman.

Basically, we're looking at a fifty/fifty proposition here, a film with as many flaws as strengths, glossy entertainment which takes the Batman (and his Batfans) for granted, yet manages to struggle by as a fantasy adventure in its own right.

Sequels: *Batman Returns*, *Batman Forever*.

Director: Tim Burton; **Producers:** Jon Peters, Peter Guber; **Screenplay:** Sam Hamm, Warren Skaaren, based on characters created by Bob Kane; **Production Design:** Anton Furst; **Editor:** Ray Lovejoy; **Photography:** Roger Pratt; **Music:** Danny Elfman, songs written and performed by Prince; **Cast:** Michael Keaton, Jack Nicholson, Kim Basinger, Robert Wuhl, Pat Hingle, Billy Dee Williams, Michael Gough, Jack Palance, Jerry Hall, Tracey Walter, William Hootkins; **Academy Award:** Best Art Direction.

Batman Forever

USA 1995 122 mins

The key words here are new and different, not better. Content with having directed the first two *Batman* pictures, Tim Burton opted for a comfortable producer's office while Joel Schumacher did all the work, labouring night and day to make this third adventure his own. For starters, there's a new Batman (in a new suit), with Val Kilmer standing in for Michael Keaton and doing just fine. Next up, we missed him in the first, missed him in the second, but third time lucky and Robin finally makes it to the big screen in the teen-dream form of Chris O'Donnell, a boy wonder with guts, an earring and a talented stunt double.

Closer in style to the 1960s TV series than the previous movies, Schumacher's *Batman Forever* favours light over dark, gags over characterization, action over plot and style over content, merrily dangling our heroes over bottomless pits and vats of acid while sending them up against the combined might of schizo-psycho Harvey Two-Face (Tommy Lee Jones) and hyperactive trickster the Riddler (Jim Carrey).

Charged with all the energy of a nuclear reactor, the movie kicks off with a spectacular battle sequence and continues to bombard the senses until the very end, yet when you can finally hear yourself think again, the chances are you'll feel short-changed.

Enthusiasm is not the problem here. The fact that you'll neither care about the characters nor notice any signs of a story is more likely to blame. In basic terms, Two-Face wants to kill Batman, the Riddler wants to kill Bruce Wayne and Robin wants to kill Two-Face, while criminal psychologist Dr Chase Meridian (Nicole Kidman, romantic bore) gets her knickers in a twist over both Bruce Wayne *and* his leather-clad alter ego. Confused? You won't be.

Medium expectations would serve you well. There's plenty here to get excited about, yet ultimately, despite in-jokes galore and action to spare, *Batman Forever* rarely reaches the heights of any one of a thousand Batman comics.

 Batfans take note that in the first movie, Harvey Dent (aka Two-Face) was played (prior to the character's disfigurement) by Billy Dee Williams, better known to generations of *Star Wars* fans as Lando Calrissian.

Director: Joel Schumacher; **Producers:** Tim Burton, Peter MacGregor-Scott; **Screenplay:** Lee Batchler, Janet Scott Batchler, Akiva Goldsman, based on characters created by Bob Kane; **Production Design:** Barbara Ling; **Editor:** Dennis Virkler; **Photography:** Stephen Goldblatt; **Music:** Elliot Goldenthal; **Cast:** Val Kilmer, Tommy Lee Jones, Jim Carrey, Nicole Kidman, Chris O'Donnell, Michael Gough, Pat Hingle, Drew Barrymore, Debi Mazar.

Batman Returns

USA 1992 127 mins

Surgeon General's Warning: the following review is excessively nitpicky. The author reserves the right to tear apart this movie since not only is it a major insult to Batfans, but also, when Hollywood pours vast amounts of cash and talent into a project, you'd expect it to be at least half-decent. Only those poor souls who know nothing of Gotham's finest have a chance of being entertained. As for the rest of us, read on...

Batman returns, but he needn't have bothered. The story, for what it's worth, covers several bases, none of them well. The Penguin (Danny DeVito), recently emerged from Gotham's sewers, plans on taking over the city, and, with the help of evil businessman Max Shreck (Christopher Walken, named after the star of F.W. Murnau's creepy classic *Nosferatu*), surprises everybody by running for mayor. Around about the same time, Max pushes feeble secretary Michelle Pfeiffer out of a window and - lo and behold - after being licked by cats, she transforms into the Catwoman, a whip-wielding, leather-clad temptress who looks a million bucks but lacks bite in the characterization department. Somewhere down the line, the two 'super' baddies join forces in a vain attempt to make up for Jack Nicholson's absence, hatching a devilish scheme to discredit the Batman, who, as millionaire playboy Bruce Wayne (still making do without his youthful ward, Robin), has a serious case of the hots for one Selina Kyle, aka Catwoman.

Written by *Hudson Hawk*'s Daniel Waters with occasional assistance from Messrs Muddled and Clumsy, *Batman Returns* was doomed from the start. Why, when the movie was still on paper, before tens of millions of dollars were spent, didn't director Tim

The suit makes the man: Michael Keaton flashes armoured pecs in *Batman Returns*.

Burton labour night and day to improve the screenplay? It doesn't cost much to scribble words on a notepad, yet Hollywood's demand for bankable new product sees one film after another rushing into production without a decent script (director Wolfgang Petersen admitted to writing scenes for his virus thriller *Outbreak* only hours before shooting). Batten down the hatches and prepare yourselves for a stormy sea of unresolved sub-plots and half-drawn eccentrics.

Batman purists are likely to be the most upset, because as good as the movie looks, it just doesn't *feel* right. A new and improved costume helps Keaton look the part, but the Dark Knight is meant to be a detective first and an action man second, and in *Batman Returns* our hero owes more to Dirty Harry than Sherlock Holmes, killing villains indiscriminately which, with his respect for the law, is something he would only do under the most extreme circumstances (likewise, this movie Batman is way too keen to reveal his secret identity).

It's ironic indeed that while Burton and friends were making the first movie they dismissed the 1960s *Batman* as camp trash, playing it dark and shadowy instead, whereas this time around they've done a complete about turn, ripping off the original show left, right and centre. Even the sub-plot of having the Penguin run for mayor is taken directly from an episode of the TV show titled *Hizonner the Penguin*.

Maybe this sounds petty and slight to everyone besides die-hard Batfans, but there's more. To start with, Burton directs with a designer's eye, focusing on the look (make-up and special effects, production and costume designs - Catwoman's outfit, the Batmobile, the Batsignal: taken individually they're the business, but they don't add up to a decent movie) at the cost of the story, characters, pace and action sequences (the climactic rocket-pack penguin assault is a major non-event).

Burton also manages to waste the title character; with the Penguin and the Catwoman hogging much of the screen time, Bats has little more than a supporting role in an ensemble cast, often simply turning up out of the blue to kill a couple of bad guys before disappearing again (not that this is necessarily a bad thing, since Keaton still seems poorly suited to the role).

DeVito, too, is a disappointment. Grotesque and deformed (courtesy of make-up master Stan Winston), with slime oozing from his mouth, he cracks dirty jokes, fools around with gadgety umbrellas, and waddles around like a true waterfowl, yet his greatest enemy is not the Batman, but the material he has to work with, and ultimately it beats the feathers out of him.

So what if the movie made money? So did *Three Men and a Baby*. In all but a financial sense, *Batman Returns* is a flop, a wasted opportunity to make the most of a classic character whose full potential has only ever been realized in the comics (personal favourites include Frank Miller's 'Batman: The Dark Knight Returns' and Doug Moench's 'Batman & Dracula: Red Rain', both of them better than anything Bats has ever done on screen).

Director: Tim Burton; **Producers:** Denise Di Novi, Tim Burton; **Screenplay:** Daniel Waters, story by Daniel Waters and Sam Hamm, based on characters created by Bob Kane; **Production Design:** Bo Welch; **Editor:** Chris Lebenzon; **Photography:** Stefan Czapsky; **Music:** Danny Elfman; **Cast:** Michael Keaton, Danny DeVito, Michelle Pfeiffer, Christopher Walken, Michael Gough, Michael Murphy, Cristi Conaway, Andrew Bryniarski, Pat Hingle.

Battle Beyond the Stars

USA 1980 104 mins

A cheap and cheerful science fiction adventure from low-budget movie mogul Roger Corman, *Battle Beyond the Stars* rips off everything from *The Magnificent Seven*

Sybil Danning models the latest in inter-galactic B-movie fashion wear in *Battle Beyond the Stars*.

to *Star Wars*, but thanks to a knowing script (courtesy of John Sayles), an enthusiastic cast and a special effects crew capable of making something out of very little, it's an acceptably silly B-grade concoction, camp, cultish and ideally suited to those of us who remember the likes of Space Invaders and *Battlestar Galactica* with a degree of nostalgia.

John Saxon gets the ball rolling as evil conqueror Sador, a gratuitously nasty piece of work who turns his attention to the peace-loving people of the planet Akir. Unable to defend themselves, they send an emissary, Shad (Richard 'John Boy' Thomas, a long, long way from Walton's Mountain), out into space to round up a gang of inter-galactic mercenaries capable of whipping Sador's butt.

Eager but inexperienced, Shad takes to the stars, sharpens his piloting skills, learns to kill and, finally, makes a whole bunch of new friends: Space Cowboy (George Peppard), whisky connoisseur and western movie buff; Gelt (as played by Robert Vaughan, one of the original *Magnificent Seven*), a lone, dispassionate bandit; Cayman (Morgan Woodward), a lizard-like creature who'd like nothing better than to see Sador dead; The Nestor, five friendly clones with a collective consciousness who think and react as one; forgettable love interest Nanelia (Darlanne Fluegel) and, dressed to kill, busty Amazonian warrior St Exmin (Sybil Danning, schwing!).

The warriors assembled, director Murakami pumps up the action as, finally, Shad and the gang return to Akir in seven (fairly) magnificent ships, dividing their forces as they battle Sador in space and his laser brained forces on *terra firma*...

Cheesy charm is the order of the day, knockabout fun for anyone willing to accept the movie warts 'n' all. Set your expectations to medium and you'll have a blast. As Bette Davis once said (in the shameless weepie *Now Voyager*), '...don't let's ask for the moon... we have the stars!'

Director: Jimmy T. Murakami; **Producer:** Ed Carlin; **Executive Producer:** Roger Corman; **Screenplay:** John Sayles, story by John Sayles, Ann Dyer; **Production Design:** Jim Cameron, Charles Breen; **Editor:** Allan Holzman, R.J. Kizer; **Photography:** Daniel Lacambre; **Music:** James Horner; **Cast:** Richard Thomas, Robert Vaughan, John Saxon, Darlanne Fluegel, George Peppard, Sybil Danning, Sam Jaffe, Morgan Woodward, Steve Davis, Earl Boen, John McGowans.

The Beastmaster

USA 1982 118 mins

*C*onan meets *Dr Dolittle* as Marc Singer talks to the animals in this enthusiastic sword 'n' sorcery adventure, a cheerful revenge saga piled high with macho heroics, witches and sorcerers, warrior hordes, flesh eating monsters and barely dressed slave girls. Played straight down the line, but good for a laugh, *The Beastmaster* should whip you up into a hyperactive frenzy cured only by excessive sofa jumping and imaginary swordplay.

Blessed with the power to communicate with the birds and the beasts, young warrior Dar (Singer) sets out on a quest to destroy the Jun Horde, a sweaty bunch of ancient biker types who trashed his entire village, and evil high priest Maax (Rip Torn), who takes great pleasure in enslaving simple villagers and sacrificing their kids. We've also got a destiny thing going on here, because Dar is unknowingly of royal extraction and destined to destroy Maax, a prophesy the vile one is determined to prove wrong.

Joining Dar on his journey are Friar Tuck wannabe Seth (John Amos), whose lengthy staff cracks many a skull along the way, future king Tel (John Milrad), a young but brave little fighter, and Kiri (Tanya Roberts), a gorgeous slave girl with a passion for swimming topless and emerging from rivers dry as a bone and fully made up. Then there are Dar's animal friends: a huge black panther who can maul with the best of 'em, an eagle who provides Dar with visions of the journey ahead, and Codo and Podo the comedy ferrets, top class thieves and cracking light entertainers.

When it comes to 'borrowing' ideas from other movies and directing without such distracting elements as subtlety and character development, Don Coscarelli is guilty as charged, but the film presents a good-natured mix nonetheless, well paced and imaginative, an exciting boy's own tale of good versus evil, of dungeons and demons, and, of course, of Tanya Roberts, the last of *Charlie's Angels*, in every way a scorching medieval babe. Marc Singer does well as the muscular hero of the piece, leaping over mountain tops, slashing open bad guys and flashing that boisterous smile of his, while Rip Torn has a ball playing the kind of guy who, after running you over, would reverse to make sure.

Sequel: *Beastmaster II: Through the Portal of Time, Beastmaster III: The Eye of Braxus.*

Director: Don Coscarelli; **Producers:** Paul Pepperman, Sylvio Tabet; **Screenplay:** Don Coscarelli, Paul Pepperman; **Production Design:** Conrad E. Angone; **Editor:** Roy Watts; **Photography:** John Alcott; **Music:** Lee Holdridge; **Cast:** Marc Singer, Tanya Roberts, Rip Torn, John Amos, Rod Loomis, John Milrad.

Best of the Best 2

USA 1993 101 mins

A blood-and-guts B-movie with A-movie trimmings, *Bloodsport* wannabe *Best Of The Best 2* improves upon its predecessor by transforming the US karate champs of the original into martial arts avengers out for justice. It ain't the most original story around, but it's a good excuse for combat, well handled by director Robert Radler and an enthusiastic cast. In fact, actor Eric Roberts even admitted once that the only reason he made this sequel was to make up for the first, and it does.

From male-bonding ritual to frantic chop-schlocky, this wild second feature makes room for every testosterone charged cliché in the book, a chamber of horrors uncluttered by intelligence and restraint, thank goodness.

The Coliseum is where the real action is, an underground club where the rich and sleazy thrill to the spectacle of gladiatorial conflict. Hosted by the irrepressibly insincere Weldon (Wayne Newton), it's a happening, showbiz place where muscle-bound men fight to the death and owner, ultimate warrior and undefeated champion Brakus (Ralph Moeller) is king. Beat him and you win the club. Lose and you die. And Travis (Chris Penn) loses, big time. Revenge is in the air, then, as best-buddies Alex Grady (Roberts) and Tommy Lee (Phillip Rhee) take on the mighty Brakus and his gang of walking beefcake, training first with drunken Uncle Sonny Landham, before charging, blasting and chopping their way straight through to the main event: Tommy takes on Brakus and a supporting trio of warriors in the arena while Alex is busy with the rest of 'em. Yee-ha.

Boosted by a healthy budget, a slight sense of humour and a profound commitment to violence, *Best Of The Best 2* is a good/bad/mad movie ideal for your most laddish mood.

Director: Robert Radler; **Producers:** Peter E. Strauss, Phillip Rhee; **Screenplay:** Max Strom, John Allan Nelson; **Production Design:** Gary Frutkoff, **Editor:** Bert Lovitt; **Photography:** Fred Tannes; **Music:** David Michael Frank; **Cast:** Eric Roberts, Phillip Rhee, Christopher Penn, Ralph Moeller, Wayne Newton, Sonny Landham, Meg Foster.

A Better Tomorrow

Hong Kong 1986 95 mins

Joining forces for the very first time, director John Woo and screen hero Chow Yun-Fat both made their names with this one, a smart and sophisticated gangster saga which, besides packing out Hong Kong cinemas, earned international critical acclaim. Much smarter and more sophisticated than your average Eastern adventure, *A Better Tomorrow* offers both epic melodrama and awesome ultra-violence, keeping the pace tight and the action explosive without sacrificing plot or characterization.

A match-chewing scoundrel with dreams of the big time, mob enforcer Mark (Chow Yun-Fat) hits the skids after his partner and best friend Ho (Ti Lung) quits the business, determined to go straight for the sake of his younger brother Kit (Leslie Cheung), an idealistic rookie cop. Following a three-year stretch in prison, Ho returns home to find a brother who blames him for their father's death and a friend who wants desperately to get back into the game...

The fact that you'll care for these characters adds greatly to the action, which comes throughout: a mighty struggle between Ho's entire family and a hulking, near-invincible assassin, a blazing one-man revenge attack as Chow slaughters a building full of bad guys, a full-on chop-socky interlude in a cab rank and, saving the best till last, a blazing gun fight which sees Chow in full macho mode, both hard and cool enough to take on an army virtually single handed.

Love, betrayal, revenge, friendship, duty, fate and male bonding: it's all here for our enjoyment, stylishly handled by Woo and his favourite leading man.

Sequels: *A Better Tomorrow II*, *A Better Tomorrow III*.

Director: John Woo; **Producer:** Tsui Hark; **Screenplay:** John Woo; **Production Design:** Bennie Liu; **Editor:** Kam Ma; **Photography:** Wong Wing Hung; **Music:** Joseph Koo; **Cast:** Chow Yun-Fat, Ti Lung, Leslie Cheung, Emily Chu, Waise Lee.

Beyond the Law

Hong Kong 1989 92 mins

Some movies are just too cheap and nasty to waste an hour-and-a-half of your life on. Fifteen minutes, maybe, twenty at a push, but no longer, which is why all you video jockeys out there should consider viewing this typically dodgy Hong Kong phooey on fast forward, stopping only for the fight scenes. There's 10 per cent of quality chop-socky action in here just waiting to be discovered, a memorable Samurai sword fight, a busy, full-contact finale, but unless you're a glutton for dim-witted, Z-grade punishment, you'd be wise to picture search the remaining 90 per cent away.

Cynthia Rothrock makes it into about half of the feature, a US FBI agent on the trail of a missing mob informer in deepest Hong Kong. Occasional brushes with Mafia and Yakuza enforcers keep our re-dubbed heroine moderately busy, while crass comic cops Dave and Chris keep tabs on the informant's sister, shamelessly ripping off the plot of *Stakeout* for want of something better to do. A tacky AIDS routine stands out among the disastrous duo's most offensive non-routines, a sledgehammer number which further degrades the cast and crew of this lobotomised trash.

Of course, you could argue that *Beyond the Law* is so darn awful it's funny, that you shouldn't judge Eastern flicks by Western standards, but then you could also argue that Elvis is alive and well and working in a Kilburn mini-mart. There's really no point, is there? Why try to justify trash when you can whiz through it instead? Why condemn your brain to a fate worse than *King Solomon's Mines* when the only thing saving this stinker from total oblivion is a fistful of martial arts? Be smart. Stick with the 10 per cent.

Director: Lau Kar Wing; **Producer:** Joe Siu; **Screenplay:** Barry Wong; **Production Design:** Eddie Chan; **Editor:** Tak-Cheung Hui; **Photography:** Chan Kong Hung; **Music:** Sai-Kit Lo; **Cast:** Cynthia Rothrock, Kirk Miu, Shing Fui On, Tong Chung Yip, Nishiwaki Michiko, Kwan Sau Mei.

The Big Boss (aka Fists of Fury)
Hong Kong 1971 98 mins

Conquering the world with his first starring role, legend-in-the-making Bruce Lee worked an alchemist's spell on *The Big Boss*, transforming a shlocky, chop-socky adventure into an influential, unforgettable martial arts classic, his powerful screen presence, strength, agility and fighting technique setting the standard for all future street-fighting action heroes.

A job at an ice factory proves more challenging than Cheng (Lee) had expected when one of his co-working cousins disappears without a trace. A lengthy and dangerous investigation reveals a drug-smuggling operation led by the 'Big Boss', a ruthless man with blood on his hands...

Technically speaking, this movie is a bit of a mess. Cheaply made with little attention paid to detail, the dubbing is crude and obvious while the sound effects are exaggerated beyond belief, particularly during fight scenes which, if you close your eyes, sound a lot like freight trains crashing into one another. Most alarming of all, however, is a worker at the factory who sounds a lot like an old, Jewish man. None of this really spoils the movie, though, it's actually quite funny and even kind of charming, in its own, peculiarly cheesy way. Still, without Lee to compensate for its faults, *The Big Boss* would have been forgotten years ago.

Fortunately, the action still packs one hell of a punch, and who among us can resist the sight of Bruce Lee leaping ten, maybe fifteen feet in the air before crashing down on hordes of shell-shocked henchmen? Only a disciplined fighter could cause this much chaos, and Lee is the best, closing the movie in style with a long and satisfying one-on-one with the Boss man, a fight to the death polished off with an outrageous knife stunt which requires the permission of a parent or legal guardian before trying at home.

Director: Lo Wei; **Producer:** Raymond Chow; **Screenplay:** Lo Wei; **Editor:** Fan Chia Kun; **Photography:** Chen Ching Cheh; **Music:** Wang Fu Ling; **Cast:** Bruce Lee, Maria Yi, James Tien, Nora Miao.

Big Trouble In Little China
USA 1986 99 mins

Do you like your pizza with everything on it, or are you strictly cheese and tomato? Certainly no stranger to cheese, but just as hungry for every other ingredient on the menu is director John Carpenter, here laying on a veritable smorgasbord of styles and genres, using a Chinese ghost story for a base and smothering it with wild chop-socky action, broad slapstick comedy, monsters on the prowl, cliffhanging adventure, flashy special effects and an extra-thin layer of ham, as supplied by campy Kurt Russell as swaggering John Wayne-type Jack Burton, a beer-swilling blockhead in love with himself, his truck, and the ever-open road.

There's a story in there too, somewhere, struggling against the odds to keep the movie from falling apart, although basically what we have here is a bunch of good guys colliding over and over with a bunch of bad guys, with non-stop comic relief from Russell, some featured martial artistry from diminutive co-star Dennis Dun, an evil sorcerer with designs on the entire universe, and a trio of end-of-level videogame baddies known as The Three Storms.

A ghostly immortal with the cosmos on his wish list, Lo Pan (James Hong) needs first to become whole again, a magic trick which involves marrying a woman with green eyes and then sacrificing her to his favourite demon. If only Lo hadn't kidnapped Wang Chi's (Dun) girlfriend, newly arrived from China with eyes 'like creamy jade', and further added to his misfortune by nabbing (for no apparent reason) Burton's beloved supertruck, the 'Pork-Chop Express', his plans might very well have gone without a hitch. As it is, he manages to upset two very violent and dim-witted people, who, along with a couple of friends, a wizard (Victor Wong), and a gang of well-armed extras, dive head first into Lo's underground lair, a labyrinth of traps, troops and things that go bump in the night.

As you might expect, Russell plays the whole thing fast and loose, over-reacting to every danger he faces, shooting off his mouth as often as his gun, while karate kid Dun kicks some serious butt, facing the enemy with impossibly high-flying gymnastics and a couple of expert chops. It's high energy stuff, this, bold and colourful, dumb and dumber, with a jokey screenplay that doesn't know when to stop and a director who refuses to put on the brakes.

If you decide to give the movie a chance, and you could certainly do a lot worse, try to keep an eye out for Fu Manchu-lookalike Al Leong, a highly capable stuntman and martial arts expert, here playing a minor henchman who is killed and later re-animated at least three times! Strange but true, and one hell of a cock-up.

Director: John Carpenter; **Producer:** Larry J. Franco; **Screenplay:** Gary Goldman, David Z. Weinstein, W.D. Richter; **Production Design:** John J. Lloyd; **Editors:** Mark Warner, Steve Mirkovich, Edward A. Warschilka; **Photography:** Dean Cundey; **Visual Effects:** Richard Edlund; **Music:** John Carpenter, in association with Alan Howarth; **Cast:** Kurt Russell, Kim Cattrall, Dennis Dun, James Hong, Victor Wong, Kate Burton, Donald Li.

Trivialists 1

SPARRING PARTNERS
Ten classic confrontations

Arnold Schwarzenegger *v* Vernon Wells, *Commando*
Bruce Willis *v* Alexander Godunov, *Die Hard*
Jackie Chan *v* Wong Jang Lee, *Drunken Master*
Sean Connery *v* Clancy Brown, *Highlander*
Jean-Claude Van Damme *v* 'Tiger' Tong Po, *Kickboxer*
Mel Gibson *v* Gary Busey, *Lethal Weapon*
Brandon Lee *v* Al Leong, *Rapid Fire*
'Rowdy' Roddy Piper *v* Keith David, *They Live*
Conan Lee *v* Gordon Lui, *Tiger on the Beat*
Bruce Lee *v* Chuck Norris, *The Way of the Dragon*

Bird on a Wire

USA 1990 111 mins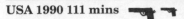

Wow! What a concept! Where do they get their ideas? Mel Gibson and Goldie Hawn - together! Do those high-priced Hollywood scriptwriters earn their pay or what? And get this! They're on the run together, making all this noise, and smashing up loads of stuff! And Mel keeps flashing that cheeky grin of his! And Goldie keeps flashing that cheeky butt of hers! Simply hilarious.

Hang on. Hold your horses. Wait just a second there. Better strike all that and start again, because, to be honest, seeing Mel and Goldie fool around is a lot like watching your parents snog. It's just too damn wholesome for public consumption. And what the hell are all those Mr Wiggly jokes about? No, what we *really* have here is a misguided star vehicle that delivers truck loads of dumb and sugar-mountains of cute. And *that's* the truth.

A misguided star vehicle with a formula plot, this saccharine adventure at least moves along so quickly you might forget to be bored. Gibson plays a guy called Rick whose cover in the witness protection programme has been blown and who is now on the run from the hitmen he once witnessed doing their job. Enter Goldie as spoiled media type and accomplished screamer Marianne, who used to have a thing with Rick until one day he suddenly disappeared (witnessing a murder can ruin your whole day, can't it?). But now he's back, ready for an odd couple romance on the road with his old flame, while all the time fleeing bad guys David Carradine and Bill Duke. And the cops. And the FBI. Like I said. Hilarious.

Oh well, at least there's enough mayhem and general destruction to pass the time. And every conceivable chase scenario you can imagine. And if you enjoy the sound of finger nails scraping down a chalk board, there's a similarly cringe-making gay hairdresser sequence featuring Mel 'Mr Comedy' Gibson.

Director: John Badham; **Producer:** Ron Cohen; **Screenplay:** David Seltzer, Louis Venosta, Eric Lerner; **Production Design:** Philip Harrison; **Editor:** Frank Morriss, Dallas Puett; **Photography:** Robert Primes; **Music:** Hans Zimmer; **Cast:** Mel Gibson, Goldie Hawn, David Carradine, Bill Duke, Stephen Tobolowsky; Joan Severance, Jeff Corey, Harry Caesar.

Black Belt Jones

USA 1974 87 mins

Welcome to the Jim Kelly experience. No woman can resist him. No man can defeat him. He's a cool, funky dude with a towering afro and a neat line in flared leisure wear. He is, as he would no doubt tell you himself, The Man. In 1973, *Enter the Dragon* made him a star, his self-assured performance coming close to stealing the show. By 1974, however, his act was wearing pretty thin. Reunited with director Robert Clouse on a low-rent blaxploitation flick which lacked the budget, class and imagination of their earlier success, Kelly was left (rather unfairly) to carry the movie, but he just couldn't do it alone.

The plot is pure TV, the quality B-grade at best: local hero Black Belt Jones (Kelly) fights to save a karate school from fiendish Mafia hoodlums, seducing every chick on earth while pounding all the bad guys.

Sledgehammer comedy and straightforward chop-socky combat is the best you can expect from this dreary, dated turkey. A couple of minutes in and any novelty value fades: laugh at the movie while you can because it soon becomes as tiresome as its leading ham, rounding itself off with a cheesy car wash climax as Jimbo takes on the enemy in a mountain of bubbles.

Not all cult movies are worth seeing. If you're feeling nostalgic for the 1970s, catch an episode of *Starsky and Hutch* instead.

Sequel: *Black Belt Jones 2.*

Director: Robert Clouse; **Producers:** Fred Weintraub, Paul Heller; **Screenplay:** Oscar Williams, story by Fred Weintraub, Alex Rose; **Production Design:** Charles Pierce; **Editor:** Michael Kahn; **Photography:** Kent Wakeford; **Music:** Luchi DeJesus; **Cast:** Jim Kelly, Gloria Hendry, Scatman Crothers, Eric Laneuville, Alan Weeks, Andre Philippe, Vincent Barbi.

Black Cat

USA 1974 87 mins

First came *Nikita* (1990), a stylish, uncompromising thriller from French director Luc Besson. The tale of a drug-addicted wild child (Anne Parillaud) turned government assassin, it's exciting and dramatic, well-characterised, intelligently played and several billion times better than John Badham's pointless shot-by-shot, English-language rehash *The Assassin*, a Bridget Fonda misfire released in 1995. Sandwiched between these two, however, came a Hong Kong remake with a mind of its own, not quite as complex, maybe, with less attention paid to the characters and their various relationships, but, in its favour, considerably more action packed than either the original or its Hollywood twin.

Snagged by the all-powerful CIA and brain-tagged with a Black Cat microchip designed to 'maximise performance', Eastern superbabe Jade Leung hits New York and Hong Kong in search of mayhem, meeting guys (cold-blooded mentor Simon Yam, sappy love interest Thomas Lam), slaughtering henchmen, and, when absolutely necessary, dashing about in a skimpy vest and panties.

Most importantly, there's violence and plenty of it, as Cat blasts her way through an army of muscle at an outdoor wedding and, rather more ingeniously, improvises a nifty construction sight assassination.

Those of you searching for depth and style will find it in *Nikita*. The faster, bloodier option, offering a meaty portion of wham-bam-kill-you-ma'am entertainment, is *Black Cat*. Sounds like a classic double bill (just don't be tempted to turn it into a triple).

Sequel: *Black Cat II: The Assassination of President Yeltsin.*

Director: Stephen Shin; **Producer:** Dickson Poon; **Screenplay:** Lam Wai-lun, Chan Boshun, Lam Tan-ping; **Production Design:** Fu Tsi-tsung; **Editors:** Wong Wing-ming, Kwok Ting-hung, Wong Chau-on; **Photography:** Lee Kin-keung; **Music:** Danny Chung; **Cast:** Jade Leung, Simon Yam, Thomas Lam.

Black Eagle

USA 1988 93 mins

When Jean-Claude Van Damme made his action movie debut as Ivan, the Russian, in *No Retreat, No Surrender*, he was entrusted with a full 20 words of spoken dialogue. Two years down the line, he returned for more punishment as the villainous

Andrei, the Russian, in *Black Eagle*, his dialogue count boosted 250 per cent to a whopping 70 words. He struggles through the screenplay and sometimes you can even understand what he's saying, but he really needn't have bothered because nothing he could do could have rescued this dreary spy thriller from the depths of Movie Hell.

Guilty of taking itself too seriously, this inaction-packed tale dangles a top secret laser-tracking device in front of both the Ruskies and the Yankies and watches as the two superpowers duke it out for posession. Ultimately, the struggle comes down to two people: CIA troubleshooter Ken Tani (Sho Kosugi), codename 'Black Eagle', and KGB big boy, Andrei. There's a tedious subplot about Tani's children (played by Kosugi's own) hooking up with their dad in Malta and getting into all sorts of trouble, but the Tani/Andrei fight is really what this style-free, non-starter is all about.

Kosugi makes a fair action man, a little past it, maybe, with an accent as thick as porridge, but he knows his stuff and kills with confidence, and that might have helped the movie had he been blessed with even a crumb of star quality. Unfortunately, though, Kosugi just doesn't have what it takes to carry a movie, and without a charismatic central presence to distract us from the film itself, we have no choice but to acknowledge just how cheap, tepid and low on thrills this B-movie bore-a-thon actually is. And that ain't good.

Director: Eric Carson; **Producer:** Shimon Arama; **Screenplay:** A.E. Peters, Michael Gonzales, story by Shimon Arama; **Editor:** Michael Kelly; **Photography:** George Koblasa; **Music:** Terry Plumeri; **Cast:** Sho Kosugi, Jean-Claude Van Damme, Doran Clark, Bruce French, Vladimir Skomarovsky, Kane Kosugi, Shane Kosugi.

Black Rain

USA 1989 126 mins

Cultures clash and bullets fly as New York City cops Nick Conklin (Michael Douglas) and Charlie Vincent (Andy Garcia) hit Osaka, Japan, on the trail of icy Yakuza psychopath Sato (Yasuka Matsuda), a vicious, fearless killer with big, scary plans.

Nick rides a hog, wears leather and shades, with big, bad hair, a mess of stubble and nothing to lose (except a double chin), he is attitude incarnate. He is also completely burnt out. His partner Charlie, meanwhile, is a lot less complicated, a free and easy type who solves crimes by day and sings karaoke by night. Once in Japan, the boys learn a lesson in honour and respect from detective Ken Takakura, a reliable drone assigned to keep an eye on them who discovers that the American way, namely excessive force and incredible rudeness, can also work wonders in a criminal investigation. Finally, for glamour and tenuous romantic interest, Kate Capshaw (the second Mrs Spielberg) lends decorative support as a sympathetic nightclub hostess.

True to form, director Ridley Scott put a lot of thought and effort into the visuals, from incredible cityscapes to neon-lit streets and dark, smoky night spots. The action, when it comes, is slick and stylishly handled, a race, a chase, a meat-packers punch up, a jungle assault and mighty final battle ensuring that we don't feel short changed in the chaos department. Ranking above watchable but below essential, *Black Rain* is an intelligent, well made and decently played thriller which manages to entertain and even surprise without ever really involving its audience.

Director: Ridley Scott; **Producers:** Stanley R. Jaffe, Sherry Lansing; **Screenplay:** Craig Bolotin, Warren Lewis; **Production Design:** Norris Spencer; **Editor:** Tom Rolf; **Photography:** Jan De Bont; **Music:** Hans Zimmer; **Cast:** Michael Douglas, Andy Garcia, Ken Takakura, Kate Capshaw, Yasaka Matsuda.

Blind Fury

USA 1990 86 mins 🔫🔫🔫🔫

The truth is out. Violence is the key to coping with new and difficult disabilities, and if you need convincing, just ask Nick Parker, blind Samurai swordsman and slayer of two-bit villains. 'I also do circumcision', jokes the Vietnam veteran who lost his sight in an explosion but had the very good fortune to be rescued and nursed back to health by a friendly band of locals who trained him to enhance his remaining senses, and most usefully of all, how to slice and dice with the best of 'em.

Years later, Nick returns to the States in search of an old army buddy, Frank (Terry O'Quinn), only to find that his pal is in a whole world of trouble. Held hostage by cash-poor casino boss MacReady (Noble Willingham), chemist Frank is being forced to make designer drugs for the mob, in exchange for which they'll allow his nine-year-old son Billy (Brandon Call) to live. Only trouble is, they haven't quite gotten their mitts on the boy yet, and our visually challenged hero makes it his business to keep it that way, dragging the kid all the way from Miami to Reno to rescue dear old dad.

A cheerful martial arts adventure from Australian director Phillip Noyce, *Blind Fury* avoids the trap of taking itself too seriously, keeping the tone light while capitalizing on Parker's blindness to add a unique twist to a variety of different action scenes. At the centre of the movie is an appealing performance from Rutger Hauer, an underrated actor who makes as convincing a blind man as Pacino, although his feats of swordsmanship tend to require a willing suspension of disbelief. Maintaining a distant look, and a cool, bemused expression throughout, Hauer takes on a variety of henchmen, most memorably human mountain Randall 'Tex' Cobb as the type of hard-hittin' heavy who scratches his butt first and asks questions later.

'Get me Bruce Lee!' screams an irate MacReady, eager to find someone capable of taking on the indestructible Parker, whose feats of daring include chopping up a gang of red necks in a cornfield, duelling with a silent but deadly assassin (Sho Kosugi), and driving at warp speeds through crowded city streets, laughing all the way.

You should definitely keep an eye out for this one.

Director: Phillip Noyce; **Producers:** Daniel Grodnik, Tim Matheson; **Screenplay:** Charles Robert Carver; **Production Design**: Peter Murton; **Editor:** David Simmons; **Photography:** Don Burgess; **Music:** J. Peter Robinson; **Cast:** Rutger Hauer, Terrance (aka Terry) O'Quinn, Lisa Blount, Randall 'Tex' Cobb, Noble Willingham, Brandon Call, Meg Foster, Sho Kosugi.

Bloodsport

USA 1987 92 mins 🔫🔫🔫

Jean-Claude Van Damme and his mighty, dancing pecs take on the world's greatest warriors, leaping into action as he kicks, chops and mashes the lot of 'em into a fine, bloody paste in the sacred name of sport. Based, believe it or not, on a true story, *Bloodsport* blows the lid off the Kumite, a top secret, full contact martial arts competition held in Hong Kong.

Eager to prove his worth at the brutal, three-day crunch-a-thon, American Ninja-type Frank Dux (Jean-Claude) takes a break from his army duties for an adventure holiday back East, signing up for the Kumite in the hope of honouring his revered martial arts instructor through glorious combat. Once there, he male-bonds with beef mountain Ray Jackson (Donald Gibb), a gigantic, hairy nutcase who demolishes bricks with his head and plans on earning 'a few more scars' at the Kumite. Elsewhere, flimsy subplots include a brief romance with nosy blonde reporter Janice (Leah Ayres), while a couple of clowns from military security (Norman Burton and *The Crying Game*'s Forest Whitaker) make it their business to try to keep Frank safely clear of the Kumite. It's pretty thin stuff, to be sure, a half-baked story which serves as little more than a distraction from the true business at hand, namely a series of brutal martial arts struggles held on an increasingly blood-stained platform, and that's where this movie really shines.

Trained to ignore as well as to inflict pain, Dux struts his stuff against a variety of different opponents, each with their own distinct style, though none more lethal than Chong Li (Bolo Yeung), undefeated champion of the Kumite, demolisher of kneecaps and all-round evil scumbag. A big, bad bully with some wicked death moves, Li needs to learn the meaning of defeat, and who better than Dux to teach him?

Take *The Karate Kid*, cut the story and characterization, skip to the climactic fight scenes, make them about a thousand times more violent and pad out the entire movie with more of the same, and you've got *Bloodsport*. Let the games begin!

Back in the real world, Frank W. Dux fought 329 matches between 1975 and 1980, retiring undefeated as the World Heavyweight full contact Kumite champion. To this day he still holds four world records, namely fastest knockout (3.2 seconds), fastest punch with a knockout (0.12 seconds), fastest kick with a knockout (72 mph) and most consecutive knockouts in a single tournament (56!). Subsequently, Dux founded the first American Ninjitsu system, Dux-Ryu, and yep, you guessed it, served as both fight co-ordinator and Van Damme's personal trainer on *Bloodsport*.

Director: Newt Arnold; **Producer:** Mark DiSalle; **Screenplay:** Sheldon Lettich, Christopher Cosby, Mel Friedman; **Production Design:** David Searl; **Editor:** Carl Kress; **Photography:** David Worth; **Music:** Paul Hertzog; **Cast:** Jean-Claude Van Damme, Donald Gibb, Leah Ayres, Roy Chiao, Bolo Yeung, Norman Burton, Forest Whitaker.

Verbal Assaults 1

If you're gonna walk the walk, you gotta talk the talk...

Angry Police Chief: 'You nearly tore that boy's arm off.'
Unruffled Action Man: 'So - he had a spare.'
- Bill Duke fails to get through to Carl Weathers in *Action Jackson*.

'The sword is not for a traitor - you die by the knife!'
- Errol Flynn at his swashbuckling best, in *The Adventures of Don Juan*.

'My dear friend, there's a little bit of Don Juan in every man, and since I am Don Juan, there must be more of it in me!'
- Flynn states the obvious in *The Adventures of Don Juan*.

'It's the car, right? Chicks love the car.'
- Caped Crusader Val Kilmer analyses his appeal in *Batman Forever*.

'I could do wonders for that boy. I would re-charge his capacitators. Stimulate his solenoids. Tingle-dingle-dangle-prangle his transistors. You know - sex!'
- Strapping Amazonian babe Sybil Danning dreams of a liaison with Richard Thomas in *Battle Beyond the Stars*.

Army Brass: 'Braddock, I'm warning you, don't step on any toes'.
Maverick Hero: 'I don't step on toes, Little John, I step on necks'.
- Chuck Norris fights the good fight in *Braddock: Missing in Action III*.

'Would you mind not shooting at the thermo-nuclear weapons?'
- John Travolta discusses bomb maintenance with a particularly moronic goon in *Broken Arrow*.

'Anything moves - kill it.'
- Sound advice from Michael Dudikoff in *Chain of Command*.

'My hair's like a woman - you treat it good, and it treats you good. You got to hold it, caress it, love it, and it'll love you right back. And if your hair gets out of line, you take a scissor and say, "Hair, I'm gonna cut you".'
- Antonio Fargas menaces a chick from beneath a vast Afro in *Cleopatra Jones*.

'This is where the law stops and I start.'
- Sylvester Stallone prepares for violence in *Cobra*.

'You're a disease and I'm the cure.'
- Stallone again, on the facts of life, and death, in *Cobra*.

'You got two choices, asshole, duck... or bleed.'

- Steve James takes on a racist boozer in *Codename: The Soldier*.

'If I want your opinion I'll beat it out of you.'
- Chuck Norris charms a bar room thug in *Code of Silence*.

'I eat Green Berets for breakfast, and right now I'm very hungry!'
- Arnold Schwarzenegger discusses his diet arrangements in *Commando*.

Virgin princess: 'I suppose nothing hurts you.'
Conan: 'Only pain!'
- Olivia D'Abo quizzes a drunken Schwarzenegger in *Conan the Destroyer*.

'Sure it's violent, but that's the way we love it - violent, violent, violent!'
- TV anchorman Junior Bruce ('The Real' Don Steele) on the *Death Race 2000*.

'Sleep tight, sucker.'
- Chuck Norris wastes a terrorist hiding under a bed in *The Delta Force*.

'Bless me father, for I have just killed quite a few men...'
- *Desperado* star Antonio Banderas reveals all.

'Yippee ki yay mother fucker!'
- Bruce Willis expresses himself in *Die Hard*, *Die Hard 2: Die Harder* and *Die Hard With A Vengeance*.

'I know what you're thinking, punk. You're thinking did he fire six shots or only five? Now to tell you the truth I've forgotten myself in all this excitement, but being this is a .44 Magnum, the most powerful handgun in the world, and will blow your head clean off [pronounced 'awf'], you've got to ask yourself a question - "do I feel lucky?" Well, do ya' punk?'
- Clint 'Snake Eyes' Eastwood, playing it cool and hard with cornered psycho Andy Robinson in *Dirty Harry*.

'Boards... don't hit back.'
- But people do, and Bruce Lee beats 'em all in *Enter the Dragon*.

'Dos Vidanya, asshole.'
- Billy Baldwin gets tough with Russian scumbag Steven Berkoff in *Fair Game*.

'Why are you pushing me?'
- Stallone demands an explanation in *First Blood*.

'This time you're eating paper - the next time it's gonna be glass!' - Little Dragon Lee lays it on the line in *Fist of Fury*.

'Flash, I love you, but we only have 14 hours to save the Earth!'
- Melody Anderson brings our hero up to speed in *Flash Gordon*

Blue Thunder

USA 1983 108 mins

Roy Scheider takes to the unfriendly skies in a hardware-heavy thriller from Gadget Heaven, blasting at the bad guys and looping the loop in the coolest of movie inventions: Blue Thunder, a heavily-armoured prototype helicopter with a handy on-board computer, a whisper mode for silent running, an infra red video camera with a 100-1 zoom lens, audio sensors that can 'hear a mouse fart at 2000 feet', and, most usefully, a 20mm electric cannon capable of firing 4000 rounds of ammo per minute. Roy is the hero, as likeable and capable as ever, but the star of the show is quite clearly Blue Thunder, a nifty invention based, we are assured, on existing technology (and this was years ago, now).

A hotshot police pilot prone to Vietnam flashbacks, Murphy gets to take Blue Thunder out for a test spin in the company of his rookie partner Lymangood (Daniel Stern). Stumbling on a massive military conspiracy involving a villain from Murphy's past, the evil, annoying Cochrane (Malcolm McDowell), our heroes film a rather damning conversation in the name of evidence, setting the wheels of action in motion for all sorts of aerial shenanigans.

Ultimately, Murphy is forced to steal the 'copter in a last ditch attempt to save the day: pursued by the cops, Murphy's main squeeze (Candy Clark) races to a local TV station with the all-important videotape, while our hero confronts a pair of F-16 jet fighters for a desperate, against-the-odds dogfight above Los Angeles, dodging heat-seeking missiles and, finally, playing a deadly game of follow-my-leader with the big man himself, daredevil helicopter pilot and cardboard psychopath Cochrane.

If you're looking for realism, you've come to the wrong place. If, on the other hand, you're up for some wild and crazy comic book action with knockout stuntwork, a fair dose of juvenile humour and a whole load of exploding buildings, then this is the movie for you.

In 1984, a feeble TV spin-off hit the airwaves starring James Farentino as pilot Frank Chaney and *Wayne's World* star Dana Carvey as his partner Clinton. Mercifully, the ABC show was cancelled after only 13 episodes. Meanwhile, CBS executives had reason to cheer: they had ripped off the idea themselves and produced a much more successful programme, *Airwolf*.

Director: John Badham; **Producer:** Gordon Carroll; **Screenplay:** Dan O'Bannon, Don Jakoby; **Production Design:** Sydney Z. Litwack; **Editors:** Frank Morriss, Edward Abroms; **Photography:** John A. Alonzo; **Aerial Photography:** Frank Holgate; **Music:** Arthur B. Rubinstein; **Cast:** Roy Scheider, Malcolm McDowell, Candy Clark, Daniel Stern, Warren Oates, Paul Roebling.

Braddock: Missing In Action III
USA 1988 101 mins

All-American hero Colonel James Braddock (Chuck Norris) charges to the rescue of his wife and kid in this routine MIA adventure, foiling the cops on the streets of Bangkok and blasting the Cong back to hell in a movie which reveals Chuck's sensitive side as he discovers fatherhood, gets re-acquainted with his other half and shepherds a priest and a flock of orphaned children through enemy-infested jungle.

Here we discover that Braddock liked at least one Vietnamese person, marrying a local girl only to lose her to a random bombing during the fall of Saigon - or so he believed. Years later, Braddock learns otherwise from a priest who tells him that his wife and child are alive, though not particularly well, and held captive by the enemy. True to form, the authorities are either unwilling or unable to help, and so, once again, it's up to Braddock to save the day, supported by a rocket gun, a turbo-charged speedboat and incredible recuperative powers which allow him to burst into action even after hours of mental and physical torture.

Director Aaron Norris steers his brother through all the same old stuff, a by-the-numbers jumble of corny drama and passable adventure which falls way short of a recommendation. Still, the opening flashback, set during the fall of Saigon, is impressive enough, while Chuck's hard-man routine prompts a smile from time to time. Crumbs of entertainment are all we're offered, though, not a loaf (that would be the first), not even a sandwich (that would be the second), but a crust, and an old one at that, representing the last and least of a trio of average actioners.

Director: Aaron Norris; **Producers:** Menahem Golan, Yoram Globus; **Screenplay:** James Bruner, Chuck Norris, based on characters created by Arthur Silver, Larry Levinson and Steve Bing; **Production Design:** Ladislav Wilheim; **Editor:** Michael J. Duthie; **Photography:** Joao Fernandes; **Music:** Jay Chattaway; **Cast:** Chuck Norris, Aki Aleong, Miki Kim, Yehuda Efroni, Ron Barker, Floyd Levine, Roland Harrah III.

Breaker! Breaker!
USA 1977 86 mins

Trouble's brewing in Texas City, California, a grotty little ghost town with delusions of grandeur where crime pays plenty. Ruled with an oily hand by Judge Joshua G. Trimmings (George Murdock), it's a wild western relic out of time in 1970s America, a square mile of lawlessness dedicated to chewing up and spitting out all passing trade. Practised in the art of luring truckers to their doom, Judge Josh and his local posse discover the true meaning of justice when J.D. Dawes (Chuck Norris, not a whisker in sight) rides into town, a one-man search party determined to find his missing brother...

Sure enough, J.D. has his hands full when he hits Texas City, a breeding farm for good ol' boys high on moonshine and hard on strangers. Slow at first, and entirely forgettable, the movie picks up just as soon as Chuck gets physical, ploughing his way through the locals with such speed and ferocity that most of the fight scenes are over within a few seconds. Fortunately, no matter how many scumbags Chuck whacks into submission, there's always a fresh batch ready to crawl out of the woodwork and give him a medium-hard time.

Cashing in on the Citizen's Band Radio craze that, for a while at least, made trucking seem like a fun profession, the movie breaks up its soft rock and country music soundtrack with occasional bursts of CB lingo supplied by the eminently qualified likes of Chuck 'The Tuna' Collins, Bob 'Red Dog' Young and last, and most probably least, Danny 'Bud Man' Delany.

Towards the end of this cheap but spirited chop-a-thon, as Chuck's trucker buddies transform into demolition men, writer/director Don Hullette makes the pretentious error of looking for some meaning in the madness, rounding off the movie with a dreary slow-motion one-on-one as a wild horse gallops frantically around our combatants. Obvious gropes for depth aside, however, *Breaker! Breaker!* is a minor but enjoyable actioner, nothing special, but chaotic enough to pass the time. Best of all is the sight of Chuck, shot in the gut but determined to press on, meditating the pain away before pulling himself up to continue the slaughter. Faith healers have since confirmed that given a weak enough script, a gun loaded with blanks, and a great, big dollop of ketchup, any one of us could perform this miracle in the comfort of our own B-movie.

Director: Don Hulette; **Producer:** Don Hulette; **Screenplay:** Terry Chambers; **Production Design:** Thomas Thomas; **Editor:** Steven Zaillian; **Photography:** Mario Dileo; **Music:** Don Hulette; **Cast:** Chuck Norris, George Murdock, Terry O'Connor, Don Gentry, Michael Augenstein.

Broken Arrow

USA 1996 86 mins

John Travolta and Christian Slater slug it out in John Woo's second US misfire, a *Die Hard*-in-the-desert adventure which passes inspection on the action front but blows it big time with a senseless plot, overblown direction and a trio of characters you'll care nothing about.

Boil the story down and what have we got? Stealth bomber pilots Vic (Travolta) and Riley (Slater) are chosen to test a top secret new toy, but Vic's bored of playing by the rules, so he tries to kill his young gun partner, crashes the plane, grabs its nuclear cargo and makes off with his henchmen buddies. Eager to save the world, Riley heads out after him, hooking up with superfluous Ranger girl Samantha Mathis (Slater's *Pump Up The Volume* co-star) so that he, too, has someone to talk to.

As directed by Woo, Travolta lays on an excess of sledgehammer cool, as corny and overplayed as Slater's perennial Jack Nicholson impersonation. Neither make much of an impression: Travolta's not worth booing, Slater's not worth cheering, and while some of the action sequences are technically impressive (explosions fill the screen as Woo trashes a variety of trains, planes and automobiles), it's hard to get excited when you don't give a hoot who lives or dies.

There's plenty of gunplay on offer and some truly nasty deaths, a wild underground mine set and all sorts of smart-ass technology, but considering this is meant to be a film about Stealth Bomber pilots, it's strange and disappointing that the action is mostly earthbound while the plane itself barely makes it ten minutes into the movie before falling to pieces.

Director: John Woo; **Producers:** Mark Gordon, Bill Badalato; **Screenplay:** Graham Yost; **Production Design:** Holger Gross; **Editors:** John Wright, Steve Mirkovich, Joe Hutshing; **Photography:** Peter Levy; **Music:** Hans Zimmer; **Cast:** John Travolta, Christian Slater, Samantha Mathis, Delroy Lindo, Bob Gunton, Frank Whaley, Howie Long.

Death Becomes Them 1

Name: BRONSON, Charles

Real name: Charles Buchinsky

Born: Ehrenfield, Pennsylvania, 1921

Characteristics: The *other* great stone-face, the Fantastic Four's Thing with hair, a single expression which says it all: 'Keep away, buddy, or I'll introduce your insides to your outsides'.

Previous professions: Streetfighter, coal-miner, sailor...

Debut feature: *You're in the Navy Now* (1951)

He's mad as hell, and he ain't gonna take it no more: Charles Bronson fights back in *Death Wish*.

Life and times: The first Buchinsky (of Lithuanian descent) to make it through high school (leaving fourteen brothers and sisters in his wake). Charles did his bit for the Second World War effort by enlisting in the Navy, picking up a fondness for flared trousers which peaked in the 1970s. Back in the early 1950s, the budding actor found steady work playing ethnic types (mostly Apaches) and heavies in a variety of Hollywood B-pictures, changing his name to Bronson in 1954 and working his way through the 1960s playing men of few words in 'boys' own' adventure movies that remain, to thisday, the best thing on Christmas TV. The 1970s spawned the Bronson/Winner partnership, a lasting commitment to screen violence which coughed up *Death Wish* and made Bronson, already well into his fifth decade, a fully-fledged movie star. Married to actress and frequent co-star Jill Ireland from 1968 until she died of cancer in 1990, Bronson continues to play it tough, turning in his most recent *Death Wish* movie (No. 5) at the golden age of 72.

Greatest contribution to action movies: Long before Eastwood adopted the grizzled look, Bronson proved that oldsters could still kick butt with the best of 'em, making the world a safer place for vigilantes by killing all the other murderers in town.

Speech, speech: 'Nobody stays on top forever. Nobody!'

Walter Hill on Chuck's mug: 'There's a lot of poetry in his face.'

Bronson enters the face debate: 'I guess it looks like a rock quarry that somebody has dynamited.'

Selected filmography: *House of Wax* (1953), *Machine Gun Kelly* (1958), *The Magnificent Seven* (1960), *The Great Escape* (1963), *The Dirty Dozen* (1967), *Once Upon a Time in the West* (1969), *Chato's Land* (1972), *The Mechanic* (1972), *The Valachi Papers* (1972), *The Stone Killer* (1973), *Death Wish* (1974),

> *Breakout* (1975), *Hard Times* (1975), *The Streetfighter* (1975), *Breakheart Pass*
> (1976), *St Ives* (1976), *Raid on Entebbe* (TV; 1976), *Telefon* (1976), *The White*
> *Buffalo* (1977), *Love and Bullets* (1979), *Borderline* (1980), *Death Wish II*
> (1982), *Ten to Midnight* (1983), *The Evil That Men Do* (1984), *Death Wish III*
> (1985), *Murphy's Law* (1986), *Death Wish IV: The Crackdown* (1987), *The Indian*
> *Runner* (1991), *Death Wish V: The Face of Death* (1993).

Bronx Warriors

Italy 1982 84 mins

Ill-fated actor Vic (*Twilight Zone: The Movie*) Morrow kicks butt and blasts brains in this shlocky but spirited B-feature 'inspired' by the likes of *Escape From New York* and *The Warriors*. We're in the future again, and, as ever, a faceless corporation runs the show with an iron hand. This time around, we're stranded in New York, with the Bronx serving as designated war zone (no change there, then), a lawless wasteland where heavily-armed soldiers duke it out with blade-wielding gang weirdos for our viewing pleasure. So, anyway, there's this chick, a wealthy, runaway heiress who turns her back on privilege in favour of life as a fugitive in the most dangerous city on earth, hooking up with biker gang The Riders and getting down with their illustrious leader, pretty boy Trash (Mark Gregory). Only trouble is, President Dad wants his precious little angel back, despatching professional son-of-a-bitch Hammer (Morrow) to retrieve her, and, while he's at it, slaughter as many trouble-makers as possible.

A psycho cop with mirrored shades, furry 'tache and poor interpersonal skills, Hammer takes life without mercy or even a second thought, 'an asshole who thinks he's god' who serves as the movie's villain, while the significantly less appealing Trash, that hog-ridin', hell-raisin', heavy metal Chippendale-type, clocks in as our hero, the lesser of several evils.

There's treachery, gang warfare and battle scenes a-plenty as director Enzo Castellari cranks up the violence and chucks in some swearing for luck. A convenient hardware shortage ensures that, in place of traditional gunplay, the action is up close and personal, with lead pipes and home-made knives responsible for more than a few bloody encounters.

As you'd expect, flaws come in all shapes and sizes, from a dodgy, humourless screenplay to a cast so wooden the Bronx becomes a forest. Only Morrow emerges unscathed, his malicious, crusty performance serving the movie well, as does an all-out combat climax, complete with flame-thrown death, cops on horseback, blood, guts and chaos. One for the kids, then.

Sequel: *Bronx Warriors II: The Battle For Manhattan.*

Director: Enzo Castellari; **Producer:** Fabrizio de Angelis; **Screenplay:** Enzo G. Castellari, Dardano Sacchetti, Elisa Livia Briganti; **Production Design:** Massimo Lentini; **Editor:** Gianfranco Amicucci; **Photography:** Sergio Salvati; **Music:** Walter Rizatti; **Cast:** Vic Morrow, Christopher Connelly, Fred Williamson, Mark Gregory, Stefania Girolami.

Bulletproof

USA 1987 94 mins

Gary Busey could have been a major star, but he blew it. The world was his hamburger as he rode high on the success of *Lethal Weapon*, his hardened performance as flame-grilled henchman Mr Joshua earning him a place in fandom and a corner in

Hollywood. A starring role in a major feature could have been his, a chance to consolidate his fame, earn some serious money, and maybe even do an Oprah special. Why then, did he make the cheap and cheerless action dud *Bulletproof*, a B-movie bomb which wiped his name off the lips of the world and sent him back to the little leagues? We may never know, or even care, why a man offered steak chooses turkey instead, but besides death and taxes, the one remaining certainty in this crazy world is that this low-grade hunk of dim-witted junk should be avoided at all costs.

As a typically unstoppable, laughably invincible, rubbery-faced LA cop with a Special Forces background and a macho, wise-ass attitude, Gary Busey plays the hero game at its most basic level. A man with a peculiar talent for getting shot, McBain (McBusey) keeps the slugs in a jar at home, a record-breaking 39 in all, a sentimental reminder of psychos past. Charm doesn't really enter into the McBain equation, but he sure loves to kill, a talent his former CIA buddies bank on when they send him out to Mexico with a view to repossessing a supertank while rescuing a bunch of US hostages (including ex-squeeze Darlanne Fluegel) from the clutches of yet another Henry Silva psycho, leader of a highly expendable army of Cuban, Nicaraguan and Arab terrorists.

The action is chaotic and frequent, the violence appropriately bloody, yet the movie remains strangely lifeless, busy and loud but about as exciting as a date with Mary Whitehouse. The whole thing's way too cheap and nasty for its own good, heavy-handed exploitation without a good/bad angle to come to its rescue. But then, what else could you expect from the men who brought us *Big Bad Mama* (director Steve Carver) and *Hollywood Chainsaw Hookers* (associate producer Fred Olen Ray), other than a like-minded stinker which labours to give schlock a bad name?

Yes, that is *Hill Street Blues*' Rene Enriquez (alias Lieutenant Ray Calletano), hanging around in the background as a stock military type.

Director: Steve Carver; **Producer:** Paul Hertzberg; **Screenplay:** T.L. Lankford, Steve Carver; **Production Design:** Adrian H. Gorton; **Editor:** Jeff Freeman; **Photography:** Francis Grumman; **Music:** Tom Chase, Steve Rucker; **Cast:** Gary Busey, Darlanne Fluegel, Henry Silva, Thalmus Rasulala, L.Q. Jones, Rene Enriquez.

Chain of Command

USA 1993 91 mins

A bog-standard B-movie with delusions of grandeur, *Chain of Command* offers a set menu of death, destruction and macho heroics, killing with confidence but falling a-over-t with the story, a needlessly complex and confused piece of work which does nothing for the movie but slow it down. Michael Dudikoff is our hero of the hour, an ex-special forces cliché who turns his back on violence only to welcome it back into his life within minutes of the movie's kick-off.

Welcome, then, to the Middle Eastern Republic of Qumir, a strange and dangerous land where terrorists are free to kidnap as many Americans as they like, provided, that is, they don't mind fighting for their worthless lives with action man Merrill Ross (our Mike), an undercover good guy with hostages to rescue and QLI (Qumiri Liberation Initiative), CIA and Mossad agents on his tail.

Supporting hams include Sam Elliott wannabe Todd Curtis, a long-haired fortysomething with a penchant for cigars and villainous behaviour, crime boss R. Lee Ermey, and secret agent/*femme fatale*/sidekick/love interest/damsel-in-distress/vacuous window dressing Maya (Keren Tishman).

Get past the plot pretensions and you might just make it: director Worth churns out the action from beginning to end, starting poorly with a dimly lit battle sequence but gaining momentum as the movie hopscotch's from gunfight to chase scene to full-on one-to-one. Knives, bayonets and other props sharp enough to take an eye out ensure a blood-and-guts bounty, with a nifty pool cue impalement proving particularly memorable.

Take your pleasures where you can: true, this film is as cheap and cheesy as they come, a quota-quickie with a dire synthesized soundtrack and actors so wooden they need fire insurance, but beyond all this badness there's a ton of mindless rough-and-tumble waiting to be discovered by anyone drunk enough to take a chance.

Director: David Worth; **Producer:** Allan Greenblatt, Asher Gat; **Screenplay:** Christopher Applegate, Ben Johnson Handy; **Production Design:** Kuly Sander; **Editor:** Alain Jakubowicz; **Photography:** Avi Koren; **Music:** Greg King, rock tracks by Slash Puppet; **Cast:** Michael Dudikoff, Todd Curtis, Keren Tishman, R. Lee Ermey, Steve Greenstein, Jack Adalist, Eli Danker.

Death Becomes Them 2

Name: CHAN, Jackie

Real name: Chan Kwong-Sang
Born: Hong Kong, 1954

Characteristics: Fast, fearless and flexible, stronger than chilli sauce with a likeable face and a kick powerful enough to send his foes into the next dimension.

Debut feature: *Big and Little Wong Tin Bar* (1962)

Hong Kong superstar Jackie Chan strikes a pose.

Life and times: An only child, Chan was packed off to live and study at the Peking Opera Academy at the tender age of seven. From child actor to stuntman (in the Bruce Lee classics *Fist of Fury* and *Enter the Dragon*) to martial arts superstar and movie maker, Chan is famous for performing his own stunts, surviving an average of one or two nasty accidents per picture. Hailed as the 'Buster Keaton of Hong Kong', Chan's comic timing, showman charm and startling martial arts ability have been put to prolific good use for more than two decades, and counting...

Greatest contribution to action movies: A hero we can believe in, mostly because, when the action gets a little hairy, it's still *him* up there on the screen, busting his chops and risking his life for our personal pleasure. Added to which, the guy can choreograph a fight like Fred Astaire on acid.

Speech, speech: 'People look at the Kung Fu films we made a few years ago and say, "That's not real. We want realism." Nowadays, we still use some of the old Kung Fu techniques, but we've added boxing techniques and use tables and chairs instead of traditional Chinese weapons. Cars, motorcycles and bicycles are also popular action aids in today's movies. In

Hong Kong now, fight scenes are as real as life itself. The opponents don't pull their punches as they used to, but hit each other with full power and often suffer real injuries. When I get hit hard and knocked flat, my stuntmen don't worry about it. They know that's what I want. Realism.'

'When I made *The Protector* they gave me two days to direct the fight scenes. Impossible! In Hong Kong, I can spend a month on just one fight. I write out the rhythm, like music: pow, pow... pow pow pow... POW! American films don't care about the action. One punch and they fall.'

Selected filmography: *Hand of Death* (1976), *Snake in the Eagle's Shadow* (1978), ***Drunken Master*** (1978), *Fearless Hyena* (+ dir; 1979), *Young Master* (+ dir; 1980), *The Cannonball Run* (1981), *Project A* (+ dir; 1984), *Wheels on Meals* (1984), ***The Protector*** (1986), ***Police Story*** (+ dir; 1986), ***Armour of God*** (+ dir; 1986), *Project A Part Two* (+ dir; 1987), *Dragons Forever* (1987), ***Police Story II*** (+ dir; 1988), *Armour of God II: Operation Condor* (+ dir; 1991), *Twin Dragons* (1991), ***Police Story III*** (1992), *Crime Story* (1993), *City Hunter* (1993), *Drunken Master II* (1994), ***Rumble in the Bronx*** (1994).

The Chase

USA 1994 94 mins

Ladies and gentlemen, please check your brains at the door. What we have here is an endearingly dumb teen-dream adventure starring the ever-ordinary Charlie Sheen and starlet Kristy Swanson - it's a comedy, it's a romance, it's a road movie too. It might even teach you a little something about yourselves. Just kidding.

Sentenced to 25 years in the slammer for a crime he didn't commit (big surprise), Jack (Sheen) escapes the law, takes pretty young thing Natalie (Swanson) hostage, and hottails it to Mexico - and freedom - in her flashy red BMW. Theirs is a match made in Hollywood heaven: he's a working class stiff, she's a rich, overprivileged brat, they share no common ground and couldn't possibly get along, so naturally they fall for one another. And so, pursued by the cops and later by the media, Jack and Natalie allow themselves about a half hour of bickering and light stunt work before they get down to business, falling in love and tearing up the highway.

The high-speed chases and auto rough-and-tumble have a familiar ring, but there's a triumphantly stupid car sex scene that's worth catching, and a lively performance from heavy metal philosopher Henry Rollins as a hick lawman whose every move is captured by a camera crew intent on producing one of those 'real life' cop shows.

Writer/director Adam Rifkin does all he can to make up for the lack of chemistry between his two leads, but quick cuts, jerky camera movements and pounding rock tracks (including something from the Rollins Band) aside, what makes this brain candy watchable is the media's frantic attempts to cover the chase, and the road-bound destruction that follows the couple all the way to the promised land.

Watch out for the 'Red Nose Robber's' *Apocalypse Now* routine after the closing credits.

Director: Adam Rifkin; **Producers:** Brad Wyman, Cassian Elwes; **Screenplay:** Adam Rifkin; **Production Design:** Sherman Williams; **Editor:** Peter Schink; **Photography:** Alan Jones; **Music:** Richard Gibbs; **Cast:** Charlie Sheen, Kristy Swanson, Henry Rollins,

John Mostel, Wayne Grace, Rocky Carroll, Miles Dougal, Ray Wise, Claudia Christian, Natalija Nogulich, Flea, Anthony Kiedis.

China O'Brien

USA 1988 90 mins

It's a man's world, alright, and Cynthia Rothrock cheerfully cripples most of them in the name of schlock movie-making and plain, old-fashioned brutality. She's a big city cop, a martial arts instructor too, who quits the force and swears off guns and violence after accidentally shooting a kid. So she heads for her roots, moving home with her Pa, the struggling sheriff of a hick town run behind the scenes by local kingpin Summers (Steven Kerby).

Now, it's as plain as a water sandwich that Daddy isn't long for this world, that pretty soon Summers will send the boys round to deal with him, and that, yes, Sheriff O'Brien's daughter China will learn to embrace homicide once more in the righteous name of revenge. 'I'll never touch a gun again', she swears, but as one of the local neanderthals note, China's 'one of them chop suey fighters', and more than capable of taking care of herself.

Running for Sheriff so that the inevitable slaughter will be good 'n' legal, our pint-sized superheroine employs the services of a couple of supporting action men, namely ex-special forces beefcake Matt (Richard Conroy) and creepy biker dude Dakota (Keith Cooke), and the carnage begins.

Cheaply produced and populated with a cast of side-burned amateurs, *China O'Brien* shares more in common with low rent 1970s exploitation than high concept 1980s adventure, a definite misfire from the team responsible for the immortal *Enter The Dragon* (director Robert Clouse, executive producer Raymond Chow). A heavy dose of hand-to-hand and foot-to-head martial arts combat boosts the movie from C to B status, but with the obvious exception of a woman in the starring role, there's nothing new to see here.

 During the final battle, there's a scene in which China's deputies jump through a window two by two, their swiftness and agility boosted by a couple of seconds of obviously sped up film.

Sequel: *China O'Brien 2*.

Director: Robert Clouse; **Producers:** Fred Weintraub, Sandra Weintraub; **Executive Producer:** Raymond Chow; **Screenplay:** Robert Clouse, from a story by Sandra Weintraub; **Production Design:** John Told; **Editor:** Mark Hurrah; **Photography:** Kent Wakeford; **Music:** David Wheatley, Paul Antonelli; **Cast:** Cynthia Rothrock, Richard Norton, Keith Cooke, Steven Kerby.

Name: CHOW, Yun-Fat

Born: Lama Island (off the coast of mainland China), 1955

Characteristics: An Eastern Eastwood, tough and moody, looks good in shades, great with a gun, even better with two.

Previous professions: Factory worker

Debut feature: *The Reincarnation* (1976)

Life and times: Although well known to TV audiences across South East Asia as the star of the popular series *Shanghai Town*, Chow Yun Fat didn't make it in the movies until director John Woo cast him as a trigger-happy mob enforcer in *A Better Tomorrow* (1986), a thriller which remains, to this day, one of the top grossing films in Hong Kong.

Death Becomes Them 3

Starring roles in *The Killer* (1989) and *Hard Boiled* (1992) earned Chow international recognition, and today he is recognised as one of the East's hottest properties, an 'acting machine' who avoided being typecast as an action hero and is now accepted in comedies and dramas as well as thrillers.

Dirty Harry heads East: Chow Yun-Fat is too cool to die in *Hard Boiled*.

Secret ambition: To play Rick in a remake of *Casablanca*.

Greatest contribution to action movies: The coolest, toughest, fastest gun in the East.

Speech, speech: 'You cannot blame [films] for the breakdown of society. It's down to the parents and the education system to teach the new generation. Not the movies!'

Selected filmography: *The Story of Wu-Viet* (1981), **A Better Tomorrow** (1986), *City On Fire* (1987), *A Better Tomorrow 2* (1987), **Tiger On The Beat** (1989), *Wild Search* (1989), **The Killer** (1989), *A Better Tomorrow 3* (1989), *God of Gamblers* (1990), *Once a Thief* (1991), **Hard Boiled** (1992), *Full Contact* (1992), *God of Gamblers 2* (1994), *Peace Hotel* (1995).

City Hunter

Hong Kong 1992 102 mins

Jackie Chan smartens up the image of sex-obsessed comicbook hero Ryu Saeba in this blockbusting, live-action adaptation, surrounding himself with fabulous, Bond-worthy babes yet keeping a lid on the more perverted stuff. Fear not, however, for though sex may not be on the agenda, quick-witted ultra-violence most certainly is, and though the story and supporting characters leave less of an impression than a bug in wet cement, Chan is as cool and capable as ever, stomping bad guys in many weird and wonderful ways.

Light, violent and fearlessly silly, *City Hunter* follows the eponymous crime-fighting whiz as he and his long-suffering partner (Joey Wong) attempt to track down a runaway heiress (Goto Kumiko), pursuing their quarry aboard a luxury ocean liner in time for extended *Die Hard/Under Siege*-style shenanigans involving a beautiful private detective (Chingamy Yau), a classy master gambler (Leon Lai) and, for spice, a well-armed gang of international terrorists with mayhem on their minds.

Never mind the plot, though, check out the set-pieces: an ambitiously choreographed skateboard chase, a punch-up at the movies in the cinematic presence of Bruce Lee, and a mighty one-to-one with Ozzie action man (and token gwailo) Richard Norton. Best of all, though, is a wacky confrontation inspired by that most classic of classic videogames, Street Fighter 2, as a shocking collision with a games console results in a serious personality crisis for Chan, who morphs into a variety of the game's best known characters, from hulking Sumo Honda to kick-crazy maiden Chun Li. It would be worth catching *City Hunter* for this scene alone (which blows Van Damme's *Street Fighter* right out of the water), but there's a hell of a lot more to keep you occupied in this one.

Director: Wong Jing; **Producer:** Wong Jing, Chua Lam; **Screenplay:** Wong Jing; **Production Design:** Hai Chung Man; **Editor:** Cheung Yiu Chung, Cheung Kai Fai; **Photography:** Lee Chi Hang, Tom Lau, Ma Ka Cheung; **Music:** Romeo Diaz, James Wong; **Cast:** Jackie Chan, Joey Wong, Chingamy Yau, Richard Norton, Gary Daniels, Leon Lam, Goto Kumiko.

Cleopatra Jones

USA 1973 89 mins

She's 'ten miles of bad road' for every hood in town, a high-kicking government agent with a wardrobe full of groovy threads, a bitchin' black corvette, a caring, sharing boyfriend (Bernie Casey) and a capacity for slang unequalled in the western world (classics include 'dig it', 'right on', 'jive', 'dude', 'cat' and 'heavy trip'). She's 'some kind of woman'. She's gonna save the day. She is, of course, the one, the only, Cleopatra Jones (Tamara Dobson), and drug dealers had better beware.

To call this movie camp barely does it justice. This is prime blaxploitation and no mistake, so bad it's good, and funny too, with outrageous performances from the likes of Antonio 'Huggy Bear' Fargas as super-pusher Doodlebug and Shelly Winters as principal villainess Mommy, an oversized blot on the landscape with a bright red wig stolen, no doubt, from Ronald McDonald.

Dated, dire and deliriously stupid, with a funky, porno-style soundtrack accompanying every shoot-out, car chase and Hapkido karate punch-up (courtesy of Master Bong Soo Han, Korean martial arts expert and technical advisor), this is a masterpiece of bad, ideal for your silliest mood.

Sequel: *Cleopatra Jones and the Casino of Gold.*

Director: Jack Starrett; **Producer:** Bill Tennant; **Screenplay:** Max Julien, Sheldon Keller; **Production Design:** Peter Wooley; **Editor:** Allan Jacobs; **Photography:** David Walsh; **Music:** J.J. Johnson; **Cast:** Tamara Dobson, Bernie Casey, Shelley Winters, Brenda Sykes, Antonio Fargas, Dan Frazer, Bill McKinney, Esther Rolle.

Cliffhanger

USA 1993 112 mins

Sylvester Stallone had hit an all-time low. *Rocky* and *Rambo*, his only two money-makers, were out for the count, while the painfully unfunny duo of *Oscar* and *Stop! Or My Mom Will Shoot* confirmed beyond doubt that Sly had an innate lack of comic timing. Then along came a movie which rescued the Italian Stallion's career, a tense, exciting action thriller set, appropriately enough, in the Rocky Mountains (although the film was actually shot in Italy's Dolomites). Mixing breathtaking scenery, gob-smacking stuntwork and an athletic pace with a standard *Die Hard* scenario, director Renny Harlin hit the jackpot with *Cliffhanger*.

A daring aerial robbery ends in disaster as three cases loaded with $100 million of Treasury cash drop over the Rockies. Crash landing in the middle of nowhere, our villains lure troubled mountain rescue ace Gabe Walker (Sly) and his estranged pal Hal Tucker (Michael Rooker, star of the chilling *Henry: Portrait of a Serial Killer*) to their stormy, snowbound location, forcing our heroes at gunpoint to guide them to the dough. Escaping from their clutches, Gabe hooks up with romantic interest Jessie Deighan (*Northern Exposure*'s Janine Turner) and regains his lost nerve by taking on the bad guys one at a time...

Sylvester Stallone and Janine Turner scale the Rocky (Balboa) Mountains in *Cliffhanger*.

Fighting for the forces of evil, John Lithgow overplays head crackpot Qualen, a psychotic Brit (how original) with a flair for theatrics, a lousy, ever-changing accent and an endless supply of cheesy one-liners (corny classics include, 'Kill a few people they call you a murderer. Kill a million and you're a conqueror. Go figure.' and 'You want to kill me, don't you Tucker? Then take a number and get in line.'). Supporting scumbags of note include crooked fed Travers (Rex Linn), vicious heavy Kynette (Leon), foul-mouthed hooligan Delmar (Craig Fairbrass) and Qualen's quick-witted girlie, Kristel (Caroline Goodall).

Compensating for a feeble arch-enemy and a dodgy screenplay, Renny Harlin keeps the pressure on and the action at fever pitch: besides several incredible climbing sequences and the occasional avalanche, jeopardy worth waiting for includes Gabe tobogganing down a mountain *on* a bad guy, a brutal, batcave punch up with a commendably juicy punchline, a full-on one-to-one as Delmar plays football with Hal's head, a dramatic (if obviously set-bound) Gabe-under-ice encounter with Travers and, saving the best until last, a cliffhanging, chopper-crashing, mountain hugging, kidney-slugging grand finale.

Director: Renny Harlin; **Producers:** Alan Marshall, Renny Harlin; **Screenplay:** Michael France, Sylvester Stallone, based on a premise by John Long; **Production Design:** John Vallone; **Editor:** Frank J. Urioste; **Photography:** Alex Thomson; **Music:** Trevor Jones; **Cast:** Sylvester Stallone, John Lithgow, Michael Rooker, Janine Turner, Rex Linn, Caroline Goodall, Leon, Craig Fairbrass, Ralph Waite, Paul Winfield.

Cobra

USA 1986 87 mins

Detective Cobretti drives a flash car, wears expensive shades and chews on a toothpick. He's a tough guy with a death wish and a smart mouth, a lawless lawman who's crazier than the bad guys he routinely sends to the morgue. They call him Cobra, we call him Sylvester Stallone, but either way he sure ain't Dirty Harry. 'In America', he slurs at the beginning of the movie, 'there's a burglary every 11 seconds. An armed robbery every 65 seconds. A violent crime every 25 seconds. A murder every 24 minutes. And 250 rapes a day.' Added to which, this fine piece of work contributes a killing every 11 seconds, a stereotype every 65 seconds, a cliché every 25 seconds, and an infinite number of macho mumblings along the lines of 'This is where the law stops, and I start.' Good sense has no place here.

There's a serial killer on the loose, a hard-working, axe-wielding maniac known as the Night Slasher, yet for some reason Cobra suspects that there's more than one psycho at work. Our hero feels this way because there's only one man alive capable of such slaughter unaided, and it's him. Besides, why send Cobra up against a single villain when he can take on a whole gang of nutters? There's no mystery here, though, just an awful lot of death and destruction, from the obligatory convenience store hold-up at the top of the picture, through to a rather tasty car chase in the middle, right on down to the wholesale slaughter of a gang of evil biker-types at the bottom.

A movie to laugh at, not with, *Cobra* shoots itself in the foot by inviting further, unflattering comparison with *Dirty Harry* by casting Reni Santoni - who played Harry's partner - as Cobra's partner, while Andy Robinson, who played wild-eyed psycho Scorpio, turns up as a typically sore-headed police chief. The film also does itself no favours by casting Brigitte Nielsen (who was Mrs Stallone at the time) as romantic interest Ingrid Knudsen (pretty name), a witless witness who develops a serious case of the hots for Mr Cobretti.

Still, we're not talking rocket science here. Either you pick this film apart, scene by scene, or you enjoy it for the brainless nonsense that it is, worthless, violent, and kinda fun.

Check out the major product placement going on in this film. Director George Cosmatos plugs everything from Coors Beer and Pepsi to Coke and Toys-R-Us. Just about the only product he isn't able to promote is Stallone: *Cobra* was not the hit the Italian Stallion had hoped for.

Director: George Cosmatos; **Producers:** Menahem Golan, Yoram Globus; **Screenplay:** Sylvester Stallone, based on the novel *Fair Game* by Paula Gosling; **Production Design:** Bill Kenney; **Editors:** Don Zimmerman, James Symons; **Photography:** Ric Waite; **Music:** Sylvester Levay; **Cast:** Sylvester Stallone, Brigitte Nielsen, Reni Santoni, Andrew Robinson, Brian Thompson, Lee Garlington.

Code of Silence

USA 1985 101 mins

Welcome to Chuck country. Keep the chatter to a minimum. Lose the facial expressions. Grow a beard. Work on those snake eyes. And beat up everyone you meet. Then, and only then, will you deserve to ride alongside the Norris machine.

As untouchable cop Eddie Cusack, Norris takes on the mob as a minor gang war erupts in the city of Chicago. Mafia bigshot Luis Comacho (Henry Silva) dedicates his life to destroying ambitious thug Tony Luna (Mike Genovese), but bad guys have to be taught that they have no place killing one another. That's Eddie's job, and he's out to prove it. Big time. Eddie also finds himself in the unusual position of trying to keep someone alive, as he struggles to protect Luna's innocent daughter Diana (Molly Hagan) from Comacho's increasingly psychotic murder attempts. There's trouble too, back at the cop shop, where Eddie risks losing his crimebusting pals by breaking the code of silence and publicly criticizing well-liked but burnt-out cop Cragie (Ralph Foody). Pretty dramatic, eh?

Chuck devotees are likely to get the most out of this modest thriller, because the action is pretty standard throughout, and while the basic story has promise, there's a shortage of imagination when it comes to the characters and the screenplay. There are several bad guys to choose from, but none are given adequate screen time, and without the proper care and attention they remain weak and only mildly villainous, not really worth booing at all.

But Chuck makes it all better. So cool he's practically comatose, he rips his way through assorted crooks, killers and dealers, casually dispensing one-liners while barely breaking a sweat.

Director Andrew Davis wisely saves his best scene till last, rounding off the movie with a commendably destructive warehouse battle in which Chuck takes on the staff of Henchmen-R-Us with the help of a heavily armed law enforcement robot (supplied to the movie by Robot Defence Systems, Inc., of Thornton, Colorado) called 'Prowler'. And guess who wins?

Director: Andrew Davis; **Producer:** Raymond Wagner; **Screenplay:** Michael Butler, Dennis Shryack, Mike Gray; **Production Design:** Maher Ahmed; **Editors:** Peter Parasheles, Christopher Holmes; **Photography:** Frank Tidy; **Music:** David Frank; **Cast:** Chuck Norris, Henry Silva, Bert Remsen, Molly Hagan, Mike Genovese, Nathan Davis, Ralph Foody, Dennis Farina.

Codename: The Soldier (aka The Soldier)

USA 1982 88 mins

The world's up the creek, but it has a paddle: The Soldier (God help us all). Only he can steer us away from nuclear devastation. Only he can pose, shamelessly, doing his damnedest to look studly while the stuntman do the real work. And only he can kill the kind of people who die in slow motion, screaming with shock, writhing in agony and coughing up vast gobs of blood while the cameras do their work, capturing each and every gory detail with the salacious glee of a lad burning ants with a magnifying glass.

We're deep in Exploitation Country now, boys, a cheap and nasty place where themes are as flat and unexplored as the characters, where humour is unheard of, style barely considered, pace thrown out the window and drama, yes drama, comes with a 'melo' prefix.

From writer/director/producer James Glickenhaus, the man who watched *Death Wish* and made *The Exterminator*, comes a sluggish tale of political intrigue starring *The Taking of Beverly Hills'* Ken Wahl, and if that's not enough to put you off, you're a man, my son.

Although we've established that, in general terms, this movie sucks, it wouldn't be fair to ignore its least forgettable moments, euphemistically described as 'highlights'. For starters, we learn how to assassinate someone using a light bulb, there's a passable ski chase (looks like someone saw *The Spy Who Loved Me* too) and numerous supporting stock action situations to pass the time, a series of lovingly filmed stunts - The Soldier leaping from an exploding cable car, The Soldier jumping over the Berlin Wall in a sports car, The Soldier remembering two lines of dialogue on the trot - and an entirely gratuitous, 'blink-and-you'd-miss-it' star cameo from Mr Understated Performance himself, *Nosferatu the Vampyre*'s Klaus Kinski. Best of all, should you decide to go with this product, our director throws in a cheerful early performance from *American Ninja*'s Steve 'You got two choices, asshole: duck... or bleed' James. Tempted as you are, now is the time to practise restraint.

Director: James Glickenhaus; **Producer:** James Glickenhaus; **Screenplay:** James Glickenhaus; **Production Design:** William De Seta; **Editor:** Paul Fried; **Photography:** Robert M. Baldwin Jr; **Music:** Tangerine Dream; **Cast:** Ken Wahl, Alberta Watson, Jeremiah Sullivan, William Prince, Klaus Kinski, Steve James.

Commando

USA 1985 88 mins

With a staggering body count of more than one on-screen death per minute, it is hard to believe that *Commando* actually marked the screen debut of the new caring, sharing Arnold Schwarzenegger.

The movie opens with three violent assassinations, courtesy of bad guy Bill Duke, and then it's off to the great outdoors to witness retired special agent Arnold, minus his shirt, chopping wood. He's got a shiny new axe in his hands, and the odds are that pretty soon he'll be using it on the person he sees sneaking up behind him in its reflection, but... the music suddenly gets sappy and he drops the weapon to pick up his young daughter, Jenny (or, as Arnold puts it in his endearingly thick Austrian accent, 'Chenny').

Arnold with a kid? The opening credit sequence proves that underneath his tough exterior, he's just a big softy: he eats ice-cream, teaches Chenny martial arts, and best of all, kneels beside a deer to stroke its fluffy little head. But while Arnold is keen to stress that he has deep feelings - his first words in the movie are 'I love you too' - the sensitive stuff doesn't last for long: Chenny is soon kidnapped by a wannabe Latin American dictator who plans to force Arnold to overthrow the President of a little island he has his eye on. If Arnold doesn't help the bad guys, Chenny will be mailed back to him 'in pieces', but he knows better than to trust them, and sets about annihilating just about everything that moves in a relentless race to destroy every villain that stands between him and his daughter.

Helping him on his way is spirited airline stewardess Rae Dawn Chong, who ditches the role of romantic interest in favour of that of the sidekick, and screams, jokes and generally reacts her way through the movie ('What is this macho bullshit?' she cries). Dan Hedaya is servicable as the potential dictator, but bad guy honours go to Bill Duke for being the coolest killer of all time, and the outrageous (not to mention overweight and clearly out of shape) Vernon Wells as a mercenary who was fired from Arnold's army unit because 'he liked killing too much'. Arnold himself is in top form: he smells intruders downwind, rips telephone boxes out of the ground, and takes on an entire army of mercenaries singlehanded. Naturally, they don't stand a chance!

Comic book violence includes standard knife and gun fights, several huge explosions, a long car chase and several painful deaths from various garden implements (the garden shed scene is a real knockout!). A brash, noisy video game of a movie with a healthy disrespect for life and liberty, *Commando* introduced the world to humour, Schwarzenegger style: 'I eat Green Berets for breakfast', Arnold threatens Duke, 'and right now I'm very hungry!'

Director: Mark L. Lester; **Producer:** Joel Silver; **Screenplay:** Steven de Souza; **Production Design:** John Vallone; **Editors:** Mark Goldblatt, John F. Link, Glenn Farr; **Photography:** Matthew F. Leonetti; **Music:** James Horner. **Cast:** Arnold Schwarzenegger, Rae Dawn Chong, Dan Hedaya, Vernon Wells, David Patrick Kelly, Alyssa Milano.

Conan the Barbarian

USA 1981 129 mins

Arnold Schwarzenegger keeps his pecs pumped and his mouth shut in this Dark Age revenge saga from in-your-face director John Milius. As Robert E. Howard's barbarian hero, Arnold pounds, chops and lumbers through his first starring role, looking every inch the savage in this heavy-handed but enjoyable sword-and-sorcery adventure. With a narrator working overtime and a talkative supporting cast, the Austrian Avenger's dialogue is

Conan the Barbarian (Arnold Schwarzenegger) poses with the two great loves of his life: his girl (Sandahl Bergman) and his sword.

kept to the barest of minimums, and when he finally does get a word in, his accent and acting inability make it a hilariously memorable experience: 'Conan', yells his teacher, 'what is best in life?' 'To crush your enemies, see them driven before you, and to hear the lamentation of the women'. What he lacks in finesse, however, he more than makes up for with gut-slashing, sword-swishing, bloodthirsty violence, and that's the most important thing.

While still a child, Conan witnesses the extermination of his entire tribe at the hands of Thulsa Doom (James Earl Jones), a wicked sorcerer whose monstrous Snake Cult spreads evil throughout the land. Growing up big, strong and dumb, Conan sets out in search of vengeance, picking up a few pals along the way: archer Subotai (Gerry Lopez), love interest Valeria (Sandahl Bergman) and even a friendly wizard (Mako).

Brutal, grim and relentless with it, *Conan the Barbarian* may not exactly speed along, and there are often long waits between action sequences, but it's all so way over-the-top that you have to see the funny side: witness Conan, crucified on the 'Tree of Woe', biting a chunk out of a vulture who shouldn't have been so eager for a taste of our hero. The most entertaining blood-bath, however, comes towards the end, as our heroes battle the forces of Doom on home ground, outnumbered six to one, but helped along the way by a variety of concealed weapons and spiked booby traps.

Men, we all have much to learn from Conan: the secret of steel, the oiling of chests, the killing of witches (after sex) and slaying of giant, animatronic snakes. There's drinking to be done, women to know and jewels to steal. A solid grounding in Dark Age laddishness, in fact, for the barbarian in us all.

Director: John Milius; **Producers:** Buzz Feitshans, Raffaella de Laurentiis; **Screenplay:** John Milius, Oliver Stone, based on characters created by Robert E. Howard; **Production Design:** Ronn Cobb; **Editor:** C. Timothy O'Meara; **Photography:** Duke Callaghan; **Music:** Basil Poledouris; **Cast:** Arnold Schwarzenegger, James Earl Jones, Sandahl Bergman, Ben Davidson, Cassandra Gaviola, Gerry Lopez, Mako, Valerie Quennessen, William Smith, Max Von Sydow.

Conan the Destroyer

USA 1984 103 mins

Welcome, once again, to the days of high adventure, to ancient, savage lands soaked in blood and scattered with body bits, where good struggles against evil on a daily basis and special effects work their magic on a variety of oversized, rubbery monsters. Life might be cheap here, but the sets are damned expensive, vast, elaborate creations which would clearly be happier in Disneyland.

Conan the Destroyer is very much a product of the 1980s, a flashy and entirely superficial action fantasy, made and played in broad comic book style, dumb as an ox, but speedy, violent and benefiting from an all-slicing, all-dicing performance from Arnold Schwarzenegger, here trying out a couple of brand new facial expressions as the world's favourite camel-trashing barbarian.

The sword-and-sorcery shenanigans continue as Conan (Arnold) agrees to accompany Jehna (Olivia D'Abo), the virgin niece of wicked Queen Shadizar (Sarah Douglas), on a long and perilous journey, in return for the promised re-animation of his dearly departed girlfriend Valeria. Joined by towering henchman Bombaata (Wilt Chamberlain), comedy sidekick Malak (Tracey Walter), friendly wizard Akiro (Mako), and fierce, shrieking warrior Zula (Grace Jones), Conan sets out to recover a magical, jewel-encrusted horn from fiendish sorcerer Thoth-Amon (Pat Roach), slaying everyone and everything that stands in his way. He'd better watch his back, though, because Bombaata has orders to kill him the moment their mission is over, and then there's Jehna's impending sacrifice to consider...

Brace yourself for a deluge of cardboard characters, plastic beasties and fibreglass sets, ignore the moronic finale and try, instead, to embrace the movie's spirit of destruction as we're bombarded with one brand of violence after another. Arnold might not be the world's greatest actor, but he can swing a sword with the best of 'em, trashing hordes of armoured competition with some spirited assistance from his motley crew of killers, thieves and magicians. It's colourful stuff, to be sure, not nearly as good as the first movie, but with a cheesy charm all of its own.

Director: Richard Fleischer; **Producer:** Raffaella De Laurentiis; **Screenplay:** Stanley Mann, story by Roy Thomas, Gerry Conway, based on the character created by Robert E. Howard; **Production Design:** Pier Luigi Basile; **Editor:** Frank J. Urioste; **Photography:** Jack Cardiff; **Music:** Basil Poledouris; **Cast:** Arnold Schwarzenegger, Grace Jones, Wilt Chamberlain, Mako, Tracey Walter, Olivia D'Abo, Sarah Douglas.

Death Becomes Them 4

Name: CONNERY, Sean

Real name: Thomas Sean Connery

Born: Edinburgh, Scotland, 1930

Characteristics: Over the years, the hairpiece moved south, the stomach moved north, but hey, he's still Sean Connery, ultimate bloke, master of manly charisma, with an accent that stands aside for no role, no matter how foreign it might be.

Previous professions: Milkman, bricklayer, lifeguard, coffin polisher...

Debut feature: *Lilacs in the Spring* (aka *Let's Make Up*; 1954)

Life and times: Turning to acting in the 1950s, Connery hit the mother lode in 1962 playing James Bond, 007, license to kill, drink, gamble and copulate in *Dr No*. Terrified of being typecast in the role, Connery quit the Bond series in 1967, returning for a one-off in 1971 when the money was too good to refuse, and then again, 12 years later, in the aptly titled *Never Say Never Again*. Determined to prove his range as an actor, Connery worked his way through the 1970s and early 1980s in a variety of low key thrillers, epic adventures, fantasy flicks and even a little experimental sci-fi (John Boorman's *Zardoz*). Winning the Best Supporting Actor Oscar in 1986 for his knockout performance in *The*

Sean Connery was, is, and always will be, the best ever Bond.

Untouchables, an older, wiser but no less rugged Connery embarked upon his current career as a major league character actor with box office clout and millions of female admirers who consider him one of the sexiest men alive.

Greatest contribution to action movies: The original, and best, big screen Bond.

Speech, speech: 'I'd always had a terrible fight to get work in Britain on account of my Edinburgh accent. And I still haven't lost it completely. I won't - I don't think it's right to lose it.'

'I don't think a single other role changes a man quite so much as Bond. It's a cross, a privilege, a joke, a challenge. And it's as bloody intrusive as a nightmare.'

Director Terence Young on Sean: 'With the exception of Lassie, Sean Connery is the only person I know who's never been spoiled by success.'

Selected filmography: *Hell Drivers* (1957), *Darby O'Gill and the Little People* (1959), *Tarzan's Greatest Adventure* (1959), *The Longest Day* (1962), ***Dr No*** (1962), ***From Russia With Love*** (1963), *Marnie* (1964), ***Goldfinger*** (1964), *The Hill* (1965), ***Thunderball*** (1965), ***You Only Live Twice*** (1967), *Shalako* (1968), *The Molly Maguires* (1970), *The Anderson Tapes* (1971), ***Diamonds are Forever*** (1971), *The Offence* (1973), *Zardoz* (1974), *The Wind and the Lion* (1975), *Robin and Marian* (1976), *A Bridge Too Far* (1977), *The Great Train Robbery* (1979), *Meteor* (1979), *Cuba* (1979), *Time Bandits* (1981), *Outland* (1981), ***Never Say Never Again*** (1983), *Highlander* (1986), *The Name of the Rose* (1986), *The Untouchables* (1987), *The Presidio* (1988), ***Indiana Jones and the Last Crusade*** (1989), *Family Business* (1989), *The Hunt For Red October* (1990), *The Russia House* (1990), *Highlander II: The Quickening* (1991), *Medicine Man* (+ exec prod; 1992), *Rising Sun* (+ exec prod; 1993), *A Good Man In Africa* (1994), *Just Cause* (1995), *Dragonheart* (voice only; 1996), ***The Rock*** (1996).

Convoy

USA 1978 100 mins

A-one, a-two, a-one, two, three, four... 'We got a great big convoy, truckin' through the night. Yeah, we got a great big convoy, ain't she a beautiful sight? Come on and join our convoy, ain't nothing gonna get in our way. We gonna roll this truckin' convoy, 'cross the U.S.A. ... CONVOY!'

10-4 good buddies, and welcome to Sam Peckinpah's blockbusting adaptation of C.W. McCall's country 'n' western classic, a rip-roarin' road movie of epic proportions starring super-cool Kris Kristofferson as trucking legend Rubber Duck.

Base a movie on a song, and what do you get? Not much of a story, that's for

Truckers Rubber Duck (Kris Kristofferson) and Spider Mike (Franklyn Ajaye) confront Dirty Lyle (Ernest Borgnine) in *Convoy*.

sure, just a whole lot of burning rubber and an excess of destruction, as the Duck flees from crooked speed cop Dirty Lyle (Ernest Borgnine, an evil glint of pleasure in his eye every time he does something mean), charging across three states, earning folk hero status along the way. Aided and abetted by hitcher Ali MacGraw and CB brothers Pig Pen (*Rocky* co-star Burt Young) and Spider Mike (Franklyn Ajaye), the Duck soon has a mile-long convoy on his hands, a legion of loyal fans eager to help out any way they can...

Road bound chaos reigns supreme as Peckinpah lays on nothing but action, turning his back on plot development and characterization, and concentrating entirely on the film's super-charged chase scenes and incredible stunt work, piling on the gags and trashing an entire Texas town for fun in this mindlessly enjoyable adventure, a daredevil tribute to 'fast trucks, fast women and fast food'.

Director: Sam Peckinpah; **Producer:** Robert M. Sherman; **Screenplay:** B.W.L. Norton, based on the song 'Convoy' by C.W. McCall; **Production Design:** Fernando Carrere; **Editor:** Graeme Clifford; **Photography:** Harry Stradling Jr; **Music:** Chip Davis, supervision and lyrics by Bill Fries; **Cast:** Kris Kristofferson, Ali MacGraw, Burt Young, Ernest Borgnine, Franklyn Ajaye, Seymour Cassel.

The Crow

USA 1994 100 mins

Following the tragic, untimely death of martial artist Brandon Lee on the set of *The Crow*, two questions were raised, one moral, one practical: the first asking whether or not the film should be completed, the second asking whether or not the film *could* be completed. The 'should' issue was tackled by Lee's mother, Linda Lee Cadwell, and his fiancée, Eliza Hutton, both of whom agreed that the film should be finished for Brandon's sake, standing forever as a testament to his athletic ability and startling screen presence. During a two-month break from filming, music video director Alex Proyas took on the 'could' issue, hiring horror writer David J. Schow (*Texas Chainsaw Massacre 3*, *Critters 4*, *Nightmare on Elm Street 5*, and counting) to re-work the screenplay, while state-of-the-art digital effects conquered the technical challenge, plucking Lee's image from previously shot footage and pasting it into brand new scenes. 'Everyone stuck with *The Crow* because of the work Brandon had done', explained executive producer Robert Rosen. 'There was no question in our minds that this was a complete performance of remarkable intensity. We felt that, as difficult as it was to go back, we knew we had an immensely powerful film'. Sadly, Lee's death will forever be linked with *The Crow*, and while that's an unfortunate cross for any movie to bear, it doesn't change the fact that it is a tremendously stylish, oppressively atmospheric piece of work which you should make the effort to see, no matter how grisly its history might be.

The world of *The Crow* is a dark, dank and dirty industrial nightmare, oozing menace and fear. Terrorized and slaughtered by a gang of thugs on 'Devil's Night', an evening of unrivalled violence and excess sponsored by exotic crimelord Top Dollar (Michael Wincott), heavy metal rocker Eric Draven (Lee) and his fiancée Shelly (Sofia Shinas) serve to boost an already mammoth body count.

Exactly one year later, Draven rises from the grave, resurrected with revenge on his mind and a crow on his shoulder, a constant companion who holds the key to his second coming. And slowly, one by one, the newly indestructible Draven picks off henchman after henchman, drawing ever closer to the supremely sick and twisted Top Dollar, a consummate psycho with plans for ultimate chaos.

Although the action relies less upon martial arts than it does upon heavy weaponry (for hand-to-hand Brandon brilliance, check out *Rapid Fire*), *The Crow* features a number of intense and often extremely bloody action set-pieces that only occasionally border on the routine. Aussie director Proyas gives the film a grim, mythical quality, focusing on the seediest side of life with occasional bursts of dark, disturbing humour. Michael Wincott serves the movie well as the chillingly sadistic Top Dollar, while curious cop Ernie Hudson and 8-year-old innocent Rochelle Davis are fine in support, although, clearly, the star of the movie is Lee, a charismatic leading man who proved to be as irreplaceable as his father.

Director: Alex Proyas; **Producers:** Edward R. Pressman, Jeff Most; **Screenplay:** David J. Schow, John Shirley, based on the comic book series by James O'Barr; **Production Design:** Alex McDowell; **Editors:** Dov Hoenig; **Photography:** Dariusz Wolski; **Music:** Graeme Revell; **Cast:** Brandon Lee, Ernie Hudson, Michael Wincott, David Patrick Kelly, Angel David, Rochelle Davis, Bai Ling, Sofia Shinas, Anna Thomson.

Cutthroat Island

USA 1995 123 mins

Yo-ho-ho and a bottle of rum, the pirate hordes of Renny Harlin's *Cutthroat Island* get to work.

$92 million is a blinding amount of dough. You could buy an island. You could buy love. You could even make a big, expensive movie: lots of action, fabulous scenery, tons of extras. But you'd better start with a decent screenplay, something with an interesting plot, intelligent dialogue and maybe even a couple of believable characters, or else you may end up making *Cutthroat Island*, and that would never do.

A swashbuckling tribute to lavish set design and shiver-me-timbers clichés, this corny pirate saga comes direct from *Cliffhanger* director Renny Harlin and his reasonably famous wife, Geena Davis, here taking the lead as fearless, fearsome pirate queen Morgan Adams, scourge of the Caribbean. Sadly, she's no more convincing than crayon-forged cash, a bawdy wench, maybe, but not much of a fighter (and that's being kind). Matthew Modine is equally miscast as William Shaw, Morgan's love interest, a dashing, well-educated Errol Flynn-wannabe who joins forces with Miss Adams in search of, you guessed it, buried treasure. Of course, there's a villain, a dastardly pirate intent on bagging the loot for himself, but even with Frank Langella in the role, Captain Dawg is, at best, a second-rate rascal.

The action sequences work a little better, pumping up the pace to keep us conscious with a rollercoaster horse-and-carriage chase and a climactic galleon battle complete with a wacky cannonball stunt. Ultimately, words like average, passable and watchable spring to mind, but why bother with Morgan Adams when you could spend the evening with Captain Blood?

Director: Renny Harlin; **Producers:** Renny Harlin, Joel B. Michaels, Laurence Mark, James Gorman; **Screenplay:** Robert King, Marc Norman, story by Michael Frost Beckner, James Gorman, Bruce A. Evans, Raynold Gideon; **Production Design:** Norman Garwood; **Editors:** Frank J. Urioste, Ralph E. Winters; **Photography:** Peter Levy; **Music:** John Debney; **Cast:** Geena Davis, Matthew Modine, Frank Langella, Maury Chaykin, Patrick Malahide, Stan Shaw.

Cyborg

USA 1989 86 mins

The world's in trouble, all plague-ridden and post-apocalyptic, and only Jean-Claude Van Damme can help. He's got a score to settle, see, with Fender (Vincent Klyn), our villain, the psycho who would be king. Much like this twisted B-movie, Fender thrives on pain and misery, a marauding pirate with a grungy band of *Mad Max* refugees at his command, a towering inferno of shades and chain mail with a daily quota of decapitations, impalements and crucifixions to meet. Fortunately, Jean-Claude, alias Gibson Rickenbacker, is no boy scout. He's a killer, one of the best, good with a gun, lethal with a blade, and, surprise, surprise, a master of unarmed combat.

Then along comes a scrap of story and, wouldn't you know it, the carnage begins. There's this girl, a cyborg who calls herself Pearl Prophet (Dayle Haddon), a RoboChick with data on curing the plague which she needs to get back to her scientist pals in Atlanta. Trouble is, she manages to get herself kidnapped in New York by a certain Mr Fender, who seems to like the world the way it is, although he wouldn't mind owning the cure for himself...

Let's not forget Jean-Claude, though, or his self-appointed sidekick Deborah Richter (Nady Simmons), a skinny-dipping wild child and slayer of warrior queens.
Together, our heroes plough through Fender's gang *en route* to the big man himself, and oh, how mindless and predictable their adventures are. A jumble of pointless flashbacks and cardboard characters, *Cyborg* enjoys its nasty side just a little too much, while the majority of the film's sets look like little more than abandoned warehouses. Still, Van Damme puts on an impressive display, and the action's pretty good, although it doesn't offer much in the way of variety.

It's watchable, but only just, and once should be enough.

Director: Albert Pyun; **Producer:** Menahem Golan, Yoram Globus; **Screenplay:** Kitty Chalmers; **Production Design:** Douglas Leonard; **Editors:** Rozanne Zingale, Scott Stevenson; **Photography:** Philip Alan Waters; **Music:** Kevin Bassinson; **Cast:** Jean-Claude Van Damme, Deborah Richter, Vincent Klyn, Dayle Haddon.

The Dead Pool

USA 1988 91 mins

The years march on, but there's no stopping Clint Eastwood, the coolest, toughest man alive. Should you ever weaken and doubt his power, however, check out this fifth and final Dirty Harry picture: no great shakes in itself, but worthwhile if only to see another great Clint performance, crusty, charismatic and capable of anything.

A pile of dead bodies at the top of the picture confirms Harry's grip on the here and now: when it comes to despatching enemies, age is a whole lot less important than a .44 Magnum and the willingness to use it. And use it he does, often and accurately, on anyone foolish enough to cross his path.

Following the successful capture and conviction of a leading San Francisco mobster, Harry divides his time between fighting off journalists eager for his life story and blowing away henchmen intent on avenging their boss's incarceration. Added to this, there's a psycho loose in the city, wasting celebrities left, right and centre (besides terminating rock star Jim Carrey, our mystery maniac also kills a film critic, so obviously he's not *all* bad), and Harry could be next. Why? Well, there's this sick bit of business doing the rounds known as the Dead Pool: invented by sleazy horror movie maker Peter Swann (Liam Neeson), it's a list of celebrities expected to die before the year is out, Harry included, and someone's taking it way too seriously...

Aiding and abetting Harry with his investigations we have romantic interest Samantha Walker (Patricia Clarkson), a pushy TV reporter who learns all the usual lessons about the evils of media intrusion, while Evan C. Kim struggles to survive as Harry's new partner Al Quan.

Miscellaneous action remains the order of the day, as Harry continues to find himself in the wrong place at the wrong time, confronting a bunch of armed robbers with the cheesy one-liner, 'You're shit out of luck' (shit out of catchphrases, more like), before cancelling their nasty butts. This scene, much like the climactic, harpoon-heavy finale, has a touch of the routines about it, but there is one action sequence which not only saves the movie, but ranks as one of the most ingenious car chases ever filmed, as Harry and Al flee a super-charged, radio-controlled miniature sports car packed with high explosives.

Director: Buddy Van Horn; **Producer:** David Valdes; **Screenplay:** Steve Sharon, story by Steve Sharon, Durk Pearson, Sandy Shaw, based on characters created by Harry Julian Fink & R.M. Fink; **Production Design:** Edward C. Carfagno; **Editor:** Ron Spang; **Photography:** Jack N. Green; **Music:** Lalo Schifrin; **Cast:** Clint Eastwood, Patricia Clarkson, Liam Neeson, Evan C. Kim, David Hunt, Michael Currie, Michael Goodwin.

Deadly Pursuit (aka Shoot To Kill)
USA 1988 110 mins

An unidentified psychopath with a big bag of diamonds is hiding out in the mountains. He may be *Dirty Harry*'s Andy Robinson. Or *Highlander*'s Clancy Brown. But he has a hostage, and she's Kirstie Alley. Anyway, there's this city boy, Warren Stantin (Sidney Poitier), a seasoned FBI agent who would do anything, even brave the great outdoors, to nab our mysterious villain. But he's going to need some help. Someone who can tie knots and ride horses, a redneck tracker with a chip on his shoulder and a hiker girlfriend (Kirstie) in mortal danger. A rugged Neanderthal with country ways, Jonathan Knox (Tom Berenger) doesn't take kindly to orders from men who bathe, and he and Warren soon have this hate thing going on, but this is a buddy movie, so you'd best prepare yourselves for a dose of grudging respect towards the end.

The male-bonding intensifies as the lads experience the death-defying thrill of the wild, climbing mountains, plunging into gorges, battling the elements, disturbing grizzly bears and, eventually, taking on the killer himself. The fish-out-of-water gags wear a little thin after a while, and it's a little too corny and predictable to really get you going, but Berenger and Poitier (still fit at 64) have fun with their roles, the action's pretty good, and there's a lot of foolishness to enjoy along the way.

Director: Roger Spottiswoode; **Producers:** Ron Silverman, Daniel Petrie Jr; **Screenplay:** Harv Zimmell, Michael Burton, Daniel Petrie Jr; **Production Design:** Richard Sylbert; **Editors:** Garth Craven, George Bowers; **Photography:** Michael Chapman; **Music:** John Scott; **Cast:** Sidney Poitier, Tom Berenger, Kirstie Alley, Clancy Brown, Andrew Robinson, Frederick Coffin, Richard Masur, Kevin Scannell.

Death Race 2000
USA 1975 79 mins

So you're sitting at home in front of the box, your eyes glued to *Death Race 2000,* famed purveyor of high-speed auto-insanity and grievous bodily gore, when suddenly your (insert aged authority figure here) walks into the living room and demands to know what on earth you're watching. Have no fear. 'It's a classic movie satire', you can explain, 'about violence and the media'. Great start, but keep going. 'Produced by low-budget maestro Roger Corman, it was directed by *Eating Raoul*'s Paul Bartel a full 20 years before Oliver Stone's like-minded, feature-length pop video *Natural Born Killers*'. Not bad, not bad at all. That ought to shut them up, and when they finally leave you alone, you can get back to this prime cut of 1970s schlock. Oh sure, if you're prepared to look for it, there's plenty of meaning behind the madness, but even if you take this movie solely at face value, you're still in for one hell of a wild ride.

This is expert exploitation and no mistake, sick to the core and a whole lot of fun, a cheerfully cheap bonanza of custom car-racing, reckless life-taking, and yes, even bondage gear-wearing perversity. This one has it all!

Welcome to America, then, circa 2000, a land of moral, spiritual and political desolation (that shouldn't be too hard to picture) where the masses are kept entertained by an annual three-day Transcontinental Death Race, a high-speed event won by the driver who clocks up the most points along the way. And how, exactly, does one earn points? Simple, by killing pedestrians (a teenager, for example, is worth 40 points, while anyone over the age of 75 makes for a whopping 100!). Only this year, sports fans, there's a rebel army committed to stopping the race for good, and all sorts of other twists and turns jammed in among the carnage as we thrill to the lunatic antics of 'swastika sweetheart' Matilda the Hun (Roberta Collins), Nero the Hero (Martin Kove), Calamity Jane Kelly (Mary Woronov), Machine Gun Joe Viterbo (a youthful Sly Stallone, here playing a thug 'loved by thousands, hated by millions') and the President's choice, audience favourite Frankenstein (David Carradine), 'who lost an leg in '98, an arm in '99, with half a face and half a chest and all the guts in the world!'

Welcome to the 1970s, man, to jazzy music and psychedelic visuals, to blood and thunder on a budget and a cast and crew who were obviously up for anything. You'd have to be crazy to make a film like this, and nuts not to like it, and I close with the immortal words of hyperactive TV anchorman Junior Bruce ('The Real' Don Steele), the best friend a death race ever had: 'Sure it's violent, but that's the way we love it - violent, violent, violent!'

Sequel: *Deathsport*.

Director: Paul Bartel; **Producer:** Roger Corman; **Screenplay:** Robert Thom, Charles Griffith, Ib Melchior; **Production Design:** Robin Royce; **Editor:** Tina Hirsch; **Photography:** Tak Fujimoto; **Music:** Paul Chihara; **Cast:** David Carradine, Simone Griffeth, Sylvester Stallone, Mary Woronov, Roberta Collins, Martin Kove, Don Steele.

Death Warrant

Canada 1990 89 mins

The inmates of Harrison Penitentiary are dropping like flies, their skulls punctured by some unknown assassin. It's a prison full of two-bit stereotypes, run the hard way by a brutal warden (Art LaFleur), and filled to overflowing with an assortment of white trash, gangland Hispanics, scavengers, pimps, killers, and, of course, that one special convict with a heart of gold (*Benson*'s Robert Guillaume). We got us a mystery here, boys, and who better to solve it than maverick cop Jean-Claude Van Damme? Well, just about anyone, really, but Colombo wasn't available and Mr Van-Damme-Thank-You-Ma'am felt like extending his range a little, tackling drama as well as the bad guys in this watchable but unremarkable thriller.

As a Canadian Mountie newly arrived in Los Angeles, Louis Burke (Jean-Claude) is the perfect choice to go undercover into Harrison, an unknown face willing to seek out and destroy whoever's responsible for the murders. But jail is a dangerous, treacherous place, and, wouldn't you know it, Louis can't help but get into one violent scrape after another, duking it out with familiar face Al Leong in a cool laundromat one-on-one before facing arch enemy The Sandman (Patrick Kilpatrick) in an extended and brutal final battle.

Without the violence we'd be talking passable TV mystery, but though you might find Van Damme's performance wanting, you certainly can't fault his ability to inflict pain upon others, and this alone makes the film worthwhile, but only just.

 Fans of *Star Trek: Deep Space Nine* are afforded a rare opportunity to see actor Armin Shimerman, alias Ferengi wheeler-dealer Quark, out of make-up and in the flesh as the troubled Doctor Gottesman.

Director: Deran Sarafian; **Producer:** Mark DiSalle; **Screenplay:** David S. Goyer; **Production Design:** Curtis Schnell; **Editor:** G. Gregg McLaughlin, John A. Barton; **Photography:** Russell Carpenter; **Music:** Gary Chang; **Cast:** Jean-Claude Van Damme, Robert Guillaume, Cynthia Gibb, George Dickerson, Art LaFleur, Patrick Kilpatrick.

Death Wish

USA 1974 94 mins

Charles Bronson checks his personality at the door and strides stone-faced into New York City to do battle with an assortment of muggers, rapists and murderers in this, his very first *Death Wish* movie. Encouraged by director Michael Winner, Bronson gives gun control the finger, condemning the police for failing to crack crime while eagerly extolling the virtues of civically minded civilians who take to blowing great big holes in the kind of scum who hang around in dark alleys and bully old ladies for fun. Liberals beware, you are not welcome here.

Following a brutal gang rape which leaves his wife dead and his daughter vegetated, mild-mannered architect Paul Kersey (Bronson) takes to slaughtering bad guys on a nightly basis. As news of the unknown vigilante spreads and the crime rate finally begins to drop, police inspector Vincent Gardenia sets out to discover the identity of the man who is rapidly becoming a national hero.

Almost interesting, almost involving, here we have a movie that's not afraid to speak its mind, yet behind the gunplay and right-wing waffle lays a schizophrenic urge to revel in the brutality it claims to condemn as Winner pours over every grisly detail with the salacious enthusiasm of a tabloid journalist. Rarely dull, but way too serious for its own good, *Death Wish* relies almost entirely upon shock and sensation and after a while the act wears pretty thin.

 Keep 'em peeled for a youthful Jeff Goldblum, seen here making his movie debut as a member of the gang who torture and terrorize Kersey's family. Oscar! Oscar!

Sequels: *Death Wish II*, *Death Wish III*, *Death Wish IV: The Crackdown*, *Death Wish V: The Face of Death*.

Director: Michael Winner; **Producers:** Hal Landers, Bobby Roberts, Michael Winner; **Screenplay:** Wendell Mayes, based on the novel *Death Wish* by Brian Garfield; **Production Design:** Robert Gundlach; **Editor:** Bernard Gribble; **Photography:** Arthur J. Ornitz; **Music:** Herbie Hancock; **Cast:** Charles Bronson, Vincent Gardenia, William Redfield, Steven Keats, Stuart Margolin, Stephen Elliott, Hope Lange.

Trivialists 2

BOND BIRD COUNT

One girl, one point, but only if they do the wild thing with James. Welcome, then, to 007's seduction scoreboard.

Sean Connery
Dr No: 3
From Russia With Love: 4
Goldfinger: 2
Thunderball: 3
You Only Live Twice: 3
Diamonds Are Forever: 1
Never Say Never Again: 4
Total: **20**

Roger Moore
Live and Let Die: 3
The Man With The Golden Gun: 2
The Spy Who Loved Me: 3
Moonraker: 3
For Your Eyes Only: 2
Octopussy: 2
A View To A Kill: 4
Total: **19**

Timothy Dalton
The Living Daylights: 2
Licence To Kill: 2
Total: **4**

George Lazenby
On Her Majesty's Secret Service: 3
Total: **3**

Pierce Brosnan
Goldeneye: 2
Total: **2**

Death Wish II

USA 1982 93 mins 🔫

How unlucky can one man be? Following the brutal gang rape and murder of his house-maid and daughter, professional architect and fervent vigilante Paul Kersey takes down every scumbag in his sights, grimly stalking those responsible for ripping off the plot of the first movie while casually annihilating a miscellaneous cast of heavies.

Kersey switches jungles (farewell New York, welcome Los Angeles) while director Michael Winner offers a batch of fresh subplots intended to distract us from the fact that this second effort is simply an ugly re-hash of the first, which wasn't all that good to begin with.

A nasty and decidedly amateurish piece of work, *Death Wish II* offers a lot more action than its predecessor, though quantity is no stand-in for quality. Eagerly fixating on the vilest side of life, the movie makes you wonder whether the various gang rapes, killings and muggings presented are intended to shock or to titillate us. The bottom line is that it's exploitation, plain and simple, salacious, crude and to be avoided like the plague.

If you thought Jeff Goldblum's screen debut in *Death Wish* warrants the most severe embarrassment, think again. Instead, why not consider budding star Laurence Fishburne III (aka Larry or Laurence Fishburne) as a junkie thug named Cutter. It's a wonder his career didn't die on the spot.

There have been those who dared suggest that director Michael Winner and film editor Arnold Crust are one and the same. One for *The X-Files*, perhaps?

Director: Michael Winner; **Producers:** Menaham Golan, Yoram Globus; **Screenplay:** David Engelbach; **Production Design:** William Hiney; **Editor:** Arnold Crust, Julian Semilian; **Photography:** Richard H. Kline, Tom Del Ruth; **Music:** Jimmy Page; **Cast:** Charles Bronson, Vincent Gardenia, J.D. Cannon, Anthony Franciosa, Jill Ireland.

Death Wish III

USA 1985 90 mins

Stone-faced vigilante Paul Kersey puts the Grim Reaper to shame as he calmly exterminates one young punk after another in the name of revenge, surely the purest of all motives. Unfortunately for our antique hero, however, he has long since run out of family to avenge, and so now it's up to his friends to get themselves killed in the name of motivation.

Quality is not an issue here. It's a corny mess, obvious and laughable, poorly played and carelessly assembled, but there's more than enough action to go around, with Charles Bronson wielding an assortment of obnoxious hardware, and if you're happy to settle for nothing but violence, there's a fair amount here to enjoy.

With Sid James and Barbara Windsor in support, Cannon could have re-titled this nonsense *Carry On Death* and no-one would have been any the wiser. Upon returning to New York, Kersey discovers a dead pal and a crumbling North Brooklyn neighbourhood terrorized by a gang of neo-nazi biker types. Someone has to make a stand, and along with hardened police chief 'Bull' Shriker (Ed Lauter), Kersey uses everything from an anti-tank missile launcher to a plank of wood with a nail in it to obliterate the likes of 'sub-human' Fraker (Gavan O'Herlihy) and his motley crew.

A note in the movie's publicity pack brought attention to the fact that special effects supervisor John Evans 'blew up three stores, one apartment house, five cars, burned down three buildings and used no less than three and a half thousand rounds of ammunition in the interests of his art'. Even more impressive is the fact that Charles Bronson hobbles through the entire movie with but a single, impenetrable facial expression, while director Michael Winner sees to it that his movie avoids such distracting elements as charm, humour, pace, intelligence, subtlety and style. Credit to production designer Peter Mullins, though, for building a convincing facsimile of New York in the heart of London's East End.

 Star spotters should be on the lookout for *Bill & Ted*'s Alex Winter as grungy thug Hermosa, while *Star Trek: The Next Generation*'s Marina Sirtis manages to get herself mugged, raped and murdered as Hispanic housewife Maria Rodriguez (a double was used in the nude scene, however).

Director: Michael Winner; **Producers:** Menahem Golan, Yoram Globus; **Screenplay:** Michael Edmonds; **Production Design:** Peter Mullins; **Editor:** Arnold Crust; **Photography:** John Stanier; **Music:** Jimmy Page; **Cast:** Charles Bronson, Deborah Raffin, Ed Lauter, Martin Balsam, Gavan O'Herlihy

The Delta Force

USA 1986 129 mins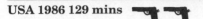

Cannon supremo Menahem Golan tripled his duties on this all-star bash, directing his heart out while co-writing the screenplay and producing with old pal and partner Yoram Globus. A crowd of familiar faces board a TWA plane, and the moment we recognize disaster veterans Shelley Winters (*The Poseidon Adventure*) and George Kennedy (*Airports '69, '75, '77, '79...*), it becomes clear as a fat chick's dance card that a hostage situation is about to arise. Sure enough, Arab terrorists soon make their presence felt, skyjacking the aircraft, scaring the passengers and making all sorts of unrealistic demands.

Hang on a second, though, this is supposed to be a Chuck Norris picture. And it is. It just takes a little while (and then a little while longer) to get started, that's all. There's a bit of rough and tumble throughout, but for the real meat and potatoes, you're going to have wait until the last half hour, when the Delta Force, an elite squad of hero types led by steely Lee Marvin and the Chuckster, finally take on the terrorists with all guns blazing. Chuck, as cool and confident as ever, even has a special bike, a James Bond special, turbo charged with front and rear rocket launchers, and boy, you gotta see those babies fly.

Mixing two parts human melodrama with one part comicbook mayhem, *The Delta Force*, though quite watchable, is much too ambitious and way too long. The action doesn't stink, though, and Chuck gets to deliver lines like 'sleep tight, sucker', so you might just get by.

Sequels: *Delta Force 2: The Colombian Connection*, *Delta Force 3: The Killing Game*, *Delta Force, Commando Two*.

Director: Menahem Golan; **Producers:** Menahem Golan, Yoram Globus; **Screenplay:** James Bruner, Menahem Golan; **Production Design:** Lucisano Spadoni; **Editor:** Alain Jakubowicz; **Photography:** David Gurfinkel; **Music:** Alan Silvestri; **Cast:** Chuck Norris, Lee Marvin, Martin Balsam, Joey Bishop, Kim Delaney, Robert Forster, Steve James, Lainie Kazan, George Kennedy, Hanna Schygulla, Susan Strasberg, Bo Svenson, Robert Vaughan, Shelley Winters.

Delta Force 2

USA 1990 111 mins

Chuck Norris clocks up a genocidal body count as Delta Force avenger Colonel Scott McCoy, slaughtering bad guys by the dozen in the jungles of South America. Directed by Chuck's brother Aaron, this mindlessly entertaining sequel dumps the drama of the original in favour of vicious ultra-violence and increasingly unlikely action, and is, as a result, a hell of a lot more fun.

Our villain *du jour* is one Ramon Cota (Billy Drago), the wealthiest drug dealer of 'em all, wanted for cocaine trafficking and murder in seventeen countries, a snake in the grass with his very own gas chamber, a hissing, sneering untouchable psycho safely tucked away in a remote jungle fortress in fictional San Carlos. Then he goes and blows it all by wasting a bunch of Chuck's best buddies. Suddenly, it's personal, and we all know what that means...

Besides a deluge of one-to-one fight scenes, car chases and skydiving stunts, *Delta Force 2* builds to a cracking, non-stop final assault which lasts a full third of the movie and sees Chuck's boys blasting Cota from the air while our hero infiltrates the boss man's stronghold for rescue and retribution duties.

Uncle Sam would be proud.

Sadly, a number of crewmen were killed in a helicopter crash during production. The film is dedicated to them.

 The third *Delta Force* movie, subtitled *The Killing Game*, is a turkey through-and-through, and not worth an hour-and-a-half of your time, unless you're bombed out on whisky and tranquillisers, in which case you might as well go for it. Even Chuck stayed away from this one, though, forcing director Sam Firstenberg to come up with a gimmick designed to save the series. His strategy was to compose a cast entirely of the sons of better known and more talented men: Kirk Norris (son of Chuck), Nick Cassavetes (son of John), Eric Douglas (son of Kirk) and Matthew Penn (son of director Arthur). Suffice to say, the plan, the boys, and the movie, failed.

Director: Aaron Norris; **Producers:** Yoram Globus, Christopher Pearce; **Screenplay:** Lee Reynolds, based on characters created by James Bruner and Menahem Golan; **Production Design:** Ladislav Wilhelm; **Editor:** Michael J. Duthie; **Photography:** Joao Fernandes; **Music:** Frederic Talgorn; **Cast:** Chuck Norris, Billy Drago, John P. Ryan, Paul Perri, Richard Jaeckel, Begonia Plaza, Mateo Gomez, Hector Mercado.

Demolition Man

USA 1993 115 mins

For several years, the undisputed king of Hollywood was Arnold Schwarzenegger. Standing in his shadow, a prince but still second best, was Sylvester Stallone. As for their fans, well, while Arnie's were legion, eagerly contributing to the box office of every movie he made, Sly's were notoriously fickle, disinterested in everything but his *Rocky* and *Rambo* flicks, though even then they were starting to lose their enthusiasm.

Then it happened: summer 1993, the blockbuster season that changed everything. Suddenly, Arnold was no longer the toast of the town, his relentless over-exposure causing something of an image whiplash, while his latest adventure, *Last Action Hero*, was a giant in-joke which bombed world-wide. The Austrian Avenger had blown it, big time, and no sooner did he stumble than the Italian Stallion enjoyed his first non-*Rocky*/*Rambo* hit with Renny Harlin's *Cliffhanger*, the film that rescued his career and propelled him, with a swift, single leap, to the top of the Hollywood heap. He had achieved the impossible, snatching the throne from the clutches of Mr Universe, and to consolidate his position as top dog of 1993, Stallone released a second winner almost immediately, the kick-ass science fiction thriller *Demolition Man*, a futuristic adventure choc-full-of gags and blazing over-the-top action.

At the top of the picture we're introduced to tough-as-nails cop John Spartan (another Sly move), a Dirty Harry type whose effective though excessive methods have earned him the 'Demolition Man' tag. In the year 1996, however, he goes too far, and in capturing super-psycho Simon Phoenix (Wesley Snipes), he seals the fate of 30 innocent hostages. Consequently, when Phoenix is cryogenically frozen for his crimes, they chuck old Spartan in the freezer with him.

Cut to 2032. San Angeles is clean, peaceful, crime-free and duller than *The Last Temptation of Christ*. The cops have it easy and they're uselessly soft, so when Phoenix escapes they are ill-equipped to deal with his particularly savage brand of violence. The only man that can help them, though, might be more trouble than he's worth, but what choice do they have? Grudgingly, the powers-that-be defrost Spartan and send him out to waste his old arch-enemy, defying authority, destroying property, and, when Phoenix springs a bunch of frozen henchman (including *Predator* hard man Jesse Ventura), killing up a storm. Battles come in all shapes and sizes, most memorably an early museum one-on-one as the boys get their mitts on some ancient - though fully operative - hardware, and, much later on, a climactic cryoprison showdown which brings a whole new meaning to the phrase, 'nerve shattering'.

Babe interest comes in the pre-*Speed* form of Sandra Bullock, a twentieth-century obsessed cop with some peculiar twenty-first-century hang-ups, offering love interest (remember Woody Allen's *Sleeper*?) and perky sidekick support while struggling to instruct our way-cool action hero in the ways of his yawn-mungus new century. *The Madness of King George*'s Nigel Hawthorne also pops up from time to time as the slippery governor of San Angeles, Dr Raymond Cocteau, who, since he has an aristocratic British accent, is obviously something of a villain himself.

All things considered, first-time director Marco Brambilla has done a pretty decent job, belting out the action sequences while making the most of the film's comic potential as well, a swarm of background details adding to the fun (check out Bullock's office for in-jokes a-plenty) as we relish the anachronistic spectacle of two wild and crazy guys battling it out in a bland and sterile environment where swearing is illegal and sex is handled electronically. As an added bonus, Stallone seems almost comfortable with the humour this time around, relaxing into his performance and having fun with it, while Snipes makes a terrific villain, crazier than Nicholson's Joker and about a thousand times more agile, a hyperactive monster with cropped blond hair and a neat line in leisure wear.

It's an imaginative brew, to be sure, self-aware and strictly tongue-in-cheek, good-looking, endlessly exciting and slicker than a greased pig in an Armani suit. You can't go wrong.

Director: Marco Brambilla; **Producers:** Joel Silver, Michael Levy, Howard Kazanjian; **Screenplay:** Daniel Waters, Robert Reneau, Peter M. Lenkov; **Production Design:** David L. Snyder; **Editor:** Stuart Baird; **Photography:** Alex Thomson; **Music:** Elliot Goldenthal; **Cast:** Sylvester Stallone, Wesley Snipes, Sandra Bullock, Nigel Hawthorne, Benjamin Bratt, Bob Gunton, Glenn Shadix, Denis Leary, Grand L. Bush, Steve Kahan, Andre Gregory.

Desperado

USA 1995 107 mins

'Bless me father, for I have just killed quite a few men...'. Texan director Robert Rodriguez presents the ultimate in movie cool, a wild and blood-stained ride of cultish proportions. A sequel of sorts to the director's *El Mariachi*, the ordinary picture with the extraordinary price tag (thousands, not millions), *Desperado* represents the apex of style over content, deliriously hip, smarter than a dolphin, and funny as hell.

A stranger carrying nothing but a guitar case full of weapons wanders resolutely through a decaying Mexican town. He is the Mariachi, a musician on a personal mission of vengeance, a killer of ugly, greasy men with Village People moustaches and hair as dirty as their minds. The drug lords responsible for murdering his woman are all but extinct. Only one remains, Bucho (Joaquim de Almeida), a moneyed spiv with an army of muscle-bound half-wits intent on pulverizing the lone vigilante.

Violence is inevitable, and you barely have to wait a minute before it erupts. Rodriguez adds a spark of invention to the action, presenting familiar scenes from a fresh perspective. A brutal saloon brawl takes a memorable turn when both the Mariachi and his final target run out of bullets, a knife-tossing mob assassin fights for his life when a gang of bad guys target him by mistake, a rooftop gun battle forces our hero to improvise an ingenious escape, while the film's climax features two additional mariachis (including Rodriguez's original, Carlos Gallardo) clocking up a massive body count with the customised assistance of machine gun and rocket launcher guitar cases.

Spiked with a dark and twisted sense of humour, *Desperado* has so much to offer it simply doesn't need a plot. Antonio Banderas takes to the lead like a bullet in a gun, smouldering his way through the most enjoyable movie of his career, tall, dark and homicidal, an air

Antonio Banderas kills with confidence in *Desperado*.

of mystery about him and jangling spurs to boot. In support, Mexican superbabe Salma Hayek supplies the sex interest, patching up the Mariachi's various knife and bullet wounds before jumping his bones, while Steve Buscemi acts up a storm as the Mariachi's only friend, a *bona fide* wind-up artist who practises his art on bartender Cheech Marin at the top of the movie. Look out, too, for a brief appearance from director Quentin Tarantino, cracking jokes and losing his brains as 'pick-up guy'.

Armed with a budget that reaches six figures, Rodriguez boosts the visuals and lays on an excellent Los Lobos soundtrack, making the most of his Hollywood trimmings without neglecting such basics as dialogue and characterization or compromising his unique, anarchic vision of the world.

Desperado is a force to be reckoned with.

Director: Robert Rodriguez; **Producer:** Robert Rodriguez; **Screenplay:** Robert Rodriguez; **Production Design:** Cecilia Montiel; **Editor:** Robert Rodriguez; **Photography:** Guillermo Navarro; **Music:** Los Lobos; **Cast:** Antonio Banderas, Salma Hayek, Joaquim de Almeida, Cheech Marin, Steve Buscemi, Quentin Tarantino.

Diamonds are Forever

GB 1971 119 mins

Cubby Broccoli and Harry Saltzman were desperate men. *On Her Majesty's Secret Service* had performed reasonably well at the box office, but it was no blockbuster. Clearly, when it came to audience popularity, Connery was an even bigger draw than Bond, and Lazenby wasn't much of anything at all. Anxious to secure Sean's services for another 'final' stab at Bondage (his first 'final' adventure, *You Only Live Twice*, came out in 1967, his third, the oh-so-unofficial *Never Say Never Again*, turned up in 1983), the producers made him an offer he couldn't refuse: $1.25 million up front, a percentage of the profits and funding for his next two pictures. Money won out, and we can all be thankful that it did, because this, the first of Bond's 1970s extravaganzas, is one of the liveliest and most entertaining movies in the whole darn series.

Connery certainly has his hands full in this one, as Bond tracks a fortune in stolen diamonds all the way from Holland to Vegas, where arch-enemy Blofeld is up to his old tricks again, kidnapping billionaires and planning world domination with help from a duped scientist, an orbital laser and several exotic henchmen.

Rugged and charming with a dry, wry wit and nerves of steel, Connery's Bond was, is, and always will be, the leader. Meanwhile, a strong supporting cast wrestles for our attention: the best of all the Blofelds, Charles Grey menaces Bond from beneath a mask of aristocratic charm, a fully qualified evil genius with manners, poise and a knack for theatrics. Oddball assassins Mr Kidd (Putter Smith) and Mr Wint (Bruce Glover) are just as amusing, glad to be gay and gainfully employed in the business of corpse production. As for the Bond girls, Jill St John plays it big and bold as diamond smuggling sexpot Tiffany Case, while the amply proportioned Lana Wood displays her wares as Plenty O'Toole.

A decade of classy, intelligent spy thrillers firmly established the Bond series, but the 1970s demanded bigger, brighter, blockbuster entertainment, driven by action, fuelled by fantasy, and *Diamonds are Forever* delivers in full. Benefiting from a sharp, knowing screenplay with a wicked sense of humour, and a director who knows exactly how to make the most of it, this is a glitzy, funny, exciting movie with several memorable set-pieces: Bond speeds through the desert in a top secret moon buggy, struggles with bikini-clad, gymnastic bruisers Bambi (Donna Garrett) and Thumper (Trina Parks), leads the cops on a merry car chase throughout Vegas, and battles Blofeld and his boys on board a converted oil rig. All this, a gang of comic Mafia goons, and a waterbed full of fish, too. Knock down a couple of Martinis and enjoy.

One of the most famous movie screw-ups of all time occurs during the Vegas chase when Bond, anxious to motor through an extremely narrow alley, balances his car on its two *right* wheels and drives on in, only by the time he emerges from the other side of the alley, his car is suddenly and mysteriously perched on its two *left* wheels instead.

The end of *Diamonds are Forever*. But James Bond will return in *Live and Let Die*.

Director: Guy Hamilton; **Producers:** Albert R. Broccoli, Harry Saltzman; **Screenplay:** Richard Maibaum, Tom Mankiewicz; **Production Design:** Ken Adam; **Editors:** Bert Bates, John W. Holmes; **Photography:** Ted Moore; **Music:** John Barry, title song performed by Shirley Bassey; **Cast:** Sean Connery, Jill St John, Charles Gray, Lana Wood, Jimmy Dean, Bruce Cabot, Putter Smith, Bruce Glover, Norman Burton, Bernard Lee, Desmond Llewelyn, Lois Maxwell.

Die Hard

USA 1988 131 mins

A peerless action classic from director John McTiernan, *Die Hard* made a movie star out of Bruce Willis and established the now-routine spanner-in-the-works scenario adopted by the likes of *Under Siege*, *Passenger 57* and *Cliffhanger*.

It's Christmas Eve in Los Angeles. A well-armed, well-organized gang of Euro baddies posing as terrorists have taken over Nakatomi Plaza, a high-rise office block with a monster vault holding $640 million in negotiable bearer bonds. An ultra-smooth criminal genius with all the yuppie trimmings, Hans Gruber (Alan Rickman) believes he has left nothing to chance. The building is locked up tight. The hostages are under control. And the authorities outside are powerless to stop him. There is, however, a fly in the ointment: a streetwise New York cop is loose in the building, determined to blast the bad guys and save the hostages, including his estranged wife, Holly (Bonnie Bedelia). With a dozen henchmen to take care of and a fiendish plot to thwart, the odds are against detective John McClane (Willis), but he's as tough as they come, with all the wits, guts and good old-fashioned fighting spirit a wise-cracking, blue-collar hero needs to survive and save the day.

Supporting players in this incredible adventure include Alexander Godunov as principal henchman Karl, enraged beyond measure when McClane wastes his brother; Reginald Veljohnson as the Twinkie-loving Sergeant Al Powell, male-bonding with McClane via radio; Paul Gleason as the incomparably dumb Deputy Chief of Police Dwayne T. Robinson; William Atherton as the arrogant, opportunistic TV reporter Dick Thornberg, and finally, Robert Davi and Grand L. Bush as gung ho FBI agents Johnson and Johnson (no relation).

As the tension mounts, the pace goes ballistic and the action follows suit, from a rooftop firefight and blazing FBI chopper assault to a gruelling one-on-one slugfest between Karl and McClane, and a dazzling, cliffhanging leap of faith.

Intelligent and inventive with a strong sense of humour, some show-stopping stuntwork and a level of excitement which starts at fever pitch and works its way up, *Die Hard* is not only better than sex, but it also lasts 131 times longer.

Sequels: *Die Hard 2: Die Harder*, *Die Hard with a Vengeance*.

Director: John McTiernan; **Producers**: Lawrence Gordon, Joel Silver; **Screenplay**: Jeb Stuart, Steven E. de Souza, based on the novel *Nothing Lasts Forever* by Roderick Thorp; **Production Design**: Jackson DeGovia; **Editors**: Frank J. Urioste, John F. Link; **Photography**: Jan De Bont; **Music**: Michael Kamen; **Cast**: Bruce Willis, Alan Rickman, Bonnie Bedelia, Reginald Veljohnson, Alexander Godunov, Paul Gleason, De'Voreaux White, William Atherton, Robert Davi, Grand L. Bush, Hart Bochner, James Shigetta.

Die Hard 2: Die Harder

USA 1990 124 mins

Startled by events, streetwise hero John McClane asks '...how can the same shit happen to the same guy twice?' Simple. *Die Hard* made a ton of cash. Its sequel, subtitled *Die Harder*, takes place the following Christmas, as, once again, Bruce Willis is left to single-handedly save the day.

This time around, terrorists, led by a fanatical Colonel (William Sadler), have taken over the airport, and since McClane's wife Holly (Bonnie Bedelia) is trapped in a plane that will crash if it isn't allowed to land, our bloodthirsty boy scout sets about terminating the bad guys and annoying the authorities, represented by stubborn airport police chief Lorenzo (Dennis Franz) and shifty special forces type Captain Grant (John Amos). Rounding off the cast, Reginald Veljohnson (alias Twinkie-gorging sergeant Al Powell) contributes a cameo, while William Atherton returns in fine, weasely form as TV S.O.B. Dick Thornberg, stranded on the same plane as arch-nemesis Holly McClane.

By allowing the action to move outside the airport, director Renny Harlin loses the claustrophobic tension that gave the original its edge, but if you don't mind settling for second best, there's lots to see here that makes the grade. Cliff-hanging ultra-violence of note ranges from in-your-face fisticuffs and frantic, machine gun shootouts to a Bond-like snowbike chase and a desperate, ejector-seat escape. Be prepared for some explosions, too, big ones, engineered with love by the special effects wizards at Industrial Light and Magic, who wisely save their best till last. As for the death scenes, Harlin lays on a couple of beauties: a chilling icicle impalement for starters, and a rotor blade mishap to leave us with a smile in our non-pureed hearts.

Keep 'em peeled for *Star Trek: Deep Space Nine*'s Colm Meaney as the pilot of the doomed Windsor aircraft, *T2*'s Robert Patrick and *Super Mario Bros*' John Leguizamo as two of Stuart's cronies, and, finally, for Bruce's own dad, David Willis Sr, as the 'Tow Truck Driver'.

Director: Renny Harlin; **Producers:** Lawrence Gordon, Joel Silver, Charles Gordon; **Screenplay:** Steven E. de Souza, Doug Richardson, based on the novel *58 Minutes* by Walter Wager; **Production Design:** John Vallone; **Editors:** Stuart Baird, Robert A. Ferretti; **Photography:** Oliver Wood; **Music:** Michael Kamen; **Cast:** Bruce Willis, William Sadler, Bonnie Bedelia, William Atherton, John Amos, Dennis Franz, Franco Nero, Reginald Veljohnson, Art Evans, Fred Dalton Thompson, Tom Bower, Sheila McCarthy, Don Harvey.

Die Hard with a Vengeance

USA 1995 128 mins

Burnt out, hung over and separated from his wife once again, hard-boiled detective John McClane (Bruce Willis, of course) struggles to survive his third run through the blockbuster mill, cussin' 'n' killin' 'n' clockin' up the mega-bucks as only the professionals know how. Die Hard director John McTiernan returns to guide McClane through the chaos, offering a familiar bombardment of laughs and ultra-violence while seizing the opportunity to widen the scope of the action still further, graduating from office block and airport settings to New York, New York in the flawed but enjoyable *Die Hard with a Vengeance*.

A mysterious villain known as Simon (Jeremy Irons, dangerous and remote) has decided to run McClane ragged, threatening to blow up selected Big Apple locations should Big John fail to solve a variety of riddles, puzzles and physical challenges that demand excessive amounts of tearing about. As the brother of dear-departed terrorist Hans Gruber, Simon is determined to see McClane suffer and die, though our hero suspects that there's more to his plan than vengeance. Several billion dollars more, in fact.

Doubling as both reluctant sidekick and comic relief, Samuel L. Jackson tags along as Harlem shopkeeper Zeus Carver, a dude with attitude who switches to killing bad guys once he runs out of startled facial expressions and wise-ass remarks.

John McTiernan wisely steered clear of making a formula rehash of the original, attempting instead to adapt the plot, characters and situations to suit a much larger setting, making the most of a variety of New York locations while boosting the humour content and adding a spark of originality to the various high-concept, big-budget action set-pieces that we have come to expect from the series.

Of the film's many highlights, a seat-of-the-pants drive through a crowded park and later against the traffic is perhaps the most memorable, although to avoid disappointment elsewhere, you'd best be prepared for a trio of lacklustre central performances, and a rushed, unsatisfying climax which leaves too many questions unanswered. The odd blot on the landscape aside, however, this is an entertaining, if not classic, action adventure.

Director: John McTiernan; **Producers:** John McTiernan, Michael Tadross; **Screenplay:** Jonathan Hensleigh; **Production Design:** Jackson DeGovia; **Editor:** John Wright; **Photography:** Peter Menzies; **Music:** Michael Kamen; **Cast:** Bruce Willis, Jeremy Irons, Samuel L. Jackson, Graham Greene, Colleen Camp.

Brainstorms 2

WHO KILLED WHO?
Match the heroes (on the left) with the villains they slaughtered (on the right), and name the movies where they met.

Winners	Losers
Connor MacLeod	Top Dollar
Harry Callahan	Screwface
Jack Burton	Damon Killian
Roger Murtaugh	Scorpio
Trash	Fraker
Eric Draven	Arjen Rudd
Matt Hunter	Lo Pan
Paul Kersey	Rostov
John Hatcher	Kurgan
Ben Richards	Hammer

Dirty Harry

USA 1971 102 mins

'Every dirty job that comes along...'. Harry's eating a hot dog in a greasy spoon when the bank opposite sounds its alarm and a gang of armed robbers spill out of the place. Lunch in hand, Harry strolls out in to the street, reaches into his jacket and pulls out the biggest god-damn gun you've ever seen. Ten seconds later and the perps are spread all over the streets of San Francisco. It's a jungle out there, man, and Harry's the great white hunter, tougher than a maths degree, snake eyes on the alert, .44 Magnum loaded and ready to take out the local wildlife. Carnage doesn't come any cooler than this, folks, and Harry delivers like no other cop in movie history.

There's a sniper on the loose, a head case by the name of Scorpio who threatens to kill a person a day until the city coughs up a hundred grand. The Mayor (John Vernon) doesn't like the idea of giving in to terrorists, but what's money when voters' lives are at stake? First things first, though. Bleeding heart liberals stand aside, police captains shut yer traps, pimps, dealers, crooks and killers start a-shakin,' 'cos 'Dirty' Harry Callahan is on the case, and he's going to see if he can't sort things out his way first...

Scorpio is one sleazy customer. As played by Andy Robinson, he's a wild-eyed psycho who gets off on the pain and terror he inflicts. A truly hissable, Grade-A villain and no mistake. Not that Harry is above inflicting pain, he's just a little more selective about his targets. Clint Eastwood delivers a 1970s icon, a superstar supercop whose movie debut inspired not just four sequels (See *Magnum Force*, *The Enforcer*, *Sudden Impact*, *The Dead Pool*) but also a hundred thousand like-minded but generally inferior imitations. Accept no substitutes: *Dirty Harry* is the genuine article.

A screenplay with a cynical edge (co-written, wouldn't you know it, by a Harry), editing sharp enough to cut you in two, a funky, jazzy soundtrack from Lalo Schifrin... we're talking superior filmmaking here, real 'in-your-face' stuff from Don Siegel, whose enthusiastic, unflinching direction draws us into the movie and keeps us handcuffed to the screen 'til the very end.

Director: Don Siegel; **Producer:** Don Siegel; **Screenplay:** Harry Julian Fink, R.M. Fink, Dean Reisner; **Production Design:** Dale Hennesy; **Editor:** Carl Pingitore; **Photography:** Bruce Surtees; **Music:** Lalo Schifrin; **Cast:** Clint Eastwood, Andy Robinson, Harry Guardino, Reni Santoni, John Larch, John Vernon.

Dirty Mary, Crazy Larry

USA 1974 92 mins

Why turn on, tune in and drop out when you can drop in, rip off and get out instead? Peace and understanding were fine in the 1960s, but by the time the 1970s rolled around, money provided the answer to all the important questions, so here we have Peter Fonda, former easy rider and veteran practitioner of free love, forsaking his hippie heritage as Crazy Larry, ripping off a supermarket and tearin' up the American South in a distinctly un-mellow getaway flick.

Speeding from the scene of the crime in a souped-up 1960s Chevy, Larry, his level-headed partner Deke (Adam Rourke) and recent conquest Mary (Susan George), race to freedom while hard-nosed police captain Franklin (Vic Morrow) makes it his personal mission in life to bring the trio to justice. Pursued by an ever-increasing number of cops, laid-back Larry puts his wheels through their paces as he breaks every speed restriction known to man, beefing up the action every once in a while with a bunch of high-flying stunts before facing off against a super-charged cop car and a police helicopter that doesn't know when to quit.

Cheap and cheerless, the movie divides its time between passable action and half-hearted character development, an endeavour which might have proved more successful had the central characters not been so entirely unpleasant, the worst of the lot being Mary, a foul-mouthed irritation who tags along for the ride and boasts the most grating and artificial American accent ever committed to film (why British actress Susan George was chosen for the role remains a mystery to this day).

There's really not too much to this curious refugee from the mid-1970s, soften its edges and it might make a decent *Dukes of Hazzard* episode, but it's just about watchable if you have nothing better to do, if only for its twisted climax which exposes the movie for what it is: an extended shaggy dog story.

Director: John Hough; Norman T. Herman; **Screenplay:** Leigh Chapman, Antonio Santean, based on the novel *The Chase* by Richard Unekis; **Editor:** Christopher Holmes; **Photography:** Mike Margulies; **Music:** Jimmie Haskell; **Cast:** Peter Fonda, Susan George, Adam Rourke, Vic Morrow, Roddy McDowall, Kenneth Tobey, Eugene Daniels.

Double Impact

USA 1991 109 mins

Jean-Claude Van Damme fights side-by-side with his favourite movie star, namely himself, playing twin brothers on the prowl in Hong Kong, eager to butcher every bad guy they can aim their fists, feet and bullets at, all in the name of sweet revenge. Van Damme was seriously hands-on with this one, with a writing and producing credit which explains why the word obnoxious best sums up this movie, and a fight choreography credit that guarantees us more than our fair share of mindlessly excessive death and destruction. You can take that as a recommendation, although Van Damme really should have made his co-star take some acting lessons.

But this is a movie about violence, plain and simple, and it's more important for Van Damme to be able to tear a guy apart than it is for him to share his feelings with his fellow man. Certainly, a degree of acting ability would have been a bonus, but when it comes to chopping a bodyguard in the throat, introducing a couple of bottles to the poor sap's skull, and then breaking his arm for luck, Jean-Claude is poetry in motion. Just don't try this at home.

There's a thinly veiled excuse for carnage hung around the movie, you might call it a story, and it goes something like this: after their parents are whacked by a Triad hit team, twin baby brothers Chad and Alex are accidentally separated, and while Alex remains in Hong Kong, where he grows to become a cigar-chomping smuggler and multi-purpose tough guy, Chad grows up in Los Angeles, where his mind turns to candy and his body turns to kickboxing. And only their barber could tell them apart.

Twenty five years pass before the two are eventually reunited on a mission of personal vengeance, and while the boys are inclined to argue among themselves, they've some male-bonding in store as they pursue 'legitimate' businessman Nigel Griffith (Alan Scarfe) and crime boss Raymond Zhang (Philip Can Yan Kin), the scum responsible for all their troubles, and also the employers of brutal martial artist Moon (Bolo Yeung), and mighty-thighed superbitch Kara, played by statuesque newcomer Cory Everson.

In the lads' corner stands Geoffrey Lewis as good old 'Uncle' Frank, a sharp-shooting strategy man who once served as their father's bodyguard (let's hope he does a better job here), while Alonna Shaw offers a healthy figure for the boys to fight over.

There's nothing new to see here, it's true, but at least it's well-recycled trash, fast and tough, with some colourful location work and capable split-screen effects (never mind the editing, though). Van Damme kicks high, the movie aims low, and both hit their targets. Chaos rules!

Director: Sheldon Lettich; **Producers:** Ashok Amritaj, Jean-Claude Van Damme; **Screenplay:** Sheldon Lettich, Jean-Claude Van Damme, Story by Lettich, Van Damme, Steve Meerson, Peter Krikes; **Production Design:** John Jay Moore; **Editors:** Mark Conte, Brent White; **Photography:** Richard Kline; **Music:** Arthur Kempel; **Cast:** Jean-Claude Van Damme, Geoffrey Lewis, Alan Scarfe, Philip Can Yan Kin, Alonna Shaw, Bolo Yeung, Cory Everson.

Death Becomes Them 5

Name: DOUGLAS, Michael

Born: New Brunswick, New Jersey, 1944

Characteristics: Kirk Douglas, only heavier, with bigger hair.

Debut Feature: *Hail, Hero!* (1969

Life and times: The son of Kirk started life as a TV star, playing opposite Karl Malden in *The Streets of San Francisco* (from 1972 to 1976). Douglas won his first Academy Award in 1975, for producing *One Flew Over the Cuckoo's Nest* (Best Picture), reaching the rank of movie star in 1984 with *Romancing the Stone* (which he also produced), and winning that all-important Best Actor Oscar for his performance as hyperactive money-maker Gordon

Michael Douglas soaks up the atmosphere in *Black Rain*.

Gekko in Oliver Stone's 1987 drama *Wall Street*. Douglas runs his own production company, Stonebridge, and tries to star in at least one 'event picture' per year (or so).

Greatest contribution to action movies: Indy lite.

> **Speech, speech:** 'Actors are paid to be selfish and self-involved.'
>
> Those British film certificates explained in full: 'Oh, I get it, it's simple. PG means the hero gets the girl, 15 means that the villain gets the girl, and 18 means everybody gets the girl.'
>
> 'Revenge is a very good motivation if you can direct it. It's healthy. Very healthy.'
>
> **Selected filmography:** *Coma* (1977), *The China Syndrome* (+ prod; 1979), *The Star Chamber* (1983), ***Romancing the Stone*** (+ prod; 1984), ***The Jewel of the Nile*** (+ prod; 1985), *Fatal Attraction* (1987), *Wall Street* (1987), ***Black Rain*** (1989), *The War of the Roses* (1989), *Basic Instinct* (1992), *Falling Down* (1993), *Disclosure* (1994), *The American President* (1995), *Ghost and the Darkness* (1996).

Dr No

GB 1962 111 mins

Way back in the good old days when smoking, drinking, gambling, sleeping around and killing foreign agents was not only acceptable but fashionable, author Ian Fleming created the ultimate man: sharp, sophisticated and intelligent, consummately British, immaculately dressed, randy as hell and deadlier than cholesterol. His name was Bond, James Bond, alias 007 of the British Secret Service, and while his licence to kill was put to prolific good use throughout the cold war and beyond, he came to make his biggest killing at the cinema, through a series of blockbusters that began with *Dr No*, a stylish spy thriller which, although rather light on action, served to introduce many of the now-classic elements that we have come to expect from the Bond series: beautiful women, larger-than-life villains, exotic locations, colossal sets, and, of course, James Bond himself, here played by the man who made him great, Sean Connery.

Ordered to Jamaica to investigate the disappearance of Secret Service Chief John Strangways, Bond hooks up with CIA hotshot Felix Leiter (here played by Jack Lord) and Cayman Islander Quarrel (John Kitzmiller). Following several attempts on his life, Bond sets sail to the mysterious Crab Key, where he stumbles upon Amazonian beauty Honey Ryder (Ursula Andress) and clashes with the evil Dr No (Joseph Wiseman) a SPECTRE (SPecial Executive for Counter Intelligence, Terrorism, Revenge, Extortion) goon of both Chinese and German parentage (so audiences of the time could hate him twice over), intent, wouldn't you know it, on world domination.

Not bad for a first attempt, quite imaginative and well played, although it all seems rather dated now, almost tame compared with later Bond adventures. But at the centre of it all is Connery, cool and hard with a roguish smile and an accent to die for, and he makes it all worthwhile.

According to Sean Connery, when *Dr No* opened in Japan, the title was translated as *No Need For Any Doctors*!

The end of *Dr No*. But James Bond will return in *From Russia With Love*.

Director: Terence Young; **Producers:** Harry Saltzman, Albert R. Broccoli; **Screenplay:** Richard Maibaum, Johanna Harwood, Berkely Mather, based on the novel *Dr No* by Ian Fleming; **Production Design:** Ken Adam; **Editor:** Peter Hunt; **Photography:** Ted Moore; **Music:** Monty Norman, Bond theme by John Barry; **Cast:** Sean Connery, Ursula Andress,

Jack Lord, Joseph Wiseman, John Kitzmiller, Bernard Lee, Lois Maxwell, Zena Marshall, Eunice Grayson, Anthony Dawson.

Dragon: The Bruce Lee Story

USA 1993 119 mins

The life and times of Bruce Lee are effectively captured by director Rob Cohen in this well-balanced biopic, an entertaining mixture of drama, romance and impressive martial arts action.

Taking care to do justice to the man, not just the legend, *Dragon* follows Lee's early life on the streets of Hong Kong and his initial struggles and successes in America, which included his interracial marriage to Linda Emery, his fight to establish a new martial art, Jeet Kune Do, and his TV success as co-star of *The Green Hornet*.

Covering the highs and lows of an incredible life, the film concludes shortly before his death (of a cerebral edema, a swelling of the brain) at the age of 32, just three weeks before the release of his only major studio film, the remarkable *Enter the Dragon*.

Lee's belief that he was being pursued by a demon is impressively visualized here in a series of dream sequences in which he struggles with a towering warrior in full battle armour. The film also recreates scenes from *Fists of Fury* and *Enter the Dragon* to great effect, while the martial arts action elsewhere is well placed, well hard and pretty damn exciting too.

Jason Scott Lee (no relation) is perfectly cast in the central role, for not only does he look and act like Lee, but he moves and fights like him too, a fact made all the more remarkable when you consider that prior to being cast in *Dragon*, Lee actually had no martial arts training at all. Lauren Holly is also impressive in a less showy but equally heartfelt role as Linda Emery (later Lee), while Nancy Kwan and Robert Wagner are fine in support.

A captivating movie about an incredible man which captures the spirit of who Bruce Lee was and what he believed in, *Dragon* should please both devoted fans of the legendary action hero, and the more sensitive members of the public (whoever they may be) who crave something a little deeper and more romantic (but don't let that put you off).

Director: Rob Cohen; **Producer:** Raffaella De Laurentis; **Screenplay:** Edward Khmara, John Raffo and Rob Cohen, based on the book *Bruce Lee: The Man Only I Knew* by Linda Lee Cadwell; **Production Design:** Robert Ziembicki; **Editor:** Peter Amundson; **Photography:** David Eggby; **Music:** Randy Edelman; **Cast:** Jason Scott Lee, Lauren Holly, Nancy Kwan, Robert Wagner.

Drop Zone

USA 1994 102 mins

Some people get their kicks on the ground, others prefer to jump out of aeroplanes and rush towards it at 120 mph, but whether you prefer to cheat death from your armchair or from several thousand feet above, this movie has all the skydiving action you could ever wish to see, and then some. Yes sir, gravity rules as Wesley Snipes pursues a high-flying gang of assorted wrongdoers through a featherlight plot constructed solely to bridge the gaps between the all-important aerial sequences. They are impressive, though, speedy and dangerous, boosted by expert camerawork and a pounding rock soundtrack, only once you've enjoyed and recovered from the first couple of jumps, don't expect what remains to be any different.

You'd think that after *Passenger 57* Wesley Snipes would have learned to stay away from aeroplanes, but here he is again, as supercool US Marshal Pete Nessip, quietly escorting convicted computer hacker Earl Leedy (Michael Jeter) to jail via a 747, when all of a sudden terrorists blow the plane half to pieces, waste Pete's partner (who also happens to be his brother) and make off with good ol' Mr Leedy. Overloaded with motivation, Pete sets out to make the bad guys pay the ultimate price , a task which - you'll never guess - involves jumping out of planes and mixing with all sorts of weird gung-ho types.

And very slick it is too, the best-looking picture that money can buy, but that doesn't make it interesting, and it doesn't compensate for two lacklustre performances, from Snipes' predictable hero to Gary Busey's mundane villain, an ex-DEA agent with a fiendish plan and a corker of a pot belly. The action is fairly well orchestrated, though, and besides the various skydiving stunts on show, the 747 shootout and *Die Hard*-style climax are both worth sticking around for, as is a particularly juicy death scene that rears its splattered head at the very end of the picture. Just don't expect too much.

Director: John Badham; **Producers:** D.J. Caruso, Wallis Nicita, Lauren Lloyd; **Screenplay:** Peter Barsocchini, John Bishop; **Production Design:** Joe Alves; **Editor:** Frank Morriss; **Photography:** Roy H. Wagner; **Music:** Hans Zimmer; **Cast:** Wesley Snipes, Gary Busey, Yancy Butler, Michael Jeter, Corin Nemec, Kyle Secor, Rex Linn, Sam Hennings, Claire Stansfield, Malcolm-Jamal Warner.

Drunken Master

Hong Kong 1978 107 mins

You're never far from a fight scene in this classic Kung Fu comedy from Yuen Woo Ping, the director of *Snake in the Eagle's Show*. Eager young action man Jackie Chan earned a lot of fans with this one, raising hell and kicking butts as legendary martial artist Wong Fei Hung (1847-1924), a real-life Chinese superhero (and subject of more than a hundred movies) whose early life is reinvented in this non-stop fist-fest.

A wayward lad with a talent for getting into (and out of) trouble, Hung is sent to train with the notorious drunken master (Yuen Hsiao Tieng), a confirmed alcoholic whose ceaseless inebriation allows him to perform a dazzling range of bizarre and brutal moves. A year of back-breaking training and strict discipline with a sadistic teacher famous for crippling his students sounds like a pretty bum deal to Hung, but once he crosses paths with kickcrazy assassin Thunderfoot (Wong Jang Lee), and his butt is well and truly kicked, he decides that there are worse fates in life than becoming a drunken master...

As fluid as the wine he guzzles, Chan doesn't stop moving for a second, working his way through a variety of tough guys (Ironhead Rat has a cranial battering ram, Mr Stick uses, well, sticks) towards a climactic re-match with the Foot man. This is martial arts slapstick at its finest: speedy and inventive with a taste for violence and a good sense of humour. You must see this movie - it's even good when you're stone, cold sober.

Sequel: *Drunken Master 2*.

Director: Yuen Woo Ping; **Producer:** Ng See Yuen; **Screenplay:** Hsiao Lung, Ng See Yuen; **Production Design:** Ting Yuen Tai; **Editor:** Pan Hsiung; **Photography:** Chang Hai; **Music:** Chow Fu; **Cast:** Jackie Chan, Simon Yuen, Wong Jang Lee.

Death Becomes Them 6

Name: DUDIKOFF, Michael

Born: Torrance, California, 1954

Characteristics: Baby-faced surfer type.

Debut feature: *The Black Marble* (1980)

Michael Dudikoff stands for truth, justice and the ultra-violent way in *American Ninja*.

Life and times: A college kid studying to become a child psychologist, Dudikoff appeared in an Adidas commercial and promptly caught the acting bug. Retreating from his studies to pursue B-movie stardom, Dudikoff hung around Hollywood for a few years until Cannon gave him a chance to prove himself in *American Ninja*. Unlike the majority of low-budget action heroes, Dudikoff was neither a martial artist nor a body builder, but he managed to make it through the movie just the same. A steady career making straight-to-video releases prepared Dudikoff for life as a TV tough guy, kicking butt on the small screen in the action adventure series *Cobra* (1995).

Greatest contribution to action movies: In *American Ninja*, he taught us just how important violence is in the male-bonding process (you beat 'em up, they respect you, end of story).

Speech, speech: 'Acting is a real challenge... I want to make it, I can make it, and I'm gonna make it.'

Selected filmography: *Bloody Birthday* (1980), *Tron* (1982), *Bachelor Party* (1984), ***American Ninja*** (1985), *Avenging Force* (1986), ***American Ninja 2: The Confrontation*** (1987), *Platoon Leader* (1987), *River of Death* (1990), *American Ninja 4: The Annihilation* (1991), *The Human Shield* (1992), ***Chain of Command*** (1993).

Name: EASTWOOD, Clint

Real name: Clinton Eastwood Jr

Born: San Francisco, 1930

Characteristics: The snake eyes. The practised drawl. The itchy trigger figure. Ladies and gentlemen, let's hear it for the hardest man alive.

Previous professions: Lumberjack, soldier

Debut feature: *Revenge of the Creature* (1955)

Life and times: A box office attraction for more than 30 years, Eastwood made his name playing Rowdy Yates in the massively popular western show *Rawhide* (1959-1966). Sergio Leone gave Clint his first taste of big screen success, casting him as The Man With No Name in a trio of groundbreaking spaghetti westerns, then along came director Don Siegel and *Dirty Harry* was born. The boss of Malpaso productions (named after a creek in Carmel),

Death Becomes Them 7

One man and his gun: Clint Eastwood blows us away as Dirty Harry.

Eastwood directed his first movie, *Play Misty For Me*, in 1971, and, 15 films later, the Academy finally sat up and smelt Clint's fresh blend: *Unforgiven* cleaned up at the 1992 Awards, winning Oscars for Best Picture, Best Director, Best Supporting Actor (Gene Hackman) and, because three statuettes are never enough, Best Film Editing (Joel Cox) too. A star on both sides of the camera, Clint has enjoyed a smorgasbord of famous damsels, from Marsha Mason, Diane Venora and Bernadette Peters to Geneviève Bujold and frequent co-star Sondra Locke. Politics beckoned for a brief spell when, in 1986, Eastwood was elected Mayor of Carmel, California. His first official act was to legalize ice cream parlours.

Greatest contribution to action movies: *Dirty Harry*, the father of every modern movie cop, from Martin Riggs to RoboCop.

Speech, speech: 'Movies are fun. But they're not a cure for cancer.'

'My old drama coach used to say, "don't just do something, stand there". Gary Cooper wasn't afraid to do nothing.'

'I do the kind of roles I'd like to see if I were still digging swimming pools and wanted to escape my problems.'

'There's always been violence in cinema, theatre and literature. But it is society's tolerance of violence in society that's probably responsible for violent behaviour more than any motion picture or television show. The attitude, at least in America, seems to be: this isn't bothering me, so why should I be bothered by it?'

Selected filmography: *Francis in the Navy* (1955), *Ambush at Cimarron Pass* (1958), *A Fistful of Dollars* (1964), *For a Few Dollars More* (1966), *The Good, the Bad and the Ugly* (1966), *Hang 'em High* (1967), *Coogan's Bluff* (1968), **Where Eagles Dare** (1968), *Paint Your Wagon* (1969), *Two Mules For Sister Sara* (1970), *Kelly's Heroes* (1970), *The Beguiled* (1971), **Dirty Harry** (1971), *Play Misty For Me* (+ dir; 1971), *Joe Kidd* (1972), *High Plains Drifter* (+ dir; 1973), **Magnum Force** (1973), *Breezy* (dir only; 1973), *Thunderbolt and Lightfoot* (1974), *The Eiger Sanction* (+ dir; 1975), *The Outlaw Josey Wales* (+ dir; 1976), **The Enforcer** (1976), **The Gauntlet** (+ dir; 1977), *Every Which Way But Loose* (1978), *Escape From Alcatraz* (1979), *Bronco Billy* (+ dir; 1980), *Any Which Way You Can* (1980), *Firefox* (+ dir; 1982), *Honkytonk Man* (+ dir; 1982), **Sudden Impact** (+ dir; 1983), *City Heat* (1984), *Tightrope* (1984), *Pale Rider* (+ dir; 1985), *Heartbreak Ridge* (+ dir; 1986), *Bird* (dir only; 1988), **The Dead Pool** (1988), *Pink Cadillac* (1989), *White Hunter, Black Heart* (+ dir; 1990), **The Rookie** (+ dir; 1990), *Unforgiven* (+ dir; 1992), *In the Line of Fire* (1993), *A Perfect World* (+ dir; 1993), *The Bridges of Madison County* (+ dir; 1995), *Absolute Power* (1997).

El Mariachi

USA 1992 80 mins

Tex-Mex first-timer Robert Rodriguez trades cash for enthusiasm in this microscopically-budgeted gun-fest, writing, directing, co-producing, editing and shooting the damn thing in a matter of weeks, while, in his spare time, serving as unit production manager, camera operator, dolly grip, special effects technician, sound man, music editor and still photographer too. And he doesn't do too bad a job, considering, although frankly, the fact that Rodriguez managed to make the movie at all is a lot more impressive than the movie itself.

A lone Mariachi musician (co-producer, unit production manager, dolly grip, special effects whiz and star of the show Carlos Gallardo) wanders innocently into a small, Mexican border town looking for work but finding nothing but trouble. Mistaken for a hit man known for packing pistols in his guitar case, our Mariachi hero is soon the target of every villain in town, courtesy of local kingpin Mauricio (Peter Marquardt), a gringo wide boy with an expendable army of trigger-happy thugs.

Cue 80 minutes of reasonably inventive bloodshed as Big M transforms from mild-mannered musician into pistol-packing avenger, running and jumping and shooting and slicing his way through the Mexican underworld, breaking only for the odd romantic pit-stop with horny bartender Domino (Consuelo Gómez), ever-present for snogging duties and the stitching of fresh, gaping wounds.

Rough, ready and cheaper than a hundred-year-old hooker, *El Mariachi* offers cultish, hit-and-run entertainment for the late night crowd. Aiming for thrills, not frills, Rodriguez keeps the action coming throughout, dumping traditional production values in favour of (frugal) style and (broad) humour. For those who believe that less is more, this is a bargain-basement classic. For those who admire the resourcefulness of an unknown filmmaker, this makes for an interesting study. If, on the other hand, you're looking for a dazzling, highly-polished blockbuster of Arnie proportions, you'd best look elsewhere.

Sequel: *Desperado.*

Director: Robert Rodriguez; **Producer:** Robert Rodriguez, Carlos Gallardo; **Screenplay:** Robert Rodriguez; **Editor:** Robert Rodriguez; **Photography:** Robert Rodriguez; **Music:** Marc Trujillo, Alvaro Rodriguez, Juan Suarez, Celilio Rodriguez, Eric Guthrie; **Cast:** Carlos Gallardo, Consuelo Gómez, Jaime De Hoyos, Peter Marquardt, Reinol Martinez.

The Empire Strikes Back

USA 1980 124 mins

Welcome to '23 reasons why *The Empire Strikes Back* is almost as good as *Star Wars...*' The gang's all back, from Luke and Han to Darth and Chewie. The inhospitable ice planet of Hoth. Stop motion snow lizard, the Tauntaun. Rebel snowspeeders. Vader's Star destroyer. The Empire's AT-AT (All Terrain Armed Transport) assault. Leia: You're not actually going into an asteroid field? Han: They'd be crazy to follow us, wouldn't they? Extra-special effects. Bounty huntin' scum Bossk, Zuckuss, Dengar, IG-88 and, coolest of the lot, Boba Fett (Jeremy Bulloch). Luke's Dagobah Vacation. Yoda, wizened 900-year-old (the Force is strong with this one). Punishing Jedi training, 'Do. Or do not. There is no try.' Han and Leia get it on. Slave 1. Choking Imperial officers. Mynocks. Bespin. Cloud City. Lando Calrisian (Billy Dee Williams), roguish administrator with a secret. The Empire strikes again. Luke and Vader's gymnastic lightsaber duel (complete with soap-style revelation), 'Obi-Wan has taught you well...' Staggering action. The cliffhanging climax. Stay tuned for *Return of the Jedi...*

Luke Skywalker (Mark Hamill) and Darth Vader (Dave Prowse) use plenty of force in *The Empire Strikes Back*.

Director: Irvin Kershner; **Producer:** Gary Kurtz; **Executive Producer:** George Lucas; **Screenplay:** Leigh Brackett, Lawrence Kasdan, story by George Lucas; **Production Design:** Norman Reynolds; **Editor:** Paul Hirsch; **Photography:** Peter Suschitzky; **Music:** John Williams; **Cast:** Mark Hamill, Harrison Ford, Carrie Fisher, Billy Dee Williams, Anthony Daniels, David Prowse, Peter Mayhew, Kenny Baker, Frank Oz, Alec Guiness, Jeremy Bulloch, James Earl Jones (voice only). **Academy Awards:** Best... Sound, Visual Effects (Richard Edlund, Dennis Muren).

The Enforcer

USA 1976 96 mins

Tact, diplomacy and political correctness take a back seat as 'Dirty' Harry Callahan (Clint Eastwood, as if you didn't know) embarks on his third screen adventure, gunning for a gang of hippie revolutionaries who deserve bumping off for their dress sense alone. The fact that they blast a big hole in Harry's partner and plant bombs all over San Francisco only serves to motivate our no-nonsense hero further.

Led by baby-faced psycho Bobby Maxwell (DeVeren Brookwalter), the People's Revolutionary Strike Force soon discover the error of messing with a man synonymous with the phrase 'excessive use of force'. In addition to keeping his know-nothing superiors firmly in their place, Harry's life is further complicated by the unwelcome presence of his new partner, a woman, and you can imagine how he feels about that. God bless him, Harry never quite made it to the twentieth century, a prehistoric male with some pretty fierce opinions who doesn't exactly hit it off with newly promoted Inspector Kate Moore (*Cagney and Lacy's* Tyne Daly).

Best not get your hopes up too high, though. Thanks to action sequences which rarely score above average and a fairly standard, no-frills plot, *The Enforcer* marks a step down in quality from the previously shot *Dirty Harry* and *Magnum Force*. Yet Eastwood remains as charismatic as ever, delivering sledgehammer justice with style and attitude, while Daly digs her heels in and delivers the best damn sidekick Harry's ever had. I'm not going to tell you whether or not they save the day, but they sure as hell save the movie.

Director: James Fargo; **Producer:** Robert Daley; **Screenplay:** Stirling Silliphant, Dean Reisner; **Production Design:** Allen E. Smith; **Editors:** Ferris Webster, Joel Cox; **Photography:** Charles W. Short; **Music:** Jerry Fielding; **Cast:** Clint Eastwood, Tyne Daly, Harry Guardino, Bradford Dillman, John Mitchum, John Crawford, DeVeren Brookwalter.

Enter the Dragon (aka The Deadly Three)

USA 1973 97mins

Bruce Lee's first and final Stateside production is a non-stop fist-fest with first-class production values and the coolest, toughest brawlers on Earth. A groovy Lalo Schifrin score takes us all the way to Funky Town as Lee dispenses justice in one of the greatest, most influential martial arts movies ever made.

A murdered sister furnishes Lee with all the motivation he needs to brave the island stronghold of omni-handed crime boss Han (Shih Kien) and exterminate the vermin within. As luck would have it, the best of the baddest are converging on Han's mysterious island to compete in a gruelling martial arts championship, presenting Lee with a perfect, plotless opportunity to while away the movie stomping competitors and henchmen alike.

Joining our hero for this wild, violent ride, John Saxon contributes combat and comic relief as cash-poor joker Roper, while Jim Kelly steals loads of the show in his big screen debut as sideburned superstud Williams, crowned by an Afro the size of Texas with an ego to match and a sex drive that could power Tokyo (when conserving energy, Williams cuts down to four hookers a night). Also, be on the lookout for Eastern heroes Samo Hung and Bolo Yeung, while US man-mountain Bob Wall can be found hulking around as bodyguard Oharra.

Complete with Bond-like sets and action set-pieces, *Enter the Dragon* is high on 1970s style, fast and fierce with Lee at his peak and a classic hall of mirrors finale that will blow you clean away.

Director: Robert Clouse; **Producers:** Fred Weintraub, Paul Heller, in association with Raymond Chow; **Screenplay:** Michael Allin; **Editors:** Kurt Hirschler, George Watters; **Photography:** Gilbert Hubbs; **Music:** Lalo Schifrin; **Cast:** Bruce Lee, John Saxon, Jim Kelly, Ahna Capri, Shih Kien, Bob Wall.

Eraser

USA 1996 114 mins

Remember when we knew what to expect from a Schwarzenegger flick? Back before political and family ties softened his edge, prompting lame-brained comedies, juvenile adventures and, to his eternal shame, *Junior*, the laugh-at-me-I'm-a-pregnant-man-mountain-in-a-pink-dress fiasco? Where's the beef? Where's the violence? Our barbarian leader must be restored. You can stuff *True Lies'* half-hearted Bond mixture. An honest-to-goodness return to limb-severing, face-blasting madness is what we want, and we want it now! Thanks then, to director Chuck (*Nightmare on Elm Street 3*, *The Blob*, *The Mask*) Russell for having the guts to drag Arnold back to form in this dumb and under-written yet spectacularly brutal death-fest.

There's this weapon, see, an assault-sized, electro-magnetic pulse rifle with X-ray sights and aluminium rounds which blast off just under the speed of light. We're in Hardware Heaven here, boys, and the bad guys are manufacturing these suckers for cashed-up terrorists the World over. Naturally, these dastardly types need a-foiling, and honest citizen Lee Cullen (1983 Miss World Vanessa Williams, M.O.R. pop sensation and run-of-the-mill actress) has enough evidence to stop them dead in their tracks, if only she can stay alive long enough to testify against them. Enter Arnold, alias US Marshal John Kruger, the 'Eraser', a specialist in witness protection who resolves to keep Lee in the land of the living, a perilous task involving jumping out of aeroplanes, tackling hungry crocodiles and strapping on a pair of "rail guns" for an explosive dockland finale which sees Arnold in full *Commando* mode, knee-deep in the dead and blowing the living hell out of all available property.

Fighting for the bad guys, James Caan has the most fun as FBI turncoat Robert Deguerin, a ruthless killer who'd stop at nothing to earn his blood money, while *Murphy Brown*'s Robert Pastorelli pitches in with helping hands and comic relief as re-located mob informer and sidekick Johnny C.

True, the movie falls apart towards the end, and the one-liners (with one hilarious exception) are pretty feeble, but the action's hard and chaotic and, besides, it's great to see Arnold playing the hero game again.

Director: Charles Russell; **Producers:** Arnold Kopelson, Anne Kopelson; **Screenplay:** Tony Puryear, Walon Green; **Production Design:** Bill Kenney; **Editor:** Michael Tronick; **Photography:** Adam Greenberg; Music: Alan Silvestri; **Cast:** Arnold Schwarzenegger, James Caan, Vanessa Williams, James Coburn, Robert Pastorelli.

Escape from New York

USA 1981 99 mins

Between *Elvis* and *The Thing*, John Carpenter and Kurt Russell joined forces on this classic cult adventure, a prison picture with a difference. We're in the future, some time soon, and the crime rate is higher than Reverend Jim. America responds to this crisis by converting Manhattan Island into a maximum security installation large enough to house a nation full of undesirables. Maintaining its reputation as the most dangerous place on Earth, New York is a dark, filthy pit full of killers and crazies. Heavily mined and surrounded by guards, it's a roach motel you can never check out of, and the President of the United States (Donald Pleasance) is missing inside, stranded in the Big Apple after a hopeless crash-landing delivers him right into the clutches of the all-powerful Duke of New York (Isaac Hayes), a bad man with a long car (sporting external chandelier upgrades) and hundreds of psychotic henchmen.

Only Snake (Russell) can save the big man. Snake Plissken. Ex-special forces, of course, with an eye-patch, an attitude, a Dirty Harry drawl and a deal with hard-boiled warden Lee Van Cleef: a full pardon (for various crimes against the State) in exchange for the Prez. Racing against an explosive 23-hour deadline, Snake hits the city that never sleeps, making friends (allies include brainbox Harry Dean Stanton, boy toy Adrienne Barbeau and cabbie Ernest Borgnine) and wasting people in this pacy, atmospheric picture.

Opportunities for violence arise with pleasing regularity, and Carpenter wisely saves the best till last: a no-holds-barred race for freedom over a heavily-mined, dilapidated old bridge. The movie belongs to Snake, though, the coolest action anti-hero of all, whose final act of twisted defiance rivals the mind-messing brilliance of *Planet of the Apes*' Liberty punchline.

Sequel: *Escape From L.A.*

Director: John Carpenter; **Producers:** Larry Franco, Debra Hill; **Screenplay:** John Carpenter, Nick Castle; **Production Design:** Joe Alves; **Editor:** Todd Ramsay; **Photography:** Dean Cundey; **Music:** John Carpenter, in association with Alan Howarth; **Cast:** Kurt Russell, Lee Van Cleef, Ernest Borgnine, Donald Pleasence, Isaac Hayes, Harry Dean Stanton, Adrienne Barbeau, Tom Atkins.

Escape to Athena

GB 1979 117mins

He gave the world *Cobra*. He gave the world *Rambo II*. He gave the world *Leviathan*. He is, of course, director George Pan Cosmatos, a Z-movie maker with A-movie money who cranked out this little beauty years before joining forces with Stallone. Recalling the lazy, hazy, crazy days of wartime Greece, circa 1944, *Escape to Athena* is a wacky, lightweight death-fest, good-looking but dumb as an ox and full of dead (and dying) Nazis. The icing on the cake is a 1970s dream team of miscast hams, including (alphabetically) cocky freedom fighter Sonny Bono, gutsy brothel madame Claudia Cardinale, hyperactive Jewish grifter Elliot Gould, Nazi-with-a-heart-of-gold Roger Moore, true-Brit archaeologist David Niven, all-singing, all-stripping sexpot Stefanie Powers, obligatory muscle man Richard Roundtree, gritty resistance leader Telly Savalas and, last and least, sadistic Nazi scum bucket Anthony Valentine.

Who knew that World War 2 could be so much fun? One minute, you're busting out of a prison camp, the next you're saving the planet from a doomsday weapon. You get to play with knives and guns, chase villains through narrow, cobbled streets on rusty old motorcycles, and maybe, just maybe, nab that priceless art treasure you've had your eye on.

Stupid, bad and brilliant with it, this is first-class nonsense for all the family, a grand adventure with its tongue in its cheek and its brain in a little jar over the fireplace.

Director: George Cosmatos; **Producers:** David Niven Jr, Jack Wiener; **Screenplay:** Edward Anhalt, Richard S. Lochte; **Production Design:** Michael Stringer; **Editor:** Ralph Kemplen; **Photography:** Gil Taylor; **Music:** Lalo Schifrin; **Cast:** Roger Moore, Telly Savalas, David Niven, Stefanie Powers, Claudia Cardinale, Richard Roundtree, Sonny Bono, Elliott Gould, Anthony Valentine.

Name: ESTEVEZ, Emilio

Real name: Emilio Sheen

Born: New York City, 1962

Characteristics: Martin Sheen, only more boyish. Tries (but fails) to compensate with a moustache.

Debut feature: *In the Custody of Strangers* (TV movie; 1982)

Life and times: Following his father, Martin Sheen, into the business, Estevez scored in the cult hit *Repo Man* (1984), made his name as a member of the 'Brat Pack' (Tom Cruise, Molly Ringwald, Rob Lowe, Demi Moore...) in a series of teenage comedy dramas (big screen *90210*), and, in 1986, became the youngest Hollywood star ever to write and direct his

Death Becomes Them 8

own pictures (with *Wisdom*). Unfortunately, he wasn't very good at it, and with only a few exceptions, the following decade was like a larder at Christmas: full of turkeys. Formerly engaged to Demi Moore, who dumped him and married Bruce Willis four months later, Estevez married singer and choreographer Paula Abdul in 1992.

The bad guys only want him for his body: Emilio Estevez defends himself in *Freejack*.

Greatest contribution to action movies:
Never directing one.

Speech, speech: 'I swore to myself that I'd make it through drive, ambition and hard work. I wanted to know I got it that way and not because of my bloodlines. And I think there is no question why I got where I am today. I'm pretty content. I have a motto: expect nothing and be pleasantly surprised.

Selected filmography: *Tex* (1982), *The Outsiders* (1983), *Repo Man* (1984), *The Breakfast Club* (1985), *St Elmo's Fire* (1985), *That Was Then, This Is Now* (+ scr; 1985), *Maximum Overdrive* (1986), *Wisdom* (+ scr/dir; 1986), *Stakeout* (1987), *Young Guns* (1988), *Men at Work* (+ scr/dir; 1990), *Young Guns II: Blaze of Glory* (1990), **Freejack** (1992), *The Mighty Ducks* (aka *Champions*; 1992), ***National Lampoon's Loaded Weapon 1*** (1993), ***Judgment Night*** (1993), *Another Stakeout* (1993), *D2: The Mighty Ducks* (1994), *The War at Home* (+ dir; 1994), *Mission: Impossible* (uncredited cameo; 1996)

Excessive Force

USA 1993 90 mins

Regardless of its irresistible title, *Excessive Force* proves entirely resistible, a routine cop thriller with brief bursts of action and an inflated opinion of itself. Action Man clone Thomas Ian Griffith plays it straight and narrow-minded, a quick-witted fighter, sure, but when did proficiency in the martial arts qualify a man to write and co-produce a movie? As predictable as a hundred thousand like-minded thrillers, there's nothing to distinguish it from the crowd, an instantly forgettable effort fronted by an inadequate Dirty Harry wannabe.

Say hello, then, to maverick cop and moody jazz pianist Terry McCain (Griffith), an obsessive type whose relentless pursuit of untouchable crime boss Sal Di Marco (*Rocky*'s Burt Young), backfires when the Italian One bites the bullet and our hero is accused of pulling the trigger. Determined to clear his name and bring the real villains to justice while avoiding both cops and mobsters, Terry hits the streets of Chicago and, well, all the same old, obvious stuff happens before the movie finally fizzles out with a poorly illuminated punch up.

An all-star supporting cast buckles from the weight of carrying the feature: Lance Henriksen, Police Captain with a secret; James Earl Jones, bartender, best friend and father confessor figure; Charlotte Lewis, estranged girlfriend in distress and *Candyman*'s Tony Todd as Terry's Kentucky Fried partner Frankie.

Heavily edited for video, *Excessive Force* delivers bland, nasty, dumb, dull, dire and little else.

Director: Jon Hess; **Producer:** Thomas Ian Griffith, Erwin Stoff; **Screenplay:** Thomas Ian Griffith; **Production Design:** Michael Z. Hanan; **Editor:** Alan Baumgarten; **Photography:** Donald P. Morgan; **Music:** Charles Bernstein; **Cast:** Thomas Ian Griffith, Lance Henriksen, James Earl Jones, Charlotte Lewis, Tony Todd, Burt Young.

An Eye for an Eye
USA 1981 106 mins

Just for a change, here's a story about a renegade ex-cop who takes the law into his own hands in the name of revenge, grimly stalking the men responsible for killing his partner. Now, there may not be an excess of originality in this leisurely paced thriller, but at least it's violent, a trademark ingredient essential to every Chuck Norris chop-a-thon. Couch potatoes enrolled in Chuck's Impossible Martial Arts class would be wise to ignore everything but the various death moves revealed here, the film's characters, plot and feeble attempt at romance mere distractions from the brutality at hand.

Besides Chuck, we have a hefty henchman to be thankful for, 'a Sherman Tank in a suit', played by none other than Professor Toru Tanaka, a veteran screen heavy who remains silent save for the odd grunt here and there, an incredible bulk of a man who never seems to make it to the end of any movie alive.

Elsewhere among the cast, satisfaction is not guaranteed. Mako overdoes it as a typically feisty martial arts instructor with a grudge of his own, while Christopher Lee pops up in a handful of scenes as menacing Brit Morgan Canfield, a thick, black ferret of a moustache chewing on his upper lip, a man with no defined character who may or may not be the villain our vigilante is searching for. Elsewhere, Richard Roundtree is similarly wasted as a typically crabby police chief who, for one reason or another, seems content to allow the mayhem to continue. As should you, but only just.

 Trekkies should keep a sharp lookout for *Star Trek: The Next Generation* and *Star Trek: Deep Space Nine*'s Rosalind Chao (aka Keiko O'Brien), here playing a TV reporter menaced by Mr Tanaka.

Director: Steve Carver; **Producer:** Frank Capra Jr; **Screenplay:** William Gray, James Bruner; **Production Design:** Vance Lorenzini; **Editor:** Anthony Redman; **Photography:** Roger Shearman; **Music:** William Goldstein; **Cast:** Chuck Norris, Christopher Lee, Richard Roundtree, Matt Clark, Mako, Maggie Cooper, Professor Toru Tanaka, Terry Kiser.

Fair Game
USA 1995 90 mins

Cindy Crawford a high-priced lawyer? Say no more. Sure, she's beautiful. Stunning, even. But since when could supermodels act? The flesh might be soft but this debut performance is solid wood, a simple case of Barbie-in-distress and nothing more. She gets her kit off from time to time, a flash of nipple here, a 'steamy' love scene there, but it's not enough. Maybe if there was even a shred of chemistry between her and co-star William Baldwin, this formulaic

Crawford's inexperience helps blow the movie out of the water, though she's by no means the only guilty party.

A brainless misfire from production whiz Joel Silver, *Fair Game* coughs up masses of brutal, bloody violence and typically impossible stuntwork, but it's a bland and predictable ride and you're not going to care whether our heroes live, die or move to Russia.

For some unbelievable reason, the KGB want Crawford dead (maybe they're film critics), despatching evil old Steven Berkoff and a squad of hi-tech heavies to do the deed. Hooking up with guardian angel Baldwin, moody cop and needless barer of butt-cheeks, the two hit the road in search of answers, running for their lives as they attempt to unravel this hopeless mystery.

Gun fights and car chases punch up the pace a little, as bullets fly and villains die everywhere from a safe house and a car park to a boat and a speeding train, but boy, is it dumb: at one stage, Crawford relaxes in her bedroom, strangely oblivious to the fact that an extremely noisy battle is raging elsewhere in the house. And it doesn't end there, but this review does: keep away.

Director: Andrew Sipes; **Producer:** Joel Silver; **Screenplay:** Charlie Fletcher, based on the novel by Paula Gosling; **Production Design:** James Spencer; **Editors:** David Finfer, Christian Wagner, Steve Kemper; **Photography:** Richard Bowen; **Music:** Mark Mancina; **Cast:** William Baldwin, Cindy Crawford, Steven Berkoff, Christopher McDonald, John Bedford Lloyd, Miguel Sandoval, Johann Carlo, Jenette Goldstein.

First Blood

USA 1982 97 mins

Invincible, unstoppable, unintelligible: Sylvester Stallone fights for his right to party as super-human killing machine John Rambo, misunderstood Vietnam veteran and mucho macho muscle-man supreme. According to Rambo's only pal, Colonel Samuel Trautman (played to the hilt by Richard Crenna, delivering dialogue in true William Shatner style, emphasizing *every* other word *and* continually pausing... in *mid*-sentence for... no... discernible *reason*), our troubled hero is 'an expert in guerrilla warfare, a man who's the best, with guns, with knives, with his bare hands. A man who's been trained to ignore pain, ignore weather, to live off the land, to eat things that would make a billy-goat puke....' and so on.

You get the picture: he's one mean mother trucker, an action man's man, a long-haired mess of trouble who you'd best leave alone, unless, that is, you're a sadistic Sheriff (Brian Dennehy, in turbo-charged, son-of-a-bitch mode) who takes exception to drifters, especially those of the mean and moody, unkempt variety who carry hunting knives the size of a small country beneath their jackets. Maybe then you'd try to run Rambo out of town, and if he refused to be bullied, maybe then you'd arrest him, let him know in no uncertain terms that his country doesn't give a damn about him, maybe even torture him a little. Only then you'd bring on a stack of nasty 'Nam flashbacks and he'd go wild, busting out of jail, heading for the hills, hiding out in the majestic wilds of America's North-West. And if you followed him, sent every man you had after him, called in the National Guard and tried to bomb the stuffing out of him, you'd have a war on your hands, my friend, with the ultimate Green Beret.

The first and finest of a trio of stunt-laden slaughter-fests, *First Blood* comes from Canadian director Ted *Uncommon Valour* Kotcheff, and while you'd be wise not to scrutinize the plot (or the politics) too closely, the fact remains that the film packs one hell of a dramatic punch, tense, exciting and often kinda funny (both intentionally and otherwise), a masterpiece of escalating violence (love those booby traps!) and wildly improbable action episodes (Rambo dives off a cliff, breaks his fall with a tree, sews up a nasty gash with a needle and thread stored in the handle of his monster knife, and rounds off the scene by taking out an aerial sniper with a rock).

Sly wisely keeps the chatter to a minimum, concentrating on the physical side of his performance and only really slipping up once, at the very end, with a climactic, teary and consummately incoherent ramble about scooping up pieces of an old friend which not even Professor Henry Higgins could decipher. Still, from a good/bad point of view, even this scene has tremendous entertainment value.

So, break out the body bags, sharpen those blades, polish your scars and settle back for the Italian Stallion's best-ever action adventure. We're talking classic, here. You know it makes sense.

Sequels: *Rambo: First Blood Part II, Rambo III.*

Director: Ted Kotcheff; **Producer:** Buzz Feitshans; **Screenplay:** Michael Kozoll, William Sackheim, Sylvester Stallone, based on a novel by David Morrell; **Production Design:** Wolf Kroeger; **Editor:** Joan Chapman; **Photography:** Andrew Laszlo; **Music:** Jerry Goldsmith; **Cast:** Sylvester Stallone, Richard Crenna, Brian Dennehy, Bill McKinney, Jack Starrett, David Caruso.

Fist of Fury (aka The Chinese Connection, The Iron Hand)
Hong Kong 1972 106 mins

Encouraged by the unparalleled success of *The Big Boss*, producer Raymond Chow cranked a second feature into production, reuniting his most valuable star with writer/director Lo Wei for *Fist of Fury*, a violent martial arts thriller with the same strengths (Bruce Lee) and weaknesses (everything else) as its predecessor.

Lumbered with a catalogue of poor production values, a headache-maker of a soundtrack and a plot which shuffles needlessly around in circles, this is a typically slapdash effort which, for all its faults, you can not afford to miss. Strange but true, and easily explained: Bruce Lee, the magic ingredient which makes even the cheapest of chop-socky actioners shine like classics.

Shot in glorious DyaliScope (whatever the hell that is), the film exploits traditional Eastern rivalries within a standard tale of revenge, painting the Chinese as honest, decent, hard-working folk while the Japanese fare rather less successfully as a bunch of scheming, arrogant, homicidal scum-buckets. Set in Shanghai around the turn of the century, the film follows the skull-cracking exploits of hot-headed Kung Fu fighter Chen Chen (Lee), a master of disguise and strained facial expressions, eager to avenge the murder of his revered mentor at the hands of the Karate-kicking Japanese.

Obvious and overlong, *Fist of Fury* redeems itself through violence, serving up twice as much hand-to-hand and foot-to-head as *The Big Boss*, rounding off the chaos with a tasty, ten-minute slaughter trail courtesy of Lee, the toughest little dragon on earth.

Bruce Lee used nunchaks for the very first time in *Fist of Fury*, introducing them to the movies and making them famous as a result. Unfortunately, since this particular weapon is banned from British screens, most of the footage it appears in winds up being censored from all certificated cinema and video releases. Outside of the UK, however, films involving nunchaks are available uncut, while bootleg copies of this movie and others like it often surface in Britain, undubbed, uncensored and just waiting to be found.

Director: Lo Wei; **Producer:** Raymond Chow; **Screenplay:** Lo Wei; **Production Design:** Lo Wei; **Editor:** Chang Yao Chung; **Photography:** Chen Ching Cheh; **Music:** Joseph Koo; **Cast:** Bruce Lee, Nora Miao, James Tien, Robert Baker.

Flash Gordon

GB 1980 114mins

Exotic space-babe Princess Aura (Ornella Muti) sets her sights on *Flash Gordon*.

Earthling director Mike Hodge takes us on a one-way trip to Mongo for a colourful, comicbook adventure with a knowing sense of humour, a flair for all things kitsch, and a top glam rock soundtrack courtesy of Queen (and Howard *Snowman* Blake).

Defending our planet from chrome-domed superfiend Ming the Merciless (malevolent Max Von Sydow), Flash Gordon (champion jock Sam J. Jones) rockets into outer space with sidekick chums Hans Zarkov (Jewish, maddish scientist Topol) and Dale Arden (distressed damsel Melody Anderson, star of TV's *Manimal*) for a rollercoaster alien encounter.

Fans of Alex Raymond's original strip (created in 1934) and Buster Crabbe's cliffhanging serials will already be familiar with Mongo's finest, and Hodge retains their services with the help of a smart supporting cast: Brian Blessed takes to the skies as rough-and-tumble Hawkman Vultan; Timothy Dalton feeds Flash to the Woodbeast as angry Arborian Prince Barin; Ornella Muti drives men wild as Ming's exotic daughter Aura; and finally, in addition to Raymond's original line-up, *Jason King*'s Peter Wyngarde plays all-new character Klytus, a menace in a golden mask working for Ming's greater glory.

'Flash, I love you, but we only have 14 hours to save the Earth...' Hilarious, ingenious and packed with action highlights, *Flash Gordon* zooms from classic plane crash to rowdy 'football' fight, from Zarkov's brain-drain horror to Flash and Barin's trial-by-combat (compete with whips, spikes and gravity), signing off with an awesome air battle and climactic palace assault. It's flash, alright. See it at least a dozen times.

Director: Mike Hodges; **Producer:** Dino de Laurentiis; **Screenplay:** Lorenzo Semple Jr, based on characters created by Alex Raymond; **Production Design:** Danilo Donati; **Editor:** Malcolm Cooke; **Photography:** Gil Taylor; **Music:** Queen, Howard Blake; **Cast:** Sam J. Jones, Melody Anderson, Topol, Max Von Sydow, Ornella Muti, Timothy Dalton, Brian Blessed, Peter Wyngarde, Mariangela Melato, Richard O'Brien.

Flesh + Blood

USA 1985 126 mins

Western Europe, 1501: folks really knew how to party back then. At least, they did according to director Paul Verhoeven, whose in-your-face English language debut is so uncompromisingly nasty that you have to admire its convictions. A bawdy medieval actioner dedicated to painful death, violent sex and the reckless destruction of property, *Flesh + Blood* delivers exactly what its title promises.

A bare-bones plot paves the way for unrivalled excess: swordsman Martin (Rutger Hauer) leads a band of mercenaries on a mission of revenge, captures a castle, kidnaps pure convent girl Agnes (Jennifer Jason Leigh) and teaches her the ropes (and chains). Though promised in marriage to feeble prince Steven (Tom Burlinson), Agnes is drawn to Martin's wickedness, and as the violence escalates and the plague comes knocking at their door, she is forced to choose between them (though not before revealing all in a hot tub scene which puts most soft porn skin flicks to shame).

Perverse humour runs throughout, adding an oddly comic edge to the horror on display, from the young lovers kissing in the shade of a hanged, decaying corpse, to a hysterical Cardinal (Ronald Lacey) who believes that just about everything is a sign from God.

Sensitive souls should run a mile. As for the rest of us, this is very strong stuff indeed, terrible, tacky and brutal. In other words, it's lots of good/bad fun, perfect for anyone with a free evening, a fridge full of beer and a sick, strange sense of humour.

Director: Paul Verhoeven; **Producer:** Gys Versluys; **Screenplay:** Gerard Soeteman, Paul Verhoeven; **Production Design:** Felix Murcia; **Editor:** Ine Schenkkan; **Photography:** Jan De Bont; **Music:** Basil Poledouris; **Cast:** Rutger Hauer, Jennifer Jason Leigh, Tom Burlinson, Jack Thompson, Fernando Hillbeck, Susan Tyrell, Ronald Lacey, Brion James, John Dennis Johnston, Simon Andreu, Bruno Kirby.

Death Becomes Them 9

Name: FLYNN, Errol

Real name: Errol Leslie Thomson Flynn

Born: Hobart, Tasmania, 1909 **Died:** 1959

Characteristics: A fine physical specimen, handsome, charming and just a little dangerous. The original scoundrel. And he knew it, too.

Previous professions: Policeman with New Guinea Constabulary

Debut feature: *In the Wake of the Bounty* (1932)

Life and times: The hunt was on at Warner Bros. for a fresh face, a bold new player capable of swashing a buckle or two, and Errol Flynn fitted the bill. A star since *Captain Blood* (1935), Flynn played the role of the dashing action hero throughout the 1930s and 1940s, though by the 1950s, he was all but burnt out by a lifetime of excess. A voracious boozer and Olympian fornicator, Flynn was the wildest party animal of 'em all, hopping from babe to bottle to scandal until his death in 1959. His autobiography, *My Wicked, Wicked Ways*, was published soon afterwards.

Greatest contribution to action movies: Heir to silent star Douglas Fairbanks, Flynn ruled the talkies, King of the Swashbucklers from *Captain Blood* to *Adventures of Don Juan*. Pirates, soldiers, cowboys and scoundrels a speciality.

Speech, speech: Jack L. Warner on Flynn: 'To the Walter Mittys of the world he was all the heroes in one magnificent, sexy, animal package.'

Gene Autry on Flynn: 'He spent more time on a bar stool, or in court, or in the headlines, or in bed, than anyone I knew.'

Basil Rathbone and Errol Flynn settle their differences, swashbuckler-to-swashbuckler, in *The Adventures of Robin Hood.*

Flynn on Flynn: 'The public has always expected me to be a playboy, and a decent chap never lets his public down.'

Selected filmography:
Captain Blood (1935), *The Charge of the Light Brigade* (1936), ***The Adventures of Robin Hood*** (1938), *The Dawn Patrol* (1938), *Dodge City* (1939), *The Private Lives of Elizabeth and Essex* (1939), *The Sea Hawk* (1940), *They Died With Their Boots On* (1941), *Desperate Journey* (1942), *Gentleman Jim* (1942), *Objective, Burma!* (1945), *Cry Wolf* (1947), ***Adventures of Don Juan*** (1948), *Kim* (1950), *The Master of Ballantrae* (1953), *Let's Make Up* (1954), *The Sun Also Rises* (1957), *Cuban Rebel Girls* (aka *Assault of the Rebel Girls*, *Attack of the Rebel Girls*; 1959).

For Your Eyes Only

GB 1981 127 mins

Following the gargantuan excess of *Moonraker*, the Bond series wisely went back to basics for a good old rough-and-tumble adventure with a half-decent plot and a hero who relies on his wits, not his weapons, to survive. Robbed of his gadgets, 007 has a much harder time in this one, no longer invincible, his hair even falls out of place, though he remains as cool and sophisticated as ever, smart too, and irresistible, of course, to the opposite sex.

The hunt is on for a top secret nugget of British technology, lost in a shipwreck at the bottom of the Ionian Sea. Should the A.T.A.C. (Automatic Targeting Attack Communicator), a device used to order British Polaris submarines to launch ballistic missiles, fall into enemy hands, all sorts of nuclear unpleasantness could follow. Obviously, a top British agent has to recover the A.T.A.C. before the Russians lay their greasy mitts on it, and who better than James Bond, newly returned from outer space with his head finally out of the clouds?

Packed off to Greece, Bond joins forces with Columbo (Topol), an 'honest' smuggler who identifies a former pal of his, Kristatos (Julian Glover), as the villain in league with the Russians. Before James can recover the A.T.A.C. and defeat his latest foe, however, he first has to find himself a gal, say, someone whose parents Kristatos had killed, a vengeful, crossbow-wielding beauty who looks great in a swimsuit. Someone, in fact, like Melina Havelock (actress and model Carole Bouquet).

Devoting extra special care to the action, director John Glen adds a welcome touch of humour and imagination to the various set-pieces on offer: trapped in a helicopter controlled by none other than Ernst Stavro Blofeld, Bond seeks to avenge his wife's murder (see *On Her Majesty's Secret Service*) before the credits roll; Glen's next trick is to blow up 007's beloved Lotus Esprit, forcing the agent into a wacky Deux Chevaux car chase on the streets and hills of Corfu; elsewhere, there's an incredible, stunt-crazy ski chase, a tense bit of business as Bond and Melina are dragged, like soap-on-a-rope, through shark-infested waters, a warehouse battle, an underwater struggle for possession of the A.T.A.C. and, as if all that weren't enough, a thoroughly passable cliffhanging, mountain-climbing finale.

Complementing Bill Conti's tacky, synthesized soundtrack with a slushy, whiny theme song, Sheena Easton made Bond history as the first singer to appear in one of Maurice Binder's trademark title sequences.

The end of *For Your Eyes Only*. But James Bond will return in *Octopussy*.

Director: John Glen; **Producer:** Albert R. Broccoli; **Screenplay:** Richard Maibaum; **Production Design:** Peter Lamont; **Editor:** John Grover; **Photography:** Alan Hume; **Music:** Bill Conti, title song performed by Sheena Easton; **Cast:** Roger Moore, Carole Bouquet, Topol, Julian Glover, Cassandra Harris, Lynn-Holly Johnson.

A Force of One

USA 1979 90 mins

California needs Chuck Norris! Drugs are on the increase while the cops are in decline, shuffling off this mortal coil thanks to the presence of a mysterious martial arts assassin. There's a secret out there, folks, and a fortune in dope, too, but the good men and women of the Narcotics Squad just aren't up to cracking the case. At the very least, they should learn how to defend themselves, and who better than Karate champ Matt Logan (Chuck) to teach them a little hand-to-hand.

With a title fight looming, an adopted kid (Eric Laneuville) to raise, a lady cop (Jennifer O'Neill) to charm, and a squad of California's finest to train against the Boogie man, Matt's a pretty busy bunny, but if we've learned anything from shaky formula thrillers, it's that things have a way of working themselves out. Somehow, you just can't shake the feeling that all the different plot lines are destined to converge, rather conveniently, near the end, and maybe, to make life even easier, the guy that Matt has to pound on for his title might also be the feared 'Karate Killer'. Two for the price of one? Wait and see...

Tales of the Unexpected this ain't, but at least it has a little action to keep things going, both in and outside the ring. It's all pretty standard, average stuff, though, nothing to get excited about, and strictly for Chuck's most devoted fans.

Although Chuck plays different characters in both movies, *A Force of One* is considered to be the sequel to *Good Guys Wear Black*, an awful thriller with too much talk and barely any action. Try not to be curious.

Director: Paul Aaron; **Producer:** Alan Belkin; **Screenplay:** Ernest Tidyman, story by Pat Johnson and Ernest Tidyman; **Production Design:** Norman Baron; **Editor:** B. Lovitt; **Photography:** Roger Shearman; **Music:** Dick Halligan; **Cast:** Chuck Norris, Jennifer O'Neill, Clu Gulager, Ron O'Neal, Eric Laneuville, Bill 'Sugarfoot' Wallace.

Forced Vengeance

USA 1982 90 mins

A blinding neon background sets Chuck Norris and a stock assailant in silhouette, pounding one another in slow motion while the opening credits roll. A promising, almost stylish, start for what turns out to be a tediously ordinary experience, a by-the-numbers, leave-your-brain-in-the-fridge, chop-fest which has the cheek to repeat the same neon sequence later on in the movie, and then a third time, during the closing credits. Fresh and imaginative it ain't, barely passable, maybe, with occasional bursts of violence offering periods of relief throughout, and, hell, let's be generous, there's nothing wrong with the performances that, say, a hundred million millennia of acting lessons couldn't put right. Give or take a century or two.

So, anyway, welcome to Hong Kong, land of adventure, the kind of place where a Vietnam veteran with a Screaming Eagles tattoo can get into a lot of trouble, especially if he's played by the Norris machine. Working as a bouncer, sorry, head of security, at 'The Lucky Dragon', a fancy casino owned and run by his adopted (half-Chinese, half-Jewish) family, Josh Randall (our Chuck) serves up a slice of mean with a side-order of nasty when the mob try to muscle in on the last honest game in town.

Infrequent offerings of average ultra-violence serve to keep us conscious throughout the opening chapters, but you'll have to wait until the majority of Randall's family are killed before our hero finally gets up enough motivational steam for a blazing display of movie-style retribution, speeding up the pace and chalking up a body count to be proud of. Prop walls shatter and stunt men fly as Chuck takes on a variety of mad, bad and gratuitously hairy henchmen, avoiding knives, fists, bullets and even the odd thrown toilet as he kits out in his army duds, pins a gross of medals on his chest and heads out into Hong Kong to do what must be done.

For fans' eyes only.

Director: James Fargo; **Producer:** John B. Bennett; **Screenplay:** Franklin Thompson; **Production Design:** George B. Chan; **Editor:** Irving C. Rosenblum; **Photography:** Rexford Metz; **Music:** William Goldstein; **Cast:** Chuck Norris, Mary Louise Weller, Michael Cavanaugh, David Opatoshu, Seiji Sakaguchi, Frank Michael Liu, Camila Griggs.

Death Becomes Them 10

Name: FORD, Harrison

Born: Chicago, 1942

Characteristics: Rugged and reliable, a likeable, regular guy with all-American hero credentials and a trademark scar (on his chin, courtesy of an age-old car crash).

Previous professions: Assistant knick knack buyer at Bullock's department store, carpenter.

Debut feature: *Dead Heat on a Merry-Go-Round* (1966)

Daredevil archaeologist Indiana Jones (Harrison Ford) picks up a bargain in *Raiders of the Lost Ark.*

Life and times: A contract player for Columbia and, later, Universal, Ford paid his dues with a decade of small-time film and TV work, training as an actor while making a living as a carpenter. Cast as roguish space ace Han Solo in the ground-breaking, blockbusting sci-fi classic *Star Wars*, Ford switched from zero to hero overnight. Consolidating his fame with a trio of Indiana Jones adventures, Ford was voted Star of the Century in 1994 (by the National Association of Theatre Owners) and has more top ten box office hits than any other actor. Eager to prove his range in a variety of comedies, dramas and serious-minded thrillers, Ford remains best suited to playing ultimate good-guy heroes, scoring most recently as stalwart CIA avenger

Jack Ryan in a pair of Tom Clancy movies: *Patriot Games* and *Clear and Present Danger*. Ford married his second wife, *E.T.* screenwriter Melissa Mathison, in 1983, and together they maintain a very private life.

Current salary: $20 million a flick

Greatest contribution to action movies: Return of the scoundrel: Han Solo and Indiana Jones, the roles he was born to play.

Speech, speech: 'I don't use any particular method. I'm from the "let's pretend" school of acting.'

'I'm famous for not doing sport. By inclination, I don't do a thing. I don't work out, I certainly don't jog, but I do have a good constitution.'

'I'm happiest when I'm in the thick of it. The running, jumping and falling down - that's fun. So is the fantasy of being someone else, living out of a dream world. But the best thing about it all is that at the end of the day I can hang up my whip and my hat and become normal again. The day I can't do that is the day I quit.'

Selected filmography: *Journey to Shiloh* (1968), *Getting Straight* (1970), *American Graffiti* (1973), *The Conversation* (1974), ***Star Wars*** (1977), *Heroes* (1977), *Force Ten from Navarone* (1978), *Hanover Street* (1979), *The Frisco Kid* (1979), ***The Empire Strikes Back*** (1980), ***Raiders of the Lost Ark*** (1981), *Blade Runner* (1982), ***Return of the Jedi*** (1983), ***Indiana Jones and the Temple of Doom*** (1984), *Witness* (1985), *The Mosquito Coast* (1986), *Frantic* (1988), *Working Girl* (1988), ***Indiana Jones and the Last Crusade*** (1989), *Presumed Innocent* (1990), *Regarding Henry* (1991), *Patriot Games* (1992), ***The Fugitive*** (1993), *Clear and Present Danger* (1994), *Sabrina* (1995).

Fortress

USA 1993 91 mins

Trading horror for science fiction without having to cut down on the gore, *Re-Animator* director Stuart Gordon puts Christopher Lambert through his paces in this futuristic prison flick, a B-movie shlocker with a healthy budget and some interesting - though hardly original - ideas and designs. The performances are neutral at best, and the screenplay doesn't work all that well, but it's an enthusiastic jumble, outrageously bloody and excessively violent, fairly well-paced and solidly entertaining. It's dumb, no doubt about it, but that's all part of the fun.

Though not quite the life of the party, Lambert proves serviceable as former 'Black Beret' John Brennick, banged up inside for getting his wife pregnant: the future, it seems, belongs to Big Brother, and population control allows each couple a single child only. A second bun in the oven means cold, hard time in a maximum security jail, a high-rise installation packed to overflowing with the fullest range of stereotypes: bullies, brainiacs (Gordon regular Jeffrey Combs), wise old men, suffering innocents and, of course, a sadistic warden, Poe (*RoboCop*'s Kurtwood Smith), not-quite-human and determined to break our John.

Assisted by super-computer Zed, Poe has the power to erase men's minds, read their dreams and blast their bellies with his precious 'intestinators'. As a last resort, he even has

Christopher Lambert turns from damsel-in-distress Loryn Locklin to hug his hardware in *Fortress*.

an army of cyborgs, slow-moving, butt-ugly and dim-witted to boot, but armed with the kind of hardware that could take out Godzilla in a flash (that is, if they could shoot straight).

Highlights among the action scenes include a hard 'n' heavy punch-up between Lambert and portly psycho Vernon Wells (of *Commando* fame), here losing his lunch in quite the nastiest way possible, a long and messy run-in with Poe's blue-blooded cyborgs and all the jail-break madness you'd expect.

We've got dismemberment. We've got gouging. Exploding 'borgs. Bursting stomachs. Lots of chaos. Lots of clichés. Laughs. Guts. Everything, in fact, but a brain. It ain't *The Great Escape*. But it'll do at a push.

Director: Stuart Gordon; **Producers:** John Davis, John Flock; **Screenplay:** Steve Feinberg, Troy Neighbours, Terry Curtis Fox; **Production Design:** David Copping; **Editor:** Timothy Wellburn; **Photography:** David Eggby; **Music:** Frederic Talgorn; **Cast:** Christopher Lambert, Kurtwood Smith, Loryn Locklin, Lincoln Kilpatrick, Clifton Gonzalez Gonzalez, Jeffrey Combs, Tom Towles, Vernon Wells.

48 Hrs

USA 1982 96 mins

Long before the world grew tired of Eddie Murphy's riot act, back in the days when no-holds-barred swearing had the power to provoke gales of nervous laughter, *48 Hrs* put the pedal to the metal and cussed up a storm, an action thriller, a buddy movie and a foul-mouthed comedy rolled up into one grand, laddish adventure.

Cop killers are on the loose in San Francisco, and homicide detective Jack Cates (Nick Nolte) can't find them alone. Jack's a cranky sort, rough around the edges. Then there's Reggie

James Remar considers ventilating Eddie Murphy's skull in *48 Hrs.*

Hammond (Murphy), a fast-talking, wheeler-dealing, well-connected convict who has the mixed fortune of being released into Jack's custody for two whole days, a taste of relative freedom provided he can help Jack bring his little 'turd hunt' to a close.

Now, teaming up with a convicted felon could hardly be described as normal police procedure, and Jack is warned in no uncertain terms that if he screws up he's 'going down', but, you see, as important as this case is for Jack, Reggie just wants to have a good time, meet the ladies, and maybe settle a little unfinished business before playtime expires.

Heavy-duty male bonding is what it's all about, a concentrated 48 hour dose of physical and verbal abuse as Jack and Reggie slowly learn to get along while pounding on the competition, chasing the bad guys and shooting up a storm on the streets of S.F. Nothing heavy, nothing complicated, just a whole lot of noisy fun.

Handling the action like a pro, director Walter Hill balances the comedy with enough violence and destruction to keep the pace good and speedy. Best of all, though, is the dynamic duo at the heart of the movie, a perfectly cast, smartly contrasted double act which allows Murphy to do his thing without diminishing Nolte's contribution. Taken separately, they're just fine, but together, they're invincible.

Sequel: *Another 48 Hrs.*

Director: Walter Hill; **Producer:** Lawrence Gordon; **Screenplay:** Roger Spottiswoode, Walter Hill, Larry Gross, Steven E. de Souza; **Production Design:** John Vallone; **Editors:** Freeman Davies, Mark Warner, Billy Weber; **Photography:** Ric Waite; **Music:** James Horner; **Cast:** Nick Nolte, Eddie Murphy, Annette O'Toole, Frank McRae, James Remar, David Patrick Kelly, Sonny Landham.

Freejack

USA 1992 108 mins

Let's get one thing straight from the beginning: this is a chase movie. It may look like a science fiction thriller, teeming with techno babble and computer wizardry, but it is, when you get right down to it, no more complicated than any one of a hundred Road Runner cartoons, though a lot less imaginative and no way near as entertaining.

Seconds before crashing and trashing his favourite race car, adrenaline junkie Alex Furlong (Emilio Estevez, average as ever) is plucked from the present - 1991 - and deposited 18 years in the future, pursued by 'bonejacking' bounty hunter Vacendak (Mick Jagger), who plans on wiping Alex's mind and handing over his fresh, young body to a rich old geezer whose mind needs a new place to hang. If you're wondering why Vacendak doesn't just pick up any old dosser off the streets of 2009, it's because the future's a mess and the public at large are an unhealthy, sore-encrusted lot, and who on earth would want to stick their old grey matter in one of them?

And so the chase begins, a cat-and-mouse cliché where each new shock revelation is clearly signposted an age in advance and the action is so entirely ordinary that you have to wonder why director Geoff Murphy bothered at all.

He certainly didn't improve the movie's chances by casting Jagger, whose last proper acting job had been in 1970 (in Nic Roeg's *Performance*), as bad guy Vacendak. The moment he appears on screen, a vision in black leather, working those lips of his around the line 'Let's do it', something strikes your funny bone and it's impossible to take him seriously. As for the remainder of the cast, Anthony Hopkins wastes his limited star appeal in a brief but supposedly key role as billionaire businessman McCandless, while Rene Russo looks appropriately surprised when boyfriend Alex, long believed dead, appears on her doorstep begging for help, terrified of losing his mind. Not that there's much to hang on to in the first place.

Now *you* have to protect *your* brain: avoid *Freejack* or else...

Director: Geoff Murphy; **Producers:** Ronald Shusett, Stuart Oken; **Screenplay:** Steven Pressfield, Ronald Shusett, Dan Gilroy, based on the novel *Immortality, Inc.* by Robert Sheckley; **Production Design:** Joe Alves; **Editor:** Dennis Virkler; **Photography:** Amir Mokri; **Music:** Trevor Jones; **Cast:** Emilio Estevez, Mick Jagger, Rene Russo, Anthony Hopkins, Jonathan Banks, David Johansen.

From Russia With Love

GB 1963 118 mins

James Bond takes on the collected might of SPECTRE in this, his second big screen adventure, a stylish cold war thriller with at least as much brain as it has brawn. You can really see the series taking shape here, and Bond fans will have a ball with the gritty location work, colourful enemy agents, rich John Barry soundtrack and other assorted trivia, including the first appearance of Q Branch's beloved weapons' master (as played by Desmond Llewellyn, in this and every Bond film since), here supplying 007 with a lethal bag of tricks in the oh-so innocent form of a briefcase.

Following Bond's victory over SPECTRE agent Dr No, sweet revenge is planned as top man Blofeld orders a 'particularly unpleasant and humiliating' death for the slick British agent. To this end, Bond is lured into an obvious trap with a valuable decoding device and a beautiful Russian agent (1960 Miss Universe runner-up Daniela Bianchi) acting as irresistible bait, and so off he goes, racing through Venice and Istanbul, enjoying the amenities of the Orient Express and battling assorted SPECTRE goons as well as hard-bodied henchman Red Grant (Robert Shaw) and brass-knuckled super-bitch Rosa Klebb (Lotte Lenya), whose venomous spiked boots claim many a fashion victim.

Following a memorable gypsy catfight there's a well-choreographed battle sequence which sees Bond in the thick of things, but you'll need a little patience after that to wait for the action highlights near the end of the movie, which start with a bone-crunching punch-up between Bond and Grant and continue with a 'copter chase and an explosive speedboat finale.

Acting honours go to Bianchi's spirited Bond girl, Pedro Armendariz as street-smart Turkish agent Ali Kerim Bey and, of course, to Sean Connery, consummate role model and sex symbol, warmed by chest hair thicker than a London fog.

There have been many more spectacular Bonds, but none are more intelligent or interesting than this one.

The end of *From Russia With Love*. But James Bond will return in *Goldfinger*.

Director: Terence Young; Producers: Harry Saltzman, Albert Broccoli; **Screenplay:** Richard Maibaum, Johanna Harwood, based on the novel *From Russia With Love* by Ian Fleming; **Production Design:** Syd Cain; **Editor:** Peter Hunt; **Photography:** Ted Moore; **Music:** John Barry, title song performed by Matt Monro; **Cast:** Sean Connery, Robert Shaw, Pedro Armendariz, Daniela Bianchi, Lotte Lenya, Bernard Lee, Eunice Gayson, Lois Maxwell.

The Fugitive
USA 1993 127 mins

Once again Hollywood plunders the small screen for its ideas, only this time around it does a bang-up job, not only in capturing the spirit and atmosphere of David Janssen's long-running 1960s TV hit *The Fugitive*, but also by improving upon it, serving up a tense, exciting action thriller with all the trimmings money can buy.

Harrison Ford takes the lead as Dr Richard Kimble, a respected surgeon who is wrongly accused (of course) and later convicted of murdering his wife. When a botched escape on the part of some other prisoners unexpectedly frees Kimble, he turns fugitive in the hope of clearing his name, searching Chicago for the one-armed man (Andreas Katsulas) he believes did the deed, all the while trying to remain at least one step ahead of an immense manhunt led by obsessive US Marshal Sam Gerard (*Batman Forever*'s Tommy Lee Jones).

Director Andy Davis followed the excellent *Under Siege* with this consummate audience-pleaser, a successful blend of edge-of-the-sofa suspense, whodunnit (and why?) mystery, well-orchestrated action and remarkable stuntwork, including an awesome train wreck (which was shot for real, although, obviously, Ford's contribution was added later on) and a death-defying plunge into a dam.

As the straight, true and ever-resourceful hero of the piece, veteran good guy Ford is perfectly cast, providing a solid central character who you will give a damn about, an old-fashioned good guy who is neither on-the-edge nor given to excess. As effective as Ford's performance is, however, it is Oscar-winner Tommy Lee's fiercely quick-witted performance which effectively steals the show, not to mention all the best lines: 'I didn't kill my wife', pleads a desperate Kimble. 'I don't care', replies an indifferent Gerard. What a star!

The final episode of the original four-season show earned a phenomenal 72 per cent share of all TV viewers on August 29 1967, a record-breaking rating which remained unbeaten for 13 years until the 'Who Shot Jr?' instalment of *Dallas* (earning close to an 80 per cent share on November 21 1980).

Director: Andrew Davis; **Producer:** Arnold Kopelson; **Screenplay:** Jeb Stuart, David Twohy, based on characters created by (executive producer and original series creator) Roy Huggins; **Production Design:** Dennis Washington; **Editors:** Dennis Virkler, David Finfer, Dean Goodhill, Don Brochu, Richard Nord, Dov Hoenig; **Photography:** Michael Chapman; **Music:** James Newton Howard; **Cast:** Harrison Ford, Tommy Lee Jones, Sela Ward, Joe Pantoliano, Andreas Katsulas, Jeroen Krabbe, Daniel Roebuck; **Academy Award:** Best Supporting Actor (Tommy Lee Jones).

The Gauntlet
USA 1977 109 mins

Take a moment to consider the real world: crime pays, terrorists run free, wars remain unresolved and smoking gives you cancer. Depressing, huh? That's reality for you - completely unreliable. Better stick to fantasy, the dependable choice. If you're looking for proof, why not check out the movies: good conquers evil, beautiful women take their clothes off, violence is strictly for fun, and smoking, well, that just makes you look cool.

In reality, a man facing 'overwhelming odds' is likely to fail. Not so in the movies, however, where the phrase merely suggests that our hero will be both indestructible and ultra-violent, leading to the spectacular deaths of a higher than average number of vil-

Clint Eastwood and Sondra Locke run *The Gauntlet*.

lains. And so we come to *The Gauntlet,* a prime slice of entertainment which stomps on reality and has a damn good time doing it.

As transparent an excuse for action as you'll ever see, the story has unremarkable cop Ben Shockley (Clint Eastwood) escorting gutsy hooker Gus Mally (Sondra Locke) from Vegas to Phoenix, where she plans on testifying against a rather important scumbag who, surprise of all surprises, would be a whole lot happier should she fail to survive the trip. One quick double cross later, and suddenly every cop and Mafia type within 500 miles of Ben and Gus clearly want them dead as dodos and as far away from Phoenix City Hall as possible.

The odds, ladies and gentlemen, are against them, a boozy and unshaven, yet tough and forever cool hero in league with an uncooperative strumpet of hidden depths, but seeing as it's Clint up there, the star *and* director of the piece, you kind of get the feeling that things might go their way, at least until they hit the streets of Phoenix in a fortified bus, driving slowly and carefully towards their objective as hundreds of misinformed cops pump thousands of bullets into their makeshift R.V. It's an amazing scene, too, expertly built up to with plenty of tension, explosive, exciting and well worth waiting for.

As for the rest, well, what comes before is fun but forgettable, neatly played, paced and written, a minor Eastwood hit distinguished by a blazing finale which'll have your granny running for cover.

Director: Clint Eastwood; **Producer:** Robert Daley; **Screenplay:** Michael Butler, Dennis Shryack; **Production Design:** Allen E. Smith; **Editor:** Ferris Webster, Joel Cox; **Photography:** Rexford Metz; **Music:** Jerry Fielding; **Cast:** Clint Eastwood, Sondra Locke, Pat Hingle, William Prince, Bill McKinney, Michael Cavanaugh.

Death Becomes Them 11

Mel Gibson and a canine chum look for trouble in *Mad Max 2*.

Name: GIBSON, Mel

Born: Peekskill, New York, 1956

Characteristics: A seasoned Hollywood hunk, with big hair, a butt that drives the ladies wild, and, yes, even a brain.

Debut feature: *Summer City* (aka *Coast of Terror*;1976)

Life and times: The son of a railroad brakeman and an Australian opera singer, Gibson was born in the States but raised, from age 12, in Oz. Studying acting in Sydney at the National Institute of Dramatic Arts, Mel's first big break came courtesy of director George Miller, who cast the 23-year-old unknown in a star-making role as futuristic road warrior Mad Max. Experiencing big-time Stateside fame as homicidal supercop Martin Riggs in Richard Donner's *Lethal Weapon* trilogy, Gibson is currently one of Hollywood's biggest wheels, a talented actor capable of shifting gears between comic book action and heavy, Shakespearean drama (playing the title role in Franco Zeffirelli's *Hamlet*). Mel first stepped behind the cameras in 1993, directing the warmly received drama *The Man Without a Face*, while his second effort, the historical adventure *Braveheart*, ruled Oscar Night 1996, winning five Academy Awards including Best Picture and Best Director.

Current salary: $20 million

Greatest contribution to action movies: Lunatic law enforcers Mad Max and Martin Riggs, violent, unstable and great fun to watch.

Speech, speech: Mel on maturity: 'I'm a guy that dances on tables, puts lampshades on his head, sticks his dick out in crowds. But I'm married now, got kids. I figure: stay healthy, live longer.'

Gibson's *Mad Max 2* experience: 'I thought it was funny. It was more like a Buster Keaton film with this stone-faced, taciturn hero. All this weird shit happening all around. I could hardly keep from laughing the whole time we were doing it. Big straight lines. Silly outfit.'

Richard Donner analyses his favourite star: 'Mel Gibson is God's gift to a director, but he tells the worst jokes in the world.'

Selected filmography: *Tim* (1979), **Mad Max** (1979), *Attack Force Z* (1981), *Gallipoli* (1981), **Mad Max 2** (aka *The Road Warrior*; 1981), *The Year of Living Dangerously* (1983), *The Bounty* (1984), *Mrs Soffel* (1984), *The River* (1984), **Mad Max Beyond Thunderdome** (1985),

Goldeneye

GB 1995 130 mins

James Bond surfs the information superhighway from Russia to Puerto Rico in search of
an orbiting super-weapon in this uneven action adventure, throwing off the shackles of
enforced political correctness while struggling to save this ever-changing world of ours from
economic armageddon and general super-villainy.

A major staff re-shuffle left several Bond regulars out in the cold while new kids on
the block Martin Campbell (director), Jeffrey Caine and Bruce Feirstein (screenwriters)
moved in to renovate the series. And boy, is Bond in for a shock. The cold war over, he's
trapped in a nightmare of friendly nations and peaceful co-operation, a land where
Moneypenny (the aptly named Samantha Bond) cites sexual harassment, and M - now a
woman (Judi Dench, commanding and capable, but way too PC) - describes Bond as a
'...sexist, misogynist dinosaur'. Be that as it may, he *still* gets the girls, tackles all the
major villains (rogue 00 agent Sean Bean, dastardly Russian General Gottfried John),
destroys acres of property and looks damn good while he's doing it. Clearly, Campbell
wants it both ways: a dominant male in a touchy-feely society, a nod to the classic elements - exotic locations (Switzerland, Monte Carlo), enormous sets (computer command
centre with a whopping great radar ideal for climactic one-on-one action), ingenious gadgetry (the ever-reliable exploding pen), fabulous women ('Bond Girl' Izabella Scorupco,
henchwoman Famke Janssen, utilizing thigh power to squeeze the life out of her victims,
getting off on evil and hamming up a storm) - while at the same time turning the series
on its head with a 'right on' 1990s attitude (Herr Bond now drives a BMW) which grates
with the Bond philosophy and doesn't do the movie any favours at all.

As for *Goldeneye*'s leading man, well, a combination of rugged good looks and winning
Irish charm served to secure the top spot for long-time Bond wannabe Pierce Brosnan,
here playing the secret agent somewhere between Connery's ruthless professionalism
and Moore's tireless hedonism, bedding the babes and blasting the bad guys yet not quite
at ease with his larger-than-life character, capable and sophisticated maybe, but lacking
the charisma and irresistible over-confidence the part demands (he does have a gimmick
though: whereas Moore relied upon his eyebrows, Brosnan prefers to wrinkle his fore-
head in concentration).

As for the action - when it comes - a standard quota of basic gunplay and hand-to-
hand combat fills in between the good bits, most memorably an outrageous pre-title
super-stunt. As the first Bond movie allowed to shoot in Russia (no mean feat, considering this is the same country that banned the previous 16 films from its cinemas),
Goldeneye takes us to St Petersburg for a wild demolition derby of a tank chase which
takes a full five seconds to appreciate the grandeur of this historical city before Bond, god
bless 'im, grinds the whole lot into rubble. Adding to the mischief, *Cracker*'s Robbie
Coltrane contributes a couple of scenes as a vaguely menacing Russian mobster, while
ancient gadget-meister Desmond Llewelyn lends his services as Q, the weapons master,
for a fifteenth gag-intensive time.

A (barely) passable Bond, a duo of forgettable villains, pace problems... dedicated sad
types obsessed with Bond (count me in!) are likely to notice the bad before the good: naff

Tina Turner track, self-conscious screenplay, restrained performances (at one stage, early on in the movie, Brosnan minces down a flight of stairs), and where in the name of tradition is John Barry? In spite of these obsessive rumblings, however, those of you who can relax and enjoy the movie without picking it to pieces might just enjoy yourselves. As light entertainment it should serve you well, but as a Bond movie, it ranks well out of the top ten.

⊕ **Rather than shoot the movie on Pinewood's famous 007 soundstage, director Martin Campbell (*No Escape*) chose instead to renovate a much larger site: an abandoned wartime plane factory and airfield in Leavesden, England. Elsewhere on the trivia trail, it turns out that *Goldeneye* was the name of Ian Fleming's Jamaican holiday home, a cosy place where the author, way back in 1952, first created the world's most famous secret agent.**

The end of *Goldeneye*. But James Bond *will* return...

Director: Martin Campbell; **Producers:** Michael G. Wilson, Barbara Broccoli; **Screenplay:** Jeffrey Caine, Bruce Feirstein, story by Michael France, based on characters created by Ian Fleming; **Production Design:** Peter Lamont; **Editor:** Terry Rawlings; **Photography:** Phil Meheux; **Music:** Eric Serra, title song performed by Tina Turner; **Cast:** Pierce Brosnan, Sean Bean, Izabella Scorupco, Famke Janssen, Joe Don Baker, Judi Dench, Robbie Coltrane, Tcheky Karyo, Gottfried John, Alan Cumming, Desmond Llewelyn, Samantha Bond; Dedicated to the memory of Miniature Effects Supervisor Derek Meddings.

Goldfinger

GB 1964 112 mins 🔫 🔫 🔫 🔫

Sing along now. Don't be afraid. *DA-DA, wa-wa-wa-wa-wa. DA-DA, wa-wa-wa-wa-wa. Da-Da, wa-wa-wa-wa-wa. Da-Da, wa-wa-wa-wa-wa. G-O-L-D-F-I-N-G-E-R, la-la-la-la-la, he's the man, the man with the Midas touch - a spider's touch, ya-ya-ya-ya-ya-ya. Such - a cold-finger, wa-wa-wa-wa-wa, beckons you to enter his web of sin — but don't go in!* Man, that felt good. How could any movie that kicks off with Shirley Bassey's belter of a theme song fail? Of course, it couldn't, and it heralds the first of the BIG Bond movies. The sets were more spectacular. The characters more exotic. The action more flamboyant. Switching the gloom and intelligence of the cold war with the bright, adventurous spirit of the US of A, this third Bond juggled all the right elements and came up with a winning formula that has served the series for more than three decades.

Packed with classic cliff-hanging situations and plenty of dry, cool wit, the film introduces us to the first of the great Bond villains: Auric Goldfinger (Gert Frobe), a wealthy businessman obsessed with gold who plans on breaking into the biggest, most heavily fortified gold reserve in the world - none other than Fort Knox itself - but not, I might add, for the most obvious reason. Helping him realize his ambition is the outrageous Pussy Galore (stunning ex-*Avengers* girl Honor Blackman), captain of an all-girl flying squadron, and mute Korean henchman Oddjob (Harold Sakata), whose razor-rimmed bowler hat shaves so close, you'll want to buy the company.

So enters Bond (Sean Connery, really in his stride now) riding into a world of trouble in the ultimate extension of a man's, uh, personality: the drop-dead gorgeous Aston Martin DB5, equipped with every deadly device a schoolboy could wish for, including, of course, that trusty old passenger ejector seat.

We're talking an overdose, here, of magic moments: there's that terrific scene at the

Goldfinger 95

Gert Frobe prepares Sean Connery for unnecessary surgery in the classic Bond flick *Goldfinger*.

beginning of the film when Bond catches Goldfinger cheating at cards and makes him lose; another, later on, when he beats him at golf by out-manoeuvring him once again; that memorable image of Jill Masterson (Shirley Eaton) lying dead on her bed, covered entirely in gold paint, and the climactic Fort Knox clash between Bond and Oddjob. And then there's the moment when Bond, strapped to a gold table with his legs apart while a laser beam slowly works its way towards his pride and joy, calls out to Goldfinger, 'You don't expect me to talk?' And Goldfinger, laughing, calls back, 'No, Mr Bond, I expect you to die!'

The end of *Goldfinger*. But James Bond will return in *Thunderball*.

Director: Guy Hamilton; **Producers:** Albert Broccoli, Harry Saltzman; **Screenplay:** Richard Maibaum, Paul Dehn, from the novel *Goldfinger* by Ian Fleming; **Production Design:** Ken Adam; **Editor:** Peter Hunt; **Photography:** Ted Moore; **Music:** John Barry, title song performed by Shirley Bassey; **Cast:** Sean Connery, Gert Frobe, Honor Blackman, Shirley Eaton, Tania Mallet, Harold Sakata, Bernard Lee, Martin Benson, Cec Linder, Desmond Llewelyn; **Academy Award:** Best Sound Effects.

Gunmen

USA 1993 90 mins

Don't trust them, not even for a second. They're greedy, they're violent, they're low down and dirty, but hell, they're the good guys, and they're here to give us what we want:

lobotomized action, and lots of it, joined at the hip with a ludicrous plot, a corn-fed screenplay, some dreadful ham acting and a bonk scene you might well describe as enthusiastic. A free-wheeling tribute to macho bullshit at its most primeval level, *Gunmen* delivers the goods in one cool, hard, chaotic package, a buddy movie with attitude from *Terminal Velocity* director Deran Sarafian.

The heat is on in sunny South America when Cockney crime boss Loomis (Patrick Stewart), crippled, dying, but cheered no end by the premature burial of his unfaithful wife, hires hyper-psycho Armor O'Malley (Denis Leary, still crazy after all these films) to find 400 million bucks of drug money ripped-off and stashed in a mystery boat by a former employee, now sadly deceased. Enter the odd couple: down-and-out opportunist Dani (Christopher Lambert, ever the scoundrel) wants Loomis dead for killing his crooked brother, and he wouldn't say no to the cash, either; strong, silent DEA bounty hunter Cole (Mario Van Peebles heads Eastwood), meanwhile, wants Loomis' arse in a sling, and then there's that money... Naturally, they're loners. Trouble-magnets too. And they can't help but hate each other. This being a movie, therefore, they have no choice but to join forces, tied together by a single, simple plot contrivance: only Dani knows which marina to head for, while only Cole knows the name of boat they have to find.

Bonded by necessity, intolerance and mutual mistrust, our trigger-happy heroes gun their way through every brand of mayhem known to man, leaping from cliff-tops, romancing the ladies, avoiding O'Malley and wasting his henchmen, taking to the sea for boat-bound shenanigans and, best of all, hanging bungee-style from a 'copter while being dragged through dense jungle and dunked in the ocean. Hey, it could happen.

Schlock scores a hat trick: loud, insane and rabidly obnoxious, it's fun and that's all, a great late-nighter for lads (you know who you are), drunks of all ages and the majority of simian life-forms.

 Keep 'em peeled for director Richard C. Sarafian, father of esteemed director Deran, acting his heart out as Chief Chavez.

Director: Deran Sarafian; **Producers:** Laurence Mark, John Davis, John Flock; **Screenplay:** Stephen Sommers; **Production Design:** Michael Seymour; **Editor:** Bonnie Koehler; **Photography:** Hiro Narita; **Music:** John Debney; **Cast:** Christopher Lambert, Mario Van Peebles, Denis Leary, Patrick Stewart, Kadeem Hardison, Sally Kirkland, Richard Sarafian, Robert Harper, Brenda Bakke.

 ## Hard Boiled
Hong Kong 1992 126 mins

A macho, maverick cop in league with a hit man? Sounds like another bloody buddy movie from director John Woo... *Dirty Harry* meets *Die Hard* head on as the excessively forceful Inspector 'Tequila' Yuen (Chow Yun-Fat) wages war on the gun-running gangsters who wasted his partner, joining forces with mysterious assassin Tony Leung in the name of truth, justice and kick-ass ultra-violence.

Slick, smart and stylish, *Hard Boiled* delivers a body count to remember, kicking off with a frantic teahouse shootout, building momentum with an explosive warehouse battle and going for broke with a long and action-packed hospital finale in which our heroes discover a basement full of weapons, a building full of bad guys and, to complicate matters further, a nursery full of new-born hostages. Armed with a baby in one hand and a gun in the other, Chow plays it cooler than ice-cream and the movie follows suit.

Director: John Woo; **Producers:** Linda Kuk, Terence Chang; **Screenplay:** Barry Wong, story by John Woo; **Production Design:** James Leung, Joel Chong; **Editor:** John Woo,

David Wu Jack, Kai Kit-Wai; **Photography:** Wong Wing-Heng; **Music:** Michael Gibbs; **Cast:** Chow Yun-Fat, Tony Leung, Teresa Mo, Philip Chan, Kwan Hoi-Shan, Anthony Wong, Philip Kwok.

Hard Target

USA 1993 95 mins

Having been hailed as a virtual god of action movie-making, Hong Kong based director John Woo stumbled badly with this, his first American feature, one of many remakes of the ancient RKO flick *The Most Dangerous Game*. Sadly, despite the talent involved, this glossy Jean-Claude Van Damme vehicle just doesn't cut it, either in the action or the story departments, and with the noted exception of Lance Henriksen's oh-so-evil bad guy, this weak

Jean-Claude Van Damme is hunted for sport in *Hard Target*.

and often silly thriller is both a dud and a disappointment.

Van Damme (who plays the same character time and time again - only the reasons for his accent are changed to protect the innocent) plays Chance Boudreaux, an unemployed New Orleans merchant sailor and - as luck would have it - master of the martial arts, who comes to the rescue of babe in distress Natasha Binder (Yancy Butler) when her father disappears. Daddy, it seems, fell foul of a scheme run by sophisticated scumbag Emil Fouchon (Henriksen), an ex-mercenary who arranges exclusive hunts - with human prey. And guess who's going to be next? Pretty soon, Chance and Fouchon come to blows and before we know it there's a hunt to the death going on, full of major explosions, impossible stunts and seriously bloody violence. Don't get too excited though, as it's not nearly as good as it sounds.

Predictably, Woo handles the action well, although there's actually little more to see here than a lot of chop socky and blazing guns. Van Damme seems to have been endowed with supernatural powers by his director, enabling him to perform some truly outrageous, often unbelievable stunts. If you like your action even remotely plausible, you're looking in the wrong place, although much of it is good for a laugh.

At least we don't have to endure Van Damme's backside, here taking an unexpected break from a busy schedule of unwelcome cameo appearances in the star's films. In its place, Wilford Brimley pops up as Chance's Uncle Douvee (pronounced, unfortunately, 'Duvet'), an OAP Rambo wannabe who provides much of the film's unintentional hilarity. At least Henriksen manages to distinguish himself, providing the movie with a little class, a commodity sadly lacking in our leading man.

And what the hell is it with that crazy hair?

Director: John Woo; **Producers:** James Jacks, Sean Daniel; **Screenplay:** Chuck Pfarrer; **Production Design:** Phil Dagort; **Editor:** Bob Murawski; **Photography:** Russell Carpenter; **Music:** Graeme Revell; **Cast:** Jean-Claude Van Damme, Lance Henriksen, Yancy Butler, Wilford Brimley.

Hard to Kill

USA 1989 96 mins

Hard to kill? More like impossible. Believe me, the critics have tried. As indestructible detective Mason Storm, Steven Seagal blasts his way through yet another corny revenge saga, this time with real-life partner Kelly Le Brock at his side, here proving with eager inefficiency that there really is someone alive today with less acting ability than her hard-boiled hubby.

Families of action types never seem to last very long, do they? Their sole function is to either get kidnapped or killed by the bad guys, supplying the movie with some drama and the hero with enough motivation to get off his butt and crack a bunch of heads. It doesn't even matter whether these relations need rescuing or avenging, just so long as their mistreatment adequately justifies the sadistic pursuit and lethal mangling of the offending villains.

And that's exactly what we have here. When supercop Storm digs a little too deeply into the affairs of a crooked senator (Bill Sadler, hardly at his best), he and his family are visited by a heavily-armed goon squad who blast them all to kingdom come. But Storm proves too stubborn to die, and after a seven-year stretch in Comaville, awakes to do battle once more, taking dim-witted nurse Le Brock along for the ride, training himself back to physical and mental perfection, and then beating the stuffing out of every suspicious character in town. And that's about it.

We're not talking quality here. The dialogue is clunky, the direction heavy-handed, and the performances, for want of a better word, are about as convincing as Rock Hudson's marriage, although the scene where Storm wakes out of his coma, coughing and spluttering all over the place while supervising nurse Le Brock doesn't notice a thing, is so wildly awful it's actually quite funny. There's also quite an obvious continuity error, and if you keep an eye on the bullet-riddled windscreen of the jeep Storm uses to escape from the Senator's pals, you can have a good laugh at the film's expense.

The action itself is fairly well handled, although the car chases and stock shoot-outs pale in comparison with the more vicious hand-to-hand encounters that Seagal so clearly enjoys, as Storm finds several new and disgusting ways to introduce a man's insides to his outsides.

Director: Bruce Malmuth; **Producers:** Gary Adelson, Joel Simon, Bill Todman; **Screenplay:** Steven McKay; **Production Design:** Robb Wilson; **Editor:** John F. Link; **Photography:** Matthew F. Leonetti; **Music:** David Michael Frank; **Cast:** Steven Seagal, Kelly Le Brock, Bill Sadler, Frederick Coffin.

Name: HAUER, Rutger

Born: Breukelen, Holland, 1944

Characteristics: Blond hair, blue eyes... the word is Aryan.

Debut feature: Turkish Delight (1973)

Life and times: When he was 16 years old, Hauer ran away to sea for a year of eye-opening adventure, and over the decade that followed managed to get himself expelled from drama school and discharged from the Dutch army on the grounds that he was 'psychologically unfit' for duty. A starring role in Paul Verhoeven's *Soldier of Orange* gave Hauer his first taste of success, and within two years he made his English language debut in the Sly Stallone thriller *Nighthawks*. Having made a world-wide name for himself playing mostly unstable villains (*Blade Runner*, *The Hitcher*) and eccentric heroes

Death Becomes Them 12

(*Flesh + Blood*, *Blind Fury*), Hauer settled down to life as a B-movie king in straight-to-video horror flicks and action adventures.

Greatest contribution to action movies: Offbeat, ambiguous characters dedicated to the weird and mysterious.

Speech, speech: 'I have a lot of energy. I'm a lot stronger than most people.'

Selected filmography: *Soldier of Orange* (1979), *Spetters* (1980), *Nighthawks* (1981), *Blade Runner* (1982), *Eureka* (1983), *The Osterman Weekend* (1983), *A Breed Apart* (1984), *Ladyhawke* (1985), **Flesh + Blood** (1985), *The Hitcher* (1986), *Wanted: Dead or Alive* (1986), *The Legend of the Holy Drinker* (1988), *Bloodhounds of Broadway* (1989), **Blind Fury** (1989), *Salute of the Jugger* (1989), *The Blood of Heroes* (1990), **Wedlock** (1991), *Split Second* (1992), *Buffy the Vampire Slayer* (1992), *Beyond Justice* (1992), *Past Midnight* (1992), *Arctic Blue* (1993), **Surviving the Game** (1994), *Nostradamus* (1994).

Rutger Hauer saves the day as a visually-impaired Samurai swordsman in *Blind Fury*.

The Hidden

USA 1988 97 mins

You never know what an alien might be after. Some crave world domination, others just want to eat your face, and then there's the friendly variety who dream of returning home. Well, you can forget about them for a start, because here we have a bug-eyed invader unlike anything you've seen before, a butt-ugly parasite addicted to fast cars, heavy metal and ultraviolence. Dedicated to having a good time, all the time, and at anyone else's expense, our bodysnatching villain takes over a variety of human hosts, running over cripples as a yuppie, robbing a record store as a middle-aged man, and, wouldn't you know it, exploring his breasts as a stripper. Welcome to LA.

Eager to avenge the murder of his wife, kids and partner, space cop Kyle MacLachlan (of *Twin Peaks* fame) pursues his parasitic nemesis from one end of the city to the other, desperate to put an end to the chaos and devastation, no matter how entertaining it might be for us. Posing as a tight-lipped FBI agent, Kyle hooks up with a typically hard-bitten homicide detective (Michael Nouri), their uneasy partnership adding a buddy element to the picture which helps bring out the humour.

All hail director Jack Sholder for fully exploiting this unique premise, an inspired and unapologetic excuse for slaughter, destruction and all-round outrageous action. It's pretty smart too, and very funny at times, but most of all, kids, it's wilder than a hungry cop in a doughnut shop.

Sequel: *The Hidden II*.

Director: Jack Sholder; **Producers:** Robert Shaye, Gerald T. Olson, Michael Meltzer; **Screenplay:** Bob Hunt; **Production Design:** C.J. Strawn, Mick Strawn; **Editor:** Michael N. Knue; **Photography:** Jacques Haitkin; **Music:** Michael Convertino; **Cast:** Kyle

MacLachlan, Michael Nouri, Claudia Christian, Clarence Felder, Clu Galager, Ed O'Ross, Richard Brooks, William Boyett, Larry Cedar.

Highlander

GB/USA 1986 119 mins

Russell Mulcahy presents 450 years in the life of an immortal, a slickly shot, tightly edited, heavy metal actioner starring Christopher Lambert as Scottish clansman Connor MacLeod, Sean Connery as his Egyptian mentor, Ramirez, and Clancy Brown as the ferociously evil Kurgan.

Now, here is a movie dedicated to swordplay. An opening battle in an underground car park teaches us that the only way to kill an immortal is to chop his head off with a sword. Excellent. Well, the year is 1986, and all remaining immortals are converging in New York to fight it out for The Prize, an all-knowing, all-seeing, meaning-of-life kinda deal which goes to the last man standing. MacLeod is our hero, and even though we hate his mock Scots accent, we want him to win because otherwise, an ancient biker type called the Kurgan will, and mankind would be doomed.

Meanwhile, over at Flashback City, we have Connor discovering his immortality (back in the good old 1530s), taking up with a wee bit o' skirt (Beatie Edney) and training with flamboyant scene-stealer Ramirez, while back in the present he's on the verge of something special with Brenda (Roxanne Hart), a weapons expert who suspects he may be a few years older than her...

Shot like a rock video with a pounding Queen soundtrack, *Highlander* offers full-on, heads-off action, with humour and romance on the side, building to a flashy, neon-lit one-to-one finale as Connor and the Kurgan seek ultimate knowledge, not through study and reflection, but through hugely destructive, ultra-violent acts of swordplay. This is what we want.

Ignore the sequels, disregard the live-action and animated TV spin-offs, and watch only this, the original, best and least moronic contribution to the ever-growing *Highlander* franchise.

Sequels: *Highlander II: The Quickening, Highlander 3: The Sorcerer* (aka *Highlander - The Final Dimension*).

Director: Russell Mulcahy; **Producers:** Peter S. Davis, William N. Panzer; **Screenplay:** Gregory Widen, Peter Bellwood, Larry Ferguson; **Production Design:** Allan Cameron; **Editor:** Peter Honess; **Photography:** Gerry Fisher; **Music:** Queen, Michael Kamen; **Cast:** Christopher Lambert, Sean Connery, Clancy Brown, Roxanne Hart, Beatie Edney, Alan North.

Hot Shots! Part Deux

USA 1993 88 mins

A wise man once remarked that stupid is as stupid does, and should you choose to apply this warped philosophy to *Hot Shots! Part Deux*, you'll find that stupid does very well, thank you. A wild and crazy spoof of action movies and most other genres besides, this shamelessly silly, hyperactive comedy fires a gag a second, and while many miss their targets, there are more than enough bullseyes to save the day. Besides, it beats the pants off its predecessor, *Top Gun* satire *Hot Shots!*

Charlie Sheen heads the insanity as all-American hero Topper Harley, sent deep into the Persian Gulf to rescue the rescue team who were themselves sent to the Gulf to rescue a group of US soldiers being held by Saddam Hussein (Jerry Haleva) following Operation Desert Storm. Obviously, the story is not what counts.

Romantic complications arise in the vampish forms of two mysterious beauties, Ramada (Valeria Golino) and Michelle (Brenda Bakke), though our hero never allows his feelings to get in the way of a good action scene. Lampooning the military father figure (Colonel Sam Trautman) he played in all three *Rambo* movies, Richard Crenna hams it up as hapless hero Colonel Denton Walters, who, trapped behind enemy lines with only a slim chance of rescue, takes his torture like a man. 'I see you're no stranger to pain', remarks a greasy interrogator. 'I've been married', explains Waters, 'twice'.

Supporting clowns include Lloyd Bridges as the hopelessly inept President Tug Benson ('The Simple Solution'), while *RoboCop*'s Miguel Ferrer steals all the best lines as a soldier who overcomes a temporary loss of confidence through excessive use of violence ('Thank-you Topper, I can kill again, you've given me a reason to live!').

No-one is safe, no movie sacred. Targets of note include *Star Wars*, *Lady and the Tramp*, and, best of all, *Apocalypse Now*, while fans of lowbrow humour should get a kick out of gags involving a rather startled chicken, an excitable on-screen body count and, you'd better believe it, a mighty underwater fart.

Good natured and fun, this is a monumentally silly adventure, ideal for anyone whose sense of humour could best be described as twisted.

Director: Jim Abrahams; **Producer:** Bill Badalato; **Screenplay:** Jim Abrahams, Pat Proft; **Production Design:** William A. Elliott; **Editor:** Malcolm Campbell; **Photography:** John R. Leonetti; **Music:** Basil Pouledouris; **Cast:** Charlie Sheen, Lloyd Bridges, Valeria Golino, Richard Crenna, Brenda Bakke, Miguel Ferrer, Rowan Atkinson.

Indiana Jones and the Last Crusade

USA 1989 127 mins

'Germany has declared war on the Jones' boys!' George and Steven's prodigal son hits the Grail trail for father/son bonding and general Hun-bashing in this third Indiana Jones adventure, a formula re-hash of the first two movies with the bonus of an extra star, Sean Connery, playing opposite Harrison Ford as Indy's eccentric dad, Henry. Returning from *Raiders* to lend our hero a hand, Denholm Elliott (Marcus Brody, slightly senile) and *Sliders*' John Rhys-Davies (Sallah, Egyptian clown) tag along as comic relief, while newcomers include Alison Doody as the dodgy Doctor Schneider and Julian *For Your Eyes Only* Glover as suspicious business-type Walter Donovan.

The Holy Grail's up for grabs and Hitler wants it bad. Grail expert Henry Jones is missing, believed kidnapped by the Nazis. The year is 1938, the world is on the brink of war, and you can't crack your bullwhip without clipping a German spy, a suicide squad, or some kind of eerie supernatural force beyond our understanding (only God and I.L.M. know the truth). With Germans to waste, a father to rescue and, hell, a planet to save, the younger Mr Jones sets out in search of the cup of Christ via a series of comic inter-ludes, male bonding moments and numerous high concept, big-budget action sequences that, as good as they are, can't quite compete with, say, the *Raiders* truck chase or the mine car madness of *Temple of Doom*.

This must be what an average *Indiana Jones* movie looks like. It's still a lot of fun, and there's some pretty decent action in there too, from a cliffhanging tank encounter and Venice speedboat chase to fun in a Nazi stronghold and a bi-plane shootout, but com-pared with Indys' one and two, number three's just a little less inventive, a little less exciting, a little less... well, everything.

River Phoenix plays young Indy in a flashback sequence at the top of the movie, battling thieves on a circus train while picking up his trademark scar, hat, whip and all-consuming fear of snakes.

 Sean may look old enough to play Harrison's dad, and he has been a star for a lot longer, but he is, in fact, only twelve years older than the *Star Wars* graduate.

Director: Steven Spielberg; **Producer:** Robert Watts; **Executive Producers:** George Lucas, Frank Marshall; **Screenplay:** Jeffrey Boam, story by George Lucas, Menno Meyjes; **Production Design:** Elliot Scott; **Editor:** Michael Kahn; Photography: Douglas Slocombe; Music: John Williams; **Cast:** Harrison Ford, Sean Connery, Denholm Elliott, Alison Doody, John Rhys-Davies, Julian Glover, River Phoenix, Michael Byrne. **Academy Award:** Best Sound Effects Editing.

Indiana Jones and the Temple of Doom

USA 1984 118 mins

The most resilient archaeologist on the face of the planet is back in his scariest adventure, chasing fortune and glory in the heart of India while battling the forces of a monstrous cult bent on world domination. This time around, story and characterization take a back seat to the action, as Steven Spielberg and George Lucas emphasize cliffhanging thrills above all else, but it's all so darn exciting that you'll barely have the time to notice.

Crammed to overflowing with voodoo rituals, human sacrifices and a soundtrack full of tortured screams, *Indiana Jones and the Temple of Doom* is easily the most violent film of the trilogy, and was single-handedly responsible for provoking a new censor certificate in the United States, PG-13. In Britain, the film was hacked at by the British Board of Film Classification (a euphemism for the censor) until it qualified as a PG, but it still has the power to shock and may not be entirely suitable for younger children, especially the wimpy ones who jump at the sight of their own shadow (come on, hurry up and get desensitized, will ya?).

First comes a spectacular nightclub shoot-out, then a wild car chase through the streets of Shanghai, and to cap it all, an outrageous skydiving escape which develops into a daring toboggan ride and white water adventure. And these are just the opening scenes (take a breath now). Suffice to say that an unlikely combination of outrageous circumstances serve to strand our hero (man's man Harrison Ford), his pint-sized sidekick Short Round (newcomer Ke Huy Quan), and dizzy blonde nightclub singer Willie Scott (the second Mrs Spielberg, Kate Capshaw) in India.

Making the most of their unusual situation, Indy and the gang set out to rescue hundreds of enslaved children as well as a trio of sacred Sankara stones from the villainous Thuggees, an ancient, wicked clan dedicated to Kali, their evil god. A visit to nearby Pankot Palace confirms Indy's worst fears when he discovers a hidden entrance to the 'Temple of Doom', underground lair of high priest Mola Ram (a supremely psychotic Amrish Puri), master of the dark light...

Not long into the movie we know who everyone is, we know what everyone wants, and we know what everyone deserves, and with all that story stuff out of the way it's time for one incredible action sequence after another, as the heroic Dr Jones struggles to save Willie from a sacrificial lava pit, takes on a hulking Thuggee guard (*Raiders of the Lost Ark*'s Pat Roach) in a blistering conveyor belt slug-a-thon, risks a death-defying, rollercoaster mine car escape and finally, puts his money where his mouth is with an edge-of-the-seat rope bridge finale which, stock footage of crocodiles aside, is a truly amazing piece of work.

Replacing snakes as the slimy creatures *du jour*, we have hundreds of thousands of bugs, a crunchy, squishy obstacle for our high-pitched heroine. A gross-out meal at Pankot Palace, consisting of 'snake surprise', eyeball soup and, to cap it all, chilled monkey brains, also proves too much for Willie, who, though she pales in comparison with *Raiders'* Marion Ravenwood, is, at the very least, as needy a damsel-in-distress as you could ever hope to rescue.

And who better to save Willie, the Sankara stones, the children, and the world than the master whip-smith himself, Indiana Jones?

George Lucas lays on a couple of *Star Wars* in-jokes for the fans, the best being the name of Shanghai nightclub where we first meet Indy, Club Obi Wan. Also, in addition to Indiana (Jones) being named after George Lucas's dog, Short Round was named after screenwriters Willard Huyck and Gloria Katz's dog, while Willie, would you believe it, was named after Steven Spielberg's dog.

Director: Steven Spielberg; **Producer:** Robert Watts; **Executive Producers:** George Lucas, Frank Marshall; **Screenplay:** Willard Huyck, Gloria Katz, story by George Lucas; **Production Design:** Elliot Scott; **Editor:** Michael Kahn; **Photography:** Douglas Slocombe; **Music:** John Williams; **Cast:** Harrison Ford, Kate Capshaw, Ke Huy Quan, Amrish Puri, Roshan Seth, Philip Stone, Roy Chiao. **Academy Award:** Best Visual Effects.

Invasion USA

USA 1985 107 mins

Double the guns, double the fun: Chuck Norris blasts the baddies in *Invasion USA*.

Chuck Norris bails out Uncle Sam in one of his most popular films, a cheerfully obnoxious testament to violence in its many forms. As action man Matt Hunter, Chuck plays the hero when a ruthless invasion force of illegal aliens drive America to its knees. Chaos rules as the conquering hordes turn their backs on military targets, choosing instead to waste countless civilians, demolish churches by the dozen and blow bus loads of school children to hell and back. And only Chuck can save them, springing out of nowhere, always just in time, delivering justice the Norris way, a whirlwind of brutal fistplay and kamikaze car chasing.

Never mind the quality, just feel the width of death and destruction on offer. Armed with dinky twin machine guns and a cool one-liner to suit every fatality, Chuck takes us on a killing spree as he guns for the leader of the pack, a top-notch psycho named Rostov (veteran scowler Richard Lynch) who harbours a special grudge against our hero.

When a movie lists more than 80 stuntmen it's safe to expect a powerful concentration of blood and devastation, and thanks to an unstoppable hero and an unspeakable villain, *Invasion USA* does not disappoint.

Director: Joseph Zito; **Producers:** Menahem Golan, Yoram Globus; **Screenplay:** James Bruner, Chuck Norris, from a story by Aaron Norris and James Bruner; **Production Design:** Ladislav Wilheim; **Editors:** Daniel Loewenthal, Scott Vickrey; **Photography:** Joao Fernandes; **Music:** Jay Chattaway; **Cast:** Chuck Norris, Richard Lynch, Melissa Prophet, Alexander Zale.

Iron Eagle

USA 1986 119 mins

Those magnificent men in their flying machines blow the living hell out of one another in this defiantly silly adventure, a testosterone-charged tribute to macho bullshit from Sidney J. Furie, journeyman director of *Superman IV*, *The Taking of Beverly Hills* and other American classics. Jason Gedrick buckles up and takes to the skies in this broad teenage fantasy, a comicbook fable which preaches that with manhood comes great responsibility, not to mention the opportunity to shoot at people and blow stuff up.

Once again, violence is the key to ultimate maturity as 18-year-old flyboy Doug Masters (Gedrick) kills a bunch of foreigners in the name of truth, justice and right-wing America. The forecast calls for excessive aerial combat throughout as Doug jets off to the Middle East to rescue his fighter pilot father (*Trancers*' Tim Thomerson) from the clutches of an evil Colonel (*Poirot*'s David Suchet) intent on teaching the Yanks a lesson in respect.

Support comes from retired Air Force Colonel Charles 'Slappy' Sinclair (Louis Gossett Jr), a stand-in father figure eager to fry some butt because 'there's something about maniacs messing with good men that always pisses me off'. Strapped into a couple of fully-armed F-16 fighters, Doug and Slappy strike a blow for lunatic heroics, flying faster than a speeding bullet from one target to the next, backed by nothing more substantial than a feeble screenplay, pedestrian direction, a minor villain and a soft rock soundtrack courtesy of Doug's trusty Walkman.

At least the action delivers, with all kinds of daring aerial manoeuvres thrown in for our amusement, although at the end of every dogfight comes a close-up of an exploding enemy jet which is so obviously a special effects model job it's as if Gerry Anderson's Thunderbirds have taken over.

Taken as a rigidly formulaic, mid-budget, lowbrow, good/bad, flag-waving actioner, *Iron Eagle* is an acceptable time-waster, dim and dopey but determined to entertain.

Sequels: *Iron Eagle II*, *Aces: Iron Eagle III*.

Director: Sidney J. Furie; **Producers:** Ron Samuels, Joe Wizan; **Screenplay:** Kevin Elders, Sidney J. Furie; **Production Design:** Robb Wilson King; **Editor:** George Grenville; **Photography:** Adam Greenburg; **Music:** Basil Poledouris; **Cast:** Louis Gossett Jr, Jason Gedrick, David Suchet, Tim Thomerson, Larry B. Scott, Caroline Lagerfelt.

Ivanhoe

USA 1952 107 mins

Step aside Robin Hood, it's time for Ivanhoe to save the day in this lavish costume bash, an all-star, Technicolor tribute to honour, love and the heat of battle. Robert Taylor takes the lead as the bravest Saxon knight of all, struggling to raise a King's ransom while locked in mortal combat with dastardly villains George Sanders and Robert Douglas. Fighting for the love of our studly hero, damsels-in-distress Elizabeth Taylor and Joan Fontaine bring Hollywood to medieval England, while director Richard Thorpe lays on some truly incredible action sequences, including a five-to-one jousting tournament, a hard 'n' heavy fight to the death between a mace-wielding Sanders and our axe-heaving hero, and, best of all, a colossal siege sequence as Ivanhoe and his new pal Locksley (aka Mr Hood) bust up a Norman castle with help from hundreds of extras, thousands of arrows, twelfth-century weaponry and twentieth-century stuntwork.

Nominated for three Academy Awards (Best Picture, Photography, Sound), *Ivanhoe* looks beautiful and the action, when it comes, is undeniably impressive, but between fight scenes the movie can't help but drag its heels. The story might be simple enough - 150,000 marks of silver is all that will free crusading King Richard from a grotty Austrian dungeon, but evil Prince John (Guy Rolfe), who wants England for himself, refuses to cash up, so it's up to Ivanhoe to save his lord and master - but there are so many sub-plots and supporting characters to deal with the movie often grinds to a halt. Let's just say that everyone either loves or hates everyone else, and leave it at that. Besides, the story isn't nearly as interesting as the swashbuckling bits, which successfully elevate the movie from plodding epic to matinee classic, and we can all be grateful for that.

Director: Richard Thorpe; **Producer:** Pandro S. Berman; **Screenplay:** Noel Langley, adaptation by Aeneas MacKenzie, based on the novel by Sir Walter Scott; **Production Design:** Alfred Junge; **Editor:** Frank Clarke; **Photography:** F.A. Young; **Music:** Miklos Rozsa; **Cast:** Robert Taylor, Elizabeth Taylor, Joan Fontaine, George Sanders, Emlyn Williams, Robert Douglas, Finlay Currie, Felix Aylmer, Harold Warrender, Guy Rolfe.

The Jewel of the Nile

USA 1985 104 mins

Cashing in on the success of *Romancing the Stone*, this first and final sequel packs Michael Douglas, Kathleen Turner and Danny DeVito off to Africa in pursuit of a mysterious jewel. Standing in for director Bob Zemeckis, Lewis Teague makes do with an average collection of action and comedy set-pieces, passing the time well enough, but failing to recapture the spirit and charm of the original.

Six months of fun in the sun with eternal bachelor Jack (Douglas) proves more than enough for Joan (Turner), who's ready for her next big adventure. Time to shake things up with a ludicrous plot, some exotic locations and a handful of colourful characters: Ralph's (DeVito) out of jail, on the streets and just as unlucky as ever (malaria, rat bites and ten weeks of rabies shots have done little to improve his mood); power-crazed smoothie Omar (Spiros Focas), meanwhile, has a plan to become Emperor of the Nile; and then there's the Jewel itself, precious, irreplaceable and number one object of desire on everybody's wish list.

Following a slowish start, the movie soon picks up with some high-concept action sequences: eager to escape Omar's clutches, our heroes drive a jet fighter through downtown Africa, blowing holes in the scenery and generally giving the enemy a very hard time; much choo-choo stuntwork follows, as Joan hangs perilously from the side of a speeding train; then there's the grand finale, as Jack, Joan, Ralph and a bunch of rebel types take on Omar and his men before it's too late...

We're looking at average here, quite entertaining, but nothing new, much more sentimental than the first, softer round the edges, too, and the characters are no way near as fresh as they once were. You will not, however, die of boredom.

Talk about your fashion disasters: one minute, while dangling from a train, Turner's wearing leather sandals. Moments later, though, when our heroine finally makes it to safety, she's sporting a pair of canvas slip-ons instead.

Director: Lewis Teague; **Producer:** Michael Douglas; **Screenplay:** Mark Rosenthal, Lawrence Konner, based on characters created by Diane Thomas; **Production Design:** Richard Dawking, Terry Knight; **Editors:** Michael Ellis, Peter Boita, Edward Abrams; **Photography:** Jan DeBont; **Music:** Jack Nitzsche; **Cast:** Michael Douglas, Kathleen Turner, Danny DeVito, Spiros Focas, Avner Eisenberg.

Joshua Tree

USA 1993 94 mins

Consider Dolph Lundgren. He's big, he's strong, he's tough. Then again, so is Frankenstein's Monster, but that doesn't mean we'd cheer him through an action flick. It may be true that as far as acting ability and basic screen presence are concerned, Dolph's a bit of a lumberer, but at least he knows how to kill and destroy, two extremely useful talents which give a helping hand to each and every action sequence in this bog-standard adventure from long-time stuntman turned director Vic Armstrong.

Prepare for a 'been there, done that' experience: framed and sent to jail by the man who killed his partner, trucker Santee (Dolph) turns fugitive, kidnapping a gorgeous lady cop (Kristian Alfonso) and heading for justice through '6000 square miles of sand and rock'. Pursued by a crooked, obsessive detective (George Segal), Santee gets into all kinds of trouble, from a high speed sports car chase to the movie's one and only action highlight, a savage, destructive and surprisingly inventive chop shop gun battle.

As for Miss Alfonso, well, at first her character hates Santee, but then, of course, she gets the hots for him, and while there's really no reason for her to be in this movie beyond window dressing, she's of Amazonian quality with a butt that won't quit and a whole lot prettier than Dolph. As for nudity, our fugitive couple almost get it on towards the end of the movie, but it's a sad case of *coitus interruptus* as the bad guys intrude upon the good stuff. Don't despair, however, for we are granted a brief view of perfection early on as Kristian strips for an entirely necessary shower scene.

Offering sex, violence and the odd gag here and there, *Joshua Tree* is an exercise in average, a passable yet entirely forgettable bit of business suitable for undemanding moods.

Director: Vic Armstrong; **Producer:** Illana Diamant, Andy Armstrong; **Screenplay:** Steven Pressfield; **Production Design:** John J. Moore; **Editor:** Paul Morton; **Photography:** Dan Turrett; **Music:** Joel Goldsmith; **Cast:** Dolph Lundgren, George Segal, Kristian Alfonso, Geoffrey Lewis, Bert Remsen, Beau Starr, Michael Paul Chan, Michelle Phillips.

> **A great, big gun, a pair of designer sunglasses, and a sharp, smart mouth are all a man needs to survive in this crazy world...**
>
> 'No! Not the bore worms!'
> - Ornella Muti ponders her fate in *Flash Gordon*.
>
> 'You keep looking at me, you're gonna see me kill you'
> - A gun-toting hobo threatens Emilio Estevez in *Freejack*.
>
> 'How does it feel to know you're about to die,'
> - Pony-tailed wonder Steven Seagal talking to the animals in *Hard To Kill*.

Verbal Assaults 2

'It's a kind of magic'
- Christopher Lambert explains himself in *Highlander*.
'War - it's fan-tastic!'
- A trigger-happy Miguel Ferrer, able to kill again, in *Hot Shots! Part Deux*.

'Time to Die.'
- Chuck Norris alerts the enemy in *Invasion USA*.

'There's something about maniacs messing with good men that always pisses me off.'
- Louis Gossett Jr throws down the gauntlet in *Iron Eagle*.

'Joe, if we go any faster, we're gonna travel back in time.'
- Damon Wayans cautions speed demon Bruce Willis in *The Last Boy Scout*.

'I like these calm little moments before the storm...'
- Drug-dealing psychopath Gary Oldman enjoys a pre-slaughter moment of peace and quiet in *Leon*.

'We're back, we're bad, you're black, I'm mad.'
- Mel Gibson clowns around in *Lethal Weapon 2*.

'I can't shoot dogs. People are OK, but not dogs.'
- Mel makes a brand new, four-legged friend in *Lethal Weapon 3*.

'Ladies and gentlemen, boys and girls, dyin' time's here!'
- Two men enter, one man leaves in *Mad Max: Beyond Thunderdome*.

'A man's gotta know his limitations.'
- Words of wisdom from Mr Eastwood in *Magnum Force*.

'Now that you're on the case, I hope we're going to have some gratuitous sex and violence!'
- Alec McCowen's Q encourages Sean Connery's Bond in *Never Say Never Again*.

'I wanna shoot you so bad, my dick's hard.'
- Obsessive cop Ice T gets busy with crime lord Wesley Snipes in *New Jack City*.

'You have a nasty habit of surviving.'
- Evil smoothie Louis Jourdan chastises Roger Moore in *Octopussy*.

'Always bet on black.'
- Sound advice from Wesley Snipes in *Passenger 57*.

'I ain't got time to bleed.'
- Jungle-bound hard man Jesse Ventura, keeping 'em peeled for a *Predator*.

'If it bleeds, we can kill it.'
- The Arnold philosophy, courtesy of *Predator*.

'I never go anywhere in South East Asia without an Uzi'
- Danny Aiello explains himself in *The Protector*.

Detective: 'You're sick, you know that don't you?'
Punisher: 'No I'm not.'
Detective: 'Well what the fuck you call 125 murders in five years?'
Punisher: 'A work in progress.'
Lawman Louis Gossett Jr questions vigilante Dolph Lundgren in *The Punisher.*

'Trust me.'
- Harrison Ford asks the impossible in *Raiders of the Lost Ark.*

'To survive a war, you gotta become war.'
- The way it is, according to Sly, in *Rambo: First Blood Part II.*

Evil Russian Colonel: 'Who do you think this man [Rambo] is? God?'
Bold American Colonel: 'No - God would have mercy. *He* won't.'
Richard Crenna talks back to Marc de Jonge in *Rambo III.*

'You should not drink and bake'
- Arnold lectures his other half in *Raw Deal.*

Judge Dredd

USA 1995 95 mins

Following years of faithful service on the streets of Mega City One and the pages of *2000AD*, judge, jury and executioner Joseph Dredd blasts away at the big screen, delivering his own special brand of kick-ass justice to a whole horde of futuristic comic book monstrosities. Kitted out in a brand new suit of armour, courtesy of rag trade supremo Gianni Versace, Dredd makes history as he finally removes his helmet, fully revealing his features for the very first time, and get this, he looks just like Sylvester Stallone. Fear not, however, for after a brief settling-in period, Sly does quite a job as the brutal, emotionless and monosyllabic lawman, a role the Italian Stallion could play in his sleep. Think of *RoboCop*, and you'll know what to expect.

Framed for a murder which naturally he didn't commit, Dredd is booted from Mega City One (aka New York, circa 2139AD) and dumped in the post-apocalyptic wasteland that is the Cursed Earth. Meanwhile, the true villains of the piece, namely Dredd's evil clone-brother Rico (Armand Assante) and corrupt Judge Griffin (Jurgen Prochnow), are hatching suitably diabolical plots of conquest and dictatorship. Now, as if the cannibalistic Angel Gang and psychotic Mean Machine weren't enough to deal with, Dredd and comedy side-kick Fergie (Rob Schneider) have to fight their way back to Mega City and somehow foil the collected plans of Rico and Griffin while battling the Special Judicial Squad, avoiding deadly city defences, and taking a can opener to the toughest robot of 'em all, the hulking, terrifying ABC Warrior, Hammerstein. Only then will Dredd's name be cleared, and he can resume a life of perp-punishing.

From the opening block war and stunning Lawmaster bike chase right through to Dredd's final encounter with arch-enemy Rico, it's clear that no expense has been spared. Designed with an eye for detail that is both spectacular and faithful to Dredd's comic book world, the movie scores on both the action and story fronts, giving us a little something to think about while cheering on the carnage.

Dredd purists are likely to breath a sigh of relief when they realize that, despite expectations, their hero has been given a fair crack of the whip by young British director Danny

Cannon and screenwriters William Wisher and Steven E. de Souza. Helping Dredd on his quest are *2000AD* favourites Judge Hershey (tentative love interest Diane Lane) and Chief Judge Fargo (Max Von Sydow), while our hero's greatest asset remains his trusty Lawgiver gun, a hand-held slice of maximum carnage which comes complete with rapid fire, armour piercing and double whammy settings.

True, the most knowledgeable of Dredd's followers should be able to pick out mistakes by the wagon load, and maybe the special effects falter every now and then, but this is pure Judge Dredd, no doubt about it, and nit-picking aside the movie packs one hell of a powerful punch.

Director: Danny Cannon; **Producers:** Charles M. Lippincott, Beau E. L. Marks; **Screenplay:** William Wisher, Steven E. de Souza, based on characters created by John Wagner and Pat Mills; **Production Design:** Nigel Phelps; **Editor:** Alex Mackie, Harry Keramidas; **Photography:** Adrian Biddle; **Music:** Alan Silvestri; **Cast:** Sylvester Stallone, Armand Assante, Rob Schneider, Jurgen Prochnow, Max Von Sydow, Diane Lane.

Judgment Night

USA 1993 109 mins

F our guys on the road, three able-bodied, one token lard-o, hopelessly lost on the wrong side of the tracks. Cue nightfall. Cue dramatic music. Cue Fallon (Denis Leary), smart-mouthed psycho killer with a henchman trio, wasting a minion for ripping him off. Wrong time, wrong place: the boys catch the entire show, witnesses the lot of 'em, and now Fallon wants them dead, pursuing our reluctant heroes through the streets, slums and sewers of Crime Central, USA.

Fiendishly clever and ingeniously plotted it ain't. You want a story? You want realistic characterization? You want basic plausibility? You're gonna have to look elsewhere. The good news, however, is that in the hands of *Predator 2* director Stephen Hopkins, *Judgment Night* is actually quite a capable chase thriller, well paced and fairly exciting, with some decent action highlights and even a little suspense.

Enduring this feature length assault course of running and jumping around, shooting bad guys and trashing property, Emilio Estevez takes the lead as former hell-raiser/newly responsible family man Frank Wyatt; macho man Cuba Gooding Jr flexes his biceps, if not his brain, as best friend Mike; wild child Stephen Dorff plays it tough but confused as Frank's brother John; rounding off the gang, meanwhile, token newcom-er Jeremy Piven fills the shoes of porky, obnoxious hanger-on Ray, a born loser and nat-ural victim whose job it is to freak out and slow the lads down as often as possible. Predictably, though, it's Leary who steals the show, as darkly hyperactive as ever, mean and spiteful with a homicidal sense of humour.

Atmospheric but empty-headed, scary but superficial, *Judgment Night* offers a palat-able mix of violence, pyrotechnics and good, old-fashioned shock treatment, building up towards an extended department store showdown, which, like the rest of the movie, man-ages to entertain without ever really involving its audience.

Director: Stephen Hopkins; **Producer:** Gene Levy; **Screenplay:** Lewis Colick, story by Lewis Colick, Jere Cunningham; **Production Design:** Joseph Nemec III; **Editor:** Timothy Wellburn; **Photography:** Peter Levy; **Music:** Alan Silvestri; **Cast:** Emilio Estevez, Cuba Gooding Jr, Denis Leary, Stephen Dorff, Jeremy Piven, Peter Greene, Erik Schrody, Michael Wiseman.

Kickboxer

USA 1989 105 mins

Jean-Claude Van Damme sets his sights on the villain who crippled his brother, raped his girl and, for the hat trick, killed his dog in this corny revenge saga, a cheap and cheerless feature saved from the brink of disaster by a couple of incredible fight scenes. Believe it or not, it took six directors to put this one together, with Mark Di Salle and David Worth credited up front, three assistants mentioned at the end, and a special 'Fight scenes choreographed and directed by' credit for Van-Damage, who contributes the only watchable portions of the movie.

Half-vegetized by kickboxing whirlwind 'Tiger' Tong Po (here playing himself), Eric Sloane (Dennis Alexio) demands vengeance, a call answered by his brother Kurt (Jean-Claude), who travels to Thailand, hooks up with a task-master, martial arts instructor (Dennis Chan), trains in the ancient, mystic art of busting people up, and finally, when he's good and motivated, takes on the big, bald and bug-ugly Po in a no-holds-barred kickboxing contest.

Often the movie seems eager to send you to sleep, a big screen Valium of mediocre characters, bargain-basement production values, cheesy soft-rock sounds (corn-fed songs include 'Never Surrender', 'Fight for Love' and the, er, classic 'Roll With the Punches') and hopeless (mis-) direction, a bland piece of nothing entirely reliant on intermittent action, a chop-socky fight scene here, a grotesque feat of endurance there, all of it building up to the one and only reason for seeing this movie in the first place (better still, why not fast-forward the first hour-and-a-bit away and just watch the good stuff?). Set in an old, underground tomb (the movie's only half-decent set), there's a slash-tastic, climactic battle to look forward to, a nifty slice of ultra-violent excess which comes a-callin' when Kurt and Tong (finally) meet to '...fight the old way, hands wrapped in hemp and resin, dipped in broken glass'.

Should you decide to accept this mission, lads, and prove your mettle by watching the movie from start to finish, best brace yourselves, first, for a typically iffy performance from Brussels' finest, a particularly horrifying disco dancing sequence and, well, a rather nasty 'hook up the arse' scene which'll bring tears to your eyes.

Sequels: *Kickboxer II: The Road Back*, *Kickboxer III: The Art of War*.

Directors: Mark Di Salle, David Worth; **Producer:** Mark Di Salle; **Screenplay:** Glenn A. Bruce, story by Mark Di Salle and Jean-Claude Van Damme; **Production Design:** Shay Austin; **Editor:** Wayne Wahrman; **Photography:** Jon Kranhouse; **Music:** Paul Hertzog; **Cast:** Jean-Claude Van Damme, Dennis Alexio, Dennis Chan, Tong Po, Haskell Anderson, Rochelle Ashana, Steve Lee.

The Killer

Hong Kong 1989 110 mins

John Woo achieved artistic nirvana with this grandiose gangster melodrama, a stylish tale of heroic bloodshed co-starring Chow Yun-Fat and Danny Lee as like-minded tough guys on opposite sides of the law: Chow's an assassin who'll only waste the wicked, Lee's a maverick cop who does more or less the same, but of the two men, only one carries a badge, and that makes all the difference. Chow means well, though, and wants out of the 'family' business, but when a botched final job leaves an innocent girl (Sally Yeh) blind, our guilty anti-hero has no choice but to further complicate his life by dashing to her rescue. Add to

Danny Lee (in pinstripes) and Chow Yun-Fat enjoy a little point-blank drama in *The Killer*.

this some extremely irritated mobsters and a textbook example of male-bonding and you have *The Killer*.

Pulp fiction with an ultra-violent edge, Woo's classic crime thriller juggles ferocious gun play and wild chase sequences with intelligent plotting and honest-to-goodness characterization without ever dropping the ball. Tense and exiting, the movie builds to a colossal shootout which sees honour served, blood spilt and Chow, cool as ever, wading through the bodies with a gun blazing in each hand. Groovy.

 Plans for a redundant US remake starring Richard Gere and Denzel Washington fell through when director Walter Hill, bless him, turned down the project.

Director: John Woo; **Producer:** Tsui Hark; **Screenplay:** John Woo; **Production Design:** Lux Man Wah; **Editor:** Fan Kung Ming; **Photography:** Wong Wing Hang, Peter Pao; **Music:** Lowell Lo; **Cast:** Chow Yun-Fat, Danny Lee, Sally Yeh, Chu Kong, Tsang Kong, Shing Fui-On.

King Solomon's Mines

USA 1985 100 mins

Could this film be any worse? Could the action be any less thrilling? Could the characters be any more annoying?

No. No. No. And, while I'm asking questions, did the Cannon boys, who produced this tiresome moronathon, honestly believe that anyone would be stupid enough to want to watch this insult to adventure movies? It's a mystery, to be sure, but not a very interesting one.

A broad (and I mean b-r-o-a-d) re-invention of H. Rider Haggard's classic adventure novel, this bargain-basement Indiana Jones wannabe settles for cheap thrills and easy laughs every time, creating a smug, sentimental hero you'd rather strangle than cheer, and a production line of tired action set-pieces that are about as thrilling to sit through as rush hour traffic.

Richard Chamberlain, who's a little too long in the tooth for this sort of thing (and that's being polite), plays great white schmuck Allan Quatermain, a dim-witted adventurer in a two-bit safari suit who, accompanied by hysterical bimbo Jessie (Sharon Stone, before her knickers travelled south and the good times rolled) and cowardly native Umbopo (Ken Gampu), races through Africa in a bid to discover King Solomon's legendary mines ahead of greedy cardboard villains Dogati (John Rhys-Davies) and Bockner (Herbert Lom). But Africa is a treacherous place, my friends, full of hungry wildlife and unfriendly locals, yet from the very beginning of this episodic baloney it's obvious that Quatermain is going to survive it all without a scratch. And where's the fun in that? Had the movie not been so completely charmless, we might have been able to forgive some of its many faults. But it's dumb, plain and simple, and best left alone.

Sequel: *Allan Quatermain and the Lost City of Gold*.

Director: J. Lee Thompson; **Producers:** Menahem Golan, Yoram Globus; **Screenplay:** Gene Quintano, James R. Silke, based on the novel by H. Rider Haggard; **Production Design:** Luciano Spadoni; **Editor:** John Shirley; **Photography:** Alex Phillips; **Music:** Jerry Goldsmith; **Cast:** Richard Chamberlain, Sharon Stone, Herbert Lom, John Rhys-Davies, Ken Gampu.

Last Action Hero

USA 1993 130 mins

Stateside reviewers were almost unanimous in their condemnation of John McTiernan's blockbusting turkey. *Variety* described it as 'a joyless, soulless machine of a movie'. Box office figures agreed. Ironically, the huge amount of publicity that Arnold Schwarzenegger indulged in to promote the film (with frequent plugs for 'his' new restaurant chain, Planet Hollywood) had an adverse effect: oversold and overkilled, *Last Action Hero* is a wretched mess of genres and ideas that disappoints on every level.

Danny Madigan (Austin O'Brien) is a movie brat with a magic ticket that enables him to enter the action-packed screen world of his hero, Jack Slater (Schwarzenegger). As he and Slater speed from one death-defying situation to the next, Danny attempts to convince his idol that they are both in a make-believe world where the good guys always win, and that Slater is actually no more than a fictional character played by a large Austrian actor named Arnold Schwarzenegger. Naturally, Slater doesn't believe a word, until he and Danny take a trip to the 'real' world, where heroes can die, and the bad guys win a little too often...

Dashing from one action set-piece to another, *Last Action Hero* devotes so much time to chaos and destruction that it forgets that a decent action movie should have at least some kind of story to go with it, and that most important of all, it needs a hero that the audience can root for. Unfortunately, Slater is as wooden as he is invincible, and about as much fun to follow as the back end of a bus. Add to this a failed attempt at self-parody, and it is clear that Schwarzenegger miscalculated the intelligence and devotion of his audience, making an action movie for kids which managed to alienate the entire planet.

Packed with an overwhelming number of star cameos and movie in-jokes, this film within a film within a film (etc. etc.) is so desperately trying to be clever that it just isn't any fun. Not even Charles Dance, who is certainly the film's most entertaining villain (and there are several), coming as he does with an ever-changing novelty glass eye, sheds any light on this gloomy project.

To be fair, the film has its amusing moments (a couple of decent lines, some imaginative killings), but they all deserve to be in a better movie because as it stands, *Last Action Hero* isn't worth watching, not even as a curiosity (could the John McTiernan who directed this mess really be the same man who made *Die Hard*?).

A running joke throughout the movie suggests that Slater can't die until 'the grosses are down'. Well Slater, the grosses are down, so push off.

Director: John McTiernan; **Producers:** Steve Roth, John McTiernan; **Screenplay:** Shane Black, David Arnott; **Production Design:** Eugenio Zanetti; **Editor:** John Wright; **Photography:** Dean Semler; **Music:** Michael Kamen; **Cast:** Arnold Schwarzenegger, F. Murray Abraham, Art Carney, Charles Dance, Frank McRae, Tom Noonan, Robert Prosky, Anthony Quinn, Mercedes Ruehl, Austin O'Brien, Sir Ian McKellen, Professor Toru Tanaka, Joan Plowright.

The Last Boy Scout

USA 1991 105 mins

Joel Silver conjures up a polished, formulaic package of sex, violence, obnoxious behaviour and, since this is a buddy movie, no end of male-bonding rituals. As written by *Lethal Weapon*'s Shane Black, and directed by *Top Gun*'s Tony Scott, *The Last Boy Scout* delivers a bounty of mindless fun, a slickly assembled action thriller with lots of laughs and a staggering body count.

Bruce Willis takes the lead as world-weary gumshoe detective Joe Hallenbeck, a former secret service man (who once saved the life of President Jimmy Carter!) with a killer punch, a lousy life, a face full o' stubble, a smart, sarcastic mouth, an estranged, adulterous wife (Chelsea Field), a superbrat daughter (Danielle Harris) and, finally, a double-murder case which leads him into the pill-popping underworld of pro-football.

Much like Joe, Jimmy Dix (Damon Wayans) has a brilliant career behind him, a former pro-footballer (with 'the best arm in the National League') with a serious drug habit and a dead girlfriend (Halle Berry), courtesy of shady Sheldon Marcone (*Blind Fury*'s Noble Willingham), owner of the LA Stallions and one mean, mercenary son-of-a-bitch.

Joining forces to bag their mutual enemy, Joe and Jimmy argue like crazy as they stomp through a veritable henchman convention, reaching warp speeds during the car chases, never turning from a gunfight, piling up the stunts, and rounding off the madness with a wild stadium finale, gory death and all

Director: Tony Scott; **Producers:** Joel Silver, Michael Levy; **Screenplay:** Shane Black, story by Shane Black, Greg Hicks; **Production Design:** Brian Morris; **Editors:** Stuart Baird, Mark Goldblatt, Mark Helfrich; **Photography:** Ward Russell; **Music:** Michael Kamen; **Cast:** Bruce Willis, Damon Wayans, Chelsea Field, Noble Willingham, Taylor Negron, Danielle Harris, Halle Berry.

Brandon Lee slaps on the foundation in the gothic slaughter-fest, *The Crow*.

Name: LEE, Brandon

Born: Oakland, California, 1965.
Died: 1993

Characteristics: A lot of Bruce, a little Linda:

an American Dragon.

Debut feature: *Kung Fu: The Next Generation*

(TV movie, 1985)

Life and times: Raised in Hong Kong, Brandon Lee was eight years old when his dad, martial arts legend Bruce Lee, died, aged 32, from an allergic reaction to aspirin. Following his father's footsteps into the business, Brandon knocked off a couple of cheapo Eastern action flicks before hitting the US in *Showdown in Little Tokyo* and *Rapid Fire*. Friendly and easy-going in person, comfortable and

Death Becomes Them 13

capable on screen, Brandon had the potential to be as big as Bruce, and, as expected, *The Crow* made him a star, but it was a posthumous honour: Brandon Lee was shot and killed in a freak accident towards the end of production. He was only 28 years old.

Greatest contribution to action movies: The best of both worlds - East meets West in one powerful, likeable package.

Speech, speech: 'I've gotten hit, kicked and punched, I broke my toe, got some stitches in my head, nothing too serious...'.

'None of my friends would come over to the house when I was a kid because they were all scared to death. There would always be six or seven grown men in the backyard screaming and throwing each other around.'

Brandon on Bruce: 'His fans say things like, "Hey, I loved your dad. C'mon, tell the truth - he's still alive, isn't he?"'

Selected filmography: *Legacy of Rage* (1986), *Lazer Mission* (1987), **Soldier of Fortune** (1989), **Showdown in Little Tokyo** (1991), **Rapid Fire** (1992), **The Crow** (1994).

Death Becomes Them 14

Bruce Lee takes a lickin' but keeps on tickin' in the martial arts spectacular, *Enter the Dragon*.

Name: LEE, Bruce

Chinese names: Lee Yuen Kam, Lee Jun Fan ('Gaining Fame Overseas'

Nickname: Lee Siu Yoong ('Little Dragon')

Born: San Francisco, 1940 (Year of the Dragon).

Died: 1973

Characteristics: Disciplined, intense and fighting fit. Screams a lot.

Debut feature: *Marlowe* (1969)

Life and times: Born in San Francisco but raised in Hong Kong, Bruce Lee returned to the States to claim American citizenship when he was 18 years old. Having studied martial arts since childhood, Lee established himself as an instructor, developing a revolutionary new method of Kung Fu known as Jeet Kune Do ('Way of Intercepting Fist'), writing several books on the subject and impressing tournament audiences with regular displays of physical prowess. Hollywood beckoned for the first time in 1967, when Lee was cast as oriental sidekick Kato in the TV adventure series *The Green Hornet*. Unfortunately, the show only lasted a single season, but it was a huge success in Hong Kong, where the series was known as *The Kato Show*. Subsequently, Lee made his first movies in Hong Kong for producer Raymond Chow, breaking more than enough box office records to rekindle Hollywood's interest in his career. *Enter the Dragon* was his first, and only, US feature, a martial arts classic which elevated him to the rank of screen legend. Sadly, three weeks before the film's release, Lee died of a cerebral edema, and while accepted wisdom has it that the swelling of his brain was caused by a severe allergic reaction to aspirin, definitive proof of this diagnosis has never been found. More than 25,000 people attended Lee's funeral in Hong Kong, and when he was finally laid to rest in Seattle, ex-students Steve McQueen and James Coburn served as pallbearers.

Greatest contribution to action movies: In cosmic terms, Lee was to martial arts adventures what the big bang was to the universe: the start of everything, from the modern chop socky flick to the high-kicking action hero.

Speech, speech: 'The martial arts are ultimately self-knowledge. A punch or a kick is not to knock the hell out of the guy in front, but to knock the hell out of your ego, your fear, or your hang-ups.'

Chuck Norris on the secret of Bruce's success: 'Bruce Lee had bad eyesight and one leg that was shorter than the other. But he had a mental image of what he wanted, and he became the quintessential martial artist and the first Chinese superstar in American films.'

Selected filmography: *Fist of Fury* (1972), *The Big Boss* (1972), *The Way of the Dragon* (1973), *Enter the Dragon* (1973).

The Legend of the Seven Golden Vampires

GB/Hong Kong 1974 88 mins

How did the world get by before the days of Kung Fu horror spectaculars? Before rubber bats, vampire masters and freshly re-animated zombies accepted the Eastern arts of stomping, mangling and exaggerated jumping into their sorry, undead lives? There's a special place in B-movie hell reserved for these freak hybrids, bad classics crafted to hilarious imperfection for the late-night cult crowd. Prepare to be terrified beyond the limits of your sanity. To experience sensations of excitement undreampt of in the human experience. To drink deep from the alcoholic well in order to fully appreciate the laugh-your-butt-off foolishness on offer. A paragon of cheesy entertainment, *The Legend of the Seven Golden Vampires* comes direct from B-movie hell for all you trash fans out there.

A bloody, mixed-up masterpiece from Hammer and the Shaw Brothers, this shocking piece of work boasts Peter Cushing's fifth and final appearance as fearless vampire hunter Van Helsing, who, in 1904, heads East to deal with an evil, immortal Chinese warlord (who is, in fact, his old pal Dracula) and his bloodsucking chums. Once in China, Van hooks up with a family of martial artists, seven brothers out for revenge, each man a living tribute to a different deadly weapon (there's axe guy, sword guy, spear guy, bow and arrow guy....). Accompanying our heroes as they wander the countryside in search of undead meat, Norwegian set decoration Julie Ege loses clothes throughout the movie, the idea being that while we're drooling over her cleavage we won't notice how lame her actual performance is (fat chance).

Basically, the dry ice is out in force as our heroes battle a variety of otherworldly foes, turning their backs on quality production values and basic common sense in favour of noisy, gory and unintentionally hilarious chaos. A culture clash of styles and ideas, this is madness incarnate, a classic good/bad experience to be savoured and relentlessly mocked.

Director: Roy Ward Baker; **Producers:** Don Houghton, Vee King Shaw; **Screenplay:** Don Houghton; **Production Design:** Johnson Tsau; **Editors:** Chiang Hising-Lung, Chris Barnes; **Photography:** John Wilcox, Roy Ford; **Music:** Wang Fu-Ling, James Bernard; **Cast:** Peter Cushing, David Chang, Shih Szu, Robin Stewart, Julie Ege.

Leon

France/USA 1995 106 mins

Luc Besson's awesome English-language debut is a class act, combining the pace and punch of a top American thriller with a European sense of style and characterisation. Jean Reno takes the lead as a milk-drinking, plant-loving hit man in New York, a role written especially for him by Besson, whose previous work with the actor includes *The Last Battle*, *Subway*, *The Big Blue* and *Nikita* (looks like these two have a Scorsese/De Niro thing going on).

Following the brutal slaying of his white trash neighbours, Léon reluctantly takes in the family's lone survivor, a spirited 12-year-old girl (Natalie Portman) in need of a little stability, even if it does come from a card-carrying killer. Besides, if she makes herself really useful, cleans the place up, teaches Léon to read, maybe then he'll share the tricks of his trade with her. Then she can avenge her family, or at least give it her best shot, as she guns for pill-popping, music-loving DEA psycho Gary 'I like these calm little moments before the storm' Oldman, a scary dude, and no mistake.

Inventive and exciting with some striking visuals, a sharp sense of humour, and a trio of knockout performances, *Léon* provides both a unique and involving central relationship and some jaw-dropping action sequences, including a long and spectacular climax as our eccentric anti-hero faces every law enforcement officer in town. Don't miss out. See this now.

Director: Luc Besson; **Producer:** Gaumont, Les Films du Dauphin; **Screenplay:** Luc Besson; **Production Design:** Dan Weil; **Editor:** Sylvie Landra; **Photography:** Thierry Arbogast; **Music:** Eric Serra; **Cast:** Jean Reno, Natalie Portman, Gary Oldman, Danny Aiello.

Lethal Weapon

USA 1987 110 mins

Superman director Richard Donner and *Predator* producer Joel Silver joined forces to present the ultimate male bonding experience, a genuine 1980s kick-ass action classic/ultra-violent cop thriller/light-hearted, odd-couple, buddy movie supreme. This is how it should be done, people, this is the real thing: if you're tired of settling for bargain-basement garbage just because the action's half-way decent, come see what happens when Hollywood manages to get it right...

Mel Gibson's application for super-stardom earned the official seal of box-office approval once *Lethal Weapon* hit the screens, switching Mad Max for Madder Martin Riggs, a homicidal supercop and ex-Special Forces killer living 'on the ragged edge' since

Danny Glover and Mel Gibson exterminate LA vermin in *Lethal Weapon*.

the death of his wife. Sharing a ramshackle trailer with trusty mutt Sam, Riggs exists on alcohol, nicotine, junk food and self-pity, a chronic Three Stooges fan who contemplates suicide on a nightly basis and, to make matters worse, strolls around in the buff (*à la* Van Damme). By day, Riggs takes out his anger and frustration on the bad guys, terrorizing the poor buggers with a variety of deadly skills, a State-registered 'lethal weapon' with lightning fists, a smokin' gun and a taste for jumping off the roofs of buildings as well as chasing cars on foot.

As for Roger Murtaugh (Danny Glover), a by-the-book homicide detective, well, he's a family man, cautious and domestic, a boat, a house, a wife, a cat and three kids to maintain, just turned fifty and feeling anything but nifty. The last thing he needs is a new partner, especially some gung-ho lunatic with blow-dried hair and a death wish, but that's exactly what he gets, a birthday gift from the LAPD in the form of wild-eyed Martin Riggs. 'I'm too old for this shit', groans Murtaugh, and the fun begins...

Besides all the buddy stuff and seat-of-the-pants miscellaneous action, Riggs and Murtaugh face off against a mercenary army of drug-dealers and assassins led by head honcho General McAllister (Mitchell Ryan), although the true villain of the piece is Mr Joshua, a blond-haired nightmare of henchman engineering played with menace and aggression by Gary Busey, who's never done anything better (the scene with the cigarette lighter, where Joshua proves his loyalty by allowing the general to toast his arm, is a real knockout).

Chemistry is the key, here, and not only up on the screen, but behind the scenes as well. Gibson and Glover make a terrific team, bitching and bonding all the way, while Donner and Silver are clearly in synch over what makes an action movie great, namely a sharp script, decent characters, plenty of violence and a healthy topping of macho bullshit.

Best of all is the climactic one-on-one between Riggs and Joshua as they drop their weapons and duke it out man-to-man in the pouring rain. It's the kind of scene that makes you want to eat red, raw meat, drink beer by the gallon and subscribe to *Soldier of Fortune*. Testosterone rules!

Fu Manchu-man Al Leong, a favourite, familiar face from dozens of classic action flicks, turns up here as Endo, a master torturer who has, according to Mr Joshua, 'forgotten more about dispensing pain than you or I will ever know'. Besides blasting Mel Gibson with electric shocks, the typically mute performer breaks his silence with a full 17 words of dialogue, not counting grunts and groans. Pointless trivia rules!

Sequels: *Lethal Weapon 2, Lethal Weapon 3.*

Director: Richard Donner; **Producers:** Richard Donner, Joel Silver; **Screenplay:** Shane Black; **Production Design:** J. Michael Riva; **Editor:** Stuart Baird; **Photography:** Stephen Goldblatt; **Music:** Michael Kamen, Eric Clapton; **Cast:** Mel Gibson, Danny Glover, Gary Busey, Mitchell Ryan, Tom Atkins, Darlene Love, Traci Wolfe, Steve Kahan, Mary Ellen Trainor.

Lethal Weapon 2

USA 1989 113 mins

Pick a nationality: Germans, Russians, Colombians - all have served the film business well in their capacity as natural born bad guys. You looking for a Nazi? A spy? A drug lord? Shop abroad, my friend, and you won't be disappointed. Only trouble is, the cinema-going public are easily bored and ever-eager for new nationalities to despise. Thanks, then, to white South Africans, who, before dumping Apartheid, were universally despised and proved instantly booable at the movies. Enter actor Joss Ackland, forever typecast as a villain from this moment on, as South African Minister for Diplomatic Affairs, Arjen Rudd, a creepy, slimy, untouchable drug dealer with an appropriately grating accent, all thick and guttural, and an equally nasty right hand henchman, Pieter Vorstedt (Derrick O'Connor), a skinny son-of-a-bitch into killing anything that moves, particularly if they're linked in some way to the good guys (brace yourselves for a sad and unnecessary plot revelation).

All we really need now are a couple of heroes to save the day, and, since their last movie did so terribly well, why not reunite super cops Martin Riggs (mighty Mel Gibson) and Roger Murtaugh (daring Danny Glover) for a second round of *Lethal Weapon* mayhem? Courtesy of director Richard Donner and co-producer Joel Silver, this wild, roller-coaster actioner knows exactly how hot a property it is, and wastes no time in boosting each and every element that made the original movie so popular: from the buddy angle and the humour to the slick style and pace with all the intense ultra-violence you can handle (beware of UK prints, however, hacked to bits by the dastardly censor).

Packed to overflowing with high-speed pursuits, homicidal one-on-ones, squishy deaths (check out the nail gun), outrageous stunts and big-budget destruction, the movie exploits the irresistible chemistry of our odd couple heroes to good effect: Roger's feeling old and thinking of retiring, Martin's not quite on the edge any more, but still about as crazy as a two-for-one pizza sale, and together they set out to demolish Rudd's evil empire, butchering bad guys and picking up co-stars along the way, from bland romantic interest Patsy Kensit (nudity alert) as Rudd's naive Dutch (so we won't hate her) secretary Rika Van Den Haas, to hyperactive comic relief Joe Pesci as self-appointed sidekick Leo Getz (as in, 'Whatever you need, Leo Getz'), a 'creative accountant' with the low-down on Rudd and his cronies.

Add to this an exploding toilet, a collapsible house and a tasty death scene involving two cars and a surf board, and you're on to one hell of an accomplished audience-pleaser. You can't go wrong.

⊕ Incidentally, if you check out what's on TV at the Murtaugh household shortly before daughter Rianne's commercial hits the airwaves, you'll catch a couple of seconds of *Tales From The Crypt*, a spooky anthology show co-produced, as it happens, by Robert Zemeckis, Walter Hill, David Giler AND... Richard Donner and Joel Silver. There. Now you know.

Director: Richard Donner; **Producers:** Richard Donner, Joel Silver; **Screenplay:** Jeffrey Boam, story by Shane Black and Warren Murphy, based on characters created by Shane Black; **Production Design:** J. Michael Rita; **Editor:** Stuart Baird; **Photography:** Stephen Goldblatt; **Music:** Michael Kamen, Eric Clapton, David Sanborn; **Cast:** Mel Gibson, Danny Glover, Joe Pesci, Joss Ackland, Derrick O'Connor, Patsy Kensit, Darlene Love, Traci Wolfe, Steve Kahan, Mary Ellen Trainor.

Lethal Weapon 3

USA 1992 118 mins 🔫 🔫 🔫

Fuelled by action, comedy and macho male-bonding, The Lethal Weapon Express was a force to be reckoned with, charging, as it did, through a duo of blockbusting cop thrillers which reminded viewers just how entertaining violence could be. For its third journey, however, drivers Donner and Silver flicked the auto-pilot switch and aimed it through all the same old territory, watching in horror as it slowly ran out of steam and ground to a halt long before the end. Reliant on formula and the loyalty of existing fans, *Lethal Weapon III* rarely rises above the average, carelessly exploiting each and every element that made the series great, only this time around the comedy seems laboured, the buddy element overdone and the action set-pieces routine. That's not to say that this is a bad movie, just that we've come to expect more from a *Lethal Weapon* flick. Basically, we're looking at a chronic case of 'been there, done that; not bad, but not good enough'.

With his house up for sale and the bliss of retirement only eight days away, the last thing Murtaugh (Danny Glover) needs is an explosive final case to shake up his plans. This, therefore, is exactly what happens, as he and action man partner Riggs (Mel Gibson) hit the trail of crooked ex-cop Jack Traven (*No Escape*'s Stuart Wilson), a dastardly piece of work selling guns with cop-killing, armour-piercing bullets to street gangs.

In other news, we find that Leo Getz (Joe Pesci) is back, this time as the estate agent roped into flogging Murtaugh's house, eager as ever to lend sidekick support no matter how badly our heroes treat him. Meanwhile, back at the station, gorgeous ex-model and *In the Line of Fire* co-star Rene Russo steals the show as Internal Affairs Detective Lorna Cole, tough, assured and sexier than the Barbi Twins in the Emperor's new clothes. Besides offering Riggs some spirited romantic interest (with a wacky game of 'I'll show you my scar, if you show me yours'), head butts and spin kicks confirm that Lorna's one gal who knows how to take care of herself, a kick-ass heroine in league with *T2*'s Linda Hamilton and *Aliens*' Sigourney Weaver.

Opening with a bang and getting straight down to business with a cool armoured car chase, the movie offers plenty of gunplay and frantic, one-on-one martial artistry, yet the odds are against the edge of your seat making contact with your backside. You won't be bored by it, but you will, more than likely, feel a twinge of disappointment that relegates this third and final effort into the realms of the standard, non-essential actioner.

⊕ After almost 20 years of cinematography work on the likes of *Die Hard*, *Black Rain* and *Lethal Weapon 3*, Dutch-born Jan De Bont turned director with a vengeance, proving his worth with the blockbusting *Speed*. As for this movie, don't be in such a hurry when the credits start to roll, and your patience will be rewarded.

Director: Richard Donner; **Producers:** Richard Donner, Joel Silver; **Screenplay:** Jeffrey Boam, Robert Mark Kamen, based on characters created by Shane Black; **Production Design:** James Spencer; **Editors:** Robert Brown, Battle Davis; **Photography:** Jan De Bont; **Music:** Michael Kamen, Eric Clapton, David Sanborn; **Cast:** Mel Gibson, Danny Glover, Joe Pesci, Rene Russo, Stuart Wilson, Steve Kahan, Darlene Love, Traci Wolfe, Mary Ellen Trainor.

Licence to Kill

GB 1989 133 mins

The moment we made friends with Russia, the Bond series was forced to re-invent itself. No more cold war, no more spy vs spy. A new breed of villain was required, someone we could hate as much as the commie trash of yesteryear. Having supplied action movies with bad guys for more than 20 years, the drug trade came to the rescue with a ruthless Latin American cocaine king, Franz Sanchez (Robert Davi), a nasty piece of work with all the hardware, henchmen and female adornments you'd expect from a Bond villain.

A straightforward revenge saga with all the trimmings, *Licence to Kill* has James (Timothy Dalton on a bad hair day), not quite as soft and politically correct as he was last time around, pursuing the scum who fed his best CIA buddy, Felix Leiter (David Hedison, who first played the role in *Live and Let Die*), to the sharks. Infiltrating Sanchez's organization with the help of surrogate uncle Q (Desmond Llewelyn), leggy CIA pilot Pam Bouvier (Carey Lowell) and stunning airhead Lupe Lamora (Talisa Soto), Bond messes with the likes of sleazy underling Milton Krest (Anthony Zerbe), double-crossing drug enforcement agent Killifer (Everett McGill), crooked TV evangelist (is there any other kind?) Joe Butcher (Wayne Newton) and wild-eyed killer Dario (Benicio Del Toro) before focusing on Mr Big with a manic, *Mad Max*-style mountain chase as our outlaw hero pursues a convoy of oil tankers loaded with nose candy...

The other action set-piece worth looking out for comes much earlier in the movie, a nautical stunt-fest with a wacky, water-skiing punchline, as James mounts a one-man assault on Krest's forces, in, under and high above the 'research vessel' Wavekrest.

Enjoyable, if not especially memorable, *Licence To Kill* vastly improves upon Dalton's first and only other Bond adventure, *The Living Daylights*.

The end of *Licence to Kill*. But James Bond will return in *Goldeneye*.

Director: John Glen; **Producers:** Albert R. Broccoli, Michael G. Wilson; **Screenplay:** Michael G. Wilson, Richard Maibaum; **Production Design:** Peter Lamont; **Editor:** John Grover; **Photography:** Alec Mills; **Music:** Michael Kamen, title song performed by Gladys Knight; **Cast:** Timothy Dalton, Carey Lowell, Robert Davi, Talisa Soto, Anthony Zerbe, Frank McRae, Wayne Newton, Desmond Llewelyn, David Hedison, Robert Brown, Caroline Bliss.

Live and Let Die

GB 1973 121 mins

Connery was out of the picture, but Bond would survive. Selected by producers Broccoli and Saltzman, debonair TV hero Roger Moore joined the series. Unlike Lazenby, however, Moore didn't try to copy Sean. Instead, he played Bond on his own terms, altering the role to make it a lighter, more comical, much less macho secret agent. As the 1970s wore on, the series grew more spectacular, funnier, flashier and more reliant on gadgetry, and while Connery would have felt out of place, Moore simply went with the flow and enjoyed himself.

As 007, licence to clown, Moore battles drug dealer Kananga (*Alien*'s Yaphet Kotto) all the way from New York City to the exotic island of San Monique, in the Caribbean. Agents are being killed, poppies are being harvested, and voodoo is in the air. Helping Kananga conquer the world with drugs, henchmen Tee Hee (Julius H. Harris), Whisper (Earl Jolly Brown) and Samedi (Geoffrey Holder) gun for Bond while beautiful fortune teller Solitaire (Jane Seymour), whose mystic powers Kananga exploits, needs rescuing - and fast - from her virginity. Meanwhile, treacherous airhead Rosie Carver (Gloria Hendry) helps our hero usher in a brave new era of sexist behaviour, as she sleeps with James and then reacts with horror as he pulls a gun on her: 'But you wouldn't, you couldn't, not after what we just done...' she pleads. 'I certainly wouldn't have done it before!' replies our randy role model in this hilarious, defining James Bond moment.

Better still, *Goldfinger* director Guy Hamilton packs the movie full of action, from an incredible speedboat chase through narrow Bayou waterways (introducing redneck Louisiana Sheriff J.W. Pepper, as played by Clifton James, comic relief) and a wacky high-speed bus adventure to a blazing final assault on Kananga's island hideout featuring snakes, sharks and the single most painful case of wind ever recorded on film. Best of all, though, is Bond's ingenious 'stepping-stone' escape from a crocodile farm ('Trespassers will be eaten'), a classic moment if ever there was one.

The end of *Live And Let Die*. But James Bond will return in *The Man with the Golden Gun*.

Director: Guy Hamilton; **Producers:** Albert R. Broccoli, Harry Saltzman; **Screenplay:** Tom Mankiewicz, based on the novel by Ian Fleming; **Production Design:** Syd Cain; **Editors:** Burt Bates, Raymond Poulton, John Shirley; **Photography:** Bob Kindred; **Music:** George Martin, title song performed by Paul McCartney and Wings; **Cast:** Roger Moore, Yaphet Kotto, Jane Seymour, Julius H. Harris, Geoffrey Holder, Gloria Hendry, Earl Jolly Brown, David Hedison, Clifton James, Bernard Lee, Desmond Llewelyn, Lois Maxwell.

The Living Daylights

GB 1987 130 mins

Following the old age spectacle of *A View to a Kill*, Roger Moore finally said goodbye to Bondage. In his place, after a lengthy, well-publicised search, Timothy Dalton was sworn in as the fourth official big screen Bond. A talented, reasonably dashing actor, Dalton had lots of potential, but somewhere hidden deep within the Bond formula, tucked away behind the super-villainy, flashy action set pieces, female window dressings and exotic location work, lurked something even more terrifying than Roger Moore's *Octopussy* safari suit: political correctness. Misguided and insidious, it contaminated our hero, transforming him from one of the cinema's few true men into that most hated of freaks, the *new* man: soft, sensitive, thoughtful, kind. Bond still gambled, for himself, and killed, for his country, but somehow you just didn't feel like cheering him on. Serious-minded yet lacking Connery's cynical edge, Bond had lost his cool.

From Eastern Europe to Russian-occupied Afghanistan, 007 follows a trail of bad guys and henchmen from two-faced KGB scoundrel General Koskov (Jeroen Krabbé) to crackpot arms dealer Brad Whitaker (Joe Don Baker), an obnoxious American with military pretensions and a booby-trapped museum reminiscent of Scaramanga's fun house. Czech cellist Kara Milovy (Maryam d'Abo), a slight, almost plain young thing, enjoys Bond's monogamous attentions throughout. Rounding off the cast, Art Malik plays Kamran Shah, leader of a gang of Afghan freedom fighters, John Rhys-Davies turns up as a mysterious KGB General, and, replacing Lois Maxwell as Moneypenny, Caroline Bliss makes her series debut.

Working on auto-pilot, director John Glen cranks out a passable, if unremarkable collection of action set-pieces (a rooftop chase, a prison break, the occasional rebel assault), only rarely rising above the ordinary with a pre-title punch-up (in Gibraltar), a nifty cello chase and some air-bound, stunt-laden shenanigans to finish.

At best, this is an average 007 adventure, moderately entertaining, rarely dull and fairly slick, but Dalton, his hands tied by an over-cautious screenplay, is simply no fun at all.

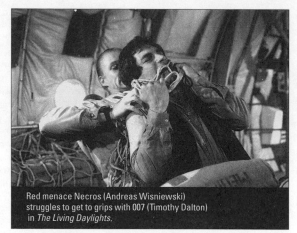

Red menace Necros (Andreas Wisniewski) struggles to get to grips with 007 (Timothy Dalton) in *The Living Daylights.*

The end of *The Living Daylights*. But James Bond will return in *Licence To Kill*.

Director: John Glen; **Producers:** Albert R. Broccoli, Michael G. Wilson; **Screenplay:** Richard Maibaum, Michael G. Wilson; **Production Design:** Peter Lamont; **Editors:** John Grover, Peter Davies; **Photography:** Arthur Wooster; **Music:** John Barry, title song performed by a-ha; **Cast:** Timothy Dalton, Maryam d'Abo, Jeroen Krabbe, Joe Don Baker, John Rhys-Davies, Art Malik, Desmond Llewelyn, Robert Brown, Caroline Bliss.

Lone Wolf McQuade

USA 1983 107 mins

Chuck's just been beaten to within an inch of his life, dumped in his jeep, shoved into a big hole and buried under quick drying cement. No problem. He finds a beer under his seat, struggles to open the can, pours the contents over his head, presumably to wake himself up, and sets to hot-wiring his super-charged cop car. Suddenly, the engine roars to life, Chuck stamps down on the accelerator and shoots out of the cement, diving to the ground before wasting a couple of bad guys with a spray of bullets.

Serves 'em right for messing with a man hard enough to cut glass, a veteran good guy who races to the rescue, gets there just in time, and gives the enemy a damn good thrashing, fighting until there's no one left alive but himself and the odd sidekick.

The name's Norris, Mr Norris, and this time he's scruffy Texas Ranger J.J. McQuade, a sharp-shooting 'lone wolf' lumbered with a new partner, a squeaky-clean native American Indian named Kayo (*Star Trek: Voyager*'s Robert Beltran), whose job it is to remind McQuade of the rules every now and then. Predictably, though, it doesn't work out that way, and pretty soon Kayo's with the program, breaking noses and torturing suspects with the best of 'em, helping J.J. track down and cut a few new holes in scumbag arms dealer Rawley Wilkes (*Kung Fu*'s David Carradine), who fancies himself as a bit of a martial arts expert and gives our hero a run for his money during a lengthy final showdown (although in 'real life', Chuck once remarked that 'David Carradine is about as good a martial artist as I am an actor', leaving us to draw our own conclusions).

Elsewhere, there's an ex-wife, a daughter in distress, a midget crime boss, a retired Ranger and a gung ho FBI agent all vying for our attention, desperate to distract us from a sappy, time-wasting romantic subplot involving Chuck and Nicaraguan temptress Barbara Carrera, a shameless over-actress who clutches gushing hosepipes while snogging and manages to slow down every single scene she appears in.

Director Steve Carver provides the movie with the grainy look and hard-bitten feel of a spaghetti western, stumbling through the humour, drama and particularly the romance (which should have been cut entirely, an oversight you can put right with the help of your trusty fast-forward button), but scoring with a variety of action set-pieces which allow Chuck to demonstrate the full range of his destructive abilities.

Director: Steve Carver; **Producers:** Yoran Ben-Ami, Steve Carver; **Screenplay:** B.J. Nelson, story by H. Kaye and B.J. Nelson; **Production Design:** Norm Baron; **Editor:** Anthony Redman; **Photography:** Roger Shearman; **Music:** Francesco De Masi; **Cast:** Chuck Norris, David Carradine, Barbara Carrera, Leon Isaac Kennedy, Robert Beltran, L.Q. Jones, R.G. Armstrong, Sharon Farrell, Dana Kimmell, Daniel Frishman.

Death Becomes Them 15

Name: LUNDGREN, Dolph

Born: Sweden, 1959

Characteristics: The Addams Family's Lurch, with a tan.

Debut feature: *A View To A Kill* (1985).

Dolph 'He-Man' Lundgren suns himself in the most violent children's movie ever made, *Masters of the Universe.*

Life and times: A Karate whiz with a master's degree in chemical engineering, Dolph Lundgren didn't plan on a movie career: while visiting girlfriend Grace Jones on the set of Roger Moore's final Bond flick, *A View to a Kill*, Lundgren was asked to fill in for a background heavy who had failed to show up. Later that year, he strapped on a Russian accent and pummelled the Italian Stallion in *Rocky IV.* Given his size and monosyllabic delivery, a career in B-movie action adventures was inevitable.

Greatest contribution to action movies: Nothing much to shout about here, but he did look good wearing a necklace of human ears in *Universal Soldier*, his only decent movie.

Speech, speech: 'I usually pick up a scar a movie.'

'My problem is that people get intimidated by someone big and beautiful like me. They hate to think I can be smart as well.'

'When I get a script I make sure that my character doesn't get badly injured in the first three reels, because then you have to limp all the way through. The last reel, yeah, go for it, blood everywhere.'

Selected filmography: *A View to a Kill* (1985), *Rocky IV* (1985), **Masters of the Universe** (1987), **The Punisher** (1989), **Red Scorpion** (1989), *Dark Angel* (1990), *Cover Up* (1990), **Universal Soldier** (1992), **Joshua Tree** (1993), *Pentathalon* (1994), **The Shooter** (1995), *Johnny Mnemonic* (1995), *Meltdown* (1995).

Mad Max

Australia 1979 90 mins

Director George Miller made his movie debut with this low-budget action classic, a fuel-injected explosion of in-your-face ultra-violence and twisted Ozzie humour. From the moment the movie starts, death and destruction reign supreme, fast, loose and wild at heart. You haven't seen a car chase till you've seen *Mad Max*.

The future is a desolate, dangerous place. Roving gangs of fearless psychos patrol Australia's streets and highways in souped-up autos and customized hogs, terrorizing the weak and innocent for fun and profit. A small band of cops do the best that they can, chasing and wasting the scum of the earth, but they're fighting a losing battle: society is screwed, and there's nothing anyone can do about it. Tired of the fight, daredevil cop Max (Mel Gibson) quits the force for the sake of his wife and child, but a startling personal tragedy forces him back on the road to Hell for a series of death-defying confrontations with the evil, brutal Toecutter (Hugh Keays-Byrne) and his lunatic gang.

With miles and miles of road to ruin, George Miller dishes out one high-speed pursuit after another, pushing the pedal to the metal as incredible stuntwork harvests a staggering variety of smashes and pile-ups. As for Max, a baby-faced tough guy with a turbocharged, Interceptor cop car, he gets to take us along for the ride.

Sequels: *Mad Max 2*, *Mad Max Beyond Thunderdome*

Director: George Miller; **Producer:** Byron Kennedy; **Screenplay:** James McCausland, George Miller, story by George Miller, Byron Kennedy; **Production Design:** Jon Dowding; **Editors:** Tony Paterson, Cliff Hayes; **Photography:** David Eggby; **Music:** Brian May; **Cast:** Mel Gibson, Joanne Samuel, Roger Ward, Steve Bisley, Tim Burns, Hugh Keays-Byrne.

Mad Max 2 (aka The Road Warrior)

Australia 1981 94 mins

This is what we want to see. No law. No order. No respect for life. Just a whole bunch of crazy, dangerous bad guys in a post-apocalyptic wasteland where only the violent survive. From director George Miller comes the ultimate in road-bound chaos, a classic cult adventure featuring some of the most incredible stuntwork you're ever likely to see, and a grimly determined hero who's just as crazy as the scum he exterminates.

Survival is the name of the game, and no one plays it better than Max (Mel Gibson). A lifetime ago he was a baby-faced cop with a family. These days he's a man of mystery, a road warrior with nothing to live for but life itself.

The most precious commodity on earth is oil. Everything else, even food, takes second place. Without oil, everyone would have to chase each other on foot, and that's not nearly as much fun as watching a guy fly off his bike at 100mph. Meanwhile, in the middle of nowhere, the inhabitants of a fortified oil refinery are desperately fending off the freakish forces of the hockey-masked Humungus (Kjel Nilsson), '...the warrior of the wasteland, the Ayatollah of rock 'n' rolla', a mean, menacing dude who wants their gasoline, and won't take no for an answer.

Only Max can save the day, a hero for hire who helps even the odds for our oil-rich pals, clashing time and again with the Humungus and his pet henchman, Wez (as played by the irrepressible Vernon Wells, dressed in black leather bondage gear with a red Mohican haircut), a hyperactive, psychopathic, endlessly homicidal maniac. You gotta love him.

Grungy, inventive and gloriously uncivilized, this peerless tribute to death and destruction builds to a totally awesome, action-packed finale as Max leads a getaway convoy in an armoured tanker loaded with gas, assisted from above by the eccentric Giro Captain (Bruce Spence), and pursued from every angle by the meanest sons-of-bitches ever born.

By far the most exciting of Max's three adventures, this is also one of the greatest action movies ever made. Prepare to be blown away.

Director: George Miller; **Producer:** Byron Kennedy; **Screenplay:** Terry Hayes, George Miller, Brian Hannant; **Production Design**: Graham 'Grace' Walker; **Editors:** David Stiven, Tim Wellburn, Michael Balson; **Photography:** Dean Semler; **Music:** Brian May; **Cast:** Mel Gibson, Bruce Spence, Mike Preston, Max Phipps, Vernon Wells, Emil Minty, Kjell Nilsson.

Mad Max Beyond Thunderdome
Australia 1985 106 mins

Max hits rock bottom in his third and final adventure, a paceless bore with a rotten plot and way too much money to spend. Any improvements are strictly cosmetic, surface gloss from Norma Moriceu's striking costumes to Graham Walker's ambitious sets, but the movie itself lacks any kind of edge, a flat and uninspired adventure which plays it soft and safe, two words that should never have been associated with a *Mad Max* feature.

An ambitious yet misguided plot leads our hero to Bartertown, a post-apocalyptic trading post run by the statuesque Aunty Entity (Tina Turner, making her big screen debut in a chainmail dress with high-rise shoulder pads). It is here that Max ends up in the Thunderdome, a gladiatorial arena where arguments are settled on a permanent basis. Two men enter, one man leaves: in this case, Max takes on a solid mass of flesh and leather known as Blaster (Paul Larrson). This is the best scene in the movie (although it does end on a rather soppy note), so make the most of it. Anyway, one thing leads to another and Max is banished from Bartertown, packed off into the desert to die. Then along comes a nomadic tribe of children and boy, the movie just grinds to a halt. A *Mad Max* movie should be a ferocious, cutting edge experience. Cute and whimsical should not enter into the equation.

Rounding off the movie (and not a moment too soon) is a passable but hardly original chase scene (ripped straight out of *Mad Max 2*) as Max flees the enemy in a train (as opposed to an oil tanker).

It's a shame the series had to end so poorly, but we'll always have the first two movies, so ignoring this one shouldn't be too hard.

Directors: George Miller, George Ogilvie; **Producer:** George Miller; **Screenplay:** Terry Hayes, George Miller; **Production Design:** Graham 'Grace' Walker; **Editor:** Richard Francis-Bruce; **Photography:** Dean Semler; **Music:** Maurice Jarre; **Cast:** Mel Gibson, Tina Turner, Helen Buday, Frank Thring, Angelo Rossitto, Bruce Spence, Robert Grubb, Angry Anderson, George Spartels, Edwin Hodgeman, Paul Larrson, Adam Cockburn.

Trivialists 3

HALL OF FAME
Action classics, the best of the best...

1. *Die Hard*
2. *Raiders of the Lost Ark*
3. *RoboCop*
4. *Commando*
5. *Enter the Dragon*
6. Star Wars

Magnum Force

USA 1973 124 mins

Clint Eastwood, long may he reign, returns for a second round of law and disorder as 'Dirty' Harry Callahan, only this time around it's another group of cops who take law enforcement too far. Endlessly at odds with the consummately uptight Lieutenant Briggs (Hal Holbrook), a pencil pushing bureaucrat who brags about never having taken his gun out of its holster, Harry shoots off his mouth as often as his .44 Magnum, making friends, influencing people, and shooting them from long distances.

Word has it that a gang of San Francisco's finest have been rubbing out hordes of so-called 'untouchable' criminals, from pimps and drug dealers to mobsters who believe they are above the law. Only trouble is, killing in cold blood is technically illegal, so Harry's on the case, sniffing out corruption in the SFPD, and blowing messy, gaping holes in whoever he finds wanting.

Faced with the unenviable position of following director Don Siegel's original, Ted Post makes the most of Briggs and Callahan's supremely antagonistic relationship, spicing up the movie elsewhere with plenty of miscellaneous action, from an hilarious aeroplane hijacking sequence to that time-honoured staple of action flicks, the convenience store bust. Best of all though, is an extended dockland chase scene, fast and noisy, with an explosion to round things off as Harry takes 'em on one at a time.

Budding talent abounds in *Magnum Force*. Not only was the film co-written by John (*Conan the Barbarian, Red Dawn*) Milius and Michael (*The Deer Hunter, Year of the Dragon*) Cimino, but it co-stars *RoboCop*'s Felton Perry as Harry's partner Early, as well as future TV cop David Soul (*Starsky and Hutch*) and future TV detective Robert Urich (*Vegas, Spencer for Hire*) as a pair of eager young cops.

Director: Ted Post; **Producer:** Robert Daley; **Screenplay:** John Milius, Michael Cimino; **Production Design:** Jack Collis; **Editor:** Ferris Webster; **Photography:** Frank Stanley; **Music:** Lalo Schifrin; **Cast:** Clint Eastwood, Hal Holbrook, Mitchell Ryan, David Soul, Felton Perry, Robert Urich.

The Man with the Golden Gun

GB 1974 125 mins

The world's in no particular danger, but James is. A million dollar hitman, the superfluously-nippled Scaramanga (Christopher Lee), is planning the crowning achievement of a brilliant career: the death of 007. Naturally, our secret agent hero has to visit a variety of exotic locations (Bangkok, Hong Kong, Macau...), battle a handful of eccentric henchmen and bed every female in town before facing his latest arch-enemy for a climactic 'fun house' duel on a secret island hideout. A solar-powered subplot throws a laser gun into the mix, but no matter what the movie lobs our way, there's no escaping the fact that this is one of Bond's least inspired outings, routine in the extreme, a feeble effort from a director (Guy Hamilton, the man behind *Goldfinger*, *Live and Let Die* and other Bond classics) who should have known better.

This time around, however, it's the bad guy who has all the gadgets, from a flying car (Chitty Chitty Bang Bang had more style, though) to the film's one impressive creation, a golden gun assembled from a cigarette case, a ball point pen, a cuff link and a lighter (with a bullet hidden in Scaramanga's belt).

Of the cast, Moore is simply adequate, which is more than you can say for Bond girl Britt Ekland (as Mary Goodnight), a scrawny, flighty thing with the sex appeal of a box of popcorn. Secondary love interest Maud Adams, as Scaramanga's mortally terrified bit-on-the-side, is a good deal more alluring. Lee, meanwhile, escapes the movie with his reputation intact, a characteristically sophisticated, menacing performance from Hammer's greatest Dracula. Finally, and perhaps most memorably, *Fantasy Island*'s Hervé Villechaize ('The plane, boss, the plane!') steals much of the show as Lee's right hand midget, Nick Nack.

From the flared clothing to the funky, tacky theme tune (courtesy of Lulu), *The Man with the Golden Gun* stands as a testament to 1970s kitsch. It's watchable enough, with a silly chop socky sequence, a surprise appearance from *Live and Let Die*'s Sheriff J.W. Pepper (Clifton James) and a wacky somersault car stunt helping to pass the time, but why settle for second best?

The end of *The Man With the Golden Gun*. But James Bond will return in *The Spy Who Loved Me*.

Director: Guy Hamilton; **Producers:** Harry Saltzman, Albert R. Broccoli; **Screenplay:** Tom Mankiewicz, Richard Maibaum, based on the novel by Ian Fleming; **Production Design:** Peter Murton; **Editors:** John Shirley, Raymond Poulton; **Photography:** Ted Moore, Oswald Morris; **Music:** John Barry, title song performed by Lulu; **Cast:** Roger Moore, Christopher Lee, Britt Ekland, Maud Adams, Hervé Villechaize, Bernard Lee, Desmond Llewelyn, Lois Maxwell, Clifton James.

Marked for Death

USA 1990 94 mins

Once again, Steven Seagal fails to suppress his natural instincts to maim, kill and destroy, and it's just as well because emotional depth doesn't suit him at all. Witness his confessional scene: 'I've lied, slept with informants, I've taken drugs, I've falsified evidence, I did whatever I had to do to get the bad guys.' Fair enough, but there's more. 'Then I realized something, that I had become what I most despised.' Boy, what a crock. Truth is, as retired Drug Enforcement Agent John Hatcher, he can't wait to get back in the game. After all, who among us could resist the urge to inflict grievous bodily harm upon others if we were officially sanctioned to do so by our President? Certainly not Hatcher, who rather sensibly leaves his brain to one side as he guns for a gang of spooky Jamaican drug dealers who plan to use their voodoo hoodoo on our hero and his family.

Co-writer Seagal has a ball with this one, running rampant through the scum-lined streets of Chicago and Jamaica, blasting, slashing and, yes, even decapitating his way to justice, ever vigilant for an opportunity to practise his own special brand of sadistic martial arts upon one sacrificial lamb after another. In the opposing corner, meanwhile, stands black magic maniac Screwface (Basil Wallace), a crime boss so pant-fillingly scary that his underlings would rather die than cross him.

Director Dwight Little allows chaos and violence to share centre stage, steering clear of common sense while dashing at kamikaze speeds through a rich maze of voodoo rituals, gratuitous nudity, casual murder and inconsequential supporting characters (tough high school coach Keith David, token black cop Tom Wright, token love interest Joanna Pacula).

For talking less and killing more. For embarking on a hugely destructive car chase which works its way through, rather than around, Chicago's unwitting pedestrians. For kicking butt and breaking bones when a stern word and a set of handcuffs might have sufficed. For all this nonsense and more, we can thank the pony-tailed wonder for what must be the best of his early movies.

Director: Dwight H. Little; **Producers:** Michael Grais, Mark Victor, Steven Seagal; **Screenplay:** Michael Grais, Mark Victor; **Production Design:** Robb Wilson King; **Editor:** O. Nicholas Brown; **Photography:** Ric Waite; **Music:** James Newton Howard; **Cast:** Steven Seagal, Joanna Pacula, Keith David, Basil Wallace, Tom Wright.

Martial Law

USA 1990 89 mins

Have you noticed how difficult it is for villains to hold onto their guns in martial arts pictures? It seems the second they brandish a piece, a chop or a kick comes from nowhere to disarm them, and they then have no choice but to fight hand-to-hand. And it's a good job too, because if a villain was born who had the good sense to shoot first, from a safe distance, and ask questions later, the streets would be lined with the corpses of action heroes.

Of course, there'll always be a couple of evil psychos per feature who are capable of giving the good guys a run for their money, but on the whole the majority of B-movie bad boys are as slow as they are ugly, and none too bright as well. Take a scene from *Martial Law*, a cheapo action thriller in which a gang of thugs manage to disarm our heroes only to blow their advantage by taunting the leading man with the question, 'What are you going to do now, tough guy?' As if we didn't know. Boy, these guys are dumb. Don't they realize they're in a martial arts movie? That within seconds of their smart remark they'll be choking on their own teeth? They never learn, and god bless them for that, because watching them suffer is just about the only thing that makes movies like this bearable.

So what's this one all about? Well, blink and you'd miss the story, but basically we have trouble-shooter cops Sean Thompson (Chad McQueen) and Billie Blake (Cynthia Rothrock) hunting down a killer who can stop a man's heart with a single punch. He also deals in stolen cars, employs none other than Sean's delinquent kid brother and, would you believe it, looks a hell of lot like David Carradine. Fists fly and cars are chased as director S.E. Cohen runs his cast through all the predictable paces, each scene looking much the same as the last, although Carradine's one-on-one with Professor Toru Tanaka is fairly memorable, and Rothrock, besides being a terrific little fighter, is a real cutie when she gets angry.

As for Chadwick Steven McQueen, son of the immortal Steve, well, he might be able to fight, but when it comes to screen presence and charm he falls way short of the mark. At 30 years old he looks like a chubby little schoolboy, no matter how cool or hard he tries to play it. Still, he's not the worst thing in the movie. That honour must surely go to actor Philip Tan for playing Carradine's cockney henchman, Wu Han. With an accent as fake as Dick Van Dyke's in *Mary Poppins* (better make that *Meery Paw-Pyns*) and Brion James' in *Tango & Cash,* Tan degrades himself with such choice cuts of dialogue as 'I fink 'e's a wenker' and 'go on guvner, kick 'is 'ed in!' Prepare yourself for an excess of unintentional stupidity. You have been warned.

Sequel: *Martial Law 2: Undercover.*

Director: S.E. Cohen; **Producer:** Kurt Anderson; **Screenplay:** Richard Brandes; **Production Design:** James R. Shumaker; **Editor:** Michael Thibault; **Photography:** John Huneck; **Music:** Elliot Solomon; **Cast:** Chad McQueen, Cynthia Rothrock, David Carradine, Andy McCutcheon, Philip Tan, Tony Longo.

Masters of the Universe

USA 1987 106 mins

From the toy shops he came, blond and muscle-bound, slayer of demons and self-appointed moral guardian of our young. Slash! 'Keep away from drugs.' Bang! 'Don't talk to strangers.' Wallop! 'Never tell a lie.' Hero to a generation of youthful consumers, He-Man flexed his way through a series of animated adventures, each week introducing a new range of heroes, villains and souped-up vehicles which, regular as clockwork, managed to appear on toy store shelves just in time for wide-eyed kids to snap them up. A marketing phenomena of world-wide proportions, *Masters of the Universe* played like a show but read like an advert and parted parents from their cash for a good couple of years before the Next Big Thing came along and stole He-Man's fickle audience.

Then came Cannon's live-action contribution to the franchise, a glossy fantasy starring monosyllabic Dolph Lundgren, an action adventure designed to breath new life into the series and return the gravy train to the fast track. Rather than act as a lifesaver, however, all the film managed to achieve was the further derailment of He-Man and his tired old chums.

Back on Eternia, the battle between He-Man (Lundgren) and Skeletor (Frank Langella) rages on, only this time around a handy piece of hardware known as the Cosmic Key transports our hero and a selection of sidekicks to modern day America, a plot twist you'll find listed under 'Hopeless Gimmicks'. Befriending a couple of teenagers (*Star Trek: Voyager*'s Robert Duncan McNeill and *Friends*' Courteney Cox) while searching for a way back home, He-Man is continually interrupted by wave after wave of expendable foes, all sent to earth by Skeletor, who comes to believe that if you want a job done right, you have to do it for yourself...

Swords clash, lasers blast and special effects rule as He-Man and company struggle to save the universe, while director Gary Goddard labours to ensure that whatever else his film is lacking, there is, at the very least, no shortage of action (for what it's worth). As bland and mediocre as the original series, *Masters of the Universe* makes a whole lot of noise and destroys everything in sight, but just isn't any fun. He-Man go home.

Director: Gary Goddard; **Producer:** Menahem Golan, Yoram Globus; **Screenplay:** David Odell, Stephen Tolkin; **Production Design:** William Stout; **Editor:** Anne V.

Coates; **Photography:** Hanania Baer; **Music:** Bill Conti; **Cast:** Dolph Lundgren, Frank Langella, Courteney Cox, James Tolkan, Christina Pickles, Meg Foster, Billy Barty, Robert Duncan McNeill, Jon Cypher, Chelsea Field.

Brainstorms 3

Twenty questions

1. What is Indiana Jones's father afraid of?

2. What does SPECTRE stand for?

3. How long are Spartan and Phoenix frozen for in *Demolition Man*?

4. What are RoboCop's prime directives?

5. What does Remo Williams have in common with Superman?

6. Where does Antonio Banderas keep his weapons in *Desperado*?

7. Who makes Martin Riggs laugh?

8. What is the number of the bus rigged to explode in *Speed*?

9. What is the name of the Voodoo drug lord in *Predator 2*?

10. Who is there a painting of on display in Dr No's lair?

11. Which planet were the aliens from in *Warlords of Atlantis*?

12. What is the name of the designer drug featured in *RoboCop 2*?

13. What is Nino Brown's favourite movie?

14. What does Michael Ironside lose near the end of *Total Recall*?

15. What are the names of all four Musketeers?

16. Who killed Helen Kimble?

17. How does henchman Milo die in *The Last Boy Scout*?

18. How old is Yoda?

19. What is highest rated TV show in 2019?

20. What is the name of the 3-D videogame Bond plays with Largo in *Never Say Never Again*?

Mighty Morphin Power Rangers: The Movie

USA 1995 95 mins

A high-energy adventure which plugs directly into the minds of hyperactive five-year-old kids, the Power Rangers' movie debut offers much the same as their TV show, an upbeat blend of Manga-style action, panto dramatics and alien creatures ripe for merchandizing. Only this time around there's a larger budget at work, boosting the special effects, sets and costumes into orbit, while such absurdities as script development, characterization and plain old common sense remain as secondary as ever.

A brightly-coloured six-pack of disagreeably wholesome do-gooders, the Power Rangers struggle to save their revered leader, Zordon (Nicholas Bell), plus the entire population of Angel Grove, now a big city, from the slimy clutches of evil ham Ivan Ooze (*Raiders of the Lost Ark*'s Paul Freeman), a butt-ugly fiend with a ghastly sense of humour and a hankering for world domination.

Every few minutes our heroes take on a fresh alien menace, eagerly defeating their enemies with a flashy combination of martial arts and gymnastics. When required to act, however, the cast proves less versatile, a series of wild gesticulations accompanying their every spoken word. Dads, meanwhile, can look forward to the arrival of Amazonian warrior Dulcea (Gabrielle Fitzpatrick), a hot bikini babe who offers a few minutes of welcome distraction before turning, inexplicably, into an owl.

Series regulars Bulk (Paul Schrier), Skull (Jason Narvy), Lord Zed (Mark Ginther) and Rita Repulsa (Julia Cortez) all make brief appearances to please the fans, while director Bryan Spicer rounds off the movie with a fairly decent battle between a set of over-sized, metallic insects and the Rangers, all safely strapped into their robotic animal Zords (it makes perfect sense to a three-year-old).

If you're an adult, *Mighty Morphin Power Rangers: The Movie* represents Hell on earth. If you're a kid, it's a slice of heaven. Go figure.

Director: Bryan Spicer; **Producers:** Haim Saban, Shuki Levy, Suzanne Todd; **Screenplay:** Arne Olsen; **Production Design:** Craig Stearns; **Editor:** Wayne Wahrman; **Photography:** Paul Murphy; **Music:** Graeme Revell; **Cast:** Karan Ashley, Johnny Yong Bosch, Steve Cardenas, Jason David Frank, Amy Jo Johnson, Paul Schrier, Jason Narvy, Paul Freeman, Gabrielle Fitzpatrick, Nicholas Bell.

Missing in Action

USA 1984 101 mins

The river is silent, still. For a moment the enemy relax, convinced that they have seen the last of Colonel James Braddock (charming Chuck Norris), Vietcong killer supreme. Suddenly, though, the movie shifts gear to slow motion and, sure enough, our hero bursts from the water, guns blazing, a face full of hate with eyes that scream 'I'll never get tired of killing you guys'. Payback time. The bullets fly and the bad guys die, one, two, three at a time, every bit as fiendish as they were during the war, but simply no match for an action man possessed. As the carnage draws to a close you can almost hear Uncle Sam cheering on the Colonel, confident beyond reason that hell has no fury like a patriotic American packing heat.

John Wayne's fabled *Green Berets* never even came close to the jingoistic heights of flag-waving political incorrectness present in *Missing in Action*, a heavy-handed 'let's do it right this time' adventure in league with the likes of *Uncommon Valour* (which came a year before) and *Rambo II* (which followed a year later).

The war was over, but not everyone went home. Imprisoned in secret jungle camps, American soldiers were made to pay for 'crimes' against the Vietcong, tortured and terrified without relief. Escaping from his captors after seven years of pain, Braddock returned to the States with one clear intention: to go back to Vietnam and rescue his pals, whether his country would help him or not...

Dramatic? No. Involving? Not really. A cracking excuse for violence? A solid Chuck Norris actioner? A film that kills first and asks questions later? That's the ticket. Low quality, high body count, you get the picture. Thicker than a blood-clot milkshake but pretty darn exciting all the same, packed with pesky assassins, dead-eyed soldiers, evil generals, explosive battle sequences and all the hand-to-hand, knife and gun-play you'd expect from the world's favourite Chuckster. Hell, he's even got a turbo-charged, bullet-proof speedboat in this one, a major bonus, even if it does come complete with an army buddy sidekick (portly wonder M. Emmet Walsh).

Determined to share more with his audience than mere death and destruction, *Invasion USA* director Joseph Zito also reaches stunning new heights of sexism, with one particular scene standing out as perhaps the single most gratuitous example of nudity ever seen on film (short of a porno flick, and closely followed by the naked lab chicks in *The Protector*): shortly after forcing information out of a sleazy Bangkok bartender, Chuck strolls out of the joint but the camera sticks with the other guy, who, a single second before the scene comes to an end, is taken by surprise when a naked woman suddenly appears from nowhere, hoisted up onto his bar for absolutely no reason other than to give us all a cheap, sexual thrill. That's not a complaint, of course, just a warning to keep your pause button at the ready so you can catch and appreciate this historic moment to the full.

 Listed among the movie's stuntmen is a gent by the name of J. Claude Van Damme. Coincidence? No way, man.

 Chuck's *Missing In Action* trilogy is a tribute to his younger brother Wieland, who was killed in Vietnam in 1970.

Prequel: *Missing in Action 2: The Beginning*. Sequel: *Braddock: Missing In Action III*.

Director: Joseph Zito; **Producers:** Menahem Golan, Yoram Globus; **Screenplay:** James Bruner, story by John Crowther and Lance Hool, based on characters created by Arthur Silver, Larry Levinson and Steve Bing; **Production Design:** Ladislav Wilheim; **Editor:** Joel Goodman; **Photography:** Joao Fernandes; **Music:** Jay Chattaway; **Cast:** Chuck Norris, M. Emmet Walsh, Lenore Kasdorf, James Hong, David Tress, Ernie Ortega.

Missing in Action 2: The Beginning

USA 1985 96 mins

Chuck Norris takes us back to the bad old days in this slow-starting prequel detailing Braddock's seven-year stretch as a prisoner of war in vengeful Vietnam. Held captive in a top secret camp hidden deep within the jungle, Braddock and his men fight to survive the twisted machinations of evil Colonel Yien (Soon-Teck Oh), a world-class sadist who gets his kicks on route sixty-sick, burning men alive, murdering pet chickens and dealing opium on the side.

When he's not busy elsewhere, Yien wiles away the hours tormenting Braddock, determined to break the spirit of the Ultimate American Hero and force his confession to some bullshit war crimes.' But Braddock is no ordinary man. Hell, even after seven years on rice and leaves in a land rife with disease, he remains as strong and as healthy as a particularly strong and healthy ox. He's so tough, not even a rat in a bag on his face worries him. We're looking at a serious case of 'Too Hard To Die Syndrome', common among movie action men but rarely seen in villains.

'I have repeatedly told you that there is no escape from my camp... unless you consider death an escape', sneers Yien, who you're going to want to see dead. 'You are surrounded by cliffs, mountains, jungles full of man-traps and a bridge that is impassable. None of you have ever escaped... and none of you ever will.' Oh yeah? Wanna bet? Who's to say what might happen if, say, after a melodramatic and vaguely suspenseful first half, the movie suddenly picks up with escapes, jungle battles, fatal beatings and a one-on-one finale with Tien? Hey, it could happen.

Somewhere in the mix you're bound to recognize Sumo lookalike Professor Toru Tanaka, here lending hefty but largely ignored support as a thuggish guard, while actor Steven Williams earns a handful of hisses as sold-out soldier Nester, in league with the enemy for an easier life.

Cheap, bloody and brutal, part exploitation flick, obsessed with cruelty and torture, part serviceable actioner, with GI Chuck doing what comes naturally, *Missing in Action 2: The Beginning* exists in that dark and scary place that only Chuck fans dare enter.

Director: Lance Hool; **Producers:** Menahem Golan, Yoram Globus; **Screenplay:** Arthur Silver, Larry Levinson, Steve Bing; **Production Design:** Michael Baugh; **Editors:** Mark Conte, Marcus Nanton; **Photography:** Jorge Stahl Jr; **Music:** Brian May; **Cast:** Chuck Norris, Soon-Teck Oh, Steven Williams, Bennett Ohta, Cosie Costa, Joe Michael Terry, John Wesley, David Chung, Professor Toru Tanaka.

The Money Train

USA 1995 110 mins

The first time Wesley Snipes and Woody Harrelson worked together was on a minor Goldie Hawn vehicle, *Wildcats*, and neither made much of a lasting impression. The second time they shared the screen, this time as leading men, the results were less than special: a feeble comedy short on laughs, *White Men Can't Jump* did *not* reveal a special chemistry between the two men. A sparkling new partnership had *not* been born. Audiences, too, did *not* cry out for more. Yet here they are again, reunited by director Joseph Ruben in this flimsy, forgettable action comedy.

As New York City transit cops, Wes and Wood play foster brothers John and Charlie, busting subway crime, fighting over women and clashing with their hard-boiled boss (Robert Blake), an obnoxious son-of-a-bitch who threatens to fuck them dead if they get in his way.

Subplots pop up all over the place, but where's the meat? Latino babe Grace Santiago (Jennifer Lopez), newly assigned to the subway, adds spice. Charlie's gambling problem gives John a chance to play 'big brother'. And there's a psycho on the loose (Chris Cooper), torching the employees. Eventually, though, Charlie announces that, rather than fight crime, he has a plan to rip off a fortune and retire in style. Collecting millions of dollars every night from every subway station in town, the money train proves way too tempting for Charlie, and even though John disapproves of the idea, it's plain as a slice of white bread that these two have a date with an extra-special choo-choo.

Delivering a minimum of action and barely a chuckle, *The Money Train* offers nothing new and rarely rises above the ordinary. Even the climactic final stunt, spectacular as it is, fails to save this morally ambiguous, by-the-numbers caper.

For Woody and Wesley, it's a straightforward case of third time unlucky.

Director: Joseph Ruben; **Producers:** Jon Peters, Neil Canton; **Screenplay:** Doug Richardson, David Loughery; **Production Design:** Bill Groom; **Editors:** George Bowers, Bill Pankow; **Photography:** John W. Lindley; **Music:** Mark Mancina; **Cast:** Wesley Snipes, Woody Harrelson, Jennifer Lopez, Robert Blake, Chris Cooper, Joe Grifasi.

Moonraker

GB 1979 126 mins

A shameless science fiction remake of *The Spy Who Loved Me*, *Moonraker* is a crass comic book adventure without a clue. Cashing in on the space craze launched by *Star Wars*, this overblown monster of a movie has no ideas of its own, wholly reliant on a bloated budget ($30 million, nearly as much as the first *eight* Bond movies combined) to smooth over the cracks in the screenplay. Excessive, ridiculous and totally recycled, this is a charmless overdose of gadgetry with barely a scrap of drama or genuine excitement on offer.

Much like Karl Stromberg, billionaire industrialist Hugo Drax is a madman with a mission: to cleanse Earth of humanity and start fresh with a master race. Karl planned to hide out under the ocean. Hugo plans to enjoy the apocalypse from space. Ready to save the world again, Bond and his bird (CIA astronaut Holly Goodhead, aka Lois Chiles) hit the road in search of bad guys to beat on, from California to Venice to Rio, and finally, to the stars for a climactic space station finale.

Having survived a dunk in Stromberg's shark pool, metal-mouthed man-mountain Jaws (Richard Kiel) makes Bondage history as the first henchman to return in a second feature, and though his presence serves to remind us just how similar this film is to the last, it's still kind of fun to see him swept over a waterfall or crushed by a falling building only to pick himself up, dust himself off and head out in to world for more super-villainy. This time around, he is treated to a whole line of dialogue and, because deep down he's not such a bad guy after all, a girlfriend.

Bombarding us with one action sequence after another, director Lewis Gilbert aims for flash over substance, hoping desperately to disguise a total lack of imagination with a variety of expensive window-dressings: Bond's pre-title skydive, a gondola chase, a hugely destructive punch-up in a glass museum, a cable-car slug-a-thon with Jaws, a speedboat chase with a hang-gliding punchline, a cheesy underwater struggle with a giant, rubbery Python and a space-bound, hare-brained laser battle. This all helps to pass the time, but Bond movies are meant to be enjoyed, not survived, and this one falls way short of the mark.

The end of *Moonraker*. But James Bond will return in *For Your Eyes Only*.

Director: Lewis Gilbert; **Producer:** Albert R. Broccoli; **Screenplay:** Christopher Wood, based on the novel by Ian Fleming; **Production Design:** Ken Adam; **Editor:** John Glen; **Photography:** Jean Tournier; **Music:** John Barry, title song performed by Shirley Bassey; **Cast:** Roger Moore, Lois Chiles, Michael Lonsdale, Richard Kiel, Corinne Clery, Toshiro Suga, Bernard Lee, Desmond Llewelyn, Lois Maxwell.

Name: MOORE, Roger

Born: London, 1927

Characteristics: From pretty boy to plastic (surgery) man in 30 years, with eyebrows that belong to the ages.

Roger Moore takes full advantage of co-stars Gloria Hendry (left) and Jane Seymour in his first Bond caper, *Live and Let Die*.

Debut feature: *The Last Time I Saw Paris* (1954)

Life and times: Roger Moore took his first professional steps at MGM during the final days of the studio system, switching tracks to British TV in the name of fame with a trio of popular shows: *Ivanhoe* (1957), *The Saint* (1963-8), and *The Persuaders* (1971). In 1973, Moore inherited the Bond series from Sean Connery, charming his way through seven blockbusting adventures as the smooth secret agent. A likeable, lightweight leading man, Moore's once action-packed career has steadily declined with age.

Greatest contribution to action movies: Bond - The Gadget Years.

Speech, speech: 'My acting range? Left eyebrow raised, right eyebrow raised.'

'I like Bond. But it's silly to take it seriously. It's just a great big comic strip.'

'It used to take them hours and hours in make-up to give me character. Now I've got the character, they take it all out.'

Selected filmography: *Interrupted Melody* (1955), *The Miracle* (1959), *The Sins of Rachel Cade* (1961), *No Man's Land* (1962), *Crossplot* (1969), *The Man Who Haunted Himself* (1970), ***Live and Let Die*** (1973), ***The Man with the Golden Gun*** (1974), *Gold* (1974), *Shout at the Devil* (1976), ***The Spy Who Loved Me*** (1977), ***The Wild Geese*** (1978), ***Escape To Athena*** (1979), ***Moonraker*** (1979), *North Sea Hijack* (1980), *The Sea Wolves* (1980), *The Cannonball Run* (1981), ***For Your Eyes Only*** (1981), ***Octopussy*** (1983), *The Naked Face* (1984), ***A View To A Kill*** (1985), *Bed and Breakfast* (1989), *Bullseye* (1990), *Fire, Ice and Dynamite* (1990), ***The Quest*** (1996).

Mortal Kombat

USA 1995 101 mins

A multi-media assault on the senses, Mortal Kombat's skull-stomping success as the toughest, bloodiest arcade 'beat 'em up' on the face of the planet scared the hell out of parents, teachers and an assortment of liberals who feared the game's corrupting influence (nutters), while, on the flip side, marketing executives went absolutely cash-in crazy, making the most of Midway's digitized baby with a second, and later a third upgraded version of the game, a set of action figures, an animated video and even a live-action stage show.

Complete with finishing moves which allowed players to rip their opponent's hearts out or pull off their heads with the spinal chord still attached, Mortal Kombat rode the band wagon all the way to Hollywood, where grand-scale, feature-length, live-action adaptation awaited. Then *Super Mario Bros* came out, and boy, did it stink. *Street Fighter* followed suit, crashing and burning at the box office, and deservedly so. Suddenly, movie adaptations of video games didn't seem like such a great idea, but then along came *Mortal Kombat* and fanboy faith was restored.

High-energy, ultra-violence for the MTV generation (that means us), this dazzling fantasy adventure combines the pace and invention of Chinese chop socky with the production values of a major Hollywood flick, offering stunning costume and production designs, startling make up and special effects, neatly shot and edited for maximum impact and polished off with a measure of gloss by true Brit Paul Anderson, director of the indie hit *Shopping*.

Following the lead of movies like *Enter the Dragon* and, to a lesser extent, *Bloodsport* and *Kickboxer*, *Mortal Kombat* offers the excuse of a no-holds-barred martial arts tournament to squeeze as much action as possible into the movie. Once a generation the world's greatest fighters gather on a secluded island near Hong Kong, making themselves at home in a shadowy comic book castle and slugging it out for the title of ultimate mortal kombatant. Trouble is, the forces of evil have won nine times in a row, and should they make it to ten, the world (as we know it) will plunge into never-ending darkness, falling prey to demons from another dimension.

Obviously, the planet needs saving, and good god Raiden (Christopher Lambert, bemused, non-violent and off-the-wall) knows exactly what to do, assembling a trio of earthly toughs to play the hero game: LA movie star Johnny Cage (Linden Ashby), Special Forces sweetheart Sonya Blade (Bridgette Wilson) and Bruce Lee wannabe Liu Kang (Robin Shou), eager to avenge the death of his brother at the hands of evil sorcerer and collector of souls Shang Tsung (*Showdown in Little Tokyo*'s Cary-Hiroyuki Tagawa). Elsewhere, fighting for the forces of badness, we have computer enhanced kombat kings Scorpion (Chris Casamassa), Sub-Zero (François Petit), and four-armed monster man Goru, a hulking marvel with more than a few 'flawless victories' to his name.

Surprisingly faithful to the spirit of the game, savage and fast though considerably less bloody, *Mortal Kombat* offers a minimum of story and an excess of action, with one incredible fight scene after another, each one set against an ever-changing backdrop of exotic locations. Best of all is the one-on-one between Johnny Cage and Scorpion, a long and well-choreographed super slug-fest, although Kang's climactic six-on-one finale is pretty darn exciting too. An enthusiastic cast, willing and able to perform their own stunts, provide the icing on the cake. This is prime entertainment, and no mistake, slick and shallow, a good-looking, state-of-the-art fantasy field-day.

Director: Paul Anderson; **Producer:** Lawrence Kasanoff; **Screenplay:** Kevin Droney; **Production Design:** Jonathan Carlson; **Editor:** Martin Hunter; **Photography:** John R. Leonetti; **Music:** George S. Clinton; **Cast:** Linden Ashby, Cary-Hiroyuki Tagawa, Robin Shou, Bridgette Wilson, Christopher Lambert, Talisa Soto, Trevor Goddard, Chris Casamassa, François Petit.

National Lampoon's Loaded Weapon 1

USA 1993 83 mins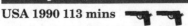

Action flicks come under fire in this cracked hit-and-miss comedy, a sledgehammer satire on cop thrillers in general and the *Lethal Weapon* series in particular. Mad, bad and kinda silly, the movie kicks off with a stock convenience store hold-up scene, as Mel Gibson wannabe Jack Colt (Emilio Estevez) comes to the rescue, blasting the bad guys fifteen feet in the air and straight through a plate glass window, but not before totally trashing the place first.

Having set the tone of the movie early on, it's clear that director Gene Quintano has done his homework and is dedicated to exposing and demolishing every single action cliché and convention there ever was. And he doesn't do too bad a job, either, delivering a solid dose of sub-*Airplane!* style entertainment, although there are those of us who believe that action pictures are already pretty darn funny, and hardly in need of a feature which points out just how dumb they can be (like, have you seen a Seagal movie lately?).

Tortured by the loss of his beloved dog Claire, Jack Colt is a hard-drinking, self-tortured maverick cop, sensitively characterized by the precinct psychologist as 'dangerous, a menace, a loose cannon, a walking time bomb, and most of all... gun happy'. Wes Luger (Samuel L. Jackson), on the other hand, is a responsible family man, a by-the book cop who's only days from retirement and eager to solve the murder of his partner before calling it a day.

What Wes doesn't need is a new partner, especially one of those on-the-edge types, and so naturally he's teamed with Jack and together they investigate piranha-eating, drug-smuggling bad guy General Mortars (William Shatner in ham mode), his henchman Jigsaw (Tim Curry, looking cute as a button in his girl scout outfit), and airhead-in-distress Destiny Demeanor (supermodel Kathy Ireland, great in a *Basic Instinct*-style interrogation scene).

We're not talking classic here, but there are enough decent sight gags, one-liners and celebrity cameos (*CHiPs'* Erik Estrada and Larry Wilcox, Whoopi Goldberg, F. Murray Abraham and a couple of hilarious surprises you're going to have to discover for yourself) to pass the time, and while there really isn't all that much action to speak of, genre fans are likely to be satisfied by the sheer volume of in-jokes cracked exclusively for them.

Director: Gene Quintano; **Producers:** Suzanne Todd, David Willis; **Screenplay:** Don Holley, Gene Quintano; **Production Design:** Jaymes Hinkle; **Editor:** Christopher Greenbury; **Photography:** Peter Dening; **Music:** Robert Folk; **Cast:** Emilio Estevez, Samuel L. Jackson, Tim Curry, Kathy Ireland, William Shatner, Jon Lovitz, Frank McRae.

Navy SEALS

USA 1990 113 mins

Charlie Sheen and Michael Biehn head the cast of this laddish no-brainer, a moderately exciting and endlessly silly tale of hyperactive boys and their ultra-violent toys. Catch the guys at work and at play, killing for a living and screwing around for fun, the best, though maybe not the brightest, gung-ho citizens of the United States of Asskickers. Joined by the likes of *Roxanne*'s Rick Rossovich and *Aliens*' Bill Paxton (here hiding out behind a moustache with barely a thing to say for himself), they're the Navy SEALS (SEa, Air, Land), an elite commando unit of Yankee trouble-shooters ever-ready to parachute, snorkel or charge their way through whatever chaos their country sends them into.

Driven by patriotism and that old, motivational chestnut, revenge, boss man Biehn and the gang take on a bunch of evil, bearded Middle Eastern terrorists who plan to blast Uncle Sam with a quantity of stolen US Stinger Missiles. The cads. They need sorting out, alright, and who better than the Navy's trained SEALS to teach them a lesson in death and destruction?

As for the players (a lifeless bunch at best), Sheen makes the most noise as Hawkins, a major macho bullshit artist with all the maturity of a processed cheese square, an adrenaline junkie with a high-school mentality who, at one point, jumps out of a speeding car, over a bridge and into a river for kicks. By comparison, Curran (Biehn) is a total square, thoughtful, responsible and probably a little too grown up for his own good, although he does get to have some fun in the arms of a half-Lebanese reporter played (but only just) by Joanne Whalley-Kilmer.

Shallow emotions run throughout, a passionless romance here, some meaningless soul-searching there, a familiar package of formula feelings mishandled by a cast of mental dwarfs. Never mind, though. The good news is that, for all intents and purposes, this is a film about combat, not emotions, no matter how many time-wasting, pace-dragging subplots director Lewis Teague hangs on the movie. Fuelled by mindless heroics and flashy pyrotechnics, the movie scrapes by with a number of lengthy GI Joe battle sequences, offering a minimum wage of entertainment which stands somewhere between 'acceptable if you're desperate' and 'not really worth the effort'.

Director: Lewis Teague; **Producers:** Brenda Feigen, Bernard Williams; **Screenplay:** Chuck Pfarrer, Gary Goldman; **Production Design:** Guy J. Comtois, Veronica Hadfield; **Editor:** Don Zimmerman; **Photography:** John A. Alonzo; **Music:** Sylvester Levay; **Cast:** Charlie Sheen, Michael Biehn, Joanne Whalley-Kilmer, Rick Rossovich, Cyril O'Reilly, Bill Paxton, Dennis Haysbert, Paul Sanchez.

Never Say Never Again

USA 1983 134 mins

The first time Connery swore 'never again' was in 1967. The second time Connery swore 'never again' was in 1971. Finally, in 1983, he learnt to keep his mouth shut, cast for the seventh time as James Bond 007 in the aptly titled adventure *Never Say Never Again*. At the golden age of 53, Sean required a little extra help impressing the ladies, but with a little powder, a little paint and a lot of extra hair he emerged as irresistible as ever, tough, confident and capable, with that same old special glint in his eye.

When Kevin McClory produced *Thunderball* in 1965, he held onto the rights and returned 18 years later with an unofficial remake, an American production unaffiliated with the rest of the series. A spirited, self-aware adventure with a wicked sense of humour, it was released the same year as *Octopussy* (Roger Moore was 56 at the time), and, thanks to Connery's polished performance, didn't suffer too much in comparison.

The plot remains much the same as it was in *Thunderball*, but it's a lighter, more entertaining version of events. Once again, smooth SPECTRE agent Largo (Klaus Maria Brandauer, cool and dangerous) holds the world to ransom with a pair of stolen, submerged nuclear missiles, and Bond is chosen to save the day. Supporting players in this little game include skinny Bond bimbo Domino (Kim Basinger), CIA hotshot Felix Leiter (Bernie Casey), irritating comic relief Nigel Small-Fawcett (Rowan Atkinson), and, most memorably, vivacious henchwoman Fatima Blush (Barbara Carrera), a deadly, exotic assassin with a pet snake and a style all of her own.

Action highlights include a slam-bang health farm punch-up between James and man-mountain Lippe (Pat Roach), a rollercoaster motorcycle chase, a nail-biting shark attack and a show-stopping horse jump. The remaining fight, rescue and battle scenes are adequate, but nothing to write home about. Ultimately, though, if you're a big Sean Connery fan, you'll enjoy this movie warts 'n' all.

Director: Irvin Kershner; **Producer:** Jack Schwartzman; **Executive Producer:** Kevin McClory; **Screenplay:** Lorenzo Semple Jr, based on an original story by Kevin McClory, Jack Whittingham, Ian Fleming; **Production Design:** Philip Harrison, Stephen Grimes; **Editor:** Robert Lawrence; **Photography:** Douglas Slocombe; **Music:** Michael Legrand; **Cast:** Sean Connery, Klaus Maria Brandauer, Max Von Sydow, Barbara Carrera, Kim Basinger, Bernie Casey, Alec McCowen, Edward Fox, Rowan Atkinson.

New Jack City

USA 1991 101mins

A traditional gangster flick dressed up as blaxploitation, *New Jack City* is a hip, slick thriller detailing the rise and fall of crack-dealing crime boss Nino Brown (Wesley Snipes), the smoothest villain in town. Mario Van Peebles made his directorial debut with this one, treating us to sex, violence and excessive living before dutifully reminding us that crime doesn't pay, that drugs are no good, and that no matter how cool the bad guys seem, they're the scum of the Earth, and they're going to Hell...

It's cops and gangstas time as on-the-edge detectives Ice-T and (token white) Judd Nelson use a junkie chum (Chris Rock) to infiltrate Nino's high-rise stronghold, your basic one-stop-crack-shop, right in the middle of town.

'You gotta rob to be rich in the Reagan era...' Besides heavy-handed political commentary and some deeply funky tunes, there are sub-plots a-plenty in this one, from Nino's deteriorating relationship with childhood homeboy Gee Money (Allen Payne), to Pookie's (Rock) struggle against addiction, and though the movie could have used a few more action scenes, what little there is (a chase, a bust, a shoot-out, a punch-up...) makes quite an impression, good, fast and violent too.

Best of all, though, is Snipes' star-making, scene-stealing performance as Nino Brown, a sharp and charismatic 'New Jack' gangster who'd fit right in with the likes of veteran scoundrels Jimmy, Bogie or Edward G.

Director: Mario Van Peebles; **Producers:** Doug McHenry, George Jackson; **Screenplay:** Thomas Lee Wright, Barry Michael Cooper; **Production Design:** Charles C. Bennett; **Editor:** Steven Kemper; **Photography:** Francis Kenny; **Music:** Michel Colombier; **Cast:** Wesley Snipes, Ice T, Allen Payne, Chris Rock, Mario Van Peebles, Judd Nelson, Michael Michele, Bill Nunn.

Trivialists 4

HEROES
Men of steel

Nick Parker (Rutger Hauer), *Blind Fury*
John Matrix (Arnold Schwarzenegger), *Commando*
John McClane (Bruce Willis), *Die Hard*
Dirty Harry (Clint Eastwood), *Dirty Harry*
Lee (Bruce Lee), *Enter the Dragon*
Snake Pliskin (Kurt Russell), *Escape From New York*
James Bond (Connery/Moore), *Goldfinger/The Spy Who Loved Me*
Mad Max (Mel Gibson), *Mad Max*
Colonel James Braddock (Chuck Norris), *Missing in Action*
Kevin Chan (Jackie Chan), *Police Story*

Indiana Jones (Harrison Ford), *Raiders of the Lost Ark*
Remo Williams (Fred Ward), *Remo: Unarmed and Dangerous*
Dalton (Patrick Swayze), *Road House*
RoboCop (Peter Weller), *RoboCop*
Jack Colton (Michael Douglas), *Romancing the Stone*
Lone Wolf (Tomisaburo Wakayama), *Shogun Assassin*
Jack Traven (Keanu Reeves), *Speed*
Han Solo (Harrison Ford), *Star Wars*
John Nada ('Rowdy' Roddy Piper), *They Live*
Jack Deth (Tim Thomerson), *Trancers*

No Escape

USA 1994 118 mins

Ray Liotta busts some heads and kicks a whole lot of butt in this lightweight no-brainer, a futuristic blend of *Papillon* and *Mad Max 2*. Having made his name playing psychopathic villains who think nothing of killing (*Something Wild*, *Goodfellas*, *Unlawful Entry*), Liotta here plays a psychopathic *good* guy who thinks nothing of killing. A lean, mean blasting machine, Ray's in fine physical form, an acceptable, though unremarkable, tough guy.

As a super-soldier who blows away his abusive commanding officer, Liotta plays John Robbins, a war-weary marine packed off to Absolom, a secret, untamed prison island offering no hope of escape. And when you get there, you stay there, for life, no matter how long, or how brief, that life may be.

Keeping the population in check is a typically ruthless scoundrel named Marek (*Lethal Weapon 3* refugee Stuart Wilson, hamming it up in yet another villainous role and stealing the show as a result), a wise-cracking killer who rules the Outsiders, a savage band of loons dedicated to chaos and destruction.

Elsewhere on the island, a former surgeon turned wise-old-man known as the Father (genre favourite Lance Henriksen) governs the Insiders, a peaceful group of blokes dedicated to survival and the pursuit of a useful life. Naturally enough, the Insiders and the Outsiders don't get along too well, as a fistful of battle sequences make all to clear. And it is here, on Absolom, that Robbins has to make a stand...

Way too straight-faced and serious for its own good (with the welcome exception of Wilson), and with holes the size of Jabba the Hutt's butt in the storyline, *No Escape* does not offer a classic adventure movie experience, although the action itself isn't too bad and there's certainly no shortage of gore, with decapitations and impalements a-plenty. Foolish and excessive, it offers light, bloody entertainment for those of us who need it.

Director: Martin Campbell; **Producer:** Gale Anne Hurd; **Screenplay:** Michael Gaylin, Joel Gross; **Production Design:** Allan Cameron; **Editor:** Terry Rawlings; **Photography:** Phil Meheux; **Music:** Graeme Revell; **Cast:** Ray Liotta, Lance Henriksen, Michael Lerner, Stuart Wilson, Kevin Dillon, Ernie Hudson, Jack Shepherd, Ian McNeice.

No Retreat, No Surrender

Hong Kong 1986 84 mins

A teenage boy learns to overcome his problems with the spectral assistance of a celebrity stiff in this cheap and cheesy but basically harmless fantasy. Newly settled in Seattle, troubled youth Jason Stillwell (Kurt McKinney) pours his heart out at the grave of his hero and role model, Bruce Lee. Bullies harass him, girls make him nervous, his martial arts training is not going well, his best friend R.J. (J.W. Falls) is a dated stereotype into early rap and breakdancing, he's stuck in a movie which can't decide whether it's *Porkies*, *The Karate Kid* or *Bloodsport*, and what's more, there's a pesky mob subplot buzzing around which is bound to end in violence (fingers crossed, anyway).

Events take a surprising turn when Jason's pleas for help are answered by none other than Bruce Lee's ghost (Kim Tai Chong), appearing in person to preach the philosophy of Jeet Kune Do while training the lad up to spec in time for a full-contact blowout with Ivan, the Russian, 'an awesome machine of annihilation' played by Jean-Claude Van Damme in his earliest action role. With only two scenes to play and no more than 20 words of unintelligible dialogue to deliver, Van Damme makes it to the end of the movie without ever having to act, although he's clearly the most capable martial artist on display (unless, of course, you count Mr Lee), as quick and deadly as lightning.

Certainly, the ghost of Sensei Lee takes quite a bit of getting used too, but if you're able to make it past this ridiculous conceit, the training scenes are actually quite interesting. An exciting finale makes up for much of the corn that comes before, as mob enforcer Ivan takes on a variety of Karate masters before Jason has his chance to save the day. Now, if only he could sort out some singing lessons with Elvis...

Sequels: *No Retreat, No Surrender 2: Raging Thunder*, *No Retreat, No Surrender 3: Blood Brothers*, *No Retreat, No Surrender 4: King of the Kickboxers*, *No Retreat, No Surrender 5: American Shaolin*.

Director: Corey Yuen; **Producer:** Ng See Yuen; **Screenplay:** Keith W. Strandberg, story by Ng See Yuen and Corey Yuen; **Editors:** Alan Poon, Mark Pierce, James Melkonian; **Photography:** John Huneck, David Golia; **Music:** Paul Gilreath; **Cast:** Kurt McKinney, J.W. Falls, Tim Baker, Kim Tai Chong, Jean-Claude Van Damme, Ron Pohnel, Kathy Sileno, Peter 'Sugarfoot' Cunningham, Kent Lipham.

No Retreat, No Surrender 2: Raging Thunder

Hong Kong 1987 92 mins

A sequel in name only, this second round of chop socky adventure bears absolutely no relation to the first, save for the tenuous exception that both films were directed by Corey Yuen, who brings in an entirely new cast and crew to run off a cheap actioner stuffed with every bargain-basement cliché and stereotype that B-movie minds have to offer, added to which, we're not even treated to a cameo appearance from the spectre of Sensei Lee. Burdened with a nonsensical plot and an ultra-geeky hero, the movie stumbles through all the usual paces, offering nothing of interest besides a deluge of death and destruction and a spirited, if broadly wooden, early performance from high-kicking heroine Cynthia Rothrock.

Prepare yourselves for the worst: 5 (think amateurish)... 4 (think corny)... 3 (think moronic)... 2 (better stop thinking now)... 1 (here goes nothing)... In a sentence, nerdy martial artist Scott (Loren Avedon) teams up with macho man Mac (Max Thayer) and mini-marauder Terry (Cynthia Rothrock) to jet to Cambodia and rescue his fiancée Sulin (Patra Wanthivanond) from a Soviet stronghold on 'Death Mountain', home of a characterless excess of muscle known as Yuri, the Russian (as played by Matthias Hues, taking over from Jean-Claude Van Damme's similarly titled Ivan, the Russian, principal heavy of movie number one), a sneering bully with a pool of hungry crocodiles to feed...

Cheap, ultra-violent and stupid, there's chaos and unintentional hilarity waiting to be discovered here, but you'd better be drunk and desperate before you begin the search.

Director: Corey Yuen; **Producer:** Roy Horan; **Screenplay:** Roy Horan, Keith W. Strandberg, Maria Elena Cellina; **Production Design:** Grisapong Hanviriyakitichai; **Editor:** Allan Poon, Kevin Sewelson; **Photography:** Nicholas Von Sternberg, Ma Kam Cheung; **Music:** David Spear; **Cast:** Loren Avedon, Max Thayer, Cynthia Rothrock, Matthias Hues, Patra Wanthivanond, Hwang Jang Lee, Nirit Sirjunya.

Death Becomes Them 17

Chuck Norris unleashes a powerful pair of snake eyes in *Missing in Action 2: The Beginning.*

Name: NORRIS, Chuck

Real name: Carlos Ray Norris

Born: Oklahoma, 1940

Characteristics: Strong, silent, blond, bearded hero-next-door.

Debut feature: *The Wrecking Crew* (1969)

Life and times: Stationed with the Air Force in Osan, Korea, Chuck Norris discovered and dedicated himself to the martial arts, training five hours a day, six days a week, returning to the States with a black belt in Karate and a brown belt in Judo. While passing on his skills as a top chop socky instructor, Norris reigned as World Middleweight Karate Champ from 1968 until 1974, retiring undefeated. Encouraged by former student Steve McQueen to work on his movie career, Chuck transformed into the action hero we now know and love. Norris made his TV debut in 1993, taking the lead and delivering weekly thrashings in his hit TV show *Walker, Texas Ranger*. He'll be 60 soon, but he could still beat the crap out of you if he wanted to.

Greatest contribution to action movies: In the distinguished field of macho martial artistry, Chuck ruled the ultra-violent 1980s.

Speech, speech: 'I don't initiate violence, I retaliate.'

Whatever luck I had, I made. I was never a natural athlete, but I paid my dues in sweat and concentration and took the time necessary to learn Karate and become world champion.'

'There are a dozen death spots, another dozen paralysing death spots, and many, many disabling spots on the body. We human beings are quite fragile, you know.'

'After years of learning to control my emotions in karate, I found it very difficult to reverse that process and fully express them. But I learn from my mistakes and develop more as an actor with each film role.'

Selected filmography: *Slaughter in San Francisco* (aka *Karate Cop*; 1973, US release 1981), ***The Way of the Dragon*** (1973), ***Breaker! Breaker!*** (1977), *Good Guys Wear Black* (1979), ***A Force of One*** (1979), ***The Octagon*** (1980), ***An Eye For An Eye*** (1981), *Silent Rage* (1982), ***Forced Vengeance*** (1982), ***Lone Wolf McQuade*** (1983), ***Missing in Action*** (1984), ***Missing in Action 2: The Beginning*** (1985), ***Code of Silence*** (1985), ***Invasion U.S.A.*** (+ co-scr; 1985), ***The Delta Force*** (1986), *Firewalker* (1986), ***Braddock: Missing In Action III*** (+ co-scr; 1988), *Hero and the Terror* (1988), ***Delta Force 2*** (1990), *The Hitman* (1991), ***Sidekicks*** (1993), *Hellbound* (1994), *Top Dog* (1995).

Northwest Frontier [aka Flame Over India]

GB 1959 130 mins

Kenneth More straps on his stiffest upper lip as the consummately British hero of this rousing boy's own adventure, a blood-and-thunder spectacular with every trimming known to man: hundreds of extras, masses of explosions, gunplay, fisticuffs and even a stab at human drama.

It's a busy movie, sure, with little time left over for a story. Instead, we're treated to an opening voice-over which explains pretty much everything that's going on without any fuss or bother. India, 1905: ordered to escort a six-year old Prince (Govind Raja Ross) across 300 miles of rebel-infested wilderness, officer and gentleman Captain Scott (our Ken) boards the ramshackle Empress of India locomotive accompanied by strong-willed governess Lauren Bacall and a colourful crew of supporting players. Then it's straight down to business, as the Empress rams the rebels and kicks off a colossal chase involving desert battles, train-top struggles and desperate, seat-of-the-pants repairs.

As for the cast, More delivers a characteristically solid performance as the hero of our tale, a decent chap under difficult circumstances, while Bacall is as desirable as an ice-cream in hell, beautiful, strong and capable of anything. Elsewhere on board, Herbert Lom menaces as a seedy reporter with a big, bad secret, Wilfred Hyde-White, looking as bemused as ever, plays a nervous British official, Eugene Deckers is Peters, the arms dealer, Ursula Jeans the resourceful Lady Windham, and finally I.S. Johar makes his presence felt as Gupta, enthusiastic engineer and occasional miracle worker.

This is the stuff that Sunday afternoon matinees are made of.

Director: J. Lee Thompson; **Producer:** Marcel Hellman; **Screenplay:** Robin Estridge, adapted from a screenplay by Frank Nugent, story by Patrick Ford, Will Price; **Production Design:** Alex Vetchinsky; **Editor:** Frederick Wilson; **Photography:** Geoffrey Unsworth; **Music:** Mischa Spoliansky; **Cast:** Kenneth More, Lauren Bacall, Herbert Lom, Wilfred Hyde-White, I.S. Johar, Ursula Jeans, Eugene Deckers, Govind Raja Ross.

Nowhere to Run

USA 1992 95 mins

A movie that never decides whether it's a thriller, a drama or an action flick, *Nowhere to Run* somehow manages to combine the weakest elements of all three genres and deliver a cheesy dish that you're not going to want to swallow. Or even take a sniff at.

A laughable, instantly forgettable waste of good film stock with a standard *A-Team* plot, this is very dodgy stuff indeed. Jean-Claude Van Damme explores his sensitive side as a cool outlaw type who's happy to read cheap skin mags (*Top Heavy* seems to be a favourite) in the privacy of his own tent, yet gentle and supportive of women in the flesh. One such damsel in distress is the quirky yet desperate Clydie (Rosanna Arquette), a single mum at odds with a gang of nasty property developers who want to eject her and her offspring (including Macaulay's brother Kieran Culkin - not a good sign) from their land. Talk about old chestnuts, this plot is positively prehistoric, a blatant *Shane* wannabe that doesn't even have the right to lick the spurs of such a classic western.

Director Robert Harmon is clearly trying to push this nowhere movie as a character-led drama, a decision that represents a milestone in the history of bad ideas: this is grade-C stuff with A-movie pretensions that won't fool anyone for a second.

Had the screenplay been even remotely interesting and not the clumsy, half-baked joke that it is, the performances might not have appeared so amateurish: Joss Ackland, perennially typecast in villainous roles since *Lethal Weapon 2*, hulks around the movie like Jabba the Hut on a bad hair day; Rosanna Arquette provides a textbook example of miscasting, a talented actress who is entirely out of place in this movie and visibly uncomfortable when called upon to strip for our hero; Van Damme, meanwhile, handles the action like a pro and the dialogue like a tree stump, parading his naked butt as if we'd never seen it before, and delivering tacked on one-liners with all the enthusiasm of a cow in an abattoir. The action, when it comes, won't send you to sleep, and there's a fairly decent bike chase in there too, but honestly, why bother?

Director: Robert Harmon; **Producer:** Craig Baumgarten, Gary Adelson; **Screenplay:** Joe Eszterhas, Leslie Bohem, Randy Feldman; **Production Design:** Dennis Washington; **Editor:** Zack Staenberg, Mark Helfrich; **Photography:** David Gribble; **Music:** Mark Isham; **Cast:** Jean-Claude Van Damme, Rosanna Arquette, Kieran Culkin, Ted Levine, Joss Ackland.

The Octagon

USA 1980 103 mins

As usual, Chuck Norris plays a Karate champ who turns his back on violence and refuses to play the hero game, but if we've learnt anything from Chuck's adventures at all, it's that he really has no choice but to get involved and waste dozens of bad guys. Clumsy dialogue and cardboard characters might serve to slow him down a little, but when there's people to be chopped and cars to be chased, Chuck has a duty to himself, as well as to his fans, to kill, kill, kill and kill some more.

Mercenaries are being taught long-outlawed Ninja techniques at a secret training centre known as the Octagon. Funded by international extremists and run by twisted killer Seikura (Tadashi Yamashita), it's a terrorist production line where new recruits are warned that if they ever cross their new masters, their 'sons, daughters, wives, brothers, sisters, will be killed without regard'. Obviously, someone has to put an end to their nefarious activities, but it won't be token pal A.J. (Art Hindle), or wasted co-star Lee Van Cleef, 'cos only Chuck can save the day, and the movie, from certain disaster.

Thick as a post but often quite stylish, *The Octagon* throws us scraps of action throughout, keeping us at bay until a devastating final assault which is well worth the wait. In case you feel inclined to follow the story, the movie comes equipped with explanatory voiceovers, Chuck's deep-down, whispered thoughts echoing throughout. At first, they're quite creepy, then you get used to them, then you get tired of them, and finally you just want to tell

Chuck's brain to shut the hell up. There's simply no place for old grey matter in a kick-fest, and that's that.

It's a good thing Chuck can dazzle us with his laid-back manner and ability to polish off two Ninjas without ever having to get out of bed. He's a star, no doubt about it, and one of the hairiest men in the business.

 Fourth Ghostbuster and *Crow* co-star Ernie Hudson pops up for a single scene, and you can check that in the credits, but for some reason, creepy character actor Tracey Walter, best known for *Conan the Destroyer*, also plays a single scene (as 'Mr Beatty') yet remains uncredited for his troubles. Strange, eh?

Director: Eric Carson; **Producer:** Joel Freeman; **Screenplay:** Leigh Chapman, story by Paul Aaron and Leigh Chapman; **Production Design:** James Schoppe; **Editor:** Dann Cahn; **Photography:** Michel Hugo; **Music:** Dick Halligan; **Cast:** Chuck Norris, Karen Carlson, Lee Van Cleef, Art Hindle, Carol Bagdasarian, Tadashi Yamashita.

Octopussy

GB 1983 130 mins

Before we get started, there's something you should know. This is a good movie, see, a little corny, perhaps, but good 'n' glossy and loaded with action. There is, however, a blot on the landscape. Something scary. Something unnatural. Something mid-1970s. It's something that you're going to have to prepare yourselves for in advance, and try hard not to let it drive you insane when it grabs you by the eyeballs and burrows into your brain. This thing, this *evil* thing, has a name. It is Roger Moore's safari suit, a fashion apocalypse which not even Elvis would have worn. Bedecked with collars so mighty, you need a pilot's licence to wear it, the suit personifies that most hated of verbs: *flared*. Alright, then. Don't say you weren't warned. Now, let's put all this unpleasantness behind us, and get on with the story...

While investigating the murder of a 00 agent, Bond travels to India for a close encounter with the mysterious Octopussy (Maud Adams), a wealthy entrepreneur with an island fortress, an all-girl army and her very own travelling circus. Meanwhile, a team of villains join forces to make a fortune, start a war and kill our hero: smooth criminal Kamal (Louis Jourdan), smuggler, forger, Afghan prince and principal thorn in James's side; lunatic warmonger General Orlov (Steven Berkoff), a mad Russian with a nuclear bomb and a dastardly plan; as for the henchmen, Kabir Bedi rules the roost as Gobinda, Kamal's personal bodyguard and assassin, while Kristina Wayborn sleeps her way to victory as the seductive Magda.

Helping James along the way, jolly sidekick Vijay (alias tennis pro Vijay Amritaj) takes us for a wild ride through busy Indian streets, fending off the bad guys with a laugh and a tennis racket. Having already played Scaramanga's ill-fated mistress in *The Man with the Golden Gun*, Maud Adams makes 007 history as the first actress to play a second Bond girl, while Lois Maxwell, who's been with the series from the very beginning, returns as the ever-reliable Moneypenny, only this time she has a younger, prettier assistant for James to flirt with: Penelope Smallbone (Michaela Clavell).

A memorable pre-title set-piece, as Bond evades a cluster of heat-seeking missiles in a mini fold-up jet plane, sets the tone (outrageous) and the standard (spectacular) for the action to come: there's a train full of villains for 007 to deal with; a jungle safari (hence the suit) with Bond as the quarry, complete with elephants and monster puns (eyeing a snake, James quips 'hiss off'); a chaotic final assault on Octopussy's stronghold as Bond, Q (Desmond Llewelyn, more hands-on than usual) and Maud's all-girl gang take on Kamal and his boys; and a ludicrous aerial one-to-one as Bond clings to the roof of a speeding jet while throwing punches at the exceptionally persistent Gobinda. Best of all, however, is an edge-of-the-seat race-against-time as James scrambles desperately to reach and disarm a nuclear bomb before Octopussy's circus, an American Air Force base and half of West Germany disappear beneath a mushroom cloud.

The end of *Octopussy*. But James Bond will return in *A View To A Kill*.

Director: John Glen; **Producer:** Albert R. Broccoli; **Screenplay:** George MacDonald Fraser, Richard Maibaum, Michael G. Wilson; **Production Design:** Peter Lamont; **Editor:** John Grover; **Photography:** Alan Hume; **Music:** John Barry, title song performed by Rita Coolidge; **Cast:** Roger Moore, Maud Adams, Louis Jourdan, Kristina Wayborn, Kabir Bedi, Steven Berkoff, Vijay Amritaj, Desmond Llewelyn, Robert Brown, Lois Maxwell.

On Deadly Ground

USA 1993 110 mins

Steven Seagal blew it big time with this one. Too big for his own boots, the pony-tailed wonder actually believed that he could direct, but he was wrong. And so we have *On Deadly Ground*, a monumental ego trip which takes itself much too seriously for its own good.

The story, for what it's worth, concerns an evil industrialist (Michael Caine) who doesn't mind ruining the planet in order to make a few bucks. Enter Forrest Taft (Seagal), a tough guy with a conscience who basically teams up with Eskimo activist Joan Chen and kills hundreds of people in the name of conservation. But by giving his film a social conscience, Seagal takes any fun there might have been out of the ensuing death and mayhem, ending up with a slow, preachy tale which seems at odds with the violence and destruction it glorifies.

Action movie fans deserve more than *On Deadly Ground*. It's a pretentious film, lazily directed, poorly written, predictable, packed with clichés and cardboard characters, and there isn't a single fight scene that lasts more than a few seconds.

Besides that, Taft is a lousy character. He's afraid of nothing, he kills and maims without ever getting a scratch himself, he has absolutely no sense of humour, and, after beating the stuffing out of yet another villain, comes out with nonsense like 'What does it take to change the essence of man?' Well, Steve, we don't know, but we'd really like you to try.

Director: Steven Seagal; **Producers:** Steven Seagal, Julius R. Nasso, A. Kitman Ho; **Screenplay:** Ed Horowitz, Robin U. Russin; **Production Design:** ?; **Editor:** Robert A. Ferretti; **Photography:** Ric Waite; **Music:** Basil Poledouris; **Cast:** Steven Seagal, Michael Caine, Joan Chen, John C. McGinley, Irvin Brink, Richard Hamilton, Sven-Ole Thorsen.

On Her Majesty's Secret Service

GB 1969 140 mins

Connery was out of the picture, but it would take more than an actor's defection to finish James Bond. Standing in for the Scottish star, Australian car salesman turned model George Lazenby strapped on the Walther PPK and stumbled through his first acting job, looking the part but struggling elsewhere. Many fans believe that, had Connery remained in the role, *On Her Majesty's Secret Service* might have been the best of all the Bonds. A return to the early days of minimal gadgetry and inventive plotting, the film delves deeper than ever into Bond's private world, as we witness him falling in love with the spirited Tracy (*The Avengers*' Diana Rigg), offering to end his career with the British Secret Service, and, finally, getting married only to experience the greatest personal tragedy of his life. The most emotional of all the Bond films, and probably the toughest to play, this sixth entry begged for Sean's participation, but all it got was George, a newcomer of minimal ability whose casual approach to the role and near-total lack of screen presence, coupled with a blockbusting ego which earned him few friends, ensured that this would be his one and only Bond adventure. Rumour has it (and even if it's not true, it's still a damn fine story) that co-star Diana Rigg took particular offence to Lazenby, so much so that she took to eating garlic before their love scenes together.

A pre-title beach battle introduces the new Bond, saving Tracy from a gang of thugs only to be left in the lurch when she escapes without a snog or even a word of thanks: 'This never happened to the other fella', jokes George directly to camera, and following a title sequence incorporating images from Bond's previous exploits, the movie gets on with the job at hand: Blofeld's back, posing as a world-famous allergist in a remote, Alpine stronghold, looking like *Kojak*'s Telly Savalas, planning germ warfare and transforming an international assembly of beautiful, female patients (including *Absolutely Fabulous* and *New Avengers* star Joanna Lumley) into brainwashed 'Angels of Death'. With help from benevolent Mafia man Draco (Gabrielle Ferzetti) and his strong-willed daughter, Tracy, Bond goes undercover hoping to polish off his old nemesis and maybe even save the world.

The movie works hard to make up for Lazenby and there are times when it succeeds with honours: a spectacular avalanche sequence, a speedy and inventive ski chase, a climactic bobsled showdown, and plenty of splendid rough and tumble throughout. Besides the showy set-pieces, Rigg shines as one of the best of all the Bond girls, while composer John Barry contributes a perfect soundtrack, a cool and pacy slice of the 1960s which shifts gears to include the rich Louis Armstrong classic 'We Have All the Time in the World', written and performed especially for the film and put to good, ironic use at the end (incidentally, the song's title comes from a line in the last paragraph of Fleming's original novel).

There's a hole at the heart of this movie that only Connery could have filled, but only a crank would dismiss it entirely. Technically impressive and often quite exciting, the film packs a middle-weight punch which, though it falls short of a knockout, you're still going to feel in the morning.

 Although he only made a single Bond movie, Lazenby returned to the role of 007 in 1983, enjoying a cameo performance as the secret service man in the nostalgic TV movie *The Return of the Man From Uncle*. Incidentally, both *Octopussy* and *Never Say Never Again* were also made in '83, offering fans a unique opportunity to see all three Bonds in a single year.

The end of *On Her Majesty's Secret Service*. But James Bond will return in *Diamonds are Forever*.

Director: Peter Hunt; **Producer:** Albert R. Broccoli, Harry Saltzman; **Screenplay:** Richard Maibaum, based on the novel by Ian Fleming; **Production Design:** Syd Cain; **Editor:** John Glen; **Photography:** Michael Reed; **Music:** John Barry; **Cast:** George Lazenby, Diana Rigg, Telly Savalas, Ilse Steppat, Gabrielle Ferzetti, Bernard Lee, Lois Maxwell, Desmond Llewelyn, Yuri Borienko, Bernard Horsfall.

Only the Strong

USA 1993 99 mins

The Brazilian martial art of Capoeira, a flashy blend of dance and combat, takes centre stage in this modest action thriller, a B-grade effort from *Double Impact* director Sheldon Lettich which offers nothing new beyond some rather aggressive acrobatics.

Strapping young lad Mark Dacascos plays a US Army Special Forces soldier stationed in Brazil who, unable to 'make a difference' in the battle against the drug lords of South America, returns home to the good old US of A. But all is not well in the State of Miami, as a visit to his former high school - now a drug infested miniature war zone - confirms. So guess what kids? Our baby-faced hero decides to stop running and 'make a stand', teaching a dirty dozen students the ancient art of Capoeira while battling local gang leader Silverio (Paco Christian Prieto). Not exactly original. Not exactly thrilling. Not exactly fun, either. But it means well, and that's the problem.

Had the movie simply concentrated on the one-to-one action that runs throughout, it might have scraped by, but it relies too heavily on a plot which barely exists and a cast of moth-eaten characters recycled from a hundred thousand other movies. Two-dimensional stereotypes abound (bad kids make good, teachers who care too much), the screenplay is dull and plodding, and the performances do little to help. Director Lettich seems satisfied with a made-for-TV feel, although even on the small screen *Only the Strong* appears cheaply made and amateurish. You won't die of boredom, but that's hardly a recommendation, is it?

Director: Sheldon Lettich; **Producers:** Samuel Hadida, Stuart S. Shapiro, Steven G. Menkin; **Screenplay:** Sheldon Lettich, Luis Esteban; **Production Design:** J. Mark Harrington; **Editor:** Stephen Semel; **Photography:** Edward Pei; **Music:** Harvey W. Mason; **Cast:** Mark Dacascos, Stacey Travis, Paco Christian Prieto, Geoffrey Lewis, Todd Susman, Jeffrey Anderson Gunter.

Our Man Flint

USA 1966 108 mins

The world is under threat from the bad guys over at Galaxy. They're bigger than SPECTRE and they have a machine that controls the weather. Violent storms and volcanic eruptions prove they mean business. A ransom is demanded. A hero is summoned. But who on earth is up to the task? Why, Derek Flint (James Coburn, having the time of his life), of course, the most capable human being on earth: martial artist, master swordsman, field doctor, ballet teacher, gambler, jet pilot, ladies man, snappy dresser, master of disguise and champion of deductive reasoning. He lives in luxury with four exotic chicks in a high-tech apartment. His reflexes are excellent. Hell, if he wants to, he can even stop his heart beating for over three hours. He is, when you think about it, the ultimate man. Beyond 007 stands a champion devoted to the satirical assassination of the superspy genre, and his name is Derek.

The Bond series takes a good-natured roasting in Daniel Mann's colourful comedy thriller, *Our Man Flint*, and although you should be prepared to survive the experience, having failed to laugh yourself to death, you should appreciate its dated charm, from the wacky action sequences and hot bikini fashions to the extravagance of the sets and hyperactivity of the villains. And who could forget Flint's one and only gadget? A gold cigarette lighter with 82 different functions. '83, if you wish to light a cigar'. Classy.

Sequel: *In Like Flint*.

Director: Daniel Mann; **Producer:** Saul David; **Screenplay:** Hal Fimberg, Ben Starr; **Production Design:** Jack Martin Smith, Ed Graves; **Editor:** William Reynolds; **Photography:** Daniel L. Fapp; **Music:** Jerry Goldsmith; **Cast:** James Coburn, Lee J. Cobb, Gila Golan, Edward Mulhare.

Out for Justice

USA 1991 86 mins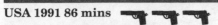

How much pain can one man inflict? How many times can the same plot be recycled? How easy is it to throw a ho-slappin' pimp head-first through a car windscreen? And what the hell is it with that pony-tail? Questions, questions everywhere, but you won't have to think. Just sit back, switch your brain onto auto-pilot, and leave everything to Steven Seagal, here playing a cop bent on a personal mission of revenge, a great departure for the actor who played a cop bent on a personal mission of revenge in *Above the Law*, and a cop bent on a personal mission of revenge in *Hard to Kill*.

This time around, Steve struts his stuff as Brooklyn cop Gino Felino, a two-bit Dirty Harry on the trail of chronic over-eater Richie (*Stone Cold*'s William Forsythe), a vicious crack-head who gunned down Gino's partner and a dozen other extras besides. The mob serve to complicate matters, but only slightly, when they also declare an interest in catching up with Richie, whose violent exploits are stirring up a lot of bad publicity for the local crime syndicate. You might say he's giving crime a bad name, and just about every Brooklyn wiseguy is after him, but if I were a betting man, I'd put all my money on Gino, because he really seems to enjoy his work, enthusiastically mashing any villain who stands between him and his stout prey.

While not exactly over-endowed on the story front, the proceedings are amply padded with a veritable wonderbra of sadistic violence, with plenty of one-to-one action, a decent car chase and an outrageous bar-room brawl in which Seagal shows off just how efficient he is by maiming dozens of minor scoundrels one at a time.

Forget the performances. As usual, Seagal plays Seagal, and while Forsyth proves he can snarl with the best of 'em, he's way too out of shape to represent any real threat to our hero. You'd also be wise to ignore the Italian-American schmaltz present in the slower sections of the movie, and concentrate on the wholesale taking of life instead. That is, after all, what Steven Seagal does best, and what this movie is all about.

Director: John Flynn; **Producers:** Steven Seagal, Arnold Kopelson; **Screenplay:** David Lee Henry; **Production Design:** Gene Rudolf; **Editor:** Robert A. Ferretti; **Photography:** Ric Waite; **Music:** David Michael Frank; **Cast:** Steven Seagal, William Forsythe, Jerry Orbach, Jo Champa.

Brainstorms 4

TAG LINES

A poster without a catchy line is like a hook without bait.
Name the films which exploited these marketing classics...

1. Don't hunt what you can't kill.

2. Crime is a disease. Meet the cure.

3. Almost Human. Almost Perfect. Almost Under Control.

4. Jack Deth is back... and he's never been here before!

5. He's an ex-cop with a bad mouth, a bad attitude, and a bad seat. For the terrorists on flight 163... he's very bad news.

6. Vigilante, city style... judge, jury and executioner.

7. Trapped in time... Surrounded by evil... Low on Gas.

8. Years of bad behaviour are about to pay off.

9. Silent. Invisible. Invincible. He's in town with a few days to kill.

10. Nick Parker is quick as a snake, strong as a bull.... not to mention blind as a bat.

Passenger 57

USA 1993 84 mins

Now here's a film that was clearly made by people who love action movies for people who love action movies: every character, every cliché and every plot development is in its proper place, all the one-liners, speeding bullets and explosions are ready to go, and from the very first second you know that this ultra-violent dash through actionland is going to be a scream.

The plot is as hilarious as it is simple (no point mucking around, after all): Wesley Snipes plays top airline security expert John Cutter, a pretty slick individual who just so happens to find himself on the same plane as airline hijacking psychopath Charles Rane (Bruce Payne), a sadistic Hannibal Lecter-like murderer whose only pleasure is killing innocent people. Groovy.

Clearly *Die Hard* aboard a plane, director Kevin Hooks' *Passenger 57* makes no excuses for piling coincidence upon coincidence: it revels in its foolishness and is totally aware of what it's doing. Reverence is given to the one-liner ('Always bet on black!'), and Snipes is given plenty of opportunities to crack jokes as well as heads. In fact, towards the end of the movie, it seems as though he stops using proper sentences entirely, conversing instead almost entirely in quips and put-downs. Gore fans might be a little disappointed by the movie's tendency to cut away from the splatter, although this doesn't make the film's various set-pieces any less exciting.

The central cast is perfect: Snipes is excellent as the ultra-cool good guy, and he handles the physical side of his role entirely convincingly. Payne too is ideal for his role: charming, dangerous - the kind of evil genius you love to hate.

Slick, fast and furious, this is a great Saturday night popcorn picture.

Director: Kevin Hooks; **Producers:** Lee Rich, Dan Paulson, Sylan Sellers; **Screenplay:** David Loughery, Dan Gordon, Stewart Raffill; **Production Design:** Jaymes Hinkle; **Editor:** Richard Nord; **Photography:** Mark Irwin; **Music:** Stanley Clarke; **Cast:** Wesley Snipes, Bruce Payne, Tom Sizemore, Alex Datcher, Bruce Greenwood, Robert Hooks, Elizabeth Hurley, Michael Horse.

The Perfect Weapon

USA 1991 112 mins

revenge *n.* **1.** punishment or injury inflicted in return for what one has suffered. **2.** a desire to inflict this. **3.** opportunity to defeat in a return game an opponent who won the first game. *-v.* to avenge; *be revenged* or *revenge oneself*, to get satisfaction by inflicting vengeance. - **revengeful** *adj.* **4.** boring John Carradine horror flick (*1986*). **5.** dreadful Kevin Costner thriller (*1990*). **6.** the kind of name you'd slap on an expensive bottle of perfume. **7.** elementary plot device, excuse for violence in action movies, *Korean mobsters killed my friend. They are many and I am only one, but this is my film and I am going to waste the lot of them.*

waste *v*. **1**. to use extravagantly or needlessly or without an adequate result. **2**. *n*. an act of wasting. **3**. (*slang*) *slay, slaughter, wipe out, execute, butcher, bump off, rub out, terminate, cancel, blow away, whack, erase, sort out*. You know, *kill*.

Perfect Weapon, The *movie*. **1**. death and destruction in the name of justice and entertainment. **2**. exaggerated description of principal hero, Jeff, played by Speakman, Jeff, in first starring role. **3**. one-off proposition, *reasonably enjoyable, loud and brutal, but not something you'd think about afterwards or ever want to sit through again.*

think *v*. (thought, thinking) **1**. to exercise the mind in an active way, to form connected ideas. **2**. unrequired exertion when viewing **Perfect Weapon, The**.

Speakman, Jeff *unshaven beefcake*. **1**. unarmed variety of movie tough guy, *a hands, elbows, knees and toes man*. **2**. Kenpo Karate boy, capable of incapacitating four muggers in five seconds flat.

Tanaka, Professor Toru *man-mountain* **1**. colossal oriental gentleman. **2**. seasoned heavy, scourge of action heroes. **3**. mute henchman Tanaka in **Perfect Weapon, The**.

alcohol *n*. **1**. a colourless inflammable liquid, the intoxicant present in wine, beer, whisky, methylated spirits and cough medicine. **2**. principal ingredient in Molotov cocktail. **3**. stimulant required to appreciate **Perfect Weapon, The**.

Director: Mark DiSalle; **Producers:** Mark DiSalle, Pierre David; **Screenplay:** David C. Wilson; **Production Design:** Curtis A. Schnell; **Editor:** Wayne Wahrman; **Photography:** Russell Carpenter; **Music:** Gary Chang; **Cast:** Jeff Speakman, John Dye, Mako, James Hong, Professor Toru Tanaka, Mariska Hargitay, Dante Basco, Beau Starr, Seth Sakai.

Police Story [aka Jackie Chan's Police Story; Police Force]

Hong Kong 1985 84 mins

The cops screw up big time and the bad guys make their escape, guns blazing as they head for the nearest getaway car. Directly in their path stands a hillside shanty town, a flimsy construction crying out to be trashed as they head through the dump without a second's hesitation. Their car wrecked, our villains hop onto a nearby bus, pulling away from the scene of their crime (the cads). Determined to salvage the operation, eager young copper Kevin Chan switches to pursuit mode, crashing down the hill, chasing them on foot, hooking onto the bus with an umbrella, climbing up the side... and that's just for starters, as martial arts miracle worker Jackie Chan bombards our senses with one complex, inventive and heart-poundingly exciting action sequence after another.

The first of a series of upbeat, upmarket cop thrillers, *Police Story* offers non-stop action, gags-a-plenty and a charismatic central performance from director Chan, an imaginative, athletic daredevil with the energy of a nuclear reactor.

A bare-bones plot paves the way for an hour and a half of supremely entertaining chaos: ordered to protect the subpoenaed secretary (Bridgette Lin) of crime boss Tom Koo (Cho Yuen), Kevin has his hands full battling a never-ending army of mobsters intent on bumping the lady off before her bean-spilling day in court. Meanwhile, romantic complications arise, as they so often do, in the pretty young form of long-suffering girlfriend May (Maggie Cheung). And that's all, folks.

Unlike your typical Hong Kong actioner, *Police Story* goes way beyond chop socky, asserting itself in the realms of the A-Movie with quality production values, brisk pacing, a strong sense of humour and tons of gob-smacking stuntwork performed by Chan himself, a fearless superbeing who parks a car like no other man on earth.

Police Story **proved so popular in Hong Kong that the police force actually ly chose to use its main theme in their recruitment commercials.**

Sequels: *Police Story 2*, *Police Story 3: Supercop*, *Project S*.

Director: Jackie Chan; **Producer:** Leonard Ho; **Screenplay:** Edward Tang; **Production Design:** Oliver Wong; **Editor:** Peter Cheung; **Photography:** Cheung Yiu Joe; **Music:** Kevin Bassinson, title song sung by Jackie Chan; **Cast:** Jackie Chan, Bridgette Lin, Maggie Cheung, Cho Yuen, Bill Tung, Kenneth Tong.

Police Story 2

Hong Kong 1988 92 mins

Everyone wants a piece of Kevin Chan, Hong Kong cop and trouble magnet: crime boss Tom Koo (Cho Yuen) is back on the street, dying of cancer and planning revenge; meanwhile, back at the cop shop, comedy duo and station supremos Raymond (Lam Kwok Hung) and Wong (Bill Tung) discipline our unorthodox hero with a demotion to traffic control; elsewhere, a gang of mad bombers hold the city to ransom, a job for Chan if ever there was one, only this time he's going to have to do it alone; and, as if there wasn't enough going on in his life already, Kevin's girlfriend May (Maggie Cheung) still doesn't understand him. And then she gets herself kidnapped.

Welcome, then, to a typical week in the life of a Jackie Chan hero, stomping on the bad guys wherever they might be, ever prepared with a kick and a joke, a combination of charm, chop-socky and impossible stuntwork seeing him through each and every excuse for action the movie dreams up.

As expected, Chan continues to find interesting locations for fight scenes, from crowded restaurant to children's playground, but while the martial arts on show are sure to entertain, *Police Story 2* isn't nearly as showy or inventive as the original, a routine effort with second rate villains (dubbed versions have terminal case Koo sounding like Brando's Godfather) and, heaven help us, a hero who's not afraid to cry.

Still, it's a damn sight better than the majority of Hong Kong actioners, slick and professional, with a memorable finale as Chan takes on a hearing-impaired henchman who clearly loves the small of napalm in the morning.

Director: Jackie Chan; **Producer:** Leonard Ho; **Screenplay:** Jackie Chan, Edward Tang; **Production Design:** Oliver Wond; **Editor:** Peter Cheung; **Photography:** Cheung Yiu Joe, Lee Yau Tong; **Music:** Michael Lai; **Cast:** Jackie Chan, Maggie Cheung, Bill Tung, Lam Kwok Hung, Charles Chao, Cho Yuen, Mars.

Police Story 3: Supercop

Hong Kong 1992 91 mins

Jackie Chan hooks up with the Royal Hong Kong Police for a third adventure as maverick 'supercop' Kevin Chan, an Eastern martial artist with a laid-back Western attitude, crazy, cool and ready for anything.

This time around, Chan is ordered to infiltrate and exterminate a vicious gang of drug-dealing killers, teaming up for the task with Chinese Chief of Security Yeung (Michelle Khan), a great little fighter, if a bit of a square. It's a mammoth undertaking of kamikaze proportions, tense, dramatic and appropriately violent. Rest assured, however, that time is consistently set aside for bouts of mood-mellowing foolishness, most memorably when trusty Inspector Wong poses in drag as Chan's loving mother. Oh yeah. And Chan's girlfriend May (Maggie Cheung), perennial damsel in distress, is kidnapped. Again.

With Chan hanging precariously from a helicopter ladder and an awe-inspiring motorcycle stunt from Khan, there's clearly no shortage of imaginatively staged action sequences, while budget-wise the film lays on all the trimmings, a glossy adventure which, though it pales in comparison with the original *Police Story*, offers plenty of audience-pleasing entertainment.

 Proving that even action heroes have their off days, out-takes shown during the end credits reveal Chan, famous for performing his own stunts, having a rather nasty run-in with a prop helicopter.

Director: Stanley Tong; **Producers:** Willie Chan, Edward Tang; **Screenplay:** Edward Tang, Filre Ma, Lee Wai Yee; **Production Design:** Wong Yue Man; **Editors:** Cheung Yiu Chung, Cheung Kar Fei; **Photography:** Andy Lam; **Music:** Lee Chung Shing; **Cast:** Jackie Chan, Michelle Khan, Maggie Cheung, Ken Tsang, Yuen Wah, Bill Tung, Josephine Koo, Wong Siu.

Posse

GB/USA 1993 111 mins

Western desperadoes Little J (Stephen Baldwin), Father Time (Big Daddy Kane), Jessie Lee (Mario van Peebles), Obobo (Tiny Lister), Weezie (Charles Lane) and Angel (Tone Loc) form a *Posse*.

Mario Van Peebles heads west as both the big bad star and super slick director of *Posse*, a mostly black, partially revisionist western which attempts to set the record straight while shooting everyone in sight and generally having a damn good time doing it. Co-starring the likes of rap star Big Daddy Kane, director Charles Lane, athlete Tiny Lister Jr, *LA Law*'s Blair Underwood and Mario's dad Melvin, himself an accomplished filmmaker (*Sweet Sweetback's Badasss Song*), this is a broad slice of gunfighting entertainment, and if you leave the movie with the knowledge that the Wild West was both white *and* black, then good for you.

Van Peebles (that's Mario, not Melvin) heads the cast as Jesse Lee, the sharp-shooting, rough-riding leader of a gang of black outlaws (plus token white Stephen Baldwin) on the run from their cruel commanding officer, Colonel Graham, a classic rotter (played by Billy Zane) who left them to die in the front line of the Spanish-American war. Returning to Jesse's hometown to settle a score (and score with a settler - the poutingly attractive Salli Richardson), he and his posse blaze a violent though moral path through the old west, all the time waiting for the evil Graham to strike.

Here we have a very stylized portrait of the old west, which attempts to tell an ignored truth that a cowboy could just have easily been black as he could white, although the film seems perfectly content to fall back on hoary old western clichés most everywhere else. Van Peebles MTV style of shooting and editing, evident in his previous feature, the first class blaxploitationer *New Jack City*, is also here in abundance, although he could have cut down on his close-ups - it's pretty clear who directed this picture. There's also a rather bizarre love scene which involves Mario's six shooter (say no more), and provides more than a couple of cheap laughs (not that there's anything wrong with cheap laughs). Elsewhere, the humour works a little more in favour of the movie, and the cast proves affable enough - and Zane villainous enough - for you to cheer with the good guys and sneer at the bad guys. Not a classic tale of the Old West, but one that passes the time well enough.

Director: Mario Van Peebles; **Producers:** Preston Holmes, Jim Steel; **Screenplay:** Sy Richardson, Dario Scardapane; **Production Design:** Catherine Hardwicke; **Editors:** Mark Conte, Seth Flaum; **Photography:** Peter Menzies Jr; **Music:** Michel Colombier; **Cast:** Mario Van Peebles, Stephen Baldwin, Charles Lane, Tiny Lister, Big Daddy Kane, Billy Zane, Blair Underwood, Melvin Van Peebles, Tone Loc, Isaac Hayes.

Predator

USA 1987 107 mins

Arnold Schwarzenegger needed a challenge. Only trouble is, when you're the hardest man on the face of the planet, worthy opponents don't exactly grow on trees. And so the Predator was born, an ugly son-of-a-bitch with a mean streak a mile wide and a portable weapons arsenal powerful enough to wipe the smile off even Arnie's grinning chops. An alien hunter with time to kill and something to prove, it jets over to Earth, sets itself up in a nasty little patch of South American jungle, and simply waits for the meat to arrive.

All the producers of this muscle-bound insanity needed was an excuse to send Arnold into the thick of things, and so they made him big chief of an allied military rescue team who, having been lured into the jungle by shady CIA operatives, find themselves at odds with an invisible creature which delights in picking them off one at a time. It's not exactly a story, but it's a good enough excuse for the ecologically unsound mayhem that follows, as Arnold and his highly-trained team of human beefcake blow apart God's green earth in the hope of maybe hitting something unfriendly.

Chaos rules the day, thanks partly to a testosterone-charged supporting cast which includes hard men Carl Weathers, Bill Duke and Indian tracker-type Sonny Landham, although it is Jesse Ventura's straight-faced, square-jawed machismo that will really blow you away: when informed of a flesh wound inflicted on his person, Jesse remarks without a hint of emotion that he 'ain't got time to bleed'. Now, *that's* cool. Let's just not forget it's Arnold who's the star.

Director John McTiernan keeps the pace tight and the action explosive, building up plenty of tension and then releasing it as noisily and as often as he can get away with, working his way towards an extended battle that, believe me, is well worth waiting for. Also, there's plenty of Predator-induced gore to enjoy, with skinned bodies hanging from trees like Christmas decorations, and a particularly juicy scene involving a disembodied arm with a tirelessly itchy trigger-finger. And, thanks to some state-of-the-art make-up and special effects, our alien friend, as played by the excessively tall Kevin Peter Hall, is the toughest customer Arnold has ever locked horns with.

Sequel: *Predator II.*

Director: John McTiernan; **Producers:** Lawrence Gordon, Joel Silver, John Davis; **Screenplay:** Jim Thomas, John Thomas; **Production Design:** John Vallone; **Editors:** John F. Link, Mark Helfrich; **Photography:** Donald McAlpine, Lein Sanchez; **Music:** Alan Silvestri; **Cast:** Arnold Schwarzenegger, Carl Weathers, Bill Duke, Elphidia Carrillo, Sonny Landham, Jesse Ventura, Kevin Peter Hall.

Predator 2

USA 1990 108 mins

He's in town with a few days to kill... Kevin Peter Hall terrorizes LA in *Predator 2.*

Arnold Schwarzenegger and the jungles of South America make way for Danny Glover and the urban war zones of Los Angeles, circa 1997, for a spectacular second round of alien-hunting adventure. Dreadlocked, fish-faced and ready to rock, our all-new Predator (played, once again, by 7'2" giant Kevin Peter Hall) heads straight for the city of angels, drawn to the chaos and combat opportunities available during a crimewave, a visitor from out of town with a deadly bag of tricks and 'a few days to kill'.

Fighting to preserve the human race is a small squad of supercops, tank girl Leona (Maria Conchita Alonso), cool cat Danny (Ruben Blades) and wide boy Jerry (Bill Paxton), a colourful, crime-busting trio led by Detective-Lieutenant Mike Harrigan (Glover), a Dirty Harry wannabe whose file describes him as prone to violence, with an obsessive/compulsive personality, a history of excessive physical force and, best of all, an aggression level that's 40 per cent above average! He's a tough guy, alright, that much is certain, and Glover does well to fill his shoes, although you can't help missing Arnold from time to time. Gary Busey, meanwhile, rounds off the cast as the boss of a mysterious federal task force, exploring LA on a top secret mission...

No expense was spared in bringing this madness to the screen, a relentlessly exciting actioner put together with a whole lot of pace and a fair amount of style by Jamaican-born Australian director Stephen Hopkins. Noisy and gory, with some amazing special effects and even a little nudity, *Predator 2* charges full steam ahead through some wild and bloody battle sequences, first on a subway train and later in a meat-packing plant, foaming at the mouth as it works its wacky way towards a kick ass finale, as Harrigan and the Predator finally come face-to-face.

Three little words: over the top. Two more: have fun.

Look closely at the alien skulls displayed like trophies on the Predator's ship, and you should be able to spot one of Geiger's *Aliens*.

Director: Stephen Hopkins; **Producer:** Lawrence Gordon, Joel Silver, John Davis; **Screenplay:** Jim Thomas, John Thomas; **Production Design:** Lawrence G. Paull; **Editor:** Mark Goldblatt; **Photography:** Peter Levy; **Music:** Alan Silvestri; **Cast:** Danny Glover, Gary Busey, Ruben Blades, Maria Conchita Alonso, Bill Paxton, Kevin Peter Hall, Robert Davi, Adam Baldwin, Morton Downey Jr.

The Protector

USA 1985 91 Mins

A man who wanted to be sued might mention, in passing, that director James Glickenhaus has, over the years, given schlock a bad name. Take a look at *The Exterminator*, or *Codename: The Soldier*. They're not funny, but they are cheap, grimmer than the reaper and what's more, the characters are usually jerks. It was with this sterling track record that, o lucky man, Glickenhaus enjoyed the biggest break of his career: the chance to direct Hong Kong hero Jackie Chan in an English-language action flick. He couldn't fail. Just switch on the cameras and leave Jackie to it. And Chan does make the picture. In fact, for what it's worth, it's almost certainly the best film Glickenhaus ever made. And yes, the drug lab full of naked chicks could well be described as gratuitous. Especially since there are actually two - count 'em, two - drug-lab-full-of-naked-chick scenes. No need to worry, though, for this excess of female flesh is both artistically valid and important to the story. Besides, where else but here, and quite possibly *The Mambo Kings*, could you enjoy a room so full of bongos?

From Glickenhaus' enchanted typewriter comes Action Movie Plot #1: Chan plays Billy Wong, a New York cop out to avenge the death of his partner at the hands of Hong Kong gangster Harold Ko (Roy Chiao, aka *Indiana Jones and the Temple of Doom*'s Lao Che). Jetting back to Kong with gung ho buddy Danny Garoni (Danny Aiello), Billy hooks up with a beautiful girl (Moon Lee) whose father was killed by Ko, and then it's straight to action stations as battles rage everywhere, from a health farm to the docks and, of course, a certain drug lab that may have been mentioned earlier. Also, there's a fairly nifty speedboat chase to look out for (complete with camera 'copter shadow on the water), a little footbound action on the streets of H.K. and all the wacky stuntwork and hands on villain-pummelling you'd expect from J.C.

Conquering evil but struggling with the dialogue, Chan just about makes it through his lines but leaves the real talking to foul-mouthed sidekick Aiello, an ever-horny, ultra-violent, Italian-American charmer with chins and hardware to spare (Too fat to fight? Does one-on-one action leave you hot, sweaty and hungry for linguini? Why not blast 'em long distance with a portable six-shot 20mm cannon?). Together, they do more damage than SPECTRE and Godzilla combined, and, wisely enough, Glickenhaus leaves them to it.

It ain't *Police Story*, but it'll do.

Director: James Glickenhaus; **Producer:** David Chan; **Screenplay:** James Glickenhaus; **Production Design:** William F. De Seta; **Editor:** Evan Lottman; **Photography:** Mark Irwin; **Music:** Ken Thorne; **Cast:** Jackie Chan, Danny Aiello, Roy Chiao, Saun Ellis, Moon Lee, Victor Arnold, Kim Bass, Richard Clarke, Ronan O'Casey, Bill Wallace.

The Punisher

USA/Australia 1990 90 mins

Dolph Lundren slays his way through *The Punisher*.

Accomplished action movie editor Mark Goldblatt, the scissors and paste behind the likes of *Commando* and *The Last Boy Scout*, eagerly tried his hand at directing a picture of his own, a good idea at the time, maybe, but a disaster of turkey-gobbling proportions once the film had hit the can. Fans of Gerry Conway's ferocious comic book creation, The Punisher, learned the true meaning of disappointment when this lame, live-action non-event limped across the screen, a dead-eyed Dolph Lundgren in the title role.

Revenge is all that matters to renegade ex-cop Frank Castle (Lundgren), the mob assassination of his wife and kids still fresh in his one-track mind. As lone vigilante The Punisher, Castle hides in the sewers and preys on the guilty, a full 125 executions to his credit. Although the film was actually shot on the streets of Sydney, Australia, the setting is Big City, USA, presumably New York, where a gang war between Mafia supremo Gianni Franco (Jeroen Krabbe) and Yakuza sweetheart Lady Tanaka (Kim Miyori) results in a great deal of gunplay and Ninja-style action. Content to let the bad guys kill one another, Castle has no choice but to get involved when Tanaka kidnaps the innocent children of mob bosses throughout the city. Meanwhile, obsessive cop Jake Berkowitz (Louis Gossett Jr) searches for his old pal Castle, a resilient gent he believes may very well be The Punisher...

Charmless and unimaginative, Goldblatt's live-action disaster looks cheap and thrown together, a big fat zero in the screenplay, production design and performance departments. To make matters worse, The Punisher's trademark skull insignia is missing from Lundgren's outfit, a further sign that this awful movie is incapable of doing justice to one of Marvel Comics' most interesting, and most violent, heroes.

Director: Mark Goldblatt; **Producer:** Robert Mark Kamen; **Screenplay:** Boaz Yakin; **Production Design:** Norma Moricuea; **Editor:** Tim Wellburn; **Photography:** Ian Baker; **Music:** Dennis Dreith; **Cast:** Dolph Lundgren, Louis Gossett, Jr, Jeroen Krabbe, Kim Miyori, Nancy Everhard, Barry Otto, Brian Rooney.

The Quest

USA 1996 93 mins

Eastwood did it. Costner did it. Trouble is, Steven Seagal thought he could do it too. So he directed a movie, *On Deadly Ground*, a self-serving, pretentious 'eco-actioner' which proved beyond any reasonable doubt that, if Seagal really had to work at all, he should at the very least operate in front of, and never behind, the cameras. A couple of years down the line, Jean-Claude Van Damme declared his intention to direct, eager, no doubt, to prove just how badly he could make a film. And boy, did he succeed...

A clumsy, self-conscious effort gorged on endless Van Damme close-ups (big surprise), *The Quest* fails on so many levels it's hard to know who or what to rip in to first. For starters, Jean-Claude is trying way too hard to impress here, drawing our attention away from the movie and towards his movie-making, which can't really stand the attention. Clichéd and corn-fed, the screenplay only makes matters worse, a production line of two-dimensional, barely tolerable characters lost in a plot so full of holes it must have been written on Swiss cheese. The cast, even those with acting ability, never stood a chance. When the movie finally ends, it's an added irritation that Van Damme doesn't even bother to finish the story properly. The good news is you won't care. Childishly shallow (no disrespect to kids intended) and cringingly sentimental, this is a premium grade turkey, a trash-fan's dream, hilarious and awful with the added attraction of violence. If you don't appreciate good rubbish, however, you'd best keep well away.

Now, if you still want to know what the movie's all about, well, it's a 1920s' period piece set mostly in Lost City, Nepal, where a secret martial arts competition has attracted an international line-up of tough guys, each with their own distinctive fighting style. There's a solid golden dragon waiting for the winner, and good guy Chris Dubois (Jean-Claude) wants it to help out his poor little orphan chums back home in New York. Meanwhile, aristocratic conman Dobbs (the one and only Roger Moore) has his own plans for the statue...

There's action, some of it decent, but mostly run-of-the-mill, with a series of *Street Fighter*-like encounters rounding the foolishness off (too much slow-motion, though). Good luck.

Director: Jean-Claude Van Damme; **Producer:** Moshe Diamant; **Screenplay:** Stuart Klein, Paul Mones, story by Frank Dux, Jean-Claude Van Damme; **Production Design:** Steve Spence; **Editor:** John F. Link; **Photography:** David Gribble; **Music:** Randy Edelman; **Cast:** Jean-Claude Van Damme, Roger Moore, James Remar, Janet Gunn, Jack McGee, Aki Aleong, Abdel Qissi, Louis Mandylor.

Rage and Honour

USA 1992 90 mins

Meet Preston (Richard Norton, tough but fair). He's an Aussie cop, a fast-talking Croc Dundee-type into martial arts and origami. Now, meet Kris (Cynthia Rothrock, fair but tough). She's an inner-city school teacher and martial arts instructor, a veteran do-gooder who's determined to make a difference. Preston's supposed to be working with the LAPD as an observer, but you know how it is with these on-the-edge types: they can never be trusted to keep out of trouble. Then along comes this plot involving drug dealers, crooked cops and a mystery videotape, and suddenly Preston's on the run from the law, framed for murder and desperate to clear his name. Of course, if he caught the real bad guys he'd be off the hook, but he's going to need help, and who can he ask? How about Kris, who's just aching to teach those bullies a lesson they'll never forget, providing, of course, they survive it at all.

Batting for the bad guys, there's Rita (Terri Treas, passable), surname Carrion (*n*. dead and decaying flesh), the big, bad crime boss responsible for all the confusion, a stereotypically fiery redhead who controls her man with incredible sex (a better way than most). That man happens to be our henchman of the hour, a blond, long-haired slab of beefcake named Drago (multi-purpose heavy Brian Thompson), first name Conrad, a twisted killer whose mannered style and tendency to work out to opera music renders him ridiculous, but that's the way we like him.

Just when you thought it was safe to read on, along comes a twist: could it be true that Drago and Kris are actually brother and sister? Could big, tall and ugly truly be related to short, pert and spunky? And, if these two do turn out to be from the same gene pool, what's going to happen when they slug it out at the end of the movie? Ah, questions, questions...

Anyway, on with the show. Sidekick duties are fulfilled by Baby (Stephen Davies, flaky), a mentally disturbed vagrant exploited for plot development and comic relief ('I'm losing my mind out here', he screams for our amusement). Elsewhere, on the side of evil stands

Hannah the Hun (Alex Datcher, slutty), a hip, 1990s chick with an all-girl gang of grungy American Gladiator-types. The 'women in positions of power' theme (could this be 'Associate Producer' C. Rothrock's handywork?) continues with our final player, Captain Murdock (Catherine Bach, extraneous), cop shop supremo and practitioner of angry chastisements.

Rest assured that with this lot running around, violent chaos is guaranteed, although you'd best be prepared for the loose ends which present themselves at the end of the movie. As for Norton and Rothrock, well, truth is they make a pretty good team. Agile, strong and likeable, they even have a little chemistry going on there for a while, and they never disappoint when it comes to administering punishment.

Speedy, slick and pleasingly dumb, *Rage and Honour* delivers in full, earning an added nod of approval for laying on a viciously inventive killing made possible by a tragically unstable trigger finger (you'll know it when you see it).

Director: Terence H. Winkless; **Producer:** Donald Paul Pemrick; **Screenplay:** Terence H. Winkless; **Production Design:** Billy Jet; **Editor:** David Byron Lloyd; **Photography:** Tom Callaway; **Music:** Darryl Way; **Cast:** Cynthia Rothrock, Richard Norton, Terri Treas, Brian Thompson, Alex Datcher, Stephen Davies, Catherine Bach.

Raiders of the Lost Ark

USA 1981 115 mins

Indiana Jones swings into action in his first and finest adventure, a whip-cracking tribute to the cliffhangers of the 1930s and 1940s from cinema supremos George Lucas and Steven Spielberg. Rarely does a movie get everything so absolutely right, but you could study it frame by frame, analyse each and every element, take a university course in advanced nit-picking and examine it further under the world's most powerful microscope, and you're still not going to find even the slightest thing wrong with *Raiders of the Lost Ark*. Smart, spirited and devoted to action, home of the coolest heroes and most hissable villains, faster than a speeding bullet and more exciting than a night with the Texas Cheerleaders, *Raiders* offers about as much entertainment as a human being is capable of receiving without expiring.

Harrison Ford takes the lead as Indy, our straight-shooting, whip-wielding, daredevil hero, world-famous 'professor of archaeology, expert on the occult, [and] obtainer of rare antiquities'. Dressed for action in a tough, brown leather jacket, and a brimmed, felt hat which he absolutely refuses to lose, Dr Jones battles the best of the worst in the name of history, rescuing treasured artefacts from a variety of crooked archaeologists, fortune hunters and goose-stepping super-soldiers. Big, hairy spiders, bottomless pits, poisonous darts and master swordsmen don't phase Indiana one bit. Snakes, on the other hand, scare him half to death, so you can imagine how he feels when confronted with around 7000 of the slimy critters in a dark, underground temple from where there may be no escape...

The year is 1936 and Adolf's army are up to no good, digging up half of Cairo in search of the fabled Lost Ark of the Covenant, resting place of the original Ten Commandments and a devastating supernatural weapon to boot. Hitler, it seems, has bought into the legend that '...an army which carries the Ark before it is invincible', which is exactly why a couple of Washington bods beg Indy to get a hold of the Ark before the Nazis can. It's not going to be easy though, and before he's through, Jones is going to need some help.

Offering a whole lot more than love interest, Karen Allen blazes across the screen as Marion Ravenwood, a hard drinking gal of the tough cookie variety, an old flame of Indy's who holds the key to the puzzle and tags along for the ride. Meanwhile, John Rhys-Davies offers ebullient support as Sallah, everyone's favourite Egyptian digger, a loyal family man who takes his sidekick and comic relief duties seriously. Then there are the bad guys, including Ronald Lacey as Toht, a pasty-faced Nazi with sadistic tastes, and Paul Freeman as Belloq, a French archaeologist and Nazi collaborator of questionable character.

John Williams contributes a soundtrack which proves as rousing as the visuals, doing his bit for the war effort as Indy plunges head first into an assortment of dangers, from a booby-trapped temple and burning bar brawl right through to a bloody one-to-one with a gigantic Nazi mechanic, and a stunt-laden truck chase which may very well be the most incredible action sequence ever filmed.

Satisfaction is guaranteed, especially if you have the opportunity to see this spectacular movie on the big screen. Video jockeys should aim for the widescreen version only, and not the TV standard, pan-and-scan version which dares to cut the movie in half.

 A five-star movie deserves five-star trivia: * Long before Harrison Ford was cast as Indiana Jones, TV star Tom Selleck was up for the role, and you can imagine what a disaster that might have been. Fortunately, however, contractual obligations kept Selleck firmly tied to *Magnum*, far away from the set of *Raiders of the Lost Ark*. ** Wrestler and *Auf Wiedersehen Pet* star Pat Roach plays duel roles here, first as a Sherpa who takes on Indy in Nepal, and second as the bald mechanic who battles our hero beside the Nazis' Flying Wing aircraft. * Producer Frank Marshall, better known today as the director of *Arachnophobia* and *Alive*, plays the Flying Wing pilot knocked out by Marion. **** Inscribed among the hieroglyphics on the wall behind the Ark in the Well of the Souls, *Star Wars'* R2-D2 and C-3PO make tiny cameo appearances. ***** Screenwriter Lawrence Kasdan, director of *The Big Chill* and *Silverado*, named the heroic Dr Jones after George Lucas's dog, Indiana.**

Prequel: *Indiana Jones and the Temple of Doom*. Sequel: *Indiana Jones and the Last Crusade*. TV spin-off: *The Young Indiana Jones Chronicles*.

Director: Steven Spielberg; **Producer:** Frank Marshall; Executive **Producers:** George Lucas, Howard Kazanjian; **Screenplay:** Lawrence Kasdan, story by George Lucas, Philip Kaufman; **Production Design:** Norman Reynolds; **Editor:** Michael Kahn; **Photography:** Douglas Slocombe; **Music:** John Williams; **Cast:** Harrison Ford, Karen Allen, Paul Freeman, Ronald Lacey, John Rhys-Davies, Denholm Elliott, Wolf Kahler. **Academy Awards:** Best... Visual Effects, Sound, Editing, Art Direction, Sound Effects Editing.

Rambo: First Blood Part II

USA 1985 95 mins

'To survive a war, you gotta become war...'. John Rambo strikes a blow for Uncle Sam by winning the only war his beloved country ever lost, re-writing history with a happy ending and cleaning up at the box office as a result. The concept of one man succeeding where an entire nation failed might seem insulting, yet America didn't see it that way at all, choosing instead to cheer on their favourite son as he slaughtered hordes of Vietnamese soldiers, striking a blow for truth and justice and securing a clear, moral victory which had even President Ray-Gun applauding in the aisles.

There were times in *First Blood* when Rambo seemed almost human, not exactly believable, but driven by emotion and the irresistible urge to survive, whereas by the time this second adventure rolled around, *Cobra* director George P. Cosmatos had opted for a pulp comic book feel which demanded an indestructible fighting machine in a black-and-white world where a single good guy can take on (literally) hundreds of heavily armed baddies (none of whom seem capable of shooting in a straight line) without such distracting elements as humour, common sense or basic charm. Still, the action rarely disappoints and you're bound to be entertained, just so long as you don't mind cheering on a brainless, mono-syllabic drone with bulging muscles and a dead-eyed look of grim determination throughout.

This time around, Rambo drops in on his Vietnamese chums for a slaughter-fest of bibli-cal proportions, slashing and blasting and blowing the hell out of any poor fool who stands between Johnny boy and his ultimate objective: the liberation of American prisoners of war held in secret jungle camps. Recruited by his old pal Colonel Trautman (Richard Crenna), Rambo has but a single question before the chaos begins: 'Sir, do we get to win this time?' '*This* time,' advises the Trautmeister, 'it's up to you'. And guess who else is coming to din-ner? None other than the cotton-pickin' Ruskies, a pesky bunch of highly armed critters led by a typically vicious and shamelessly over-played Steven Berkoff villain, a sneering Red who knows his way around a flying gunship and aims to prove it to J.R. Subplots include a short-lived romance between Hambo and lady guide Julia Nickson, while Charles Napier (who you might remember as the guard whose face Hannibal the Cannibal 'borrows' in *Silence of the Lambs*) offers his services as a double-crossing US agent who strands the big man in the middle of a war zone, forcing him to fight his way through a never-ending pro-duction line of moving targets.

If you thought the first movie was outrageous, wait till you get a load of this one: we're talking mid-1980s, caution to the wind, excessively forceful, pre-politically correct macho bullshit complete with non-stop jungle madness and a thirst for blood and thunder matched only by such savoury historical figures as Vlad the Impaler and Atilla the Hun.

 Keeping it in the family, Sly had his brother Frank sing the movie's title song, 'Peace in our Time', though what this sequel has to do with peace is a mystery of *Murder, She Wrote* proportions. You have been warned (TV's on mute, if you know what's good for you). Oh yeah, for an extra nugget of trivia, check out who co-wrote the picture with Stallone.

Director: George P. Cosmatos; **Producer:** Buzz Feitshans; **Screenplay:** Sylvester Stallone, James Cameron, story by Kevin Jarre, based on characters created by David Morrell; **Production Design:** Bill Kenney; **Editor:** Mark Goldblatt, Mark Helfrich; **Photography:** Jack Cardiff; **Music:** Jerry Goldsmith; **Cast:** Sylvester Stallone, Richard Crenna, Charles Napier, Steven Berkoff, Julia Nickson, George Kee Cheung, Andy Wood, Martin Kove.

Rambo III

USA 1988 101 mins

Way back in 1988, the Mujaheddin triumphed against the Russians, forcing their with-drawal from Afghanistan. Check it out, it's called history. Anyway, with the Reds out of the picture the conflict was pretty much resolved, which was good news for the world, but not quite so wonderful for producer Buzz Feitshans, whose latest feature, *Rambo III*, dealt with the muscled-one's efforts against the Russians in, you guessed it, Afghanistan. Now, had the war raged for just a few months longer, the movie could have played the topicality card and cashed in big time, but as it turned out, it kind of missed the boat with that one, earning respectable if not phenomenal returns at the box office which ensured that this third adventure would be John Rambo's last.

Exaggerated beyond all boundaries of reality, *Rambo III* weighs in as one of the most outrageous action pictures of all time, a tribute to mindless macho bullshit in its many var-ied forms, a magic carpet ride of unintentional comedy, deeply caricatured characters and good, old-fashioned, 1980s ultra-violence. In other words, it's a scream, hugely enjoyable for all the wrong reasons and perfect for all the family (so long as your family is made up entirely of young male adults).

As for the story, well, it's terribly complicated, but here goes. Colonel Samuel Trautman's (Richard Crenna) in some serious trouble, having been captured during a mission in Afghanistan. Held captive in a Russian fortress by the fiendish Colonel Zaysen (Marc de Jonge), there's only one man who can save him: a full-blooded combat machine with the social skills of a zombie, a barely intelligible super-soldier whose passion for destruction draws him away from his Buddhist buddies for a third round of ultra-unlikely rough and tumble, this time in the desert, and with a supporting cast of Mujaheddin buddies to back him up.

Let's hear it then, for action and nothing but, as jolly John Rambo kicks off with a blazing stick fight in Thailand, presses on through various invasions and mountaintop struggles (watch out for an excellent death scene involving a makeshift noose and a well-timed grenade!), takes time to cauterize a nasty arrow wound and finally stands tall against the entire Russian army. Faced with tanks, flying gunships and hundreds of troops, Colonel Sam looks at Rambo, his partner in arms against the world, and asks, 'What do you say, John?' The reply: ' Fuck 'em!'

A perfect union of bloodthirsty fantasy and solid gold idiocy, *Rambo III* is so far over-the-top it's in orbit.

Director: Peter MacDonald; **Producer:** Buzz Feitshans; **Screenplay:** Sylvester Stallone, Sheldon Lettich, based on characters created by David Morrell; **Production Design:** Bill Kenney; **Editors:** James Symons, Andrew London, O. Nicholas Brown, Edward A. Warschilka; **Photography:** John Stainer; **Music:** Jerry Goldsmith; **Cast:** Sylvester Stallone, Richard Crenna, Marc de Jonge, Sasson Gabai, Kurtwood Smith, Spiros Focas.

Rapid Fire

USA 1992 95 mins

Undressed and unarmed, Brandon Lee sizes up a lamb-to-the-slaughter opponent (Jeff McCarthy) in *Rapid Fire*.

Brandon Lee's energetic performance in this wildly violent martial arts flick looked likely to establish him as one of the most successful 'chop socky' leading men of the 1990s. Stepping out of his father's shadow, Lee proved more likeable, versatile and charismatic than most other action heroes of the day, while his remarkable fight choreography (in association with Jeff Imada) elevated what might have been an ordinary B-picture into something his fans will remember forever. Today we can only speculate as to how successful Lee might have been had he not died on the set of *The Crow*, yet it seems clear from his incredible work in *Rapid Fire* that eventually he would have risen to the top of his field.

The story, while it doesn't contribute to the movie in any significant way, does at least provide several excuses for mortal combat. Lee plays an art student - and martial arts expert - who witnesses a mob killing, and subsequently spends the rest of the movie trying to stay alive, while the mobster - your usual common or garden mad dog variety (with a twist of Italian, as played to the hilt by Nick Mancuso) - spends the rest of the movie trying to kill him. There's also a pretty extraneous sub-plot which starts with a flashback of Jake (Lee) witnessing his father's death in Tienanmen Square, which provides our hero with a fair helping of mental anguish. 'Will he ever be able to commit himself to a cause?' we ask ourselves. And, 'When will he stop running away - from himself?' Then along comes butch father figure Powers Boothe, a maverick cop with plenty of attitude, and hey presto, Jake is given plenty of opportunities to work out his problems. Never mind the psychiatrist's couch: if you really want to get your head straight, it's best to kill or at least maim as many people as possible in a number of strange and interesting ways.

Lee brought the inventiveness and frenetic pacing of Eastern action movies to the West, surprising hardened fans of the genre with moves that were ten times sharper than a switchblade. While each and every fight scene has something new to offer, Lee's one-on-one with Fu Manchu lookalike and master stuntman Al Leong is just about the most incredible thing you'll ever see, a dazzling display of martial arts technique which ranks right up there with the best of Bruce Lee and Jackie Chan.

Ultimately, what we have here is a great 'good time' movie: there's no social message, no deep undercurrents of meaning, just lots and lots of action. And Brandon Lee is the absolute business.

Director: Dwight H. Little; **Producer:** Robert Lawrence; **Screenplay:** Alan McElroy; **Production Design:** Ron Foreman; **Editor:** Gib Jaffe; **Photography:** Ric Waite; **Music:** Christopher Young; **Cast:** Brandon Lee, Powers Boothe, Nick Mancuso, Raymond J. Barry, Kate Hodge, Tzi Ma.

Raw Deal

USA 1986 106 mins

Death is in the air as Arnold Schwarzenegger takes on the mob in this heavy-handed thriller, a brutal and bloody vehicle for the world's favourite Austrian, here in full *Terminator* mode as unstoppable crime buster Kaminski, a guy you most definitely wouldn't want to mess with. Sporting slicked-back hair and a black leather jacket, Arnold plays it cool and confident all the way, a weapons arsenal strapped tightly to his chest (think *Commando*) as he sails from one violent confrontation to another, stumbling occasionally over the odd dead body and awkward one-liner ('You should not drink and bake' is just about the best the movie can manage).

When we first lay eyes on our hero he's marking time as the cigar chomping Sheriff of a nowhere hick town. Formerly a crusading FBI agent, Kaminski (Arnold) was set up by the mob and busted right out of the Bureau. But now he has a chance to get back in the game, only he has to do an old friend a favour first. Eager to avenge the murder of his son, Police Chief Shannon (Darren McGavin) offers Kaminski a fresh start if only he'll infiltrate the powerful Petrovita family (led by a smoothly dangerous Sam Wanamaker) and basically trash the lot of them for wasting his boy. Kill 'em all and let God sort 'em out, that sort of thing. So naturally Kaminski agrees, and it's hell and thunder from there on in.

Director John Irvin makes the most of his star on the action front, sending Arnold into one car chase, gun fight and punch up after another. Particularly memorable is the gravel pit showdown, in which Kaminski tears through the dump in a flashy convertible, The Rolling Stones' 'Satisfaction' blaring out of the car stereo as he shoots every bad guy in sight. Now *that* takes class, yet when it comes to the straighter acting portions of the movie, Arnold seems a lot less confident. Maybe when you're working with a script as dire as the one this movie is lumbered with, an awkward performance is only to be expected. The supporting cast do what they can, but without a commanding central presence, there's little to distract us from the fact that there isn't much to see here that's new or exciting. The film simply gets by without hitting too many highs or too many lows. Expect anything more and you're going to be disappointed.

Director: John Irvin; **Producer:** Martha Schumacher; **Screenplay:** Gary M. DeVore, Norman Wexler; **Production Design:** Giorgio Postiglione; **Editor:** Anne V. Coates; **Photography:** Alex Thomson; **Music Design:** Cinemascore; **Cast:** Arnold Schwarzenegger, Kathryn Harrold, Darren McGavin, Sam Wanamaker, Paul Shenar, Steven Hill, Ed Lauter, Robert Davi.

Red Dawn

USA 1984 114 mins

Ask not what your country can do for you, but what you can do for your country... Taking a break from the heartache of teen romance, youthful rebellion, parents, homework and zits, The Brat Pack sign up for a tour of duty with director John Milius, kicking butt for Uncle Sam as they defend their homeland against an invading army of foreign stereotypes.

The land of the free and home of the Twinkie makes up for almost missing the first two world wars by hosting the third on home ground. As a shifty assortment of Russian, Cuban and Nicaraguan militia launch a series of surprise attacks throughout the once-United States, a handful of Colorado school boys and girls head for the hills, fleeing for their lives. Stuck 40 miles behind enemy lines in occupied territory located 'right smack dab in the middle of World War III', our young heroes come to try their hand at freedom fighting, forming a rather destructive and fiercely inventive guerrilla force known as the Wolverines, which as we all know, is a small, ferocious animal, and by an amazing coincidence, the name of the local sports team as well.

Leading the Wolverines against consummate military man Colonel Bella (Ron O'Neal), a baby-faced Patrick Swayze joins the likes of C. Thomas Howell, Lea Thompson and Charlie Sheen in combat, enjoys a pre-*Dirty Dancing* fling with Jennifer Grey, and takes manly advice from arrogant ultra-right wing colonel Powers Boothe who bemoans Europe's wartime non-involvement with a simple, 'I guess they figured that twice in one century was enough'.

Anyway, it's all very heroic, bloody stuff, this war business, spun around a strict formula which alternates political tosh and violence with sentimental tosh and violence. There's certainly no shortage of action, with a helitank sequence and a climactic assault on the town providing two of the highlights.

But, you know, it's hard to figure out why the forces of evil invaded Colorado in the first place, unless, that is, they were planning on doing a little mountain climbing and white-water river rafting while they were there.

Director: John Milius; **Producers:** Buzz Feitshans, Barry Beckerman; **Screenplay:** Kevin Reynolds, John Milius; **Production Design:** Jackson DeGovia; **Editor:** Thom Noble; **Photography:** Ric Waite; **Music:** Basil Poledouris; **Cast:** Patrick Swayze, C. Thomas Howell, Lea Thompson, Charlie Sheen, Jennifer Grey, Powers Boothe, Ben Johnson, Harry Dean Stanton, Ron O'Neal, William Smith.

Red Heat

USA 1988 104 mins

We're talking motivation, here. Arnold Schwarzenegger, bless him, plays Ivan Dankow, a stern Russian policeman whose partner dies at the hands of wicked Ruskie drug dealer Viktor Rostavili (Ed O'Ross in full sneer mode). That makes one vendetta. Adding to the body count, Viktor's wayward brother manages to get himself shot (several times, actually) by our Ivan, doubling the score to two vendettas, and we're not even ten minutes into the movie yet. Out of luck, Viktor flees to the States in search of contacts who can help him smuggle that Western poison, 'cocainum', back home, and so Ivan, having no life or sense of humour about drugs, pursues our villain all the way to Chicago. Once there, we're introduced to bog-standard smart-ass detective Art Ridzik (James Belushi, playing it TV cop show all the way), whose partner, wouldn't you know it, gets blown away by one of Viktor's new friends. That, then, makes three vendettas, and a whole lot of motivation, as Ivan and Art form another one of those queasily uneasy alliances, tearing up the town in search of the ultimate Red Menace and his goon-like chums.

Fine, so we can all see how well motivated Ivan, Art and Viktor are, but can we say the same about director Walter Hill, whose decision to devote a year of his life to this anaemic feature remains a mystery? And does anyone have any idea why the Soviet authorities granted *Red Heat*, of all films, the honour of being the first Western production allowed to shoot (film) in Moscow's historic Red Square? Questions, questions everywhere, and all of them more interesting than the movie itself.

If you're tuning in for action, there's a moderately destructive bus chase to look forward to, while devoted Arnold fans might squeeze a laugh out of the spectacle of our hero wrestling semi-naked in the snow with a miscellaneous bad guy. Other than that, the film is pretty ordinary really, but that's only to be expected from a buddy movie in which you neither like the buddies nor believe in their friendship.

Director: Walter Hill; **Producer:** Walter Hill, Gordon Carroll; **Screenplay:** Harry Kleiner, Walter Hill, Troy Kennedy Martin; **Production Design:** John Vallone; **Editor:** Freeman Davies, Carmel Davies, Donn Aron; **Photography:** Matthew F. Leonetti; **Music:** James Horner; **Cast:** Arnold Schwarzenegger, James Belushi, Peter Boyle, Ed O'Ross, Larry Fishburne.

Trivialists 5

T & A
Baring more than their souls...

Girls
Rosanna Arquette, *Nowhere to Run*
Tia Carrere, *Showdown in Little Tokyo*
Cindy Crawford, *Fair Game*
Linda Hamilton, *The Terminator*
Patsy Kensit, *Lethal Weapon 2*, *Timebomb*
Jennifer Jason Leigh, *Flesh + Blood*
Kelly Lynch, *Road House*
Tanya Roberts, *The Beastmaster*
Sharon Stone, *Action Jackson*, *The Specialist*
Vanity, *Action Jackson*

Boys
Mel Gibson, *Lethal Weapon*, *Bird on a Wire*
Rutger Hauer, *Flesh + Blood*
Christopher Lambert, *Highlander*
Dolph Lundgren, *Showdown in Little Tokyo*
Kurt Russell, *Tango & Cash*
Arnold Schwarzenegger, *The Terminator*, *Red Heat*
Sylvester Stallone, *Tango & Cash*, *The Specialist*
Patrick Swayze, *Roadhouse*
Jean-Claude Van Damme, *Bloodsport*, *Universal Soldier*
Denzel Washington, *Ricochet*

Red Scorpion

USA 1989 102 mins

Scraping the barrel of entertainment on the backside of B-movie schlock, director Joseph Zito and big, bad beefcake Dolph Lundgren pool their limited resources to create something not only cheap and nasty, but dull and with a lousy sense of humour, too.

As a Soviet officer packed off to Africa to waste pesky rebel leader Sundata (Ruben Nthodi), Dolph reads the riot act as relentless killing machine Nikolai, the Red Scorpion. But the Russians are an evil lot, brutal slayers of women and children, the lot of 'em, and so Nikolai throws in with the rebels against his former comrades. Or something like that. Actually, it's not always clear exactly whose side Dolph is on, and we can all thank the screenplay for that, hopeless jumble that it is.

Violence is clearly the name of the game here, and there's certainly no shortage of the stuff, with extras a-plenty to slaughter at will and heavy-duty hardware to waste them with, but it's a flat and cheerless process, at best, and drags much too often.

Then there's the cast you'll care nothing about, starting with Lundgren and working on down to *Missing in Action*'s M. Emmet Walsh as a Red-hating journo and *Tango & Cash*'s Brion James in a typically scummy, villainous role (complete with dodgy accent).

Oddly enough, Zito aims to give the madness some meaning, a failed attempt which sees Lundgren seeking to find himself, questioning his life and choice of career when really, what he should have done, was quit the movie and write a body-building book instead. Worse still, Dolph spends much of the movie in a semi-naked state, wandering around the desert in little more than sandals and a torn pair of boxers.

All this and a Little Richard soundtrack too..

If it sounds like torture, that's because it is. A heavy-handed flop, in fact, worth missing by all.

Director: Joseph Zito; **Producer:** Jack Abramoff; **Screenplay:** Arne Olsen, story by Robert Abramoff, Jack Abramoff, Arne Olsen; **Production Design:** Ladislav Wilhelm; **Editor:** Dan Loewenthal; **Photography:** João Fernandes; **Music:** Jay Chattaway; **Cast:** Dolph Lundgren, M. Emmet Walsh, Al White, T.P. McKenna, Carmen Argenziano, Alex Colon, Brion James, Regopostaan, Ruben Nthodi.

Red Sonja

USA 1985 89 mins

Before Stallone, the implants, the settlement, and the tabloid feeding frenzy, Brigitte Nielsen launched a bungled screen career with this crass, puerile and hopelessly ham-handed sword and sorcery adventure, a turkey of the first order which had the nerve to relegate Arnold Schwarzenegger to a supporting role, that of sidekick and, god help us all, tenuous romantic interest. Director Richard Fleischer laboured beyond all reason to prove that he was capable of making a motion picture that was even worse than *Conan the Destroyer*, and boy, did he succeed with *Red Sonja*, an ugly jumble of ludicrous costume and set designs, dim-witted dialogue, useless non-performances and the kind of bug-eyed monsters which can only be found at the bottom of the special effects food chain, below even the cardboard creations of *Dr Who* and the rubbery foolishness of *Warlords of Atlantis*.

Conan the Barbarian's Sandahl Bergman makes an ass of herself as evil Queen Gedren, a tyrannical ham with a brand new toy, a stolen talisman with enormous destructive powers. Naturally, someone has to stop her before she blows up the planet, and who better than fiery warrior Red Sonja (Nielsen), whose entire family was slaughtered by Gedren years earlier? Enough with the plot, already, 'cos it's clobbering time, a task Sonja sets to with occasional assistance from obnoxious youth Prince Tarn (Ernie Reyes Jr), his ever-patient guardian Falkon (Paul Smith), and randy marauder Kalidor (Arnold), who slaughters hundreds of men hoping to impress Sonja, and when she finally reveals that '...no man may have me unless he has beaten me in a fair fight', he gets out his sword and battles her for a shag. Classy.

They don't come any dumber than this, that's for damn certain. Arnold's not in the movie nearly enough, Nielsen shouldn't have been in it at all, the action is passable but offers nothing that we haven't seen a million times before, and the violence isn't nearly gory enough.

Time for the bottom line: cut out all the bad stuff and you've got a 15-minute classic. Sit through all 89 minutes, however, and all you'll get is a headache.

Director: Richard Fleischer; **Producer:** Christian Ferry; **Screenplay:** Clive Exton, George MacDonald Fraser, based on the character created by Robert E. Howard; **Production Design:** Danilo Donati; **Editor:** Frank J. Urioste; **Photography:** Giuseppe Rotunno; **Music:** Ennio Morricone; **Cast:** Brigitte Nielsen, Arnold Schwarzenegger, Sandahl Bergman, Paul Smith, Ernie Reyes, Jr, Ronald Lacey, Pat Roach.

Remo: Unarmed and Dangerous (aka Remo Williams: The Adventure Begins)

USA 1985 122 mins

Fred Ward hangs out with Lady Liberty in *Remo: Unarmed and Dangerous.*

From director Guy Hamilton, the man behind such classic Bond flicks as *Goldfinger* and *Live and Let Die*, comes a new breed of blue collar superhero, Remo Williams, a slob-cop turned New York avenger, likeably played with lots of clumsy charm by Fred Ward. Inspired by Richard Sapir and Warren Murphy's 'Destroyer' novels, *Remo* is a goofy, comic-book actioner, good-natured and exciting, with a spirited student/sensei relationship at its core.

Recruited by a covert crime-busting agency dedicated to bringing untouchable villains to justice (no matter what it takes), our hero is sent to train (and bond) with a master of Sinanju (*Cabaret*'s Joel Grey, completely hidden under heavy Oriental make-up), an eccentric Korean of advancing years whose back-breaking instruction transforms Remo from your basic couch potato into a quick-witted, bullet-dodging martial artist with a sturdy sense of humour and a new, *eleventh* commandment to enforce: 'You shall not get away with it'.

As Remo's skills increase, the movie lays on greater challenges, from a brief encounter with three brainy Dobermans, to an acrobatic battle with a henchman trio on a scaffolded Statue of Liberty. Unfortunately, Remo's adventures began and ended with this single, promising film. It's far from perfect, but loaded with potential, and could have developed into an enjoyable series. As it is, *Remo* is a one-off diamond-in-the-rough.

Director: Guy Hamilton; **Producers:** Dick Clark, Larry Spiegel, Mel Bergman; **Screenplay:** Christopher Wood, based on the 'Destroyer' novels by Richard Sapir and Warren Murphy; **Production Design:** Jackson de Govia; **Photography:** Andrew Laszlo; **Music:** Craig Safan; **Cast:** Fred Ward, Joel Grey, Wilford Brimley, J. A. Preson, Charles Cioffi, Kate Mulgrew, George Coe.

Renegades

USA 1989 105 mins

By the numbers, then: **1.** Pursued by cops and mobsters alike, misunderstood undercover cop *Buster McHenry (Kiefer Sutherland) resolves to clear his name by bringing Mafia goon Marino (Rob Knepper) to justice. **2.** Lakota Indian **Hank Storm (Lou Diamond Phillips), smouldering guardian of his tribe's sacred lance, randomly crosses paths with said gangsters, losing both his brother and the lance in the process. **3.** Awesome car chase***. **4.** Our heroes meet. **5.** They hate each other (it's a cultural thing). **6.** Guns, guns, guns and a pretty cool train stunt. **7.** They hate but respect each other. **8.** They team up. **9.** Another personal tragedy. **10.** They jump off a roof. **11.** Dirty cops subplot. **12.** Blazing buildings, horseplay, forest frolicking... **13.** Feeble Hollywood resolution.

* Easily disgruntled Dirty Harry wannabe with serious moustache problems.

** Super-cool Native American Indian hero, proud of his heritage, even if going on about it kills the movie.

*** An undercover screw-up sees Buster driving getaway for Marino, who's being pursued - on foot - by Hank. Lots of screaming, fleeing civilians, car wrecks and flashy stunt work. Shame it's at the beginning, though: following this rousing early climax, it's downhill all the way.

He directed *The Hidden*, but you can't hit the bullseye every time: Jack Sholder, who can do a whole lot better, didn't. It's not that *Renegades* is unwatchable, but it is about as bog-standard as they come, a testosterone charged buddy flick which would have worked a whole lot better had Sholder cut out everything but the violence and slapped the auto-action at the end.

Director: Jack Sholder; **Producer:** David Madden; **Screenplay:** David Rich; **Production Design:** Carol Spier; **Editor:** Caroline Biggerstaff; **Photography:** Phil Meheux; **Music:** Michael Kamen; **Cast:** Kiefer Sutherland, Lou Diamond Phillips, Rob Knepper, Bill Smitrovich, Peter MacNeil, Jami Gertz.

Return of the Jedi

USA 1983 132 mins

Welcome to '34 reasons why *Return of the Jedi* is almost as good as *The Empire Strikes Back*...' A brand new Death Star. Luke visits the homeland. Jabba the Hutt, vile, tubby gangster. Jabba's palace (cantina sequence, take two). Bib Fortuna's (Michael Carter) head. Boushh. The Rancor. Solo decarbonized. The pit of Carkoon, nesting place of the all-powerful Sarlacc, in whose belly 'you will find a new definition of pain and suffering, as you are slowly digested over a thousand years'. Leia in a super-skimpy outfit. Jabba's sail barge rumble. Boba Fett's cameo. Yoda's cameo. Ben's cameo. Admiral Ackbar (Dermot Crowley), vertical salmon. The Emperor (Ian McDiarmid), evil wizard-type with a skin disorder. The Imperial Shuttle Tydirium. Luke, Leia, Solo, Chewie and the Droids visit the forest Moon of Endor. Enter the Ewoks, spear-chucking teddy bears with tremendous merchandising potential. Ewok superstar Wicket (*Willow*'s Warwick Davis). The high-speed, forest-bound, speeder bike pursuit. Threepio impersonates a deity, 'I never knew I had it in me'. Further soap-style revelations. Luke confronts Vader (only then, a Jedi will he be). General Solo and the Ewoks take on the Empire to take out the energy shield. AT-ST (All Terrain Scout Transport) adventures. Lando and the rebel fleet hit outer space for incredible dog-fighting action. Wedge (Denis Lawson) returns, again. The Emperor confronts Luke, 'If you will not be turned, you will be destroyed'. Vader confronts himself. The Falcon invades the Death Star's rusty innards. Vader's face. Serious excitement. Amazing effects. The Force will be with you... always.

Director: Richard Marquand; **Producer:** Howard Kazanjian; **Executive Producer:** George Lucas; **Screenplay:** Lawrence Kasdan, George Lucas; **Production Design:** Norman Reynolds; **Editors:** Stuart Barton, Marcia Lucas, Duwayne Dunham; **Photography:** Alan Hume; **Music:** John Williams; **Cast:** Mark Hamill, Harrison Ford, Carrie Fisher, Billy Dee Williams, Anthony Daniels, David Prowse, Peter Mayhew, Sebastian Shaw, Ian McDiarmid, Kenny Baker, Frank Oz, Alec Guiness, Jeremy Bulloch, James Earl Jones (voice only). **Academy Award:** Best Visual Effects (Richard Edlund, Dennis Muren, Ken Ralston, Phil Tippett).

Ricochet

USA 1991 102 mins

Supercop Denzel Washington enforces the law in *Ricochet*.

Denzel Washington enjoys the full benefit of an action makeover, looking cool and hard in a lunatic thriller directed by *Highlander*'s Russell Mulcahy, scripted by *Commando*'s Steven E. de Souza and produced by jolly Joel Silver, the driving force behind such monster hits as *Die Hard*, *Predator* and *Lethal Weapon*. Not a bad pedigree for any movie, but a lot to live up to as well, and if it doesn't quite meet the same high standards set by the classics of the genre, it sure as hell gives it its best shot.

As golden boy Nick Styles, Washington plays a cop whose flashy apprehension of premium psychopath Earl Talbot Blake makes him famous, a public crusader with a future as bright as Blake's is dark. A couple of years down the line, and Nick has it all: he's handsome and athletic, hip and wholesome, wealthy, popular, married to the prettiest gal in town, father of two beautiful daughters and assistant district attorney to boot. Sickening, really, especially for Blake, who dedicates himself to Styles' downfall, planning a terrible revenge that kicks off with a brutal jail break and gathers momentum as our hero's life slowly falls apart.

Washington does well as Styles, lending weight to a character who might have seemed cardboard in less capable hands, while John Lithgow goes way overboard as Blake, which is acceptable, but he's capable of more and a little extra effort would have been welcome. In support, Ice T pops up as a rising young drug lord with a heart of gold, while as Styles' amiable partner Larry, Kevin Pollak does one of the greatest Captain Kirk impressions ever commited to film. And for all you TV trivia buffs out there, yes, that is *The Bionic Woman*'s Lindsay Wagner as Styles' boss, the district attorney.

There are plenty of excuses for action here, and rest assured that Mulcahy exploits each one to its fullest, killing extras at random and blowing buildings sky high as he works his wild and wicked way towards a climax that earns the movie a major thumbs up. It's all pretty stupid stuff, overdone and excessive, but that's all part of its charm, and besides, who cares whether you laugh *with* it or *at* it, so long as you enjoy it?

Director: Russell Mulcahy; **Producers:** Joel Silver, Michael Levy; **Screenplay:** Steven E. de Souza, story by Fred Dekker, Menno Meyjes; **Production Design:** Jaymes Hinkle; **Editor:** Peter Honess; **Photography:** Peter Levy; **Music:** Alan Silvestri; **Cast:** Denzel Washington, John Lithgow, Ice T, Kevin Pollak, Lindsay Wagner.

Road House

USA 1989 114 mins

Patrick Swayze and Marshall Teague duke it out in *Road House*.

If ever a movie was designed to exclude the fairer sex, this would have to be the one. As obnoxious an action flick as you're ever likely to find, *Road House* is a feature for guys who dig chicks in tight skirts, drink beer by the barrel and approve of violence without reason. You know, the kind of picture where men are men, and women are grateful (Feminists take note: if you think this review is offensive, you should see the film).

Patrick Swayze is in full macho mode as professional bouncer Dalton, trained in philosophy and the martial arts, a strong, silent type who takes care of troublemakers in swanky night-spots and sews up his own cuts come closing time. He is, of course, the best, and just the man for the job of cleaning up a red neck road house called the Double Deuce, which is, we're warned, 'the type of place where they sweep up the eyeballs after closing'.

So there's a new sheriff in town, name of Dalton, and the teeth soon start a-flyin' as he makes his presence felt. Bar brawls are kept to a minimum, knife fights and punch-ups optional, no drugs allowed. Then along comes local 'businessman' Brad Wesley (Ben Gazzara having fun), a delightfully smug SOB with an ego the size of Texas and a dirty hand in every cash register in town, and the fireworks let loose. The town of Jaspar, it seems, ain't big enough for the both of them, and you just know that, after a healthy dose of destructive chaos (and the odd Miss Wet G-String contest), there's gonna be an extended and satisfyingly bloody showdown.

Proving that there's life in the old horse yet, grizzled tough guy Sam Elliott wanders into the movie as veteran bouncer Wade Garrett, while in Wesley's corner stands young hell raiser Jimmy (Marshall Teague), a hard-hitting psycho who, after beating on Dalton for a while, reveals for some curious reason that 'I used to fuck guys like you in prison'. Oh well, it takes all sorts. As for love interest, make way for superbabe doctor Kelly Lynch, a fun-lovin' gal who knows when to take her clothes off.

Be prepared, however, for a Patrick Swayze bare butt shot. Considering that *Road House* is aimed almost entirely at a male audience, why director Rowdy Herrington included something like this is anyone's guess, but there's no need to question the abundance of naked female flesh on show, all of which, you'll be pleased to hear, is justified and integral to the plot.

Producer Joel Silver works his magic once again and the result is a seriously frantic mix of sex and violence. And if you've ever wondered what a man having his throat ripped out looks like - and sounds like - you've come to the right place.

Director: Rowdy Herrington; **Producer:** Joel Silver; **Screenplay:** David Lee Henry, Hilary Henkin; **Production Design:** William J. Durrell Jr; **Editors:** Frank J. Urioste, John F. Link; **Photography:** Dean Cundey; **Music:** Score by Michael Kamen, featured musical performance by The Jeff Healey Band; **Cast:** Patrick Swayze, Ben Gazzara, Kelly Lynch, Marshall Teague, Sam Elliott, Kathleen Wilhoite.

Robin Hood: Prince of Thieves

USA 1991 138 mins

A Californian Yankee in King Richard's Court: Kevin Costner sorts out medieval England in *Robin Hood: Prince of Thieves.*

Kevin Costner robs from the rich and gives to the poor in true Hollywood style, a Yank in Sherwood Forest with long, flowing locks, an accent out of time and, in place of Errol Flynn's figure-hugging green tights, a pair of brown suede trousers. He does, however, swash a pretty mean buckle, being good with a sword, great with a bow, and simply irresistible to the ladies.

Slick and expensive, *Robin Hood: Prince of Thieves* gives the twelfth-century tale a 1990s twist (for better and for worse), pumping up the action with some incredible stuntwork (see the boys' catapult over a castle wall) and a steady supply of battles, rescues and high-speed horseback pursuits. Costner is able but uninspiring, allowing the movie to be stolen by Alan Rickman's hyperactive Sheriff of Nottingham, an amateur Satanist with a caustic sense of humour and a talent for violence shared by most modern movie villains. For romantic diversion and damsel-in-distress duties, Mary Elizabeth Mastrantonio delivers gutsy sweetheart Maid Marion, while Morgan Freeman stands out among the Merry Men as grateful Moor Azeem.

The news for nitpickers is that the accents, ranging from broad American to fake English, may very well drive you crazy, while huge leaps in logic (Robin walks from Dover to Nottingham in less than a day, even though the two locations are 196 miles apart) and unnecessary changes to the legend (token teen Christian Slater has a soap-style secret to reveal as Will Scarlett) confirm that director Kevin Reynolds was more interested in flash than substance.

Still, a good, dumb movie never did anyone any harm, and though it may be shallow and underwritten, it is also glossy, exciting and reasonably well-paced. You won't be bored. You will be entertained. But nothing could take the place of Flynn's 1938 spectacular, *The Adventures of Robin Hood*.

Director: Kevin Reynolds; **Producers:** John Watson, Pen Densham, Richard B. Lewis; **Screenplay:** Pen Densham, John Watson; **Production Design:** John Graysmark; **Editor:** Peter Boyle; **Photography:** Doug Milsome; **Music:** Michael Kamen; **Cast:** Kevin Costner, Morgan Freeman, Mary Elizabeth Mastrantonio, Alan Rickman, Christian Slater, Geraldine McEwan, Michael McShane, Brian Blessed, Michael Wincott, Nick Brimble, Pat Roach.

RoboCop

USA 1987 103 mins

The all-time greatest, goriest death scene in the history of motion pictures: Emil (Paul McCrane) takes a toxic shower and melts likes mozzarella in *RoboCop*.

Describing this awe-inspiring adventure as perfect barely does it justice. Directed by Paul Verhoeven, *RoboCop* works on so many levels it truly is a champion among action movies: outrageously violent, savagely funny and deeper than Anna Nicole Smith's cleavage, it's as wild and entertaining as any experience on Earth.

The brainchild of cut-throat executive Bob Morton (Miguel Ferrer), RoboCop rises from the remains of Officer Alex J. Murphy (Peter Weller), shot, quite literally, to pieces by homicidal loon Clarence Boddicker (Kurtwood Smith) and his goon squad. The property of Omni Consumer Products, an all-powerful, multi-national corporation, RoboCop is a cyborg designed to offer '...the best of both worlds: the fastest reflexes modern technology has to offer, onboard computer-assisted memory, and a lifetime of on-the-street law enforcement.' His memory wiped, Robo's sole purpose is to crack crime in Old Detroit, but something of the man remains, a glimmer of humanity, and with it, the urge to avenge his own death...

Multiple-target scenarios abound as RoboCop plies his trade, taking down a drug lab, blowing up half the city, bathing henchmen in chemical waste and gunning for twisted, malicious, best-bad-guy-ever Clarence. Armed with a fearless, hilarious screenplay, a sporting supporting cast (disgruntled exec Ronny Cox, ambitious 'Old Man' Dan O'Herlihy, loutish henchman Paul McCrane, butch lady cop Nancy Allen...), some knockout special effects (stop-motion animation fans should be on the lookout for Ed 209, a cannon-fisted enforcement droid with firepower a-plenty) and a wild imagination, Paul Verhoeven blew us all away with this one, the original and best Robo adventure.

 Designed by special effects wizard Rob Bottin, whose credits include *The Howling* and *The Thing*, Peter Weller's Robo suit took 20 people ten months to develop and six months to build. When completed, it took an hour and a half to put on every day, and with temperatures inside reaching 128 degrees, Weller lost around three pounds of water weight every single day.

Sequels: *RoboCop 2*, *RoboCop 3*. TV: Live action and cartoon series.

Director: Paul Verhoeven; **Producer:** Arne Schmidt; **Screenplay:** Edward Neumeier, Michael Miner; **Production Design:** William Sandell; **Editor:** Frank J. Urioste; **Photography:** Jost Vacano; **Music:** Basil Poledouris; **Cast:** Peter Weller, Kurtwood Smith, Nancy Allen, Ronny Cox, Daniel O'Herlihy, Miguel Ferrer, Robert DoQui, Ray Wise, Felton Perry, Paul McRae; **Academy Award:** Best Sound Effects Editing.

RoboCop 2

USA 1990 116 mins

RoboCop did everything right. *RoboCop 2* does everything wrong. It's as simple as that. Only the second time round, and already the series has lost its edge. The humour is broader, the characters are weaker, the action is much less intense. Robo remains obsessed with his humanity. Psychos and businessmen continue to co-exist in harmony. And funny ads still play on TV. But the magic is gone. In the hands of director Irvin Kirshner, this feeble sequel lacks the courage of the first, unwilling to shock, unable to thrill, machine-made in Hollywood for premium disappointment.

What do you get when you cross a mad scientist, a designer drug, and the brain of a psychopath? The answer is *RoboCop 2*, a monstrous cyborg with a habit to feed and a bone to pick with Delta City's finest, RoboCop.

There are times when the movie doesn't stink, when the action rises above average, when a clever line manages to surface, but it's just not enough. After all, why waste your time with this one when you could be watching the original instead? *2* is a loser.

Director: Irvin Kershner; **Producer:** Jon Davison; **Screenplay:** Frank Miller, Walon Green, based on characters created by Edward Neumeier, Michael Miner; **Production Design:** Peter Jamison; **Editors:** Deborah Zeitman, Lee Smith, Armen Minasian; **Photography:** Mark Irwin; Music: Leonard Rosenman; **Cast:** Peter Weller, Nancy Allen, Daniel O'Herlihy, Belinda Bauer, Tom Noonan, Gabriel Damon, Felton Perry, Willard Pugh.

RoboCop 3

USA 1991 (Originally released 1993) 105 mins

The tin man returns for a third round of public service in this moderately enjoyable action-er, a so-so, sci-fi spectacular which improves upon the last entry in the series, although neither could ever hope to improve upon (or even equal) the original. Tired of the title role, Peter Weller passed the Robo suit on to Hal Hartley regular Robert Burke (*The Unbelievable Truth*, *Simple Men*), although, to be honest, you could be forgiven for not noticing the change.

It's the future again, and Detroit is on the verge of demolition thanks to the guys and girls at Omni Consumer Products, a gang of corporate cut-throats intent on building a shiny new metropolis over the dingy, old city. Before construction begins, however, there's a population to sweep out of the way, with thousands of terrified innocents being forced out of their homes and onto the streets, a merciless operation overseen by evil military type Paul McDaggett (John Castle), who clearly doesn't give a damn how it's done. Enter RoboCop, who, after a startling personal tragedy, decides to join the resistance and battle OCP in the name of truth, justice and slum housing.

Obviously, the bad guys aren't about to give up without a fight, and besides utilizing the entire police force against Robo, they also have a back-up batch of dirty tricks to fall back on, including a gang of Japanese Ninja Terminator-types intent on taking a can-opener to our hero, providing, of course, he first survives Detroit's psychotic criminal element, youth-ful gangs of killers, thieves and rapists known as 'Splatterpunks'.

With all the usual elements fitting neatly into place, *Night of the Creeps* director Fred Dekker lays on a passably tongue-in-cheek adventure with some ropy - though reasonably imaginative - special effects (the one to look out for is the Robo rocket pack, a flying marvel which looks a lot like a giant tin-opener).

Now for the bad news: besides a run-of-the-mill feel and mediocre screenplay, the big problem with the movie is that Robo keeps getting beaten up. He's slow, his responses are sluggish, and practically every scumbag who comes along manages to take a piece of him. Consequently, our metallic chum spends around half the movie recovering - in pieces - from various beatings, and the pace often grinds to a sleep-inducing halt.

At best, though, the movie's quite exciting, fairly slick, you know, perfectly watchable but nothing to write home about, so adjust your expectations accordingly.

Director: Fred Dekker; **Producer:** Patrick Crowley; **Screenplay:** Frank Miller, Fred Dekker; **Production Design:** Hilda Stark; **Editor:** Bert Lovitt; **Photography:** Gary B. Kibbe; **Music:** Basil Poledouris; **Cast:** Robert Burke, Nancy Allen, Rip Torn, John Castle, Jill Hennessy, C.C.H. Pounder, Mako, Robert Do'Qui, Felton Perry.

The Rock

USA 1996 129 mins

Blockbuster boys Don Simpson and Jerry Bruckheimer came, saw and conquered Hollywood with a string of flashy, formulaic mega-hits which cleaned up at the box office and set the standard for slick, brainless entertainment throughout the 1980s and beyond. From *Beverly Hills Cop* and *Top Gun* right up to Michael Bay's *Bad Boys*, Don and Jerry remained loyal to the glossy, the foolish and the downright outrageous, churning out male-bondathons with a pleasing disregard for common sense.

As wild and crazy as any of his movies, Simpson's rock 'n' roll lifestyle caught up with him in 1996 when, aged just 52, his heart threw in the towel. *The Rock* was his final movie, co-produced by Bruckheimer, directed by Bay, and a fitting tribute to a man who believed that nothing succeeded quite like excess.

Backed by a squad of psychotic commando types (Tony Todd, John C. McGinley, David Morse), a military crackpot (Ed Harris) intent on squeezing $100 million of 'war reparations' from Uncle Sam has seized control of Alcatraz Island, taking tourists hostage and aiming some rather nasty chemical weapons at San Francisco. With thousands of lives at stake, and a 40-hour deadline to play around with, the powers that be leave it to off-beat chemical weapons expert Stanley Goodspeed (Nicolas Cage) and former Alcatraz inmate John Mason (Sean Connery), the only man ever known to escape the famous prison, to save the day.

An adrenaline-charged buddy movie with a *Die Hard* twist, Bay's second feature packs in the action (a lunatic car chase, lots of Indiana Jones-style stuntwork and stacks of inventive killings) while making the most of Goodspeed and Mason's tempestuous relationship, and though the movie falters with the screenplay and supporting characters, it remains a lot of good, clean, silly, violent fun.

Director: Michael Bay; **Producers:** Don Simpson, Jerry Bruckheimer; **Screenplay:** David Weisberg, Douglas S. Cook, Mark Rosner; **Production Design:** Michael White; **Editor:** Richard Francis-Bruce; **Photography:** John Schwartzman; **Music:** Nick Glennie-Smith, Hans Zimmer; **Cast:** Sean Connery, Nicolas Cage, Ed Harris, Michael Biehn, William Forsythe, Tony Todd, John C. McGinley, David Morse.

Romancing the Stone

USA 1984 105 mins

Michael Douglas and Kathleen Turner trip out on adrenaline in *Romancing the Stone.*

Back in the days when Robert Zemeckis was an unknown director of minor-league comedies, before Marty McFly, Roger Rabbit and Forrest Gump elevated him to the rank of Major Hollywood Player, Oscar-winning producer Michael Douglas made him an offer he couldn't refuse: the chance to make his very first blockbuster. He was young, it was the 1980s, what else could he do? The stars of the show would be Kathleen Turner, Douglas himself and his old pal Danny DeVito, still best known for TV's *Taxi*, and eager for big-screen success. The chemistry between the three was strong enough to remove even the most stubborn of bathroom stains.

The movie itself worked out just as well, a spirited adventure with several sharp, enthusiastic performances and a busy quota of stunt-intensive action (a rollercoaster mud-slide escape, the ever-popular rope bridge scenario, a great jungle car chase, a spectacular waterfall gag...), heavy on laughs, light on sentiment and always lots of fun.

A best-selling romantic novelist whose quiet, unremarkable lifestyle takes a back seat to daydreams of passion and excitement, heroine-in-waiting Joan Wilder (Turner) gets to live out her fantasies, for better or worse, when a treasure map pops through the post and leads her to Colombia (Hey, it could happen). On the trail of a priceless emerald ('El Corazon' - 'The Heart') in a 'third world toilet' full of crooks and cut-throats, Joan and new-found hero-for-hire Jack Colton (Michael Douglas) get acquainted with their supporting cast: hapless scoundrel Ralph (DeVito), corrupt secret policeman Zolo (Manuel Ojeda) and crime-boss-with-a-heart-of-gold Juan (Alfonso Arau).

Inspired by the exploits of Indiana Jones, but bang up to date (for 1984) with a racy sense of humour (sex, drugs, you name it...), *Romancing the Stone* is one of those movies that made the 1980s worthwhile.

And boy, what a blinding punchline.

Best known for playing long-suffering LAPD shrink Stephanie Woods in the *Lethal Weapon* trilogy, small-time character actress Mary Ellen Trainor nabbed a minute or so of screen time in this earlier flick as Joan's kidnapped sister Elaine.

Sequel: *The Jewel of the Nile*.

Director: Robert Zemeckis; **Producer:** Michael Douglas; **Screenplay:** Diane Thomas; **Production Design:** Lawrence G. Paull; **Editors:** Donn Cambern, Frank Morriss; **Photography:** Dean Cundey; **Music:** Alan Silvestri; **Cast:** Michael Douglas, Kathleen Turner, Danny DeVito, Zack Norman, Alfonso Arau, Manuel Ojeda, Holland Taylor, Mary Ellen Trainor, Eve Smith.

The Rookie

USA 1990 121 mins 🔫 🔫 🔫 🔫 1/2

Clint Eastwood and Charlie Sheen board the Male Bonding Express for a two hour trip through Actionland, steering well clear of logic and restraint in order to fully focus on ultra-violent death, destruction and big screen foolishness. A quality cast overplay their roles to perfection, from Clint's grizzled, cigar-chewing cop, to Raul Julia's greedy, kill-crazy crook, and a good time is had by all.

Nick Pulovski (Clint) is a hard-drinkin', cigar-chompin', barrel o' bad habits with the LAPD's Grand Theft Auto division. True to formula, he's after the man who killed his partner, and to make matters even more stereotypical, he's just been saddled with a brand new one, David Ackerman (Charlie), a rookie with a troubled past, a wealthy, over-protective dad (Tom Skerritt) and a capacity for violence which sets him free. Together, our heroes explore the meaning of macho as they fight amongst themselves in true buddy movie style while gunning for the chop shop king of Southern Los Angeles, Strom (Julia), and his exotic, psychotic hench-girlfriend, Liesl (Julia's *Kiss of the Spider Woman* co-star, Sonia Braga).

Sit back, relax, and enjoy the chaos. There's a wild freeway chase to get things started, some excellent punch-ups and an excess of obnoxious behaviour to follow, a classic moment for Charlie, asserting himself in a biker bar by trashing the place and beating on the regulars, a daredevil escape, a whole bunch of shoot-outs, a brief spell of bondage and a full-on airport finale to round things off. All this, and a wealth of wacky one-liners too: 'There's gotta be a hundred reasons why I don't blow you away', hisses Clint to his prey, 'but right now I can't think of one.'

As directed by Eastwood, *The Rookie* is a deliberately silly, knockabout adventure which aims for outrageous and hits a bullseye. We're talking good, dumb, fun. Get your brains out and the beers in, and you're all set.

Director: Clint Eastwood; **Producers:** Howard Kazanjian, Steven Siebert, David Valdes; **Screenplay:** Boaz Yakin, Scott Spiegel; **Production Design:** Judy Cammer; **Editor:** Joel Cox; **Photography:** Jack N. Green; **Music:** Lennie Niehaus; **Cast:** Clint Eastwood, Charlie Sheen, Raul Julia, Sonia Braga, Lara Flynn Boyle, Tom Skerritt.

Death Becomes Them 18

Cynthia Rothrock kicks the hell out of a pair of Neanderthal males in *China O'Brien*.

Name: ROTHROCK, Cynthia

Chinese name: Law Fu-lock

Born: Wilmington, Delaware, 1961

Characteristics: Small (5'3"), blonde and perky, Doris Day with balls (metaphorically speaking).

Debut feature: *Yes, Madam* (1985)

Life and times: The founder and proprietor of martial arts schools in Pennsylvania and California, five times undefeated World Female Karate Champion (1981-5) Cynthia Rothrock first flexed her acting muscles in a Kentucky Fried Chicken commercial ('I'm the number one in Karate, and Kentucky Fried is number one in chicken!'). After a couple of years of chop socky training in Hong Kong, Cynthia joined forces with *Enter the Dragon* director Robert Clouse on the B-movie beat-'em-up *China O'Brien*, a massive video hit which established Rothrock as the undisputed Queen of Martial Arts.

Secret ambition: To work with Kenneth Branagh: 'You know, he'd make a great action movie director. I'd love him to direct one of my movies. But I can forget that, right?'

Greatest contribution to action movies: Rothrock proved that sisters, even short ones, could do it for themselves.

Speech, speech: 'I weigh about 111 pounds, [and] the public feels that you have to be big and strong, but it actually doesn't matter what your body weight is as long as you know the correct technique and know where to hit.'

Cynthia considers her male following: 'The ones who have a crush on me say, "If you don't marry me, nobody else will marry you because I'll make sure of it." Of course, I know I could take anyone who came up to me, but I don't want to hurt someone. And I don't want to get a lawsuit.'

Selected filmography: *Yes, Madam* (1985), ***No Retreat, No Surrender 2: Raging Thunder*** (1987), *The Inspector Wears Skirts* (aka *Top Squad*; 1988), ***China O'Brien*** (1989), ***Beyond the Law*** (1989), ***Martial Law*** (1990), *China O'Brien 2* (1990), *Karate Cop* (1991), *Lady Dragon* (1991), *Triple Cross* (1991), *Tiger Claws* (1991), *Fast Getaway* (1991), ***Rage and Honour*** (1992), *Angel of Fury* (1992), *Guardian Angel* (1993), *Fast Getaway II* (1994), *Eye for an Eye* (1996).

Rumble in the Bronx

Hong Kong 1995 105 mins

Hong Kong supercop Jackie Chan heads way out west for a New York story, trying to take things slow but making enemies really fast, battling street gangs, dodging mob enforcers and generally making this world of ours a better, more violent, place. Anxious to beat up foreigners on their home turf, Jackie starts their engines with classics like 'Don't you know you're the scum of society?' Subtlety may be in short supply, the performances broad, the direction pedestrian, but Chan, as ever, saves the day with a cool new variety of action situations, counteracting the movie's shortcomings with a vengeance.

There's a crippled lad with a big bag of underworld diamonds stashed in his wheelchair. A supermarket targeted for mob demolition. A possible romance with a gang leader's dame. In other words, a multitude of excuses for flashy, brutal set-pieces. For our amusement, then... Jackie battles thugs on motorcycles, in their hideout, on a pool table... He waterskis like a pro, but in trainers, and takes on hovercrafts' single-handed, driving them through city streets on a destructive rampage in the name of justice. This is fun, and nothing but. If you're a Chan fan, climb aboard.

 Mountains in New York? Busted. *Rumble* wasn't even shot in the States, but in Vancouver, hence the scenery.

Director: Stanley Tong; **Producer:** Leonard K.C. Ho; **Screenplay:** Edward Tang, story by Stanley Tong, Ma Mei-ping; **Production Design:** Oliver Wong; **Editor:** Peter Cheung; **Photography:** Jingle Ma; **Cast:** Jackie Chan, Anita Mui, Bill Tung, Yip Fong-wa, Bai Cheun-wai, Marc Akerstream.

Runaway

USA 1984 100 mins

Between *Westworld* and *Jurassic Park* came another Michael Crichton tale of technology-gone-awry, only this time it has a helping hand from Kiss front man Gene Simmons, here making his big screen debut as techno psycho Luther, a bad, mad scientist with an army of robot spiders and a whole case of Tracers, the bullet with your name on it.

Obviously, we're in the near future with this one, and it's a world full of machines. They cook, they clean, they put the kids to bed, and sometimes they go crazy, which is when the Runaway Squad go to work. Enter Jack Ramsay (Tom Selleck) and his rookie partner Karen Thompson (Cynthia Rhodes), saving the likes of Kirstie Alley from crackpot droids while taking on the might and menace of Dr Luther.

Written and directed by Crichton himself, *Runaway* is, at heart, a deeply silly movie, but that's all part of its charm. The hi-tech stuff is fun, if not always plausible, the performances are adequate, if not exactly gripping (except for Simmons - he's a blast!), and the action sequences are pretty decent too, from some neatly explosive road-bound chaos to a cliff-hanging finale set in a high rise construction site where Jack, our troubled hero, has to finally face his fear of heights...

It ain't brain surgery, but it is a lot of fun, *if* you're prepared to go along with it (just try not to blow chunks during the slushy end credit snog scene).

Director: Michael Crichton; **Producer:** Michael Rachmil; **Screenplay:** Michael Crichton; **Production Design:** Douglas Higgins; **Editor:** Glenn Farr; **Photography:** John A. Alonzo; **Music:** Jerry Goldsmith; **Cast:** Tom Selleck, Cynthia Rhodes, Gene Simmons, Kirstie Alley, Stan Shaw, G. W. Bailey, Chris Mulkey, Joey Cramer.

Runaway Train

USA 1985 111 mins

Imagine you're a convict, a real killer's killer, so bad, in fact, that for the last three years your cell door has been welded shut. Suddenly, from out of nowhere, comes a chance to escape, and you take it, fleeing for your life alongside another prisoner, an idiot, although he does have his uses. Anyway, the pair of you hop aboard a train, a couple of stowaways in for a shock: it's a runaway. see, vast and unstoppable, charging through the bleak, Alaskan wilderness towards what promises to be a very big bang indeed.

So, what do you do? Fight amongst yourselves, admire the scenery, struggle against the odds to stop the darn thing, or pretend you're in an art movie and ponder the meaning of life, death, fate and other distractions? Why not stretch yourself thin by doing all these things, and while you're at it, how about taking the only other person on the train hostage, a girlie engineer who'll scream in all the right places and keep the conversation rolling when you're feelin' philosophical? Oh yeah, and you'd better keep 'em peeled for the warden, that sadistic son-of-a-bitch, 'cos he's on your tail and he wants you dead...

Based on a screenplay by celebrated Japanese director Akira Kurosawa, *Runaway Train* divides its time between thought-provoking artiness and spectacular action sequences, as escaped convicts Manny (Jon Voight), Buck (Eric Roberts) and engineer Sara (Rebecca DeMornay) face all kinds of peril as they fight to stop the train before it reaches the end of the line.

Both Voight (the monster) and Roberts (the simpleton) earned Academy Award nominations for this one (as did editor Henry Richardson), although DeMornay deserves a special mention for holding her own against the boys and making her presence felt.

Sometimes the movie tries way too hard to be deep, a mannered pretentiousness creeping into the dialogue and performances, although mostly it's just a cracking adventure, directed with pace and an excess of style by Andrei Konchalovsky. Top honours go to Alan Hume's photography, however, for fully capturing the forbidding Alaskan wilderness, providing the movie with an eerie, doom-laden atmosphere which draws us in and keeps us shivering till the end.

Director: Andrei Konchalovsky; **Producers:** Menahem Golan, Yoram Globus; **Screenplay:** Djordje Milicevic, Paul Zindel, Edward Bunker, based on a screenplay by Akira Kurosawa; **Production Design:** Stephen Marsh; **Editor:** Henry Richardson; **Photography:** Alan Hume; **Music:** Trevor Jones; **Cast:** Jon Voight, Eric Roberts, Rebecca DeMornay, Kyle T. Hefner, John P. Ryan, T.K. Carter, Kenneth McMillan.

The Running Man

USA 1987 101 mins

Arnold Schwarzenegger fights the power in this near-futuristic tale of television violence from Detective Dave Starsky himself, Paul Michael Glaser. It's 2017 and America is screwed, oppressed beyond belief by a totalitarian government which uses TV to sedate the masses, gluing them to the idiot box with sensational trash like *The Hate Boat* and *Pain American Style*. The most brutal show of all, *The Running Man*, is also the highest rated, presented and produced by the despicable Damon Killian (*Family Feud* host Richard Dawson). Convicts run for their lives through a large, burned-out section of Los Angeles, desperately searching for a way out while vicious, well-armed Stalkers hunt them down. Now, that's entertainment.

Fighting for the bad guys in the blessed name of broadcasting, Stalkers include Fireball (Jim Brown), a human flame-thrower, Buzzsaw (Gus Rethwisch), a chainsaw-wielding redneck, Dynamo (Erland Van Lidth), an opera-singing fatboy with the dress sense of a Christmas tree and a talent for throwing lightning bolts, and Subzero (Professor Toru Tanaka), '...the incredible ice man, who slices his enemies limb from limb into quivering, bloody sushi' with a razor-sharp hockey stick and exploding pucks.

Framed for mass murder and forced to run on the show, Ben Richards (Arnie, our hero) plans to survive the experience, break Killian in half, and maybe even overthrow the government with the help of his revolutionary running buddies, Laughlin (Yaphet Kotto), Weiss (Marvin J. McIntyre) and romantic interest Maria Conchita Alonso.

There's action here, and plenty of it, from prison breakout to rebel assault (keep 'em peeled for Mick Fleetwood and Dweezil 'Don't touch that dial' Zappa) with a whole bunch of stalk-and-slash in the middle. It's funny too, full of cheesy one-liners and sledgehammer satire. We're not talking classic, here, but it may be the next best thing: a lightweight excuse for violence with lots of laughs thrown in. Arnold certainly seems to be enjoying himself. The chances are, you will too.

Director: Paul Michael Glaser; **Producers:** Tim Zinnemann, George Linder; **Screenplay:** Steven E. de Souza, based on the novel by Richard Bachman (aka Stephen King); **Production Design:** Jack T. Collis; **Editors:** Mark Roy Warner, Edward A. Warschilka, John Wright; **Photography:** Thomas Del Ruth; **Music:** Harold Faltermeyer; **Cast:** Arnold Schwarzenegger, Maria Conchita Alonso, Yaphet Kotto, Richard Dawson, Jim Brown, Jesse Ventura, Erland Van Lidth, Marvin J. McIntyre, Gus Rethwisch, Professor Toru Tanaka, Mick Fleetwood, Dweezil Zappa.

Name: RUSSELL, Kurt

Born: Springfield, Massachusetts, 1951

Characteristics: Classic leading man material, tall and tough for action roles, cheekily likeable in comedies, capable of straight-faced drama, the works. An all-round decent chap.

Debut feature: *The Absent-Minded Professor* (1961)

Life and times: A child actor for the Walt Disney Studios, Kurt Russell started making movies when he was nine years old. Fortunately, there's only so much harmless family entertainment a kid can churn out before growing up and trying to make it as an adult lead. Russell's breakthrough picture was *Elvis*, one of the highest rated TV flicks of all time, directed in 1979 by John Carpenter, who picked Kurt for the title role and worked with him throughout the 1980s on a trio of big screen adventures: *Escape From New York*, a dark, futuristic thriller which made him famous, *The Thing*, a terrifying monster movie with a neatly subversive sense of humour, and *Big Trouble in Little China*, a martial arts comedy adventure. Once married to actress Season

Death Becomes Them 19

Harry Dean Stanton and Kurt Russell do whatever it takes to *Escape From New York*.

Hubley, Russell now lives in sin with actress Goldie Hawn.

Greatest contribution to action movies: The greatest Dirty Harry impression of all time: *Escape From New York*'s Snake [eyes] Pliskin, ultra-cool, anti-hero supreme.

Speech, speech: 'My generation couldn't stand me and I couldn't stand them. In high school I was to the right of being straight. I believed in the work ethic, making money, and they all had this beef with the Nation. Vietnam disappointed me because we *didn't* win.'

'To go on about acting as art is ridiculous. If it is an art, then it's a very low form. You don't have to be gifted just to hit a mark and say a line. And as far as I'm concerned, hitting my marks and knowing my lines is 90% of the job. I'm always criticised for talking like that. Maybe the reason I do it is that I never got the chance to develop a real desire to act. I was acting by the time I was nine so it seemed a natural thing to do. Anyone who finds acting difficult just shouldn't be doing it.'

Selected filmography: *It Happened at the World's Fair* (1963), *Follow Me, Boys!* (1966), *The One and Only, Genuine , Original Family Band* (1968), *The Horse in the Grey Flannel Suit* (1968), *The Computer Wore Tennis Shoes* (1970), *The Barefoot Executive* (1971), *Charley and the Angel* (1973), *The Strongest Man in the World* (1975), *Elvis* (TV movie; 1979), *Used Cars* (1980), ***Escape From New York*** (1981), *The Thing* (1982), *Silkwood* (1983), *Swing Shift* (1984), *The Mean Season* (1985), *The Best of Times* (1986), ***Big Trouble in Little China*** (1986), *Overboard* (1987), *Tequila Sunrise* (1988), *Winter People* (1989), ***Tango & Cash*** (1989), *Backdraft* (1991), *Unlawful Entry* (1992), *Captain Ron* (1992), *Tombstone* (1993), *Stargate* (1994), *Executive Decision* (1996), *Escape from L.A.* (1996).

Name: SCHWARZENEGGER, Arnold

Nickname: Conan the Republican

Born: Graz, Austria, 1947

Characteristics: Fiercely ambitious man-mountain with an accent thicker than his biceps.

Debut feature: *Hercules in New York* (aka *Hercules Goes Bananas*, Arnie billed as Arnold Strong; 1970).

Death Becomes Them 20

Arnold Schwarzenegger fights the power in *The Running Man*.

Life and times: When Arnold Schwarzenegger was 15 years old he decided to become a champion bodybuilder. Five years later, he won his first Mr Universe competition. In total, Arnold nabbed 13 world titles, more than any other bodybuilder in history, winning the coveted Mr Olympia muscle-fest an unprecedented seven times before retiring undefeated. Shrewd, confident and determined to succeed, Arnold tore his way into the movie business, winning a Golden Globe Award for Best Newcomer in Films (with his performance in Bob Rafelson's *Stay Hungry*) before slashing and blasting his way to movie stardom as barbarian beefcake Conan and cyborg assassin *The Terminator*. Winning the Grand Prize at the Avoriaz Film Festival in France, James Cameron's *Terminator* slayed 'em world-wide, prompting the National Association of Theatre Owners to pronounce Arnold International Star of 1985. Determined to prove that there was more to Arnold, the actor, than Arnold, the action hero, Schwarzenegger made his (intentional) comedy debut in *Twins*, a deeply goofy but passable feature. Five years later, Arnold, over-confident to the point of bursting, slugged his way through one of most expensive and least popular movies of all time: *Last Action Hero*. Still, everyone needs a flop from time to time, and Arnold soon bounced back in the Cameron-directed actioner *True Lies* and Ivan Reitman's politically correct 'comedy' *Junior*, in which our hero falls pregnant and mocks his hard-man image for a couple of (extremely painful) hours. As for directing, Arnold is taking it very slowly indeed, limiting his output to an episode of *Tales From The Crypt* and a TV movie, *Christmas in Connecticut*, made in 1992. The author of several best-selling books on bodybuilding, Arnold's business interests extend way beyond movie production, from real estate to the Planet Hollywood restaurant chain. An American citizen since 1983, Schwarzenegger married into the most powerful Democratic clan in the country (Kennedy offshoot Maria Shriver) yet remained deeply in league with the Republicans, hitting the campaign trail in 1988 with George Bush, who, once elected President, appointed Arnold chairman of the President's Council on Physical Fitness and Sports in 1990. As for Arnold's next big step? How does President Schwarzenegger sound?

Current salary: $17.5 million

Greatest contribution to action movies: Vast and indestructible comic book heroes who shoot first and ask questions later.

Speech, speech: 'If I wasn't happy, I'd be an idiot.'

'I experienced a *lot* of prejudice. The people in Hollywood had many reasons why I could not make it: my accent, my body, my long name. You have to establish yourself in such a way that no one else can compete with you.'

'In most action movies, women are in the way.'

Arnold on bodybuilding (courtesy of *Pumping Iron*): 'It's as satisfying to me as coming is, you know, as having sex with a woman and coming. So can you believe how much I am in heaven? I am getting the feeling of coming in the gym, I'm getting the feeling of coming at home, I'm getting the feeling of coming backstage when I pump up, [and] when I pose out in front of 5000 people I get the same feeling, so I'm coming day and night! I mean, that's terrific, right?'

'I have a love interest in every one of my films - a gun.'

Selected filmography: *Stay Hungry* (1976), *Pumping Iron* (1977), *The Villain* (1979), ***Conan the Barbarian*** (1982), ***Conan the Destroyer*** (1984), ***The Terminator*** (1984), ***Red Sonja*** (1985), ***Commando*** (1985), ***Raw Deal*** (1986), ***Predator*** (1987), ***The Running Man*** (1987), ***Red Heat*** (1988), *Twins* (1988), ***Total Recall*** (1990), *Kindergarten Cop* (1990), ***Terminator 2: Judgment Day*** (1991), ***Last Action Hero*** (1993), ***True Lies*** (1994), *Junior* (1994), ***Eraser*** (1996).

Death Becomes Them 21

If you think you're *Above the Law,* expect a visit from Steven Seagal.

Name: SEAGAL, Steven

Born: Detroit, Michigan, 1951

Characteristics: Straight-faced and self-important with a charisma bypass and, from time-to-time, a pony-tail. Chop socky a speciality.

Debut feature: *Above the Law* (aka *Nico*; 1988)

Life and times: A kick ass martial artist with alleged secret service ties, Steven Seagal made history as the first and only non-oriental to establish a dojo in Japan, his home for almost 15 years. Returning to the States, Seagal played sensei to the stars, teaching a variety of rich and influential people how to bust heads, including super-agent Mike Ovitz, who encouraged Steve to get into the movie business and even helped him secure the lead in his very first film, *Above the Law.* A string of mid-budget blockbusters came next, bloody revenge sagas which established Seagal as a hot property and, following the incredible success of *Die Hard* wannabe *Under Siege,* powerful enough to demand a crack at directing. The results were rather less than encouraging: muddled, mindless and pretentious,

On Deadly Ground did *not* herald the arrival of a major new directing talent. Formerly married to *Hard to Kill* co-star Kelly Le Brock, Seagal whiles away his free time organizing special investigations and security task forces to protect public figures.

Greatest contribution to action movies: Sadistic ultra-violence. Why settle for knocking a bad guy unconscious when his arms and legs are screaming to be broken?

Speech, speech: The Depth of Steve: 'The secret is not to act, but to be.'

The Mystery of Steve: 'I can't really give out any details, but I've had to use much of what I've learned practically in the field.'

The Philosophy of Steve: 'Action films are great, but an action film that has characters that are compelling and a story that people can care about is something even better. We love to see action heroes that are vulnerable, that are sensitive, that are family people, that are accessible' (So says the man who, in *Under Siege 2*, falls off a cliff, gets himself shot, beaten and blown up, yet escapes with barely a scratch. Now, *that's* vulnerability).

Selected filmography: *Above the Law* (aka *Nico*; + co-prod; 1988), *Hard to Kill* (+ co-prod; 1990), *Marked For Death* (1990), *Out For Justice* (1991), *Under Siege* (1992), *On Deadly Ground* (+ dir/co-prod; 1994), *Under Siege 2: Dark Territory* (+ co-prod; 1995), *Executive Decision* (1996).

The Shadow

USA 1994 107 mins

Even in his earliest incarnation, as a disembodied voice on the radio some 60 years ago, The Shadow struck fear in the hearts of man. With the power to cloud minds and render himself invisible, Lamont Cranston reigned supreme as the original crime-fighter, aided by a vast underground communications network and a theatrical streak a mile wide. Cursed with a sordid past of his own, The Shadow understood evil only too well, and lived solely to bring justice to those whose crimes could not be ignored. It was a mysterious, dark and dangerous time, with a sprinkle of Eastern mysticism, and seemed ideal for 1990s blockbuster treatment.

The trouble is, despite some wonderful production values (great art deco design, sharp costumes, cool special effects) the film fails to set the right tone, ditching mystery and danger for high-camp and self-conscious humour, which suggests that Mulcahy and screenwriter David Koepp didn't have the guts to play it straight. Had the action been more spectacular we could be more forgiving, but sadly there's little here to get excited about.

And so, as we witness the struggle between The Shadow (Alec Baldwin) and the last living descendant of Genghis Khan (John Lone), we are amused but not

Who knows what evil lurks in the hearts of man? The Shadow (Alec Baldwin), that's who.

thrilled, and ultimately disappointed as the film fails to capitalize on its more promising elements.

That said, there are times when director Russell Mulcahy gets it right, but neither he nor his cast (supporting players include tepid love interest Penelope Anne Miller, absent-minded scientist Ian McKellen, sidekick Peter Boyle and a typically slimy Tim Curry) seems confident enough with their source material to entrust *The Shadow* to a 1990s audience. Consequently, the cast and crew add too much unnecessary spice to the film, ruining it for those of us whose evil hearts craved a more faithful approach.

Director: Russell Mulcahy; **Producers:** Martin Bregman, Willi Baer, Michael S. Bregman; Writer: David Koepp; **Production Design:** Joseph Nemec III; **Editor:** Peter Honess; **Photography:** Stephen H. Burum; **Music:** Jerry Goldsmith; **Cast:** Alec Baldwin, John Lone, Penelope Ann Miller, Peter Boyle, Ian McKellen, Jonathan Winters, Tim Curry.

Death Becomes Them 22

Name: SHEEN, Charlie

Real name: Carlos Irwin Estevez

Born: New York, 1965

Characteristics: He's the boy next door, folks, with a scrap of attitude. Stick him in a suit and you'd think he was an estate agent.

Debut feature: *The Execution of Private Slovik* (1974)

Charlie Sheen goes gun-crazy in *Hot Shots! Part Deux.*

Life and times: Inspired, quite possibly, by the wicked, wicked ways of Errol Flynn, Charlie Sheen dedicated his youth to booze, broads and bad behaviour. During these years of sin, Charlie managed to get a little work done, from the WWIII flick *Red Dawn* to sci fi super-flop *The Wraith. Platoon* gave Sheen his first real taste of screen fame, but the wild times continued until finally, his family (especially his father, Martin Sheen, and elder brother, Emilio Estevez) stepped in to help him clean up his act and re-launch his career on a much more even keel. Scoring a bullseye at the box office in Jim Abrahams wacky *Top Gun* spoof *Hot Shots!,* Sheen was clean, sober and popular enough to keep on working, a star again, just not a very bright one.

Greatest contribution to action movies: Hot Shot hero Topper Harley, young, dumb and eager to kill.

Speech, speech: 'Life just used to be one big party with a few films thrown in.'

'I have trouble with romantic, sexual scenes. I'm far more comfortable killing somebody.'

'How does Keanu Reeves work with Coppola and Bertolucci and I don't get a shot at that, know what I'm saying?'

Selected filmography: *Red Dawn* (1984), *The Boys Next Door* (1985), *Lucas* (1986), *The Wraith* (1986), *Platoon* (1986), *No Man's Land* (1987), *Wall Street* (1987), *Young Guns* (1988), *Eight Men Out* (1988), *Major League* (1989), *Navy SEALS* (1990), *Men at Work* (1990), ***The Rookie*** (1990), *Hot Shots!* (1991), *Beyond the Law* (aka *Fixing the Shadow*; 1992), ***Hot Shots! Part Deux*** (1993), ***The Three Musketeers*** (1993), *Deadfall* (1993), ***The Chase*** (1994), *Major League II* (1994), ***Terminal Velocity*** (1994), *Martin Eden* (1996), *The Shadow Conspiracy* (1996), *Loose Women* (1996), *The Arrival* (1996).

Shogun Assassin

Japan/USA 1980 86 mins

Starting out with a couple of features from Japan's *Sword of Vengeance* film series, US producer David Weisman chopped the footage to pieces then re-edited and re-dubbed all the best stuff to produce a single masterpiece, *Shogun Assassin*, a savage tale of death and vengeance admired by gore hounds the world over as one of the bloodiest martial arts movies ever made.

By the time the credits are over and done with, the scene has already been set, and the story neatly explained. Feudal Japan is the time and place, a cheery locale where folks would just as soon slice your guts open as they would offer you a bowl of rice. Our hero, Lone Wolf (Tomisaburo Wakayama), is a double-chinned whirlwind of sword-swishing fury, a masterless Samurai whose refusal to pledge allegiance to Kurando, a vicious Shogun, costs his wife her life.

Vengeance is sworn, swords are sharpened, and, accompanied by his young son, Tizuro, Lone Wolf hits the road, slicing and dicing his way to justice through an assortment of Ninjas, extras and a trio of Kurando's offspring, the terrifying Masters of Death.

Narrated by Tizuro, whose baby carriage hides a multitude of sharp surprises, this furious adventure surfs a crimson wave of blood from one outrageous battle to another, a mountain of body parts left dripping in its wake.

Considering the film's patchwork origins, *Shogun Assassin* is a surprisingly stylish piece of work. Backed by a chorus of squishy sound effects, the violence is as devastating as it is frequent, and more than enough to make up for any dramatic or technical weaknesses. At the end of the day, it's the slaughter that's important, and you can bet your innards that this stomach-churning classic does not disappoint.

Directors: Kenji Misumi (original version), Robert Houston (American version); **Producers:** Shintaro Katsu, Hisaharu Matsubara (original version), David Weisman (American version); **Screenplay:** Kazuo Koike, Robert Houston, David Weisman; **Production Design:** Akira Naito; **Editor:** Lee Percy; **Photography:** Chishi Makiura; **Music:** Hideakira Sakurai, Mark Lindsay, W. Michael Lewis; **Cast:** Tomisaburo Wakayama, Masahiro Tomikawa, Kayo Matsuo, Minoru Ohki, Shoji Kobayashi, Akhiro Tomikawa.

The Shooter

USA 1995 104 mins

It's long, it's lame and it's melodramatic. Too serious, too stagy, and way too pretentious. But hey, it's set in Prague, Czech beauty spot and natural born location, so it must be good - right? Wrong. No, what we have here is a straightforward action thriller with a self-important Euro dressing, a minor effort with a matt finish which marks, for its sins, the 'all grown up and serious' acting debut of Swedish colossus Dolph Lundgren, a capable tough guy but lacking muscle in the thesp department.

As US Federal Marshal Michael Dane, Lundgren hits Prague in search of lady killer Simone Rossett (Maruschka Detmers), a skilled assassin who may, or may not, be planning to strike at the impending Cuban/American summit. They meet, they fight, they chase: part travelogue, part adventure, cityscapes and statues, gunfights and car stunts. Then emotions enter the arena, and Dolph, no longer the cool, hard, killing machine, cries. Please, let's say no more about this.

From the director of *First Blood*, Mr Ted 'He'll never make another film that good again' Kotcheff, comes *The Shooter*, a movie which misfires in almost every direction, smothering a couple of decent action sequences with awkward dialogue, bland performances, predictable plotting and a soundtrack from Elevator Hell. The good stuff never had a chance.

Director: Ted Kotcheff; **Producers:** Paul Pompian, Silvio Muraglia; **Screenplay:** Yves Andre Martin, Meg Thayer, Billy Ray; **Production Design:** Brian Eatwell; **Editor:** Ralph Brunjes; **Photography:** Fernando Arguelles; **Music:** Stefano Mainetti; **Cast:** Dolph Lundgren, Maruschka Detmers, Assumpta Serna, Gavan O'Herlihy, John Ashton.

Showdown in Little Tokyo

USA 1991 76 mins

'You have the right to remain dead', quips crazy LA cop Johnny Murata (Brandon Lee), shortly before incinerating a mobster (he deserved it, though). Elsewhere, Detective Kenner (Dolph Lundgren) is impaling, inflating, slicing, dicing and generally laying waste to an entire army of Yakuza psychos, led by icy lunatic Yoshida (Cary-Hiroyuki Tagawa), whose hobbies include drug dealing, rape, torture, decapitation, extortion and murdering the parents of small children (Kenner) who consequently grow up with violent revenge on their minds. And all in an hour-and-a-quarter! Talk about busy.

A truly mindless overdose of hyperactive macho bullshit, *Showdown in Little Tokyo* frees itself from the restraints of reality and feasts on sex and violence, treating women like brainless playthings and thug extras like lambs to the slaughter. Be warned, though, for it also has a down side: the story sucks, the screenplay, even by B-movie standards, is embarrassing, and the performances are so wooden the actors are in danger of contracting Dutch Elm Disease. But what the hell: it ain't Shakespeare - or even Jackie Collins - but it's sick and obnoxious and cheaper than a lobotomy.

Raised in Japan, Kenner is a hulking supercop with Samurai ways. Raised in the Valley, Murata is a high-kicking bimbo who likes McDonald's and MTV (fair enough). Neither work well with partners, and so naturally they are thrown together to patrol the streets of Little Tokyo, Los Angeles, where they get to wipe out wave after wave of vicious Japanese mobsters, rescue fair maidens in distress (the gorgeous Tia Carrere, here honing her thespian skills with a nude hot tub scene), and, of course, bond in an entirely male and bloodthirsty manner.

Blessed with a truly massive body count, this excessive flesh-and-blood-fest offers a bounty of quick fix entertainment, speeding from gory death to martial arts battle to naked party girl to impossible stunt at a speed that leaves no time for intelligent thought. So kick off your shoes, down a couple of six-packs, and accept this madness for what it is.

Director: Mark L. Lester; **Producers:** Mark L. Lester, Martin E. Caan; **Screenplay:** Stephen Glantz, Caliope Brattlestreet; **Production Design:** Craig Stearns; **Editors:** Steven Kemper, Robert A. Ferretti; **Music:** David Michael Frank; **Cast:** Dolph Lundgren, Brandon Lee, Carey-Hiroyuki Tagawa, Tia Carrere, Toshiro Obata.

Sidekicks

USA 1993 100 mins

The Secret Life of Walter Mitty meets *The Karate Kid* head on in this enjoyable, family-oriented fantasy from the Norris boys. Aaron call the shots while brother Chuck supplies the action, taking on a variety of B-movie bad guys in a role that calls for our hero to play the ultimate role model, namely himself.

Jonathan Brandis, teenage star of the disastrous *SeaQuest DSV*, takes the lead as Barry Gabrewski, a sickly high school geek and chronic daydreamer who spends his days imagining what it might be like to fight side-by-side with his beloved hero, Chuck Norris. A variety of action sequences follow, tough, but not too violent, and always played for laughs, as Barry and Chuck fight their way through every genre from Ninja chop-socky and sharp-shootin' western to futuristic cop thriller and, of course, Vietnam war movie.

Real life intrudes when booming karate instructor Stone (Joe Piscopo) mocks Barry's meagre talents, but then along comes friendly martial arts instructor and multi-purpose sage Mr Lee (Mako) to help restore the lad's confidence. Meanwhile, mean old Mr Stone has the honour of appearing as almost every villain Barry can dream up, but when the lad's fantasies develop into hallucinations it's time to get some serious help. Unfortunately, Barry's Dad (Beau Bridges) proves pretty feeble on the solution front, but let's not forget the impending Karate tournament, and who knows who might turn up, in the flesh, to help sort out his troubled fan?

Calling all non-believers. If you've ever doubted Norris's acting ability, just take a look at how upset he looks after Piscopo boxes him illegally during their big scene together. After that, if you still can't give the guy a break on the thespian side, you can at least admire the man's mighty fighting skills in this harmless chunk of wish fulfilment.

Director: Aaron Norris; **Producer:** Don Carmody; **Screenplay:** Donald G. Thompson, Lou Illar; **Production Design:** Reuben Freed; **Editor:** David Rawlins, Bernard Weiser; **Photography:** Joao Fernandes; **Music:** Alan Silvestri; **Cast:** Chuck Norris, Jonathan Brandis, Beau Bridges, Joe Piscopo, Mako, Julia Nickson-Soul, Danica McKellar.

Smokey and the Bandit

USA 1977 97 mins

Burt Reynolds puts the pedal to the metal in this 1800-mile ego trip, a wealth of dumb one-liners and plush hair enhancements at his command, a cheesy grin, a cheeky laugh and a pair of comedy flares juiced up and ready for action. Back in the 1970s, Burt was the biggest star on the face of the planet, a consummate charmer who conquered the box office playing an assortment of easily-digestible, cocky and likeable heroes like the Bandit, a Georgia bootlegger with a need for speed and a personal soundtrack of country hits, courtesy of co-star Jerry Reid, singing his praises.

Hal Needham made the transition from stuntman to movie director with *Smokey and the Bandit,* and, as you'd expect from a man who spent the first half of his career falling off, jumping over and crashing into all sorts of scary stuff, action is his first priority, with laughs coming in second and storytelling finishing last, a lame distraction from the chaos at hand.

Get ready for one long, comedy car chase, a lightweight blend of the *Big Book of Auto Stunts* and *Corny Jokes: A Refresher Course,* as the Bandit races to complete an 1800-mile journey in just 28 hours, a cargo of bootleg beer to deliver and a whole horde of smokeys to avoid. Joined by the Snowman (Reid), a natural sidekick with a canine chum and a truck full of hooch, the Bandit scouts ahead in a classic black Trans-Am, clearing the road of law enforcers unfamiliar with the new 110mph speed limit. Sally Field plays it cute and quirky in support, hitchhiking her way into the Bandit's trousers as the film's designated romantic interest, while *The Honeymooners'* Jackie Gleason goes way overboard as Yosemite Sam wannabe Sheriff Buford T. Justice, a rootin', tootin' Texas lawman who dedicates his life to catching our free-wheelin' hero.

Easy on the brain and lots of cheerful, unpretentious fun, *Smokey and the Bandit* is an acceptable time-waster. You'd be wise to avoid the sequels, though.

How about a little CB translation to help you keep up with the Bandit (thanks to Hot Pants, Little Beaver and Sugar Bear)? Handle - Name; Smokey - Cop; 10-4 - Yes; Copy - Understand; Choke 'N' Puke - Roadside Cafe; Go-Go Juice - Petrol; You Got Your Ears On? - Are You Listening?

Sequels: *Smokey and the Bandit II* (aka *Smokey and the Bandit Ride Again*), *Smokey and the Bandit III.*

Director: Hal Needham; **Producer:** Mort Engelberg; **Screenplay:** James Lee Barrett, Charles Shyer, Alan Mendel, story by Hal Needham, Robert L. Levy; **Production Design:** Mark Mansbridge; **Editor:** Walter Hannemann, Angelo Ross; **Photography:** Bobby Byrne; **Music:** Bill Justis, Jerry Reid; **Cast:** Burt Reynolds, Sally Field, Jerry Reid, Jackie Gleason, Mike Henry, Paul Williams, Pat McCormick.

Sniper

USA 1993 97 mins

Billy Zane keeps 'em peeled for a rival *Sniper.*

It does the heart good to see men acting like men for a change. Out in the jungle, overloaded with weaponry, looking for people to kill: you just can't beat it. No women to slow the plot down with extraneous romances, just a lot of blood, sweat and dirt. Of course, there has to be some psycho-babble: Tom Berenger and Billy Zane are on the edge and they know it, but ignore the psychological foolishness and concentrate on the action, because that's where this movie really hits the bullseye.

Master Gunnery Sergeant Tom Beckett (Berenger) is a sniper who is repeatedly sent - unofficially, of course - into the jungles of Panama to dispose of various drug dealers and petty dictators. It's a pretty dangerous business, so he's lost more than a few partners over the years, and keeps their dog tags as a constant reminder to the audience that underneath all that grit and muscle, there's a tortured guy just waiting to explode. The last thing he wants is another partner, especially one with absolutely no experience, which is, of course, exactly what he gets: government agent Richard Miller (Zane), who is supposed to be in charge of a very risky mission that they have to go on together, not that Beckett recognizes his authority. Naturally, they don't get along, and since this ain't a buddy movie, that can only lead to trouble...

OK: so it sounds like director Luis Llosa doesn't quite score with the psychological stuff, which he doesn't, but the good news is that *Sniper* turns out to be an extremely tense, exciting movie. It doesn't seem to matter that the characters don't quite work, and the performances don't exactly electrify the screen, because the pacing, the originality, and the sheer machismo of it all makes the film worthwhile. Keep 'em peeled for the cracking sniper *v* sniper shootout.

Director: Luis Llosa; **Producer:** Robert L. Rosen; **Screenplay:** Michael Frost Beckner, Crash Leyland; **Production Design:** Herbert Pinter; **Editor:** Scott Smith; **Photography:** Herbert Pinter; **Music:** Gary Chang; **Cast:** Tom Berenger, Billy Zane, J.T. Walsh, Aden Young, Ken Radley, Reinaldo Arenas, Carlos Alvarez, Roy Edmonds.

Death Becomes Them 23

Name: SNIPES, Wesley

Born: New York, 1963

Characteristics: Striking, talented, African-American superstar-type. Dig that attitude, man.

Debut feature: *Wildcats* (1986)

Wesley Snipes takes a trip to Macholand in *Passenger 57*.

Life and times: A classically trained actor with a lively interest in the martial arts, Wesley Snipes began his career on Broadway. Michael Jackson's *Bad* video, directed by Martin Scorsese in 1987, featured Snipes in gangsta mode, menacing Jacko off the screen with a charismatic performance that caught Hollywood's eye. Two years later, Snipes resurfaced to steal the show in the baseball comedy *Major League*, turning next to drama for the first of two Spike Lee collaborations, *Mo' Better Blues* (followed by *Jungle Fever*). Fame came at last when *New Jack City* hit the streets, a wild blaxploitation thriller showcasing Snipes as smooth criminal Nino Brown, mad, bad, dangerous to know and dynamite at the box office. Wes played his first action hero in Kevin Hooks' *Die Hard*-in-the-sky slugfest *Passenger 57*, wowing fight fans with some ultra-slick martial artistry. Accepted by his fans in any number of different genres, these days, Snipes is riding very high indeed.

Greatest contribution to action movies: The perfect acting range, from solid heroics to maniacal villainy.

Speech, speech: 'I like being the bad guy because I know how to look at a person and make them feel like, "here's someone I shouldn't mess with". Sometimes, I've been standing around in a club, bopping my head to the music, and women have told me I look real mean, like I'm ready to hurt people.'

Selected filmography: *Streets of Gold* (1986), *Critical Condition* (1987), *Major League* (1989), *Mo' Better Blues* (1990), *King of New York* (1990), *Jungle Fever* (1991), **New Jack City** (1991), *The Waterdance* (1992), *White Men Can't Jump* (1992), **Passenger 57** (1992), *Rising Sun* (1993), *Boiling Point* (1993), *Sugar Hill* (1993), **Demolition Man** (1993), **Drop Zone** (1994), *To Wong Foo, Thanks For Everything, Julie Newmar* (1995), **The Money Train** (1995), *Waiting to Exhale* (1995), *The Fan* (1996), *One Night Stand* (1997).

Soldier of Fortune

USA 1989 85 mins

The world's leading expert in laser weaponry is missing, believed kidnapped, by some ghastly foreign power, and only Special US Agent Michael Gold (Brandon Lee) can save the day. Original, eh? And get this: he's a lone wolf, a maverick with attitude and a master of unarmed combat. Bet you didn't see that coming. And there's more: the absent Professor Braun (Ernest Borgnine) has a bimbo daughter, Alissa (Debi Monahan), who insists on joining Gold (cue sexual tension) to keep abreast of the situation. Jet with us, then, to the fictional country of Namibia and the sandy wastes of the Skeleton Coast, where B-movie madness awaits.

A trophy room full of human heads and third-rate villains refusing to die contribute to the schlocky feel of this mindless but cheerful adventure, a Z-grade actioner saved from the scrapheap by Lee, who manages to rise above the material and deliver far more than the movie deserves (close to 40 confirmed kills, and his acting doesn't stink, either).

There's a jail break, a car chase, multiple shoot-outs and hand-to-hand insanity, but that's about it. Besides Brandon and the action, the remainder of the cast are as lame as a frog in a French restaurant, while the movie itself, in terms of screenplay, direction and production values, is about as appealing as an all-you-can-drink cod liver oil party. For Lee's most devoted fans only.

Director: Beau Davis; **Producer:** Claus Czaika; **Screenplay:** Phillip Guteridge, story by David A. Frank; **Production Design:** Ruth Strimling; **Editor:** E. Selave; **Photography:** Hans Kuhle, Jr; **Music:** David Knopfler; **Cast:** Brandon Lee, Ernest Borgnine, Debi Monahan, Warner Pocath, Graham Clarke, Maureen Lahoud, Pierre Knoessen.

The Specialist

USA 1994 110 mins

Sylvester Stallone braves new ground in this erotic action thriller, a flawed but laughably enjoyable revenge saga set in sunny Miami, land of drug dealers, old people and crazy Latin rhythms. Despite a number of well-orchestrated action sequences, the accent here is on sex, suspense and the steamy relationship that develops between explosives expert Ray Quick (Stallone) and *femme fatale* May Munro (Sharon Stone).

Obsessed with avenging the murder of her parents at the hands of some evil underworld types, chain-smoker May contacts reclusive Ray and begs him to incinerate several members of the local Cuban-American crime syndicate led by heavy breather Joe Leon (Rod Steiger), who tends to snort like a pig when he gets emotional. Joe's son Tomas (Eric Roberts) is equally outrageous, treating women like dirt, slapping people around and generally acting like spoilt white trash with too much cash. Then there's Ned Trent (James Woods), a blast from Ray's chequered past, an old enemy in league with the Leons who would like nothing more than to round off Ray's life with a bang.

At first, May goes undercover, establishing a relationship with Tomas which she believes will serve to get her close enough to those she wishes to blow away, but Ray soon gets involved, and the scene is set for a satisfying dose of destruction, much double-crossing and the occasional shower scene.

Luis Llosa directs with energy and enthusiasm, boosting the movie with some incredible stunts and explosions, trashing everyone and everything he can get his hands on, from bridges and buildings to bad guys by the truck load. Unfortunately, the erotic tone of the movie is way too self-conscious to be genuinely sexy, with shots of Ray working out and May lolling around in her lingerie proving rather less sensuous than silly, although Sharon Stone remains one hell of a horny babe, as gorgeous and desirable as ever, and if you still get a kick out of seeing her naked, then this is the movie for you.

John Barry's soundtrack is considerably less appealing, intrusive and overbearing, sounding like something rejected from one of his old James Bond scores. Similarly awful are cringe-makers Steiger and Roberts, overdoing every moment of every scene they appear in, although they're not exactly helped by a screenplay which all too often resorts to cliché.

Stallone and Stone fare rather better, though, a match made in Hollywood heaven, slick, professional and lovingly photographed, although it is James Woods, as the ultimate hyperactive killer-cum-explosives genius, who walks away with the movie.

Director: Luis Llosa; **Producer:** Jerry Weintraub; **Screenplay:** Alexander Seros; **Production Design:** Walter Martishius; **Editor:** Jack Hofstra; **Photography:** Jeffrey L. Kimball; **Music:** John Barry, Emilio Estefan; **Cast:** Sylvester Stallone, Sharon Stone, James Woods, Rod Steiger Eric Roberts.

Speed

USA 1994 115 mins

Keanu Reeves and Sandra Bullock
feel a need for *Speed*.

Adrenaline junkies prepare yourselves for *Speed*, a kick ass actioner that has secured for itself a permanent place in our very own Action Movie Hall of Fame. Simply put, it's the business, and if you have even the slightest hint of a pulse, you'd better prepare for it to beat harder than it ever has before.

The story is uncomplicated because what matters is the action: Jack Traven (Keanu Reeves) is a reckless cop, a good guy who isn't afraid to do what it takes (you know the type). Howard Payne (Dennis Hopper), meanwhile, is a mad bomber with a chip on his shoulder who wants a lot of money rather badly (forget world domination, this guy's in it for the cash). Put 'em together, and what have you got? How about a crowded LA bus wired to explode if it slows below 50 mph? And somehow, Traven has to climb aboard the bus and, while negotiating with Payne, keep the vehicle speeding through heavy rush hour traffic.

Not bad, eh? And that's not even the end of it...

Despite the majority of the movie taking place both on and around the bus, screenwriter Graham Yost and director Jan De Bont sustain the action brilliantly, keeping the audience guessing, gasping and begging for more. And the movie delivers in full: imaginative, exhilarating and brilliantly executed, it tears along faster than a speeding bullet and passes two hours in what seems like a couple of minutes.

As with *Die Hard*, the movie is the real star, although the cast perform admirably: Reeves' earnest, monosyllabic cop, coupled with Hopper's well-practised psycho are perfectly in keeping with the movie's no-nonsense philosophy, although Sandra Bullock adds a little light as a gutsy sweetheart who helps out by driving the bus through some pretty terrifying situations.

The edge of your seat doesn't have a chance.

Director: Jan De Bont; **Producer:** Mark Gordon; **Screenplay:** Graham Yost; **Production Design:** Jackson De Govia; **Editor:** John Wright; **Photography:** Andrzej Bartkowiak; **Music:** Mark Mancina; **Cast:** Keanu Reeves, Sandra Bullock, Dennis Hopper, Joe Morton, Jeff Daniels, Alan Ruck, Glenn Plummer; **Academy Awards:** Best... Sound, Sound Effects Editing.

The Spy Who Loved Me

GB 1977 125 mins

Bright and spectacular, *The Spy Who Loved Me* is classic Bond. Sharply written, cleverly played, and designed with an eye for the awesome, this mighty slice of prime entertainment lays on some truly groundbreaking, breathtaking action set-pieces, none more impressive, however, than the pre-title sequence, a rollercoaster ski chase and shoot-out as James rushes from the arms of a bimbo ('But James', she pleads, 'I need you.' Our hero's reply: 'So does England!') towards a mighty, 3000ft drop...

There's microfilm to be found and middle-eastern locations to explore as 007 forms an uneasy and often treacherous alliance with KGB counterpart XXX, also known as Major Anya Amasova (Barbara Bach), a bitchin' Russian babe whose secret agent boyfriend died at the hands of an unknown British operative...

The trail soon leads to dastardly shipping magnate Karl Stromberg (Curt Jurgens), a genocidal megalomaniac with an aquatic fortress, a pool full of sharks, a trio of stolen nuclear submarines and, of course, a lunatic cause: the destruction of mankind, save for a handful of perfect specimens set aside to re-populate the planet - Stromberg's planet.

Fighting for the good guys, Roger Moore shines as Bond, fairly tough and very funny, witty innuendo a speciality. Just as good, Barbara Bach ranks among the best of all the Bond girls, sexy, strong, intelligent and, here's the bonus, a whole lot more than window dressing. Without XXX there'd be no movie, and that's the truth. On the side of villainy we have an adequate evil genius, courtesy of Mr Jurgens, and one of the greatest henchmen of all time, the huge and hulking, metal-mouthed Jaws (Richard Kiel), as indestructible as Superman, if not quite as smart.

Two stars remain: Bond's Lotus Esprit, a flashy white sports car which transforms into a mini-submarine, complete, of course, with a staggering variety of deadly gadgetry. Also worth a mention is the interior of the super-tanker Nostromo: large enough to swallow three submarines (much like Blofeld's rocket-gobbler in *You Only Live Twice*), it required a sound stage so large (374 feet long, 160 feet wide, 53 feet high), production designer Ken Adam had to build the thing from scratch (forever after known as the 007 Stage). Once completed, director Lewis Gilbert proceeded to blow it apart, as Bond leads the Navy against Stromberg's well-armed forces in an epic, climactic battle. Carly Simon said it best: Nobody does it better.

The end of *The Spy Who Loved Me*. But James Bond will return in *Moonraker*.

Director: Lewis Gilbert; **Producer:** Albert R. Broccoli; **Screenplay:** Christopher Wood, Richard Maibaum, based on the novel by Ian Fleming; **Production Design:** Ken Adam; **Editor:** John Glen; **Photography:** Claude Renoir; **Music:** Marvin Hamlisch, title song performed by Carly Simon; **Cast:** Roger Moore, Barbara Bach, Curt Jurgens, Richard Kiel, Caroline Munro, Walter Gotell, Geoffrey Keen, Bernard Lee, Shane Rimmer, Desmond Llewelyn, Lois Maxwell.

Death Becomes Them 24

Sylvester Stallone conquers Vietnam in *Rambo: First Blood Part II*.

Name: STALLONE, Sylvester

Real name: Michael Sylvester Stallone

Nickname: The Italian Stallion

Born: Hell's Kitchen, New York, 1946

Characteristics: Sly said it best. 'I'm not handsome in the classical sense. The eyes droop, the mouth is crooked, the teeth aren't straight, the voice sounds like a Mafioso pallbearer, but somehow it all works.' Add to this a frame of straining muscles and a dialogue-unfriendly slur (the result of a forceps accident at birth which left his vocal chords partially paralysed), and you've got yourself one Italian Stallion, slightly used.

Previous professions: Gym teacher and dorm bouncer at a Swiss boarding school for girls, lion cage cleaner.

Debut feature: *A Party at Kitty and Stud's* (1970; re-named *The Italian Stallion* for 1985 re-release)

Life and times: Despite an early bit part in Woody Allen's *Bananas* in 1971, Sylvester Stallone found that acting jobs did not come easily, and by 1973 he had auditioned for almost every casting agent in New York. While waiting for his big break, Stallone turned more and more to writing, and several screenplays later, in 1974, his perseverance finally paid off with a major role (as well as an 'additional dialogue' writing credit) in Brooklyn gang movie *The Lords of Flatbush*. With the money earned from that project, Stallone moved to Hollywood, where he played small parts in various TV shows and movies, most notably three exploitation features for legendary low-budget producer Roger Corman: *Capone*, *Death Race 2000* and *Cannonball*. By 1976, Stallone was desperate for stardom, and with virtually no cash left in the bank, he wrote the boxing melodrama *Rocky*. Remarkably, he not only sold the script, but managed to keep the lead role for himself, turning down offers of several thousand dollars to give up the part to an established star. This proved to be a very smart move: with a little help from director John G. Avildsen, the film was a phenomenal critical and commercial success, which won three Academy Awards (Best Picture, Director and Editor) and made a star of out Stallone. Subsequent projects fared much less favourably at the box office, and it wasn't until Sly wrote, directed and starred in *Rocky II* that he was back in business. A pattern was already beginning to form: the public loved Rocky Balboa, but were unprepared to accept Stallone in any other role. That was, until John Rambo came along in director Ted Kotcheff's gripping action thriller, *First Blood*. From that point on, Stallone's fans cheered for Rocky and Rambo, they showed great interest in his failed marriages (Sasha, the mother of his two children, and the publicity hungry Brigitte Nielsen), but were generally disinterested in anything else he tried his hand at. Often criticized for taking himself too seriously, Stallone tried to brighten his image with the semi-spoof actioner *Tango & Cash*, and two comedies, *Oscar* and Golden Turkey award winner (for worst movie of 1992) *Stop, Or My Mom Will Shoot*. The mixed responses to these prompted him to go straight for the commercial jugular with two no-nonsense action movies that drew in the punters and saved his career: *Cliffhanger* and *Demolition Man*. Besides his movie interests, Stallone is a keen artist ('I don't know where the world would be without art.'), and, as anyone who's ever eaten a hamburger knows, co-owner of the Planet Hollywood restaurant chain along with fellow movie tough guys Bruce Willis and Arnold Schwarzenegger.

Current salary: $20 million

Greatest contribution to action movies: John 'I kill therefore I am' Rambo.

Speech, speech: 'I see a body as a classy chassis to carry your mind around in.'

'When President Reagan stood up and said, "Having seen Rambo I know what to do with Libya", it was the kiss of death. He made Rambo a Republican.'

'People don't credit me with much of a brain, so why should I disillusion them?'

Selected filmography: *The Lords of Flatbush* (+ co-scr; 1974), *Capone* (1975), ***Death Race 2000*** (1975), *Rocky* (+ scr; 1976), *F.I.S.T.* (+ co-scr; 1976), *Paradise Alley* (+ dir/scr; 1978), *Rocky II* (+ dir/scr; 1979), *Nighthawks* (1981), *Escape To Victory* (aka *Victory*; 1981), ***First Blood*** (+ scr; 1982), *Rocky III* (+ dir/scr; 1982), *Staying Alive* (dir/co-scr/co-prod only; 1983), *Rhinestone* (+ co-scr; 1984), ***Rambo: First Blood Part II*** (+ co-scr; 1985), *Rocky IV* (+ dir/scr; 1985), ***Cobra*** (+ scr; 1986), *Over The Top* (+ scr; 1987), ***Rambo III*** (+ co-scr; 1988), *Lock Up* (1989), ***Tango & Cash*** (1989), *Rocky V* (+ scr; 1990), *Oscar* (1991), *Stop! Or My Mom Will Shoot* (1992), ***Cliffhanger*** (+ co-scr; 1993), ***Demolition Man*** (1993), ***The Specialist*** (1994), ***Judge Dredd*** (1995), ***Assassins*** (1995), *Daylight* (1996).

Star Wars

USA 1977 121 mins

Luke Skywalker (Mark Hamill), Princess Leia (Carrie Fisher), Chewbacca (Peter Mayhew) and Han Solo (Harrison Ford) battle the dastardly Empire in *Star Wars*, the best movie ever made.

Welcome to '34 reasons why *Star Wars* is the greatest film of all time...' The epic establishing shot. Cowardly protocol droid C-3PO (Anthony Daniels), fluent in over six million forms of communication. Spirited astromech droid R2-D2 (Kenny Baker), Threepio's beepy comedy comrade. The Force, '...an energy field created by all living things. It surrounds us and penetrates us. It binds the galaxy together'. The evil, all-powerful Empire, galactic conquest a speciality. Darth Vader (Dave Prowse's brawn, with the voice of James Earl Jones), Dark Lord of the Sith, Master of the Dark Side of the Force, bad guy in black.

Dykstra and Edlund's groundbreaking special effects. Stormtroopers. Princess Leia Organa (Carrie Fisher), big cheese with the Rebel Alliance, a spunky gal and no mistake. Jawas. Luke Skywalker (Mark Hamill), Tatooine farmboy turned intergalactic hero. Banthas. Tusken Raiders. Lightsabres. Luke's favourite Jedi Knight, Obi-Wan Kenobi (Alec Guiness). Mos Eisley Spaceport, a '...wretched hive of scum and villainy'. Aliens a-plenty in the classic Cantina sequence. Han Solo (Harrison Ford), Corellian space cowboy, smuggler, scoundrel, reluctant hero. Chewbacca (Peter Mayhew), Han's towering, 200-year-old Wookie partner. Greedo. The Millenium Falcon, fastest hunk of junk in the galaxy. The Death Star, spherical space station, destroyer of planets, top rebel target. The Grand Moff Tarkin (Peter Cushing), villainous station commander. Alderaan's demise. Holographic fun and games. Leia's rescue and garbage chute escape ('what an incredible smell you've discovered...'). Luke, Leia and a length of rope. Ben and Vader's lightsaber duel. John Williams' magnificent soundtrack. Luke and Han's Tie Fighter target practice. The Fourth Moon of Yavin. Rebel X-Wing fighters. The climactic Death Star assault, dogfights and trench warfare, 'Use the Force, Luke', 'Now let's blow this thing and go home...' And finally, writer/director George Lucas, whose godlike creation of an entire exotic, swashbuckling universe has given us all a reason to live. 'May the Force be with you'.

Sequels: *The Empire Strikes Back*, *Return of the Jedi*.

Director: George Lucas; **Producer:** Gary Kurtz; **Screenplay:** George Lucas; **Production Design:** John Barry; **Editor:** Paul Hirsch, Marcia Lucas, Richard Chew; **Photography:** Gilbert Taylor; **Music:** John Williams; **Cast:** Mark Hamill, Harrison Ford, Carrie Fisher, Peter Cushing, Alec Guiness, Anthony Daniels, David Prowse, Peter Mayhew, Kenny Baker, James Earl Jones (voice only). **Academy Awards:** Best... Original Score, Art Direction, Costume Design (John Mollo), Editing, Sound, Sound Effects (Ben Burtt), Visual Effects (John Dykstra, Richard Edlund).

Stone Cold

USA 1991 90 mins

All-American jock Brian Bosworth embraces excessive force in *Stone Cold*.

A glorious career behind him, American football ace Brian Bosworth tackled this by-the-numbers actioner, custom-made for a jock in need of a career change. Wisely ignoring the messy business of acting, Bosworth diverts most of his energy into creating the perfect image: He's the coolest. He's the toughest. He has balls of steel and a bike to kill for. As undercover cop Joe Huff, 'Boz' gets to play one of those mean, moody types who insist on doing things their way, or not at all. And under the circumstances, he doesn't do half bad.

Enlisted by the FBI, Huff is asked to infiltrate an outlaw gang of Redneck bikers who call themselves 'The Brotherhood'. Led by the increasingly vicious Chains (Lance Henriksen), they do all the usual macho biker stuff, but besides booze, babes and beating on each other for fun, they're in league with the mob, peddling drugs, refusing to wash or shave themselves, and killing anyone who gets in their way. Then along comes our good friend Joe Huff, only now he's jailbird rebel John Stone, out to join a gang of Neanderthals with names like Gut, Tool and Mudfish, hoping to win approval from Chains, and waiting for the right moment to destroy The Brotherhood from the inside out.

What *Stone Cold* lacks in subtlety it makes up for with enthusiasm. When guns aren't being fired, fists are being thrown (no martial arts, just a lot of brute force), and there's a memorable bike chase between our hero and Chains' enthusiastic henchman Ice (William Forsythe), whose ample beer gut and range of automatic weaponry endears him to his simian chums. Director Craig R. Baxley seems equally committed to destruction, delivering a body count to be proud of, and a climactic State House battle - between Joe and roughly a hundred heavily armed bikers - which is violent enough to justify the entire movie alone.

Of the cast, Bosworth does all that he is required to do, but we're not seeing the making of a new action hero here. Only Lance Henriksen, as the joyfully sadistic Chains, makes a lasting impression: 'It's better to be first in Hell', he preaches, 'than second in Heaven!' Right on, brother.

Director: Craig R. Baxley; **Producer:** Yoram Ben Ami; **Screenplay:** Walter Doniger; **Production Design:** John Mansbridge, Richard Johnson; **Editor:** Mark Helfrich; **Photography:** Alexander Gruszynski; **Music:** Sylvester Levay; **Cast:** Brian Bosworth, Lance Henriksen, William Forsythe, Arabella Holzbog, Sam McMurray.

Street Fighter

1994 USA 100 mins

Why slap around a real person when you can do it at home on TV? Thanks to wholesome beat 'em ups like Streetfighter II, couch potatoes around the world have been able to work off their aggression without resorting to physical exercise. Would you believe that an hour spent playing video games is better for you than wasting an entire morning in the gym? You simply cannot afford to underestimate the therapeutic value of going a few rounds with Blanka, a growling mutant killer with green skin, orange hair and a violent disposition. In fact, ever since our very first match together, when I had him sink his fangs deep into Ken's skull and bleed him like a pig, I knew we had something special. I felt fitter than I had in years, and later, when I discovered that a Streetfighter movie adaptation was being prepared by gifted screenwriter Steven E. de Souza (*Commando*, *The Running Man*...), who would also be trying his hand at feature directing for the first time, I crossed my fingers and hoped for the best. Fat lot of good that did.

It can't be easy to adapt a video game, but if someone is crazy enough to try, they should at least attempt to capture its spirit. Streetfighter may not have delivered much in the way of story or characterization, and those elements obviously had to be created from scratch for the movie, but what the game did have to offer was seriously intense hand-to-hand combat, fast, bloody and inventive, which is exactly why it proved so popular.

Why then, make a kids' movie, with muted action, goofy characters and hardly a drop of the red stuff in sight? This is not Streetfighter. This is a live-action, Saturday morning kids' cartoon, drawn in bland primary colours and directed with broad, careless strokes. What it does have going for it is a lot of energy, a pace that rarely drags, and a spirited (final) performance from Raul Julia as jolly tyrant General Bison, a power mad warlord with 63 hostages and a pressing need for $20 billion ransom money. The ruler of Shadaloo, an Asian nation torn apart by civil war, Bison is also developing his own mutant army (Blanka makes a very poor prototype) with whom he plans to take over the entire planet.

Determined to make the world a safer place by blasting Bison and his forces out of their heavily fortified island hideaway are the 'street fighters': Colonel Guile (Van Damme), an all-American good guy with a funny accent and a 'stars and stripes' tattoo; TV reporter Chun Li (Ming-Na Wen), a spirited young thing eager to avenge her father's death at the hands of Bison's forces; Ken (Damian Chapa) and Ryu (Byron Mann), two crazy conmen enlisted by Guile to infiltrate bad guy Sagat's (Wes Studi) arms network, and so the list wears on. With this many characters to attend to (and there are at least ten more not mentioned here), the movie fails to do justice to any of them, although at the end of the day it is Guile and Bison who duke it out for the future of all mankind.

Technically speaking the movie is a mess. De Souza's camera tends to get too close to the action, and combined with some of the clumsiest editing I've ever seen, the fight scenes are often impossible to follow. You want drama? Forget it. But it's bright and light and if you take it as a kids' movie you might just get by. The humour is broad and self-deprecating, the action fast if not particularly exciting, and the cast play it *Power Rangers* all the way. Only trouble is, it's meant to be Streetfighter.

 Ken and Ryu join forces against Bison in *Street Fighter II: The Animated Movie*, directed by Gisaburo Sugii. If you're a fan of the original game, and 'anime' gets you going, you might try this as an alternative to the live-action distraction reviewed above.

Director: Steven E. de Souza; **Producers:** Edward R. Pressman, Kenzo Tsujimoto; **Screenplay:** Steven E. de Souza; **Production Design:** William Creber; **Editors:** Dov Hoenig, Anthony Redman, Robert F. Shugrue, Ed Abroms, Donn Aron; **Photography:** William A. Fraker; **Music:** Graeme Revell; **Cast:** Jean-Claude Van Damme, Raul Julia, Ming-Na Wen, Wes Studi, Damian Chapa, Byron Mann, Kylie Minogue, Roshan Seth, Grand L. Bush, Peter Tuiasosopo, Jay Tavare, Andrew Bryniarski, Simon Callow, Gregg Rainwater, Miguel A. Nunez Jr., Robert Mammone.

Street Knight

USA 1993 87 mins

From the time-honoured convenience store hold-up scene to the climactic martial arts one-on-one, *Street Knight* is every bit the standard Cannon actioner. Ever the professional, Yoram Globus clocks in as co-executive producer, taking care of business while ensuring that the film reaches appropriately high levels of stupidity and ultra-violence. No face is left unmashed. No pint of blood left unsplattered. Expect the expected and you won't be disappointed.

Jeff Speakman kicks, chops, slices and dices his way through the movie as troubled ex-cop Jake Barett, haunted by memories of the 8-year-old hostage he couldn't save, comforted solely by the injuries he routinely inflicts upon the local lowlife. Blessed with a depth that rivals that of any wading pool, Barett soon shrugs off his self-doubt and straps on his guns to lay waste to a group of villains led by the mysterious James Franklin (Christopher Neame), a trigger-happy ham whose half-baked British accent is only slightly less ridiculous than his plan to provoke a full-scale gang war on the streets of Los Angeles.

And boy, does the blood flow. While Franklin busily shoots his enemies not once, not twice, but fifteen times, Barett proves more economical, demolishing two psychos at a time with but a single shot. The performances, dialogue and direction are ripped straight from the worst TV cop shows, but what truly matters here is that Speakman slays with confidence and style, slitting a throat here, breaking a neck there, quoting Schwarzenegger with abandon and looking steely-eyed throughout.

We've seen it all before and we'll see it all again, but as an obnoxious time waster *Street Knight* does just fine.

Director: Albert Magnoli; **Producer:** Mark DiSalle; **Screenplay:** Richard Friedman; **Production Design:** Curtis Schnell; **Editor:** Wayne Wahrman; **Photography:** Yasha Sklansky; **Music:** David Michael Frank; **Cast:** Jeff Speakman, Christopher Neame, Jennifer Gatti, Bernie Casey, Lewis Van Bergen, Ramon Franco, Richard Allen, Richard Coca.

Striking Distance

USA 1993 101 mins

Bruce Willis strikes out in this disappointing misfire from *Road House* director Rowdy Herrington, a corny cop thriller which plays its ace early on in the game, knocking us for six with an elaborate car chase, only to find it has nothing left to offer later on, a humdrum non-event reliant on cheap shocks, ancient clichés and a school of obligatory red herrings.

Willis plays it tough and misunderstood as a typically cynical, hard-bitten cop (time to dust off that well-worn phrase, 'over-the-edge') who publicly challenges the Pittsburgh police force (most of whom he seems to be related to) over the identity of the serial killer who nailed his dad (*Frasier*'s John Mahoney). Consequently, he's busted down to river rescue patrol and (get ready for a surprise...) after two years of playing Popeye the Sailor, a new series of murders convince him that his father's killer is alive, and well, and at it again. And so, with a new partner in tow ('quirky' actress and apparent swim-suit model Sarah Jessica Parker), he breaks every rule in the book in pursuit of his old nemesis. Yawn.

Tired, tiresome and an hour-and-a-half too long, *Striking Distance* is a murder mystery of interest only to itself, a lifeless combo of routine action (save for the opening chase), bland characterization and by-the-numbers movie-making which struggles to keep its head above water but drowns long before the end.

Director: Rowdy Herrington; **Producers:** Arnon Milchan, Tony Thomopoulos, Hunt Lowry; **Screenplay:** Rowdy Herrington, Martin Kaplan; **Production Design:** Gregg Fonseca; **Editors:** Pasqualle Buba, Mark Helfrich; **Photography:** Mac Ahlberg; **Music:** Brad Fiedel; **Cast:** Bruce Willis, Sarah Jessica Parker, Dennis Farina, Tom Sizemore, Brion James, Robert Pastorelli, Timothy Busfield, John Mahoney.

Verbal Assaults 3

A final celebration of obnoxious behaviour...

'No man may have me unless he has beaten me in a fair fight.'
- Brigitte Nielsen lays down the law in *Red Sonja*.

'I used to fuck guys like you in prison!'
- A psychotic Marshall Teague, telling Patrick Swayze rather more than he should, in *Road House*.

'Cancel the kitchen scraps for lepers and orphans, no more merciful beheadings, and call off Christmas!'
- Sheriff of Nottingham Alan Rickman hams it up in *Robin Hood: Prince of Thieves*.

'Locksley - I'm gonna cut your heart out with a spoon.'
- Rickman again, threatening blunt-edged nastiness in *Robin Hood: Prince of Thieves*.

'Your move creep - dead or alive you're coming with me.'
- Peter Weller enforces the law in *RoboCop*.

'That's life in the big city.'
- Ambitious executive Miguel Ferrer, shortly after the gooey death of a fellow employee, in *RoboCop*.

'There's gotta be a hundred reasons why I don't blow you away, but right now I can't think of one.'
- Justice, Eastwood style, courtesy of *The Rookie*.

'It's time for me to stop being scared, and for other people to start.'
- Charlie Sheen toughens up in *The Rookie*.

'Kenner, just in case we get killed, I wanted to tell you, you have the biggest dick I've ever seen on a man.'
- Male bonding, according to Brandon Lee (and directed towards Dolph Lundgren) in *Showdown In Little Tokyo*.

'May the Force be with you.'
- The space-age equivalent of 'Shalom', from *Star Wars*, *The Empire Strikes Back* and *Return of the Jedi*.

'I will peel your skin off with a knife dipped in shit.'
- Psycho biker Lance Henriksen gets mean in *Stone Cold*.

'It's better to be first in Hell than second in Heaven.'
- Henriksen again, sharing his thought in *Stone Cold*.

'Go ahead - make my day.'
- Definitive Dirty Harry, delivered by Clint in *Sudden Impact*.

Mocking cop: 'He thinks he's Rambo.'
Yuppie detective: 'Rambo... is a pussy.'
- Sylvester Stallone mocks his alter-ego in *Tango & Cash*.

'I'll Be Back.'
- The Arnold Schwarzenegger classic, in almost every movie he's made since *The Terminator*.

'Hasta la vista, baby.'
- Arnie again, so damn cool, in *Terminator 2*.

'I promise I will not kill anyone.'
- Arnold resolves to respect life and stick to crippling people instead, in *Terminator 2*.

'I have come here to chew bubblegum and kick ass - and I'm all out of bubblegum!'
- Rowdy Roddy Piper, getting nasty with alien invaders in *They Live*.

'Brother, life's a bitch - and she's back in heat!'
- Rowdy Roddy again, at his deepest, in *They Live*.

'All for one and one for all.'
- *The Three Musketeers* prepare to swash their buckles.

'All for one and more for me.'
- Tim Curry in dastardly mode as Cardinal Richelieu in *The Three Musketeers* (1993).

'Nobody beats me in the kitchen.'
- Killer cook Steven Seagal asserts himself in *Under Siege 2*.

'I just want to eat.'
- Jean-Claude Van Damme, dead hungry, in *Universal Soldier*.

'I'll shove that bat up your ass and turn you into a popsicle'
- James Remar makes friends in *The Warriors*.

'Don't just stand there - kill something!'
- Warrior-priest Dennis Hopper, looking for a piece of the action in *Waterworld*.

Sudden Death

USA 1995 110 mins 🔫

Timecop's Peter Hyams drags out, dusts off and carbon copies the (tried, tested, abused and now sadly tired and stale) *Die Hard* formula for his old pal Jean-Claude Van Damme, here playing it tough - yet sensitive - as a blue collar hero whose life has no meaning until he gets to kill a bunch of bad guys in a sports stadium.

Prepare yourself for the latest in a long line of increasingly tedious cat-and-mouse adventures as troubled fireman Darren McCord (McDammage, trying to act and, as usual, failing miserably) struggles to rescue 17,000 screaming ice hockey fans, the Vice President of the United States (Raymond J. Barry) and, of course, his beloved daughter Emily (Whittni Wright) from the dastardly clutches of smooth master criminal Joshua Foss (Powers Boothe, hardly trying, but who can blame him?). The venue is Pittsburgh's Civic Arena, a towering dome packed to capacity for the final game of the Stanley Cup. And Foss has it wired to explode, threatening major detonation unless the powers that be cough up a couple of billion bucks before the end of the match.

It's a noisy flick, gory too, with lots of explosions. Despite this trio of virtues, however, *Sudden Death* is way too predictable to be exciting and, oddly enough, rather slow and short on action.

An early encounter has Jean-Claude wrestling a 7-foot penguin. Then things get *really* silly: fisticuffs break out in the kitchen and our hero, in true cliffhanging style, has his head forced towards a razor-sharp meat slicer. Escaping this, he soon has his head positioned dangerously close to a deep fat fryer. Avoiding that, he then has to face a burning hot grill, and so the B-movie madness continues from feeble chase scene to half-hearted punch-up right up until a rooftop extravaganza rounds off the show with a Tarzan swing-along and a fake crashing 'copter.

If only it were as funny as it sounds, and not a dire, plagiaristic knock-off.

Director: Peter Hyams; **Producers:** Moshe Diamant, Howard Baldwin; **Screenplay:** Gene Quintano, story by Karen Baldwin; **Production Design:** Philip Harrison; **Editor:** Steven Kemper; **Photography:** Peter Hyams; **Music:** John Debney; **Cast:** Jean-Claude Van Damme, Powers Boothe, Raymond J. Barry, Whittni Wright, Ross Malinger, Dorian Harewood.

Sudden Impact

USA 1983 117 mins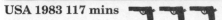

Older, wilder and harder than a granite pasty, Dirty Harry hit the 1980s with bigger sunglasses and a brand new catchphrase, blasting his way through Generation X with snake-eyed cunning, a .44 Magnum and five words that changed the world forever: 'Go ahead - make my day'.

Besides calling the shots on screen, standing every bit as tall as the younger generation of action heroes (Arnie, Sly, Chuck, Mel...), Clint Eastwood played boss behind the scenes as well, producing, directing and generally making sure that this fourth Harry adventure was very much his own.

So, what's it like? Well, there's a lot more action than usual, with Harry wasting a random selection of criminals throughout the picture, which is, unfortunately, a little grim at times, quite heavy and long-winded, and urgently in need of further doses of violence to see it through. Eastwood the star, however, is in top form, guaranteeing a top time for his fans if not especially for regular moviegoers.

Highlights come early on in the movie, as Harry crashes a wedding party to harass the father of the bride, a mobster who's none too pleased at the intrusion and suffers a fatal heart attack as a result. Following this immortal moment, irate mobsters flock to kill our hero, signing their own death warrants as they riddle his car with bullets, wasting their ammo on an indestructible cop who only needs one bullet per man to finish the job.

As a result of Harry's exploits, bewildered Captain Briggs (Bradford Dillman) packs the Dirty One off on 'vacation' to a small California coastal town, where, true to form, he immediately involves himself in a murder investigation, much to local police Chief Jannings' (Pat Hingle) distress.

Scrawny, pale and tortured by memories of the brutal gang rape which wrecked her life and vegetized her sister, vengeful artist Jennifer Spencer (Sondra Locke) slowly works her way through the men (and the woman) who destroyed her life ten years earlier. A vigilante cleansing the streets of poor, white, evil trash, Spencer's methods aren't all that dissimilar to Harry's, who, as he slowly works his way towards the truth, comes to realize that, this time around, the line between victim and villain is blurred...

Offering us something to think about alongside respectable doses of drama, comedy and suspense, Eastwood covers all the bases, some better than others, a worthy effort with a decent body count, but not quite as much fun as his earlier adventures.

Director: Clint Eastwood; **Producer:** Clint Eastwood; **Screenplay:** Joseph C. Stinson; **Production Design:** Edward Carfagno; **Editor:** Joel Cox; **Photography:** Bruce Surtees; **Music:** Lalo Schifrin; **Cast:** Clint Eastwood, Sondra Locke, Pat Hingle, Bradford Dillman, Paul Drake.

Surviving the Game

USA 1994 96 mins

Way back when in 1932, an evil Count hunted humans for sport in a wild little horror flick called *The Most Dangerous Game*. Based on a short story by author Richard Connell, the film has since inspired a legion of rip-offs and remakes, including *Game of Death* (1945), *Kill or be Killed* (1950), *Bloodlust* (1961), *To Kill A Clown* (1973), *The Running Man* (1987), *Hard Target* (1993) and now, for our viewing pleasure, the not-nearly-as-bad-as-it-sounds *Surviving the Game*.

Originality is not an issue here. This latest version of the tale is as trite and formulaic as all the others, but what saves it from a fate worse than daytime TV is *Juice* director Ernest Dickerson, former Spike Lee cameraman supreme, present purveyor of such wild and pacy adventures as *Demon Knight*, here pumping up the movie with quick, sharp cuts, expert steadicam action and a well-known cast of genre favourites.

Head out with us, then, to forbidding Hell's Canyon, home to mountain, river, forest and cliché alike, it's the wilderness, men, and there's trouble afoot. Enter down-and-out with attitude Ice-T, hunted like a dog for the thrill of the chase by a team of bloodthirsty civilians who've each paid $50 grand for the privilege of killing another human being.

Wealthy, mysterious and bad to the bone, head honcho Burns (Rutger Hauer) leads a motley crew of professional types through the Canyon in search of the increasingly resourceful and aggressive Mason (Ice). John C. McGinley's in there somewhere, F.Murray Abraham and Gary Busey too, and they all have their precious acting moments, a mistake for Abraham, who's way too camp when he's angry, but surprisingly successful for Gary Busey, clearly at ease playing a meat-eating monster with a belly full of red neck charm. As for Ice-T. Well, he's Ice-T. Again. And it's a good act, if a little familiar by now.

The opening third of the movie is all it takes to set the wheels in motion, leaving a whole hour free for all the human drama, gut-wrenching scares (dig that trophy room!) and increasingly manic action you can handle.

Guys with guns, lunch-spewing gore, testosterone a-plenty and a cracking punchline too: surely this is the stuff that drunken lads' nights are made of.

Director: Ernest Dickerson; **Producer:** David Permut; **Screenplay:** Eric Bernt; **Production Design:** Christiaan Wagener; **Editor:** Sam Pollard; **Photography:** Bojan Bazelli; **Music:** Stewart Copeland; **Cast:** Ice-T, Rutger Hauer, Charles S. Dutton, John C. McGinley, William McNamara, Jeff Corey, Gary Busey, F. Murray Abraham.

The Taking of Beverly Hills

USA 1991 118 mins

This motion picture is entirely fictitious and is not based on any real persons or events...'. There are times when this familiar disclaimer hardly seems necessary, especially when the movie in question is a piece of lobotomized trash which has about as much chance of delivering a realistic moment or a convincing, well-rounded character as Santa has of getting next Christmas off.

Once again we're in *Die Hard* territory, as a fake chemical spill serves to evacuate the residents of Beverly Hills, leaving their ostentatious homesteads and garish belongings to the mercy of a well-organized gang of crooked ex-cops who plan to rob the town blind. Predictably enough, there's a fly in their ointment, a single, unarmed man the bad guys failed to relocate before getting down to some serious law-breaking. Still, what can one man do? Yeah, right. Obviously he's a hero type, tough, resourceful and fit as a fiddle, entirely capable, in fact, of taking on an invading force of well-armed and highly-motivated thieves and killers. His name is Boomer Hayes (Ken Wahl, as wooden, and as interesting, as a pencil), a famous footballer turned champion of justice who makes the most of his professional skills by throwing rocks at the enemy and tackling anyone who stands between him and saving the day.

A supporting cast of movie stereotypes add to the malaise. Robert Davi sleepwalks through the movie as the coolly dangerous Robert Masterson, our villain. Harley Jane Kozak plays the smart and spirited Laura, our romantic interest and, when the movie embraces yet another cliché, our damsel-in-distress. *Max Headroom*'s Matt Frewer tries not to look too embarrassed as Boomer's comic sidekick Kelvin, a cowardly lion, a bit of a weed and a definite 'glass is half empty' type: 'Boy', he quips, 'I can hardly wait to see the look on their faces when we die right in front of them'. Easily the worst and consequently most entertaining player is our henchman of the day, Benitez (Branscombe Richmond), a raging psycho so desperate to waste Boomer that he even pursues him in a cop shop tank, trashing house after house in a vain attempt to wreck more of the neighbourhood than our demolition man hero, who's supposed to be saving the place, but knows how to make Molotov cocktails and can't help getting carried away sometimes.

A B-movie with delusions of grandeur, *The Taking of Beverly Hills* is so entirely lame and pedestrian that it does have a certain good/bad value, though rather than search through the wreckage of this turkey for scraps of entertainment, why not just watch a good movie instead?

Director: Sidney J. Furie; **Producer:** Graham Henderson; **Screenplay:** Rick Natkin, David Fuller, David J. Burke; **Production Design:** Peter Lamont; **Editor:** Anthony Gibbs; **Photography:** Frank Johnson; **Music:** Jan Hammer; **Cast:** Ken Wahl, Matt Frewer, Harley Jane Kozak, Robert Davi, Lee Ving James, Branscombe Richmond.

Tango & Cash

USA 1989 101 mins

Kurt Russell, Teri Hatcher and Sylvester Stallone hit the dirt in *Tango & Cash*.

Let's do it!' croaks Stallone at the beginning of this macho, muscle-bound adventure, a sledgehammer comedy offering gratuitous nudity, unintentional stupidity, mindless destruction of property and, naturally, lots and lots of comic book ultra-violence.

Brigitte Nielsen's ex-husband and Goldie Hawn's main squeeze ham it up as a pair of *Odd Couple* cops framed for murder by their enemies and banged up in the big house. Sly stands in for Felix Unger as yuppie detective Tango, neat, tidy and addicted to action. As expected, Kurt Russell invokes the spirit of Oscar Madison as slob cop Cash, great at his job if not the social graces. Together, our heroes plan to bust out of stir and prove their innocence by gunning down dozens of miscellaneous bad guys on their way to the big three: crime bosses Quan (James Hong), Lopez (Mark Alaimo, aka *Star Trek: Deep Space Nine*'s Cardassian hotshot Gul Dukat), and, right at the top, boss of bosses Yves Perret (Jack 'The Lad' Palance), a heavy-breathing, scheming kingpin.

Elsewhere among the cast, there's a babe alert out on *The New Adventures of Superman*'s Teri Hatcher as Tango's sister and Cash's love interest, a toupee alert out on *Double Impact*'s Geoffrey Lewis as Tango's captain, a quirky alert out on Michael J. Pollard as Owen, the weapons master, and a full-blow damn-would-you-look-at-that-freak alert out on the square-jawed horror that is The Face (*Maniac Cop*'s Robert Z'Dar). Best of all, though, is Brion James' idiotic performance as Requin, Peret's pet henchman, a wild-eyed, pony-tailed plonker with a cockney accent even Dick Van Dyke wouldn't stoop to (favourites include 'I'll cut your bloody froat', 'piss awf', 'up yours arsole, you ain't werf a toss' and 'e's the guvner').

Wild, silly and over-the-top from the stunts and the gags to the Italian Stallion's lumbering comedy debut, *Tango & Cash* puts its brain to one side and simply enjoys itself, a prison punch-up here, a garage shoot-out there, lots of dumb, harmless, bloody fun (with a little cross-dressing thrown for laughs) with a blazing, action-packed 'RV' finale as our heroes storm Peret's stronghold with a view to killing the villains, saving the girl, and getting the hell out before the whole place self-destructs. Have a good/bad time.

Director: Andrei Konchalovsky; **Producers:** Jon Peters, Peter Guber; **Screenplay:** Randy Feldman; **Production Design:** J. Michael Riva; **Editors:** Hubert de La Bouillerie, Robert Ferretti; **Photography:** Donald E. Thorin; **Music:** Harold Faltermeyer; **Cast:** Sylvester Stallone, Kurt Russell, Teri Hatcher, Jack Palance, Brion James, James Hong, Mark Alaimo.

Tank Girl

USA 1995 104 mins

Jamie Hewlett and Alan Martin's post-punk, post-apocalyptic comic book heroine blasts her way into the movies, slaying deadbeats, chugging beer, playing it cool and making out (in the biblical sense) with mutant kangaroos. Sound good? Are you kidding? It's a big, noisy misfire, irreverent and energetic, maybe, but dumber than Squeeze Cheese and curiously dull.

Following another one of those cosmic cataclysm-type events, which, this time around, robs the world of its water, the earth of 2033 is a typically bleak, inhospitable and sandy place where death-defiance is a way of life and the big bad boss of the all-powerful Water and Power Company, Keslee (Malcolm McDowell), is king. Basically, the world's in a state, and there's no one left to do anything about it...except maybe Tank Girl (*Point Break*'s Lori Petty, wild 'n' crazy with a shaven head), her brainy pal Jet Girl (sidekick Naomi Watts) and an oddball gang of genetically altered kangaroos known as Rippers (Ice-T and Scott Coffey among them). Together, they stand up to Keslee, dividing their time between witless comedy and poorly choreographed ultra-violence, a feeble hash of old ideas and new mistakes graced by two tasty ingredients (which, impressive as they are, don't even come close to saving the movie): Stan Winston's creature effects and Petty's customized wonder-tank, mobile pop culture exhibit and hardware-heavy battle beast.

Beware though, of cheapo comic art links between scenes, of lame, careless characterization and of a blatantly hopeless plot which couldn't find its way even if it had a map, compass, Indian guide, sniffer dog, metal detector, radar and divining rod at its disposal. Trying desperately to be hip, clever and crazy, *Tank Girl* comes up shorter than a eunuch at an orgy.

It's possible that fans of the original strip might enjoy what director Rachel Talalay has to offer, but for the rest of us it's a charmless bag of tricks at best.

Director: Rachel Talalay; **Producers:** Richard B. Lewis, Pen Densham, John Watson; **Screenplay:** Tedi Sarafian; **Production Design:** Catherine Hardwicke; **Editor:** James R. Symons; **Photography:** Gale Tattersall; **Music:** Graeme Revell; **Cast:** Lori Petty, Ice-T, Naomi Watts, Malcolm McDowell, Don Harvey, Reg E. Cathey, Scott Coffey, Jeff Kober.

Teen Agent (aka If Looks Could Kill)

USA 1991 88 mins

A simple misunderstanding is all it takes to plunge reckless youth Michael Corbin into a fantasy world of fast cars, hot babes and wild adventure, territories more commonly explored by superspy James Bond, whose larger-than-life exploits are relentlessly spoofed in this foolish but likeable comedy from William Dear, director of *Harry and the Hendersons*.

Richard Grieco turned his back on the security of episodic TV (*21 Jump Street, Booker*) to play the hero in question, a super-cool high school stereotype who manages to get himself mistaken, as teenagers so often are, for an undercover CIA operative.

Muddling through a world-weary plot involving power mad politician Augustus Steranko (*Cheers'* Roger Rees), whip-cracking assassin Ilsa Grunt (diminutive Rosa Klebb wannabe, Linda Hunt), and Manska (Gabrielle Anwar), a pretty young thing bent on revenge, Corbin survives a variety of exciting, Bond-like action sequences through a combination of pretty boy charm, ultra-flash gadgetry and honest-to-goodness dumb luck.

Weapons' mistress Geraldine James mimics Q just long enough to supply Corbin with such secret service goodies as x-ray specs, explosive chewing gum and, of course, a scorching red sports car with rocket launchers as standard. He'll need them, too, if only to survive the broad performances, corny dialogue and hit-and-miss gags on offer throughout this flawed but good-natured bar of brain candy.

 Rock star Roger Daltrey makes a rare screen appearance as ill-fated secret agent Blade, eliminated before the end of his one and only scene.

Director: William Dear; **Producers:** Craig Zadan, Neil Meron; **Screenplay:** Darren Star, story by Fred Dekker; **Production Design:** Guy J. Comtois; **Editor:** John F. Link; **Photography:** Doug Milsome; **Music:** David Foster; **Cast:** Richard Grieco, Linda Hunt, Roger Rees, Robin Bartlett, Gabrielle Anwar, Geraldine James, Roger Daltrey.

Teenage Mutant Ninja Turtles

USA 1990 93 mins

The title really says it all. Eastman and Laird's bizarre comic book creations, those villain-stomping, pizza-loving heroes in a half-shell, enjoyed their first taste of live-action mayhem in this safe but enjoyable mix of martial arts adventure and *Bill and Ted*-type comedy. Mutated teen turtles Raphael, Michaelangelo, Donatello and Leonardo burst into the real world thanks largely to Jim Henson's world-famous Creature Shop, whose dazzling animatronic creations work wonders for the lean, green, Ninja machines.

Living a secret existence in the sewers beneath New York City, the turtles spend their time watching TV, eating snacks and training with Master Splinter, a wise and oversized Japanese rat. When a crime wave sweeps the city clean of valuables, our sheltered champions get a chance to hit the streets, kicking butt all the way to Master Shredder (James Saito), an evil Darth Vader wannabe with an army of pint-sized crooks and killers at his disposal.

Joined by spunky TV reporter April O'Neil (Judith Hoag) and excitable vigilante Casey Jones (Elias Koteas), the Turtles make the most of their only decent movie to date, cracking jokes and busting crime as only juvenile super-heroes know how.

Sequels: *Teenage Mutant Ninja Turtles II: The Secret of the Ooze, Teenage Mutant Ninja Turtles III.*

Director: Steve Barron; **Producers:** Kim Dawson, Simon Fields, David Chan; **Screenplay:** Todd W. Langen, Bobby Herbeck, based on characters created by Kevin Eastman and Peter Laird; **Production Design:** Roy Forge Smith; **Editors:** William Gordean, Sally Menke, James Symons; **Photography:** John Fenner; **Music:** John Du Pre; **Cast:** Judith Hoag, Elias Koteas, James Saito, Toshishiro Obata, voices of Kevin Clash, Robbie Rist, Brian Tochi, David McCharen, Corey Feldman.

Terminal Velocity

USA 1994 102 mins

Charlie Sheen and Nastassja Kinski take the plunge in *Terminal Velocity*.

One minute you're a skydiving wild man, a macho throwback of prehistoric proportions who's hooked on adrenaline and chock full o' hormones, then along comes a plot device and suddenly you're an all-action hero with a pocket full of secret plans and a bone to pick with the Russian Mafia. It's funny how some days turn out.

Case in point, the high-flying misadventures of Richard 'Ditch' Brodie, a super-cool skydiving instructor and veteran practitioner of the vintage one-liner whose private investigation into the 'accidental' death of a fellow thrill-seeker leads him blindly into a whole world of trouble which lies somewhere between the macho bullshit of *Point Break* and the international espionage of the Bond flicks.

And very exciting it is too, with a conventional 'good guys versus the bad guys' plot that cleverly disguises itself as a mystery while wisely laying on plenty of standard action fare as well as some of the most spectacular aerial stunts you are ever likely to see, which is really what this movie is all about.

Slick and efficient, the film scores highly in all the technical areas, with some truly epic cinematography from Oliver Wood and impressive special effects which allow the cast to boldly fall where no one has fallen before. The screenplay proves less capable, and while writer David Twohy deserves credit for at least trying something different, a spell in dialogue school wouldn't have hurt him one bit. Of the cast, Charlie Sheen sleepwalks as Ditch, delivering an indifferent performance which passes the physical but fails the intelligence test, while the lad's screen pairing with Nastassja Kinski, here playing mystery lady Chris, is about as lively as a tortoise with a broken leg and a pounding tequila hangover. Oh well, at least we're given a decent villain to jeer at called Kerr, a snarling, muscular Mafia man played with masses of thuggish enthusiasm by Christopher McDonald. Kill first, ask questions later (or something like that, anyway).

The phrase 'terminal velocity', if you're at all interested, refers to the speed a body picks up as it falls through the air (around 110/120 kph), and true to the spirit of the title, director Sarafian puts the peddle to the metal and lays on all the G-forces we can handle, with an explosive escape sequence serving as the movie's half-time highlight, and a high-flying, free-falling, death-defying finale that ends the movie on a real high and is guaranteed to overload your brain, pop your eyes right out of your head and slacken that normally heroic jaw of yours. In other words, it's the business, and even if the rest of this movie was a pile of trash (which it isn't), I'd recommend it to you on the strength of its climax alone.

Director: Deran Sarafian; **Producers:** Scott Kroopf, Tom Engelman. **Screenplay:** David Twohy; **Production Design:** David L. Snyder; **Editor:** Frank J. Urioste, Peck Prior; **Photography:** Oliver Wood; **Music:** Joel McNeely; **Cast:** Charlie Sheen, Nastassja Kinski, James Gandolfini, Christopher McDonald, Melvin Van Peebles.

The Terminator

USA 1984 108mins

Arnold Schwarzenegger aims to obliterate the entire human race in this ingenious early offering from director James Cameron, a mind-messing sci-fi chase flick with lots of funky make-up and visual effects (courtesy of Stan *Predator* Winston), intense and uncompromising ultra-violent action, and a neatly emotionless, cold, hard and expressionless performance from our favourite man-mountain, destined, from birth, to play a robot monster.

A cyborg from a future where the machines rule, has travelled to the past to kill a man before his birth. Sarah Connor (Linda *Beauty and the Beast* Hamilton) will give birth to a boy whose destiny is to save mankind from extinction, and the Terminator wants her dead before the bun is even in her oven. A soldier, Kyle Reese (Michael Biehn), heads from 2029 to 1984 to protect her, but hell, he's only human. The Terminator, on the other hand, is one tough, metallic son-of-a-bitch. 'It can't be bargained with', explains Kyle. 'It can't be reasoned with. It doesn't feel pity, or remorse, or fear, and it absolutely will not stop - ever - until you are dead.'

Arnold's relentless pursuit of the troubled, young couple harvests mayhem a-plenty, from a nightclub rumble and virtuoso cop shop shootout to an explosive high speed pursuit and scarifying exoskeleton finale. Hard, fast and smart, with an all-time classic bad guy, *The Terminator* is wildness incarnate.

 Arnold utters 'I'll be back' (for the very first time) and leaves the police precinct. There's a screeching noise, and the Desk Sergeant looks up startled, his face illuminated by, we assume, headlights. But, fellow nit-pickers, when the movie cuts to Arnold driving through the precinct wall, his lights are clearly off.

 Supporting, supporting cast members with familiar faces include *Aliens'* Lance Henriksen and (spiky blue-haired punk) Bill Paxton, Paul *Wrath Khan* Winfield, Rick *Navy SEALS* Rossovich and Corman/Dante regular Dick Miller.

Sequels: *Terminator 2: Judgment Day.*

Director: James Cameron; **Producer:** Gale Anne Hurd; **Screenplay:** James Cameron, Gale Anne Hurd; **Editor:** Mark Goldblatt; Photography: Adam Greenberg; **Music:** Brad Fiedel; **Cast:** Arnold Schwarzenegger, Michael Biehn, Linda Hamilton, Paul Winfield, Lance Henriksen, Rick Rossovich, Bess Motta, Earl Boen.

Terminator 2: Judgment Day

USA 1991 136 mins

Shortly before gunning down a precinct full of cops in *The Terminator*, Arnold Schwarzenegger uttered the now-immortal line 'I'll be back.' True to his word, he and director James Cameron re-united, and, along with a budget ten times the size of the original, made this long-awaited super-sequel.

As different from the first as *Aliens* was from *Alien*, *T2* focuses on the big, the bold and the strangely safe, as Arnold, once the villain, shifts to hero mode, too concerned about his public image to play another baddy.

Schwarzenegger's original Terminator had failed. Sarah Connor (Linda Hamilton) had survived and given birth to Kyle Reese's son, a boy destined to lead the human race to victory against the machines. But now another Terminator, the all-new shape-shifting T-1000 (Robert Patrick) has travelled back in time to kill John Connor (Edward Furlong) while he is still a boy.

With his mother banged up in a high security mental institute, teen-dream John seems destined for an early grave until, as if by magic, a second Terminator hits the scene, an old Arnold model reprogrammed to protect him. And so the chase begins, again, as John and Arnie's T-101 team up to spring Sarah from hospital, trash the T-1000, and prevent Cyberdyne Systems from creating the super-computer which came close to wiping out mankind...

Arnold, suddenly a good guy, allows his character a few shreds of humanity. For starters, he swears never to kill again, choosing, instead, to cripple his enemies (well, it's a start). As his relationship with John develops, he learns to smile and even picks up a little slang - 'Hasta la vista, baby!' Compared with this new, caring, sharing Terminator, Sarah Connor seems positively robotic, her humanity slipping away as the pretty, young innocent of the original transforms into a grim and humourless survivalist, weighed down by the knowledge of what the future holds. Edward Furlong, meanwhile, does well to make his presence felt as a rebel with a new cause, while Robert Patrick plays it straight and lets

Linda Hamilton toughens up in *Terminator 2: Judgment Day*.

Dennis Muren's special effects do most of the work, as his liquid-metal form 'morphs' from one shape to another with startling results.

Blazing shoot-outs, bust-ups and chase sequences unite to blow us away as Cameron adds unique and imaginative touches to each and every action sequence. Smart, intense and wildly exciting, *T2* is a remarkable sequel.

Director: James Cameron; **Producer:** James Cameron; **Screenplay:** James Cameron, William Wisher; **Production Design:** Joseph Nemec III; **Editors:** Conrad Buff, Mark Goldblatt, Richard A. Harris; **Photography:** Adam Greenberg; **Music:** Brad Fiedel; **Cast:** Arnold Schwarzenegger, Linda Hamilton, Edward Furlong, Robert Patrick, Earl Boen, Joe Morton; **Academy Awards:** Best... Visual Effects, Sound, Sound Effects Editing.

They Live

USA 1988 94 mins

There are a couple of things that you need to know about *They Live* before seeing it, or else you're sunk. Call it survival trivia. First of all, you have to consider director John Carpenter's devotion to the time-honoured sport of wrestling. This explains why he cast World Wrestling Federation superstar 'Rowdy' Roddy Piper as his blue-collar hero. It also explains why there's a long, tough and extremely well-choreographed punch up/wrestling match somewhere around the middle of the movie.

The second point you need to take on board is that while this movie appears to be, at least for the first half hour or so, rather ingenious and serious science fiction in the time-honoured tradition of E.C. Comics, *The Twilight Zone* and paranoid 1950s fare along the lines of *Invasion of the Body Snatchers*, it is in fact a rather elaborate and increasingly frantic shaggy dog story. Take the film too seriously and you're cruising for a serious bruising. Take it with a pinch of salt (and a belly full of beer and doughnuts) and you might just get by.

Truth is, the movie would have been a whole lot better had Carpenter not played it so fast and loose, but there's a bounty of mindless action to enjoy, and, believe it or not, a capable central performance from Piper, whose easy charm, macho charisma and willingness to deliver outlandish one-liners with deadly earnest makes him a natural. 'Brother', he warns, face straighter than a ruler, 'life's a bitch - and she's back in heat!'

There's trouble brewing on Earth, and only one man can save us. Word has it that pizza-faced aliens from another dimension have been colonizing this fair planet of ours for several years now, using mind control to disguise their alarming appearance while planting subliminal messages in the populace along the lines of 'Conform', 'Consume', 'Sleep' and 'Obey'. The only way to block the pizza-creatures' signal and see them as they really are is to wear a special pair of designer sunglasses (what else?), and guess who comes across a pair? None other than struggling labourer John Nada (Piper), a drifter, loner and multi-purpose tough guy who makes it his mission in life to sabotage the aliens' subliminal transmitter, killing as many of them as possible along the way.

Witness Nada as he strolls into a bank, shotgun in hand, trusty sunglasses revealing half the clientele as alien scum. 'I have come here to chew bubblegum and kick ass', he announces to the crowd, 'and I'm all out of bubblegum!' Subtle it ain't, but it grows on you.

Director: John Carpenter; **Producer:** Larry Franco; **Screenplay:** Frank Armitage, based on the story 'Eight O'Clock in the Morning' by Ray Nelson; **Production Design:** Daniel Lomino, William J. Durrell Jr; **Editors:** Gib Jaffe, Frank E. Jiminez; **Photography:** Gary B. Kibbe; **Music:** John Carpenter, Alan Howarth; **Cast:** Roddy Piper, Keith David, Meg Foster, George 'Buck' Flower, Peter Jason, Raymond St. Jacques, Jason Robards III.

The Three Musketeers: The Queen's Diamonds

GB 1974 105 mins

Director Richard Lester does Dumas for laughs in this irreverent comic swashbuckler, a grand, glorious adventure prone to extended bouts of swordplay, slapstick and bawdy romance. Duty, honour and friendship co-exist with gluttony, lust and violence in the name of knockabout entertainment, and it's a spirited mix indeed, polished off with an all-star cast of familiar faces and a lively, British sense of humour.

The flimsiest of plots has Cardinal Richelieu (Charlton Heston) seeking to damage the throne by exposing the Queen's (Geraldine Chaplin) extra-marital activities, and, as ever, the Three Musketeers, namely Athos (Oliver Reed), Aramis (Richard Chamberlain) and the laddish Porthos (Frank Finlay), dash to the rescue, accompanied by their new-found pal D'Artagnan (Michael York).

Providing distraction along the way, supporting players include Raquel Welch, surprisingly funny as the gorgeous yet accident prone Constance, Faye Dunaway as secondary schemer Milady, Christopher Lee as Richelieu's creepiest henchman, Jean-Pierre Cassel as the foppish King, Spike Milligan as Constance's lawfully-wedded dirty old geezer, and Roy Kinnear as D'Artagnan's personal dogsbody, a loyal slave, accomplished fool and, when push comes to shove, handy target.

There's lots to see and plenty to be enjoyed, from the Musketeers' unique style of food theft to a wild, inventive wash house fight. It's a circus movie, really, full of clowns and acrobats, a light-hearted spectacle made back-to-back with *The Four Musketeers*, a like-minded sequel which you'll have to catch if you want to see what happens to the baddies.

Sequels: *The Four Musketeers: The Revenge of Milady*, *The Return of the Musketeers*.

Director: Richard Lester; **Producer:** Alex Salkind; **Screenplay:** George MacDonald Fraser; **Production Design:** Brian Eatwell; **Editor:** John Victor Smith; **Photography:**

David Watkin; **Music:** Michel Legrand; **Cast:** Michael York, Oliver Reed, Richard Chamberlain, Frank Finlay, Raquel Welch, Geraldine Chaplin, Spike Milligan, Faye Dunaway, Charlton Heston, Christopher Lee, Jean-Pierre Cassel.

The Three Musketeers

USA 1993 106 mins

D'Artagnan (Chris O'Donnell) and Athos (Kiefer Sutherland) horse around in *The Three Musketeers*.

Sheen and Sutherland: The Next Generation join forces with fellow showbiz youngsters Oliver Platt and Chris O'Donnell for yet another run through the Dumas mill, unnecessary, sure, but a perfect excuse for swashbuckling thrills, sweeping romance (if you want that sort of thing) and broad, knockabout comedy. A lightweight adventure from director Stephen Herek, *The Three Musketeers* offers a standard collection of forest chases, daring rescues, last minute escapes, rooftop struggles and, of course, lots of flashy, well-choreographed swordplay.

A familiar plot sets the wheels of action in motion: eager young swordsman D'Artagnan (O'Donnell), newly arrived in Paris, sets out to join the King's Musketeers, only to find that they have been disbanded by principal schemer Cardinal Richelieu (Tim Curry). Only three loyal Musketeers remain, suave Aramis (Sheen), broody Athos (Sutherland) and lusty Porthos (Platt) who, along with their brand new pal, fight to protect the throne from Richelieu, the treacherous Milady (Rebecca De Mornay) and vile henchman Rochefort (*The Crow*'s Michael Wincott). Elsewhere among the cast, Hugh O'Conor and Gabrielle Anwar make an acceptable King/Queen combination, while Euro-babe Julie Delpy wins D'Artagnan's heart as the lovely Constance.

This is very much a Disney movie, lively, colourful and safe, with a good-looking cast of youngsters, a screenplay chock full of slang and no end of American accents. If you're in the market for bland, brainless family fun, your search is over.

Director: Stephen Herek; **Producers:** Joe Roth, Roger Birnbaum; **Screenplay:** David Loughery, based on the novel *The Three Musketeers* by Alexandre Dumas; **Production Design:** Wolf Kroeger; **Editor:** John F. Link; **Photography:** Dean Semler; **Music:** Michael Kamen; **Cast:** Charlie Sheen, Kiefer Sutherland, Chris O'Donnell, Oliver Platt, Tim Curry, Rebecca De Mornay, Gabrielle Anwar, Michael Wincott, Paul McGann, Julie Delpy, Hugh O'Conor.

3 Ninjas

USA 1992 84 mins

A huge box-office success in the States, Disney's knockabout adventure *3 Ninjas* is a perfect kids' flick: silly, short and obnoxious to adults. The *Home Alone* formula strikes again as three young brothers defend their household and take the offensive against a variety of toon-like bad guys, best of all veteran henchman Professor Toru Tanaka (*An Eye For An Eye*, *The Perfect Weapon*, *The Running Man*...), using the martial arts skills taught to them by their wise old grandfather (*Big Trouble in Little China*'s Victor Wong), the only grown-up who doesn't act like a fool throughout the movie.

Slick, manipulative and, yes, pretty enjoyable too, the film introduces us to brothers Rocky (Michael Treanor), Tum Tum (Chad Power) and Colt (Max Elliott Slade), a trio of hyperactive youngsters turned Kung Fu fighters who exercise their new-found skills on evil Ninja master Snyder (Rand Kingsley), a champion trouble-maker in desperate need of pint-sized punishment.

The movie's highlight serves up everything but Macaulay Culkin as the boys deal painfully and hilariously with three dastardly Bill and Ted types who dare invade their home. As you'd expect, the chop-socky action is played strictly for laughs, although parents of particularly impressionable, boisterous children would be well-advised to tread carefully around the house for a day or two, just in case.

Unimaginative and shamelessly plagiaristic it may be, but kids looking for an entertaining hour-and-a-half aren't going to moan about such things: they'll be too busy enjoying the spectacle of three miniature Ninjas out-thinking, out-manoeuvring and out-fighting the adults.

Sequels: *Three Ninjas Kick Back*, *Three Ninjas Knuckle Up*.

Director: John Turteltaub; **Producer:** Martha Chang; **Screenplay:** Edward Emanuel, story by Kenny Kim; **Production Design:** Kirk Petruccelli; **Editor:** David Rennie; **Photography:** Richard Michalak; **Music:** Rick Marvin; **Cast:** Victor Wong, Michael Treanor, Max Elliott Slade, Chad Power, Rand Kingsley, Alan McRae, Margarita Franco, Professor Toru Tanaka.

Thunderball

GB 1965 129 mins

SPECTRE returns to menace the world in this waterlogged adventure, a good-looking but unimaginative thriller which remains the dreariest of all the Bond flicks. The pre-credit sequence, in which Bond knocks the stuffing out of an enemy agent before jet-packing his way to safety, might suggest better things, but don't be fooled: this movie is about as exciting as, Satan preserve us, an art movie. And that's during the *good* bits.

With a matching pair of stolen nuclear missiles hidden safely away in the waters off funky Nassau, SPECTRE gives NATO a week to hand over £100 million (or $280 million - now that's what I call an exchange rate) or suffer the consequences. Pretty soon every 00 agent is on the case, but it's blindingly obvious that only one of them is going to see any action, so the others might as well have stayed at home while good old number seven checks out the Bahamas. Intent on ruining Bond's summer vacation is moneyed Eurotrash Emilio Largo (Adolpho Celi), a SPECTRE heavy who seems more concerned with Bond's interest in his girlfriend Domino (French beauty queen Claudine Auger) than he does with the business of international extortion.

Hold the drama. Hold the style. What we have here is a cosy, overconfident mistake: the good guys know who the bad guys are, the bad guys know who the good guys are, and all they seem to do is skate coyly around the issue. As James Bond, Sean Connery goes through the usual paces, working his way towards an extended but confusing underwater battle via a swimming pool full of hungry Golden Grotto Sharks, but his heart just doesn't seem to be in it. The same goes for bad guy Celi, all accent and eye patch, the weakest of all of Bond's adversaries.

There's plenty of sex, a lot of harpooning and a painful overdose of cute, knowing dialogue. The movie's only highlight comes when Bond, ever the misogynist, jumps in the sack with beautiful SPECTRE assassin Fiona Volpe (Luciana Paluzzi), only to tell her afterwards that he did the deed solely for King and Country. 'You don't think it gave me any pleasure do you?' Nice try, James, but it's too little, too late. Besides, everyone knows guys can't fake it.

The end of *Thunderball*. But James Bond will return in *You Only Live Twice*.

Director: Terence Young; **Producer:** Kevin McClory; **Screenplay:** Richard Maibaum, John Hopkins, based on the novel by Ian Fleming; **Production Design:** Ken Adam; **Editor:** Peter Hunt; **Photography:** Ted Moore; **Underwater Photography:** Lamar Boren; **Music:** John Barry, title song performed by Tom Jones; **Cast:** Sean Connery, Claudine Auger, Adolfo Celi, Luciana Paluzzi, Rik Van Nutter, Bernard Lee, Martine Beswick, Desmond Llewelyn, Lois Maxwell. **Academy Award:** Best Visual Effects.

Trivialists 6

HALL OF SHAME

1. *King Solomon's Mines*
2. *Black Eagle*
3. *Bulletproof*
4. *Death Wish II*
5. *Black Belt Jones*
6. *Excessive Force*
7. *On Deadly Ground*
8. *The Punisher*
9. *American Cyborg: Steel Warrior*
10. *Bird on a Wire*

Dishonourable mentions...

11. *Braddock: Missing In Action 3*
12. *Codename: The Soldier*
13. *Fair Game*
14. *Last Action Hero*
15. *Freejack*
16. *The Money Train*
17. *Nowhere to Run*
18. *The Shooter*
19. *Striking Distance*
20. *Sudden Death*

Tiger on the Beat

Hong Kong 1988 89 mins

Alcohol-fuelled violence saves the day as mismatched Hong Kong cops Chow Yun-Fat and Conan Lee learn that the partners who slay together, stay together. Fat's the gun man of the operation, a typically casual, maverick sort into booze by the crate and raw eggs by the carton. Balancing one character stereotype with another, Lee plays a fighting fit tempest of Kung Fu fury dedicated to bringing down drug lord Gordon Lui. Chow, meanwhile, has his eye on *femme fatale* Nina Li Chi, sister of the crime boss in question and one seriously squeezable babe.

Overplayed comic interludes break up the action, scattering gags among the chaos as Chow blasts his way through an army of henchmen while Lee chops their cotton-pickin' socks off. The laughs are easily forgotten, though, and contribute little to the movie. Best to concentrate on the bloodshed, then, well paced and executed by veteran director Liu Chia Liang, who wisely saves the best till last...

With Chow busy elsewhere, tying loose ends and slaughtering extras, Lee and Lui come face-to-face for one of the most vicious showdowns in action movie history, a swashbuckling masterpiece involving that most versatile of household gadgets, the chainsaw.

You are not going to want to miss this.

Sequel: *Tiger On The Beat 2.*

Director: Lau Kar Leung; **Producer:** Wellington W. Fung, Tsang Kwok Chi; **Screenplay:** Tsang Kwok Chi; **Production Design:** Eric Lee; **Editor:** Wong Ming Lam; **Photography:** Cho On Shun, Joe Chan Kwong Hung; **Music:** Teddy Robin Kwan; **Cast:** Chow Yun Fat, Conan Lee, Ti Lung, Nina Li Chi, Gordon Lui, Tsui Sui Keung.

Timebomb

USA 1991 96 mins

Brace yourself for yet another good-guy-on-the-run-trying-to-save-the-day flick, this time with a *Total Recall* twist: inexplicably pursued by a squad of high-powered henchmen, mild-mannered watchmaker Eddy Kay (Michael Biehn) freaks out as long-lost skills and memories slowly begin to re-surface. Kidnapping local shrink Anna Kolmar (Patsy Kensit) for therapy, sidekick support and eventual love interest, Eddy sets out to unravel the mystery of his erased earlier life. Naturally, a lot of people have to die - and die horribly - before this is possible. Particularly special is the pay-off to one particular punch-up, where Eddy swiftly wraps a villain's head in a clean, white sheet and proceeds to elbow-pummel his face into a crimson mash. Now *that's* entertainment.

It's not all good news, though. Watch closely as - before your very eyes - a promising sci-fi spy flick loses both credibility and momentum as an increasingly silly series of plot developments come into play. Director Avi Nesher proves himself a reliable blood-and-guts man, scoring well with the action sequences but faring rather less successfully in the (way overblown) story and screenplay departments.

As for Biehn and Kensit, while they're not exactly Mr and Mrs Personality, they manage, at least, to make it to the end of the movie without laughing out loud, as our hero re-discovers new and interesting ways to break important bones and Kensit, well, takes her clothes off. Elsewhere, Richard Jordan discovers an acting state beyond ham as token military creep Colonel Taylor, while Tracy Scoggins (as Ms Blue) and B-movie muscle man Billy Blanks (as Mr Brown) keep the dialogue to a minimum as assassins who'd choose war over peace any day of the week.

We've reached the realms of the passable, people, where movies are just about watchable but by no means re-watchable, a shlocky adventure which, though it loses its way and verges on the nutty, manages, at the very least, to serve up the kind of brutal and entirely gratuitous ultra-violence that we love and admire.

Director: Avi Nesher; **Producer:** Raffaella de Laurentiis; **Screenplay:** Avi Nesher; **Production Design:** Greg Pruss, Curtis A. Schnell; **Editor:** Isaac Sehayek; **Photography:** Anthony B. Richmond; **Music:** Patrick Leonard; **Cast:** Michael Biehn,

Patsy Kensit, Tracy Scoggins, Robert Culp, Raymond St Jacques, Richard Jordan, Billy Blanks, Jim Maniaci, Stephen J. Oliver.

Timecop

USA 1994 98 mins

Jean-Claude Van Damme strips for action in *Timecop*.

Here we have a science fiction thriller with the intelligence to allow its star, Jean-Claude Van Damme, the freedom to do what he does best, namely punch, kick, jump and basically beat the living hell out of a whole army of villains. Sure, there's a little acting in there too, and a plot which may very well exercise a fraction of your old grey matter, but what really counts here is, of course, the action, and there's a truck load: mostly macho hand-to-hand (or, more accurately, foot-to-head) stuff with the muscled one doing all manner of spectacular martial arts moves, moving with speed and agility and coming down on the bad guys like a ton of Belgian bricks.

The year is 2004 and time travel is a dangerous reality, with ambitious villains changing the past to make the most of their future, altering history, manipulating world finances and generally messing things up. Travelling to the past is therefore outlawed, making it an obvious target for every criminal who can get his hands on the technology. And so we have the timecops, guardians of the past who travel back in time to deliver twenty-first century justice to those who dare break the law. People such as wicked Senator McComb (Ron Silver), whose ruthless political ambitions bring him head-to-head with the greatest timecop of 'em all, Max Walker (Jean-Claude, of course), whose wife Melissa (Mia Sara) dies following a mysterious attack in Walker's past...

What follows is one time travel paradox after another, with people dying and coming back to life, history changing and so on until, as good as the story is, you come to concentrate on the action. And it is amazing. Van Damme is in his finest form ever, performing stunts that will leave you breathless, while Ron Silver delivers a deliciously hissable bad guy, complete with a major bad attitude, some deadly one-liners and an inexhaustible supply of henchmen. And director Peter Hyams pulls it all off perfectly.

Director: Peter Hyams; **Producers:** Moshe Diamant, Sam Raimi, Robert Tapert; **Screenplay:** Mark Verheiden, based on a story and comic book series by Mark Verheiden and Mike Richardson; **Production Design:** Philip Harrison; **Editor:** Steven Kemper; **Photography:** Peter Hyams; **Music:** Mark Isham; **Cast:** Jean-Claude Van Damme, Mia Sara, Ron Silver, Bruce McGill, Gloria Reuben, Scott Bellis, Jason Schombing.

Total Recall

USA 1990 109 mins

Paul Verhoeven messes with our minds in this ingenious 21st century adventure based on the classic Phil Dick tale 'We can remember it for you wholesale'. Arnold Schwarzenegger battles a tyrant on Mars, but is it real, or really a dream? A major-league budget endeavours to amaze with incredible sets and set-pieces, weird mutant aliens and wacky, new contraptions (Johnny Cab, anyone?), and, for the most part, it's successful. Some of the make-up effects are a little rubbery, sure, and the Martian landscapes are pretty obvious miniatures, but a lot of time, thought and effort has been invested in this one, and even if it does slip up every now and then, it's a wild, inventive ride, just the same.

Blessed with a near-total lack of restraint, the director of *RoboCop* and *Flesh + Blood* does it again, going for broke with a vicious sense of humour, paying keen attention to all things violent and, best of all, grossing us out at every opportunity (Arnold's bug-up-the-nose trick is almost as disgusting as the squishy-dead-guy-on-the-escalator sequence).

Schwarzenegger is in fine, fighting shape as the muscled, troubled Doug Quaid, zooming to Mars with a brain full of resurfacing memories, eager to make sense of an erased former existence and maybe save the planet while he's there. Of course, he could be nuts, with everything happening in his mind, but it's a pretty good fantasy either way, with top acting support from despicable Mars boss Ronny Cox (aka *Robo*'s Dick Jones), high-kicking earth-bitch Sharon Stone, bloodthirsty henchman Michael Ironside, and, because Doug needs a friend, romantic interest Rachel Ticotin.

A twisted adrenaline rush of action and ideas, *Total Recall* aims to overload your senses, so you might as well give in and enjoy the show.

Director: Paul Verhoeven; **Producer:** Buzz Feitshans, Ronald Shusett; **Screenplay:** Ronald Shusett, Dan O'Bannon, Gary Goldman, story by Ronald Shusett, Dan O'Bannon, John Povill, based on the short story 'We Can Remember It For You Wholesale' by Phillip K. Dick; **Production Design:** William Sandell; **Editor:** Frank J. Urioste; **Photography:** Jost Vacano; **Music:** Jerry Goldsmith; **Cast:** Arnold Schwarzenegger, Rachel Ticotin, Sharon Stone, Michael Ironside, Ronny Cox.

Toy Soldiers

USA 1991 112 mins

Teenage rebels follow the yellow brick road of violence all the way to well-adjusted manhood in director Daniel Petrie Jr's 'homage' to *Die Hard*, a deeply foolish adventure addicted to Hollywood formula, boyish angst and enthusiastic bursts of impossible action. It's a slay-ride, alright, a couple of hours of youthful wish-fulfilment as a band of pretty boy rejects take on - wait for it - a gang of cut-throat Colombian drug dealers (complete with regulation pony-tails).

When South American kingpin Enrique Cali (Jesse Doran) ends up in a Stateside jail, his evil, vicious son Luis (Andrew Divoff) jets to the US with a handful of terrorists intent on taking the students of an exclusive prep school hostage. Using the kids of important citizens as bargaining chips, Luis hopes to spring dad and bugger off back to poppy paradise, but - shock horror surprise of the century - these are no ordinary boys: they're deadbeats the lot of 'em, anti-authority problem cases, law-breakers, drinkers, smokers, sex-chat phone-line abusers, and, as such, are eminently qualified to make like Bruce Willis and, through a combination of strategy, force and manipulative direction, fight back with a vengeance.

Twelve-year-old girls are advised to check out this dreamy cast: leading the pack is Sean Astin, still clinging on to his puppy fat, on the surface a real bad lad, but underneath, ladies, he's all heart (and when the plot demands he take his clothes off, all butt). Loyal egghead Wil Wheaton (*Star Trek: The Next Generation*'s boy-genius Wesley Crusher, fully-clothed throughout, thank goodness) follows close behind, playing it smart and tough, or at least trying to, while supporting merry men include relative unknowns Keith Coogan, George Perez and T. E. Russell. Old farts of note (aka grown-up window dressing) include kindly headmaster Denholm Elliott, no-nonsense dean Louis Gossett Jr, and, playing a military type for the hundred billionth time (more or less), R. Lee Ermey.

Silly is a good word. Male bonding a fine expression ('...you're fucking morons, you know that, you're fucking morons...'). Learning to kill in devious and devilish ways a worthwhile pursuit for young minds. And it's all here, in glorious, lightweight cheese-e-vision. You'll laugh. Oh yes. You'll cry. If you're peeling onions. And hey, you might even emerge from the movie a better person. Or you might just have a fairly good time and forget this flick the moment the TV fades to black. Either way, you could do a lot worse.

Director: Daniel Petrie Jr; **Producers:** Jack E. Freedman, Wayne S. Williams, Patricia Herskovic; **Screenplay:** Daniel Petrie Jr, David Koepp, based on the novel by William P. Kennedy; **Production Design:** Chester Kaczenski; **Editor:** Michael Kahn; **Photography:** Thomas Burstyn; **Music:** Robert Folk; **Cast:** Sean Astin, Wil Wheaton, Keith Coogan, Andrew Divoff, R. Lee Ermey, Mason Adams, Denholm Elliott, Louis Gossett Jr, George Perez, T. E. Russell.

Trancers (aka Future Cop)

USA 1985 85 mins

A low-budget, science-fiction adventure with a *Terminator* plot and a *Blade Runner* hero might not sound like such a great idea, and considering the film's director, Charles Band, lists among his credits the likes of 3-D turkeys *Parasite* and *Metalstorm: The Destruction of Jared-Syn*, you could be forgiven for expecting the worst, but, surprise of surprises, *Trancers* turns out to be a minor classic, cheap and cheerful, often quite funny, and hell, even inventive, in a plagiaristic kind of way.

Besides Band, the man to thank for this B-movie miracle is comedian Tim Thomerson, here filling the shoes of our hard-bitten hero, Jack Deth, a twenty-third century cop with a chip on his shoulder and a knack for getting into trouble. Besides striking matches on his teeth, Deth prefers not to shave, wash or change his clothes, although he's always willing to contribute an explanatory voice-over, just so long as it's in the style of a 1930s private eye. Naturally enough, he has an arch-enemy, a psychic psycho by the name of Martin Whistler (Michael Stefani), a nasty piece of work with blank, staring eyes and the ability to twist the minds of the weak and transform them into Trancers, pale-faced, zombie-like slaves described by Deth as 'not really alive, and not dead enough'.

Just as you'd expect from an evil genius, Whistler has a dastardly plan, to travel 300 years back in time to Los Angeles, build an army of Trancers, take over the planet and, while he's at it, knock off the ancestors of a trio of troublesome twenty-third century council members who will consequently cease to exist. Fearing eternal nothingness, the council sends Deth's mind back to 1985 where he inhabits the body of an identical ancestor and promptly sets out to stop Whistler and his Trancers once and for all, ably assisted by sidekick, damsel-in-distress and perky love interest Helen Hunt.

The action is enjoyable if generally unremarkable, with the odd twenty-third century gadget popping up to help Deth on his mission (the 'long-second' watch is particularly useful), and a great deal made of his efforts to adapt to twentieth-century life. All things considered, this is probably the best movie Charles Band has ever made, spirited, stylish and exciting, with some neat comic touches, an eye for the unusual and enthusiasm to spare.

Sequels: *Trancers II: The Return of Jack Deth*, *Trancers III: Deth Lives*, *Trancers IV: Jack of Swords*, *Trancers V: Sudden Deth*.

Director: Charles Band; **Producer:** Charles Band; **Screenplay:** Paul de Meo, Danny Bilson; **Production Design:** Jeff Staggs; **Editor:** Ted Nicolaou; **Photography:** Mac Ahlberg; **Music:** Mark Ryder, Phil Davies; **Cast:** Tim Thomerson, Helen Hunt, Michael Stefani, Art Le Fleur, Telma Hopkins, Richard Herd, Anne Seymour, Miguel Fernandez, Biff Manard.

Trespass

USA 1992 101 mins

Ice Cube and Ice T ooze inner-city attitude in *Trespass*.

Director Walter Hill treads familar action territory in this routine thriller which owes more than a little to the now classic *Die Hard* scenario, but doesn't stint when it comes to the pyrotechnics. Bill Paxton and William Sadler play a couple of fireman who discover from a dying man that a fortune in stolen gold has been hidden in a burned out, ramshackle factory on the outskirts of East St Louis. With riches in mind, the two make their way to the factory, where they have the misfortune of witnessing a gang murder carried out by the local crime syndicate, namely King James, Savon (Ices T and Cube, respectively) and an assortment of other gangster types. As it turns out, heavily-armed, drug-dealing scumbag psychos don't mix too well with greedy, suspicious fortune hunters who know too much, and consequently the two groups clash time and time again, with King James calling in hired hands to exterminate the trespassers on his turf, and Paxton and Sadler wracking their brains for a way to escape the factory alive, and with their loot. A couple of guys trapped in a building with baddies all around them is by no means an original idea, but what makes *Trespass* different and also why it ultimately fails is that there are no good guys. King James (Ice T in fine, butt-kicking form) and his gang are the most obvious villains, but Paxton and Sadler aren't exactly wholesome, mom-and-apple-pie guys either. Technically, the film is well made and rarely dull, but without a good guy to root for you just can't get into it. Still, the action packs a pretty hefty punch, and there are more than enough gun fights and explosions to pass the time. Just don't expect to cheer, boo or laugh too much.

Director: Walter Hill; **Producer:** Neil Canton; **Screenplay:** Bob Gale, Robert Zemeckis; **Production Design:** Jon Hutman; **Editor:** Freeman Davies; **Photography:** Jon Hutman; **Music:** Ry Cooder; **Cast:** Bill Paxton, Ice T, William Sadler, Ice Cube, Art Evans, De'Voreaux White, Bruce A. Young, Glenn Plummer.

True Lies

USA 1994 141 mins

A turkey of *Last Action Hero* proportions might have been enough to kill the career of a lesser mortal, but Arnold Schwarzenegger simply came back for more. A multi-million dollar project with extravagant tastes, *True Lies* dares, like its predecessor, to blend action with comedy in equal doses, a tricky procedure which, fortunately for Arnold, his fans, and director Jim Cameron, works a whole lot better this time around.

Armed with a tuxedo, an arsenal of hardware and a neat line in gadgetry, Arnie is in full Bond mode as super secret agent Harry Tasker, who, along with his foul-mouthed, continually wise-cracking partner Gib (Tom Arnold), saves the world on a daily basis. The only trouble is, while Arnie is out blasting the bad guys, his wife (Jamie Lee Curtis) and teenage daughter (Eliza Dushku) have no idea what he actually does, believing instead that he sells computers for a living. But secrets, no matter how well kept, have a habit of revealing themselves at awkward moments, such as when Harry is on the trail of a group of psychotic terrorists led by the despicable Aziz (Art Malik), and his wife is being wooed by a used car salesman (Bill Paxton) who, to make himself seem more exciting, pretends to be a secret agent (talk about ironic).

Expert special effects and kamikaze stunt work combine to create some incredible action sequences, from Arnold's indoor horse race to a chase along a Florida Keys highway, and while Cameron's efforts to lighten the movie work fairly well throughout, *True Lies* is at its best when it doesn't seem to be trying too hard: occasional forays into slapstick and ultra-violence seem out of place and spoil the rhythm of the movie. Fortunately, the film gets back on track for a spectacular climax, as Arnold commandeers a Harrier Jet and tears off after the bad guys, while the performances help distinguish the movie further: Jamie Lee Curtis is fabulous in a role that calls for her to be both homely and awkward as well as gorgeous and sexy, while Tom Arnold (once known as Roseanne's other half) is surprisingly funny, reacting well off of Arnie, who plays it straight and tough all the way, just as he should do.

Director: James Cameron; **Producers:** James Cameron, Stephanie Austin; **Screenplay:** James Cameron, based on the French movie *La Totale*, written by Claude Zidi, Simon Michael and Didier Kaminka; **Production Design:** Peter Lamont; **Editors:** Conrad Buff, Mark Goldblatt, Richard A. Harris; **Photography:** Russell Carpenter; **Music:** Brad Fiedel; **Cast:** Arnold Schwarzenegger, Jamie Lee Curtis, Tom Arnold, Bill Paxton, Art Malik, Tia Carrere, Eliza Dushku, Charlton Heston.

Under Siege

USA 1992 102 mins

Steven Seagal hit the jackpot with this one: not only a successful movie, but a good one too. He may not be able to act, or pull off a successful one-liner, but put him in a room with a sharp knife and a bad guy and you simply can't go wrong. Better yet: strand him on a nuclear battleship with a whole gang of wrongdoers, call the movie *Under Siege*, and you're onto a winner.

Casey (Seagal) is a violence expert: what he doesn't know about killing people and blowing stuff up isn't worth knowing. Oh yeah, he also cooks (talk about a three-dimensional character). So he's on a boat, and maybe *Die Hard* is his favourite action flick, and when terrorists (Tommy Lee Jones, Gary 'Mr Joshua' Busey) take over his battleship, he decides to take them on, with only an incredibly beautiful *Playboy* playmate (who just happened to be on the ship, semi-naked, looking suspiciously like former Baywatcher Erika Eleniak) at his side. Hey, it could happen.

For his part, Seagal clearly attempted to do something different, something a little special, in this picture. Sure, he talks the same, he kills and crushes and smashes and bashes the same as he always has, but something has changed, and the movie is all the better for it. Yes folks, after careful thought and serious consideration, Seagal finally cut off his pony tail. Not surprisingly, he grew (or stuck) it back in later movies, but at least he proved that, when pressed, he can survive without it. Samson eat your heart out.

Gloriously dumb and obnoxiously violent, *Under Siege* relishes the painful and inventive deaths of a number of bad guys, from fatal saw wounds and impalements, to a fabulous high speed knife fight which rounds off the movie and leaves a certain bad guy with a bitch of a headache.

The first (and, to date, only) Seagal film that doesn't take itself too seriously, *Under Siege* offers flippant killing, naked women (super babe Eleniak) and hilarious one liners. It truly is a meat-and-potatoes, leave-your-political-correctness-at-the-door kind of flick.

Director: Andrew Davis; **Producers:** Arnon Milchan, Steven Seagal, Steven Reuther; **Screenplay:** J.F. Lawton; **Production Design:** Bill Kenney; **Editor:** Robert A. Ferretti; **Photography:** Frank Tidy; **Music:** Gary Chang; **Cast:** Steven Seagal, Tommy Lee Jones, Gary Busey, Erika Eleniak, Patrick O'Neal, Damian Chapa, Troy Evans, David McKnight, Lee Hinton.

Under Siege 2 (aka Under Siege 2: Dark Territory)

USA 1995 99 mins

Steven Segal hunts for terrorists on the roof of the Grand Continental choo-choo in *Under Siege 2*.

He did it before, he can do it again. The world needs saving from a curly-haired psycho with a doomsday weapon, and only one man can save the day. A man who laughs in the face of danger. A man compelled to kill, maim and destroy for our amusement, an arsenal of weaponry his to command, from hunting knives and flare guns, to home made bombs and his own bare hands. A man possessing supernatural powers, able to fall off a cliff, get punched, kicked, and yes, even shot, yet escape without a scratch, immaculately dressed in black, calm, composed and ready for action. Call him excessive. Call him artificial. Hell, call him a god, because that's the way this movie treats him, a stirring, heroic soundtrack complementing his every move, a fawning series of close-ups capturing every solid, expressionless glance. 'I guess he's a hero', notes his niece with pride, and what's more, he's a wizard in the kitchen, too. The name is Casey Ryback, an ego with a gun whose sole saving grace is his yearning, unquenchable thirst for bloody conflict.

Freejack director Geoff Murphy dusts off the old *Die Hard* scenario for another round of 'spanner-in-the-works' adventure, setting his sights on the luxurious Grand Continental, a five-star choo-choo charging through Colorado's magnificent wilderness when, all of a sudden, mad hacker Travis Dane (*Talk Radio*'s Eric Bogosian) and his mercenary army take charge, holding the passengers hostage and the world to ransom: speeding undetected through the Rockies, Dane gains control of an orbiting super-weapon which he threatens to use on Washington DC unless the government coughs up a billion dollars, and fast. The situation seems bleak, even hopeless, but guess what? By some amazing coincidence Casey Ryback is aboard (bet you never expected that, eh?), enjoying a brief vacation with his niece (Katherine Heigl) when the script hits the fan and the ex-Navy SEAL has no choice but to strap on his weapons and play action man for an hour and a half.

'Good evening ladies and gentleman', announces Dane with a grin, 'I'll be your captor this evening.' Part mad scientist, part game show host, Dane delivers a lively blend of cornball humour and techno-babble, deadly with a computer, but not all that scary in the flesh, a physical shortcoming the movie compensates for with the addition of a gang of professional cut-throats, ably led by chief henchman Penn (Everett McGill), a stern-faced Aryan-type who's just aching to tear Ryback a new personality. Elsewhere among the supporting cast, Heigl is not only pretty, but pretty pointless too, as Ryback's niece Sarah, while Morris Chestnut takes Erika Eleniak's place as Casey's inexperienced sidekick, a porter with a nervous disposition who, much like the *Baywatch* babe, doesn't contribute all that much to the movie, although at least Erika had breasts to keep us happy.

Under Siege 2: Dark Territory delivers everything but the unexpected, a big-budget, by-the-numbers action extravaganza, slickly shot and speedily paced, with every scene well sign-posted in advance, every cliché fondly embraced, and macho-bullshit to spare. The story and performances might count for very little, but the action delivers non-stop and the stunt-work is incredible, with fights and shoot-outs taking place all over the train, the occasional pit-stop for a cliffhanging punch-up or kick-ass truck chase, and a shamelessly over-the-top, collision-course climax which is as exciting as it is unbelievable.

Best of all, though, is (co-producer) Seagal's continued willingness to embrace ultra-violence, slashing, burning, shooting and pounding the enemy with the wild abandon of an action superstar who refuses to tone down his blood-lust just to please a bunch of impressionable kids, letter-writing pensioners and whining, social-working, wishy-washy liberals. Thumbs up, also, to director Murphy for boosting the gore wherever possible, and for refusing to cut away at the last minute to spare us from the splatter, so that when a disposable bad guy falls in front of the train, we actually get to see him liquidized on the tracks, and when a villain falls hundreds of feet down a cliff, the camera follows him all the way to the bottom (leave your imagination at home, because you're not going to need it). Added to which, there's not even a whiff of romance to slow things down.

Ultimately, there's little more to *Under Siege 2* than a ton of well-orchestrated, blood-splattered action and a whole lot of under-written, over-played, exaggerated silliness which is, at the very least, worth a laugh. Alter your expectations accordingly and enjoy the mayhem.

Director: Geoff Murphy; **Producers:** Steven Seagal, Steve Perry, Arnon Milchan; **Screenplay:** Richard Hatem, Matt Reeves, based on characters created by J.F. Lawton; **Production Design:** Albert Brenner; **Editor:** Michael Tronick; **Photography:** Robbie Greenberg; **Music:** Basil Poledouris; **Cast:** Steven Seagal, Eric Bogosian, Everett McGill, Katherine Heigl, Morris Chestnut, Brenda Bakke, Nick Mancuso, Andy Romano.

Universal Soldier

USA 1992 102 mins

Desperate to break out of B-movie bondage, Jean-Claude Van Damme and Dolph Lundgren joined forces to deliver a dose of death and destruction in probably the most exciting and enjoyable feature that either of them hiade. Macho men, to your posts...

Kicking off in Vietnam some time during the war, the movie treats us to the unexpected sight of good guy Jean-Claude and psycho nutcase Lundgren (dig that necklace!) getting into something of a scuffle and blasting each other to Hell. Hours later, a mysterious military convoy swings by to pick up the corpses and put them on ice. Cut to the present day, where the chaps re-emerge as two members of a small band of re-animated super soldiers, kind of like *Night of the Living Rambo*. As if being a zombie weren't bad enough (although it's well within his acting range), Jean-Claude's carelessly wiped memory slowly begins to return, and while his former existence remains a bit of a blur, he does, at least, remember that he hates Dolph's guts, and before you know it they're at each others throats again, Vietnam flashbacks 'n' all.

There's a girlie (Ally Walker) in there somewhere, too, a nosy photo-journalist who tags along with Van Damme to unravel the mystery of his existence and teach him what it means to be human (the diner scene is a classic), and while she serves well in the comic relief, damsel-in-distress and window dressing departments, she is not about to be romanced by a dead guy. Hollywood, it seems, is not quite ready for necrophilia.

A decent-sized budget gave (pre-*Stargate*) director Roland Emmerich the opportunity to pump up the action scenes with some spectacular location work, a truck load of hardware, explosions a-plenty and enough time during production to add an imaginative twist onto every car chase, shoot-em-up and brutal one-on-one that the movie has to offer.

As for the story, it clearly rips off both *RoboCop* and *The Terminator*, a shameless Hollywood patchwork of other people's ideas, but at least it does it well enough not to spoil the film. Best of all, *Univeral Soldier* keeps from ever taking itself too seriously, with both leads cracking jokes, albeit in their own deadpan way.

This may not be the most original, or least predictable, movie that you'll see all day, but it's a pacy, kick-ass adventure just the same.

Director: Roland Emmerich; **Producers:** Allen Shapiro, Craig Baumgarten, Joel B. Michaels; **Screenplay:** Richard Rothstein, Christopher Leitch, Dean Devlin; **Production Design:** Holger Gross; **Editor:** Michael J. Duthie; **Photography:** Karl Walter Lindenlaub; **Music:** Christopher Franke; **Cast:** Jean-Claude Van Damme, Dolph Lundgren, Ally Walker, Ed O'Ross, Jerry Orbach, Leon Rippy.

Name: VAN DAMME, Jean-Claude

Real name: Jean-Claude Van Varenberg

Nickname: The Muscles From Brussels, Van Dammage

Born: Brussels, Belgium, 1961

Characteristics: Ace martial artist, firm and flexible. That's the good news. Here's the rest: better actors have been discovered in roach motels (like, have you ever seen him try to smile? It's painful). And if you took his personality and turned it into a movie, you'd have to call it *Attack of the 50 Ft Ego*.

Jean-Claude Van Damme defies gravity in *Bloodsport*.

Previous professions: Bouncer, carpet layer, limo driver, waiter...

Debut feature: *Monaco Forever* (1980)

Life and times: A skinny, feeble kid with lousy eyesight, Jean-Claude Van Damme dedicated himself to physical self-improvement at the age of nine, taking up karate, weight-lifting and even ballet. Leaving school at 17, Van Damme ran his own gym, and very successfully too, but something was missing: movie stardom, his ultimate dream. So, he dumped the first of three wives, moved to Los Angeles, learned to speak English (well, kind of) and struggled like hell to impress the right people. A chance meeting with Cannon supremo Menahem Golan prompted a spontaneous display of martial arts from Van Damme, who was rewarded with a starring role in the $2 million revenge flick, *Bloodsport*. A half-dozen bog-standard B-movies later, Van Damme hit the big time with *Universal Soldier*, his best film to date. *Timecop*, released in 1994, confirmed Van Damme's box-office prowess, earning more than $135 million world-wide. In 1996, Jean-Claude made his directorial debut on the historical actioner *The Quest*, a film he believes will come to be considered as 'the *Ben Hur* of martial arts' movies. Modest as ever, Van-Damme will always be his greatest fan.

Greatest contribution to action movies: Ten years of wild-eyed violence.

Speech, speech: 'I love challenges. If you don't have any and can do whatever you want, then it's probably time to die.'

'My dreams came true in America. It's not possible in Belgium. I grew up sadly. Skinny kid. Big, thick glasses. Everything I've done is a miracle.'

' I am one of the most sensitive human beings on Earth - and I know it.'

Rosanna Arquette spills the beans: 'He does what he does very well, kickboxing and stuff, but acting is not his forte. Neither is being humble.'

Selected filmography: *No Retreat, No Surrender* (1986), *Black Eagle* (1988), *Bloodsport* (1988), *Kickboxer* (1989), *Cyborg* (1989), *A.W.O.L.* (1990), *Death Warrant* (1990), *Double Impact* (+ co-scr; 1991), *Universal Soldier* (1992), *Nowhere To Run* (1993), *Timecop* (1994), *Street Fighter* (1995), *Sudden Death* (1995), *The Quest* (1996).

A View to a Kill

GB 1985 131 mins

Octopussy should have been Roger Moore's swan-song as Bond. He could have quit while he was still ahead, but no, he had to spoil it all by hanging on for a desperate seventh feature, almost six decades old and ravaged by some of the most obvious, uncomfortable-looking plastic surgery ever committed to film; even his trademark mole is missing (where it ended up on his body is anyone's guess). It's sad to see him go this way, an anti-quated hero in his final, feeble adventure.

Christopher Walken hams it up as genetic superfiend Max Zorin, a billionaire industri-alist with a diabolical plan to destroy Silicon Valley and snap up the world's microchip monopoly for himself. With hundreds of thousands of people to save, not to mention the computer trade, Bond travels the world in search of glamorous locations (England - France - America...), gunning for the bad guys while bedding a bewildering number of women, including devious Russian agent Pola Ivanova (Fiona Fullerton), striking, severe hench-woman May Day (Grace Jones), and official Bond girl Stacey Sutton (as played by Charlie's last Angel, Tanya Roberts), a bona fide bimbo with nothing to do but scream for help. Completing the cast, *Avengers* star Patrick Macnee adds a welcome touch of class to his role as portly sidekick Tibbett, intended, no doubt, to make Moore look fitter by comparison. The only problem with this strategy is that the moment Roger stands next to a beautiful, young lady, he suddenly seems as old as sin all over again.

Ultimately, this is Bond for the sake of Bond, routine and commonplace, lacking ener-gy, invention and a decent screenplay, resorting instead to crude, broad humour and in-your-face action which, though quite exciting, fails to save the movie. Just for the record, though, set-pieces of note include an opening, snowbound stunt-fest, a manic Parisian pur-suit (complete with Eiffel Tower parachute jump), an underground flood disaster (which has Zorin pumping bullets into his drowning ex-employees, laughing all the way), a Keystone Cop-style fire truck escape on the streets of San Francisco and, finally, a crazy zeppelin showdown atop the Golden Gate Bridge.

 Keep an eye out for Grace Jones' ex-boyfriend Dolph Lundgren, here making his movie debut as beefy henchman Venz.

The end of *A View to a Kill*. But James Bond will return in *The Living Daylights*.

Director: John Glen; **Producers:** Albert R. Broccoli, Michael G. Wilson; **Screenplay:** Richard Maibaum, Michael G. Wilson; **Production Design:** Peter Lamont; **Editor:** Peter Davies; **Photography:** Alan Hume; **Music:** John Barry, title song performed by Duran Duran; **Cast:** Roger Moore, Christopher Walken, Tanya Roberts, Grace Jones, Patrick Macnee.

Warlords of Atlantis

GB 1978 96 mins

For a lad growing up in the 1970s, eagerly taking in all the science fiction and adventure fantasy his young brain could handle, choosing an appropriate role model was of prime importance. James Bond was always a favourite, as were Han Solo and Superman, but how many kids can you think of who realistically aspired to become sophisticated secret agents when they grew up, let alone space pirates or costumed superheroes?

No, when it came to picking a hero that we could not only identify with, but whose abilities were fully within our reach, Doug McClure was the obvious choice. Not too smart, not too handsome, and not too fit, the veteran star of such classic TV westerns as *The Virginian* still managed to attract the babes in droves, and when it came to fending off oversized, rubbery monsters, Doug was the main man, and no mistake. Stocky and average, McClure played a variety of everyman heroes throughout the 1970s, struggling with not-so-special effects while battling all manner of beasties in such cheerfully cheesy British fare as *The Land That Time Forgot* and *At The Earth's Core*, although his finest hour surely came in 1978 when he discovered a fabled underwater city, romanced a busty damsel with gills behind her ears, and battled everything from a prehistoric sea-serpent to a flying band of chunky piranha fish in *Warlords of Atlantis*. Be warned, though, for only those of us reared

Doug McClure experiences a close encounter of the rubbery kind in *Warlords of Atlantis*.

on this kind of nonsense can even hope to enjoy it today, the mists of nostalgia clouding our minds and impairing our critical faculties almost completely.

A nineteenth century yarn in which seabound adventurer Greg (our Doug) and his brainy pal Charles (*The Onedin Line*'s Peter Gilmore) discover Atlantis, trash a variety of mutant creatures, take on a twisted alien master race (including 1950s musical star Cyd Charisse) and defend themselves from a trio of crooked sailors (look out for *Cheers*' John Ratzenberger), *Warlords of Atlantis* is to the cinema what the stylophone is to the music business: a ropy 1970s creation, kind of naff, but fondly remembered. And besides, the giant octopus finale is a real humdinger.

Director: Kevin Connor; **Producer:** John Dark; **Screenplay:** Brian Hayles; **Production Design:** Elliott Scott; **Editor:** Bill Blunden; **Photography:** Alan Hume; **Music:** Mike Vickers: **Cast:** Doug McClure, Peter Gilmore, Shane Rimmer, John Ratzenberger, Michael Gothard, Lea Brodie, Cyd Charisse, Daniel Massey.

The Warriors

USA 1979 90 mins

A motley crew of teenage weirdos fight for their right to ransack in this hard-nosed action thriller from director Walter Hill, shot at night on the streets of New York City, a wham-bam-mug-ya'-ma'am experience shot in mid-budget Grit-O-Vision with plenty of action to go round.

If it's an excuse for violence you're looking for, welcome to *The Warriors*. There's this guy, see, a sort of heavy metal visionary named Cyrus (Roger Hill) who wants to unite the gangs and take a whopping great bite of the Big Apple. Later, when the scum of the city converge in the Bronx for a mass meeting, Neo-Nazi Luther (David Patrick Kelly), leader of The Rogues, blows away the Big C, and, to save his own skin, frames rival gang the Warriors for the killing. The remainder of the film plays out as expected: stranded in town without weapons, 100 miles from home, our youthful scapegoats leg it all the way to Coney Island, hotly pursued by every cop and gang member alive. Pretty dramatic, eh?

Leading a young cast of dedicated over-actors, Michael Beck calls the shots as mean and moody Warriors supremo Swan, while James Remar delivers attitude a-plenty as second-fiddler Ajax, a hyperactive loon who'd rather fight than run. Dedicated to giving our lads (with hearts of gold) a hard time, oddball gangs of skinheads, mimes, sluts and baseball players all get a chance to kill them some good guys, running rampant from a cracking park punch-up to a bloody restroom rumble and beyond.

As ever, Hill pulls no punches and the result is a seriously tough movie, speedy, intense and even kinda scary. If you're looking for depth, however, you'd better go jump down a well.

Director: Walter Hill; **Producer:** Lawrence Gordon; **Associate Producer:** Joel Silver; **Screenplay:** David Shaber, Walter Hill, based on the novel by Sol Yurick; **Production Design:** Don Swanagan, Bob Wightman; **Editor:** David Holden; **Photography:** Andrew Laszlo; **Music:** Barry de Vorzon; **Cast:** Michael Beck, James Remar, David Patrick Kelly, Thomas Waites, Dorsey Wright, Brian Tyler, Deborah Van Valkenburgh, Mercedes Ruehl, Roger Hill.

Waterworld

USA 1995 135 mins

A jumble of recycled plots, characters and production design, Kevin Reynolds' *Waterworld* is saved from the murky depths by a combination of epic cinematography and inventive action sequences. Publicity for the film claimed that it was 'the first major motion picture to be filmed almost entirely on water', a complicated and troublesome undertaking which explains how a $60 million picture cost upwards of $180 million. Do not be discouraged, however, for despite a multitude of flaws and a penchant for plagiarism, the film features a collection of explosive battle scenes and death-defying stunts which more or less justify the price of a video rental, if not quite the price of the budget.

The planet is ours, but the setting is straight out of Sea World. Submerged under water following centuries of neglect and abuse (leading to the melting of the polar ice caps), Earth is little more than a gigantic ocean floor, while dry land is widely regarded as mythological. Huge, floating fortresses and a variety of sailing craft are all that remains of civilization, while a population of scavengers and pirates, known as Smokers, fight endlessly for territory and supplies.

Playing it somewhere between The Man From Atlantis and The Man With No Name on a bad hair day, Kevin Costner heads the cast as The Mariner, a mutant human with gills, webbed toes and a seriously cool boat who rescues a couple of ladies in distress (well-proportioned love interest Jeanne Tripplehorn and mysterious tattooed youth Tina Majorino) who may or may not hold the key to discovering dry land. Assuming bad guy duties with good humour if not true style, Dennis Hopper chews up the scenery as hard-living, one-eyed warrior-priest Deacon, maniacal leader of a vile gang of Hell's Angels wannabes who hang out on a huge oil tanker. They too are on the lookout for dry land, and so harass The Mariner and his female chums from one side of Waterworld to the next, although in reality their time would have been better spent searching for a decent screenplay.

No sense crying over spilt salt water, though. *Waterworld* may not work terribly well as a movie, but as a collection of nautical thrills it remains pretty darn impressive, from squads of jetskis leaping through the air to a bungee jump finale which will leave you thoroughly gob-smacked..

We've all put up with Disney on Ice. Why not, then, *Mad Max* on Water?

Director: Kevin Reynolds; **Producers:** Charles Gordon, John Davis, Kevin Costner; **Screenplay:** Peter Rader, David Twohy; **Production Design:** Dennis Gassner; **Editor:** Peter Boyle; **Photography:** Dean Semler; **Music:** James Newton Howard; **Cast:** Kevin Costner, Dennis Hopper, Jeanne Tripplehorn, Tina Majorino, Michael Jeter.

Trivialists 7

VILLAINS
Bad to the bone

Sir Guy of Gisbourne (Basil Rathbone), *The Adventures of Robin Hood*
Sador (John Saxon), *Battle Beyond the Stars*
Sato (Yasuka Matsuda), *Black Rain*
Thulsa Boom (James Earl Jones), *Conan the Barbarian*
Top Dollar (Michael Wincott), *The Crow*
Simon Phoenix (Wesley Snipes), *Demolition Man*
Ernst Stavro Blofeld (Charles Grey), *Diamonds Are Forever*
Hans Gruber (Alan Rickman), *Die Hard*
The Scorpio Killer (Andy Robinson), *Dirty Harry*
Ming the Merciless (Max Von Sydow), *Flash Gordon*
The Kurgan (Clancy Brown), *Highlander*
Arjen Rudd (Joss Ackland), *Lethal Weapon 2*
Charles Rane (Bruce Payne), *Passenger 57*

The Predator (Kevin Peter Hall), *Predator*
Clarence Boddicker (Kurtwood Smith), *RoboCop*
Dr Luther (Gene Simmons), *Runaway*
Yoshida (Cary-Hiroyuki Tagawa), *Showdown in Little Tokyo*
Darth Vader (Dave Prowse/James Earl Jones), *Star Wars*
Chains (Lance Henriksen), *Stone Cold*
Terminator (Arnold Schwarzenegger), *The Terminator*

The Way of the Dragon [aka Return of the Dragon]
Hong Kong 1973 99 mins

Bruce Lee proved his superiority over all living things by meeting and beating an inter-national selection of bad guys, thumping his way through Italy in his first and final film as writer and director. Obligated to make a movie for his largest audience, the Chinese, Lee had no choice but to churn out an easily-digestible, chop-socky effort for producer Raymond Chow, playing it safe with the home crowd rather than investing more thought and money in something which might have had a chance to succeed abroad.

Taking advantage of his added responsibilities, Lee crowns himself the close-up king, occupying almost every frame of film in this self-serving adventure, a lone hero whose accompanying chop and kick sound effects boom twice as loudly as everyone else's.

It's fish out of water time as unsophisticated country boy Tang Lung (Lee) travels to Rome to help prevent the mob from muscling in on a friend's restaurant. Suffering from a serious case of culture clash, Tang breaks up the drama with a little light comedy, stum-bling through an alien land of loose women and complicated menus. It's pretty obvious stuff, though, mishandled in true sledgehammer fashion by Lee in all three of his creative capaci-ties. And, you know, it's not easy to appreciate the language barrier angle when the entire cast share a common tongue of dubbed American slang.

Still, no amount of shoddy production values could distract us from the film's single strength: not Lee the director, Lee the actor or Lee the writer, but Lee the fighter, and he's as fast and inventive as ever. Best of all is the Colosseum showdown, a graceful, disciplined fight to the death between Tang and the toughest dude the mob have in stock, an American troubleshooter (with an inconveniently hairy chest) played by Karate champ Chuck Norris, here making his big screen debut.

Dismiss the movie, not the star. However brief and infrequent the action might be, it's worth waiting for just to see Lee do his stuff. Clearly, though, if you're not a fan you should keep your distance.

Director: Bruce Lee; **Producer:** Raymond Chow; **Screenplay:** Bruce Lee; **Editor:** Chang Yao-Chung; **Photography:** Ho Lan-Shan; **Music:** Joseph Koo; **Cast:** Bruce Lee, Chuck Norris, Nora Miao, Wei Ping-Ao, Huang Chung-Hsin, Whong In-Sik.

Wedlock [aka Deadlock]
USA 1991 95 mins

From *Alligator* and *Navy SEALS* director Lewis Teague comes a well-played and reason-ably inventive made-for-cable adventure inspired by Hitchcock's *The 39 Steps*, only instead of handcuffs forcing hero and heroine together, we're offered something a little more hi-tech.

Rutger Hauer plays an expert safe-cracker whose partners in crime double-cross him in the worst way, blasting him full of holes and leaving him for dead, but he's a resourceful, resilient bloke, and so instead of going to Hell, Frank Warren (Hauer) ends up in a maximum security prison with a twist - there are no walls and no guards. Instead, every inmate is made to wear an explosive collar which swiftly separates heads from shoulders should the prisoner wearing it venture more than a hundred yards (metrically, we're talking 91.44 metres) away from his 'wedlock' partner, namely a fellow, unidentified, convict. Now (and this is the clever bit), since no one knows who their partner is, the inmates pretty much guard one another, remaining well within Camp Holliday's perimeters and keeping an eye out for any stir-crazies who might be desperate enough to make a break for it, since one man's futile escape attempt means the splattered death of two. Boom!

Following a number of unpleasant encounters with psycho inmate Emerald (*Marked For Death*'s Basil 'Screwface' Wallace) and corrupt Warden Stephen Tobolowsky, Frank hooks up with rough-and-tumble, good-time gal Tracy Riggs (Mimi Rogers), wrongly imprisoned (of course), eager to escape, and, wouldn't you know it, our (anti) hero's wedlock partner, so off they go, closely pursued by the cops and Frank's former accomplices, scheming minx Noelle (*On Deadly Ground*'s Joan Chen) and half-wit Sam (*48 Hours*' James Remar), both of them desperate to get their filthy hands on the $25 million worth of diamonds that Frank had the presence of mind to hide before they shot him (clever boy).

With the story explained and the characters introduced, *Wedlock* swiftly gets on with the action, hurling Frank and Tracy through a minefield of double and triple-crosses, an odd-couple of escapees whose lives depend on remaining within a hundred yards of one another. Rest assured, therefore, that Teague takes great pleasure in splitting them up whenever possible (sticking one on a bus and the other on foot, stranding one on a hotel rooftop while the other heads for the ground floor in an express elevator...), watching them sweat as they race to, quite literally, save their necks in this well-paced and exciting tale of the near-future.

Director: Lewis Teague; **Producer:** Branko Lustig; **Screenplay:** Broderick Miller; **Production Design:** Veronica Hadfield; **Editor:** Carl Kress; **Photography:** Dietrich Lohmann; **Music:** Richard Giggs; **Cast:** Rutger Hauer, Mimi Rogers, Joan Chen, James Remar, Stephen Tobolowsky, Basil Wallace, Grand L. Bush, Denis Forest, Glenn Plummer.

Where Eagles Dare

GB 1969 155 mins

There's nothing on earth more fulfilling than viewing the wholesale slaughter of wave after wave of Nazi vermin. Nazis do, after all, make perfect movie villains: they're evil to the core and easy to hate, and it is our moral, God-given right - nay, it is our duty - to take pleasure in their extermination. Sure, after two world wars and one world cup, we're all friends now, but there's nothing wrong with a quick trip down memory lane in the company of a good war movie. And *Where Eagles Dare* is a classic. Not particularly stylish, it's true, and director Brian G. Hutton seems to be one of those singularly uninspired 'point the cameras at the action and see what happens' types, but any movie which features Richard Burton and Clint Eastwood mowing down a never-ending parade of Nazis has got to be good for a laugh, and with second unit direction from legendary stuntman Yakima Kanut, the action is particularly well handled and commendably destructive.

There's trouble in store for a team of Allied Paratroopers intent on rescuing a captured American General from the forbidding Schloss Adler, a seemingly impregnable fortress which towers high above the Bavarian Alps and surrounds itself with several platoons of well-armed troops, a thousand casualties just waiting to happen. But there's more to this mission than meets the eye, as Burton, Eastwood, Mary Ure and the rest encounter dastardly double agents, fiendish Gestapo officers and an assortment of enlisted lambs to the slaughter as they attempt to sneak their way in and blast their way out of the 'Castle of the Eagles'.

Eastwood is as cool as ever, blowing away Nazis as casually as he might blow his nose, but there's no doubt that this movie belongs to top dog Burton, surely the consummate iceman, lovingly described in the movie as having more than a sixth sense, but a 'seventh and an eighth sense' as well, whatever the hell that means.

Anyway, following an hour and a half of well-paced twists and turns courtesy of boys' own novelist and screenwriter Alistair MacLean, it's down to business as our heroes get into every conceivable scrape with the enemy, shooting, stabbing and blowing up everything that moves, battling it out on the roof of a cable car, and taking a spectacular rollercoaster ride through some pretty treacherous terrain on a bus that lays waste to everything in its path.

Now that's what I call fun.

Director: Brian G. Hutton; **Producer:** Elliott Kastner; **Screenplay:** Alistair MacLean, based on his novel; **Production Design:** Peter Mullins; **Editor:** John Jympson; **Photography:** Arthur Ibbetson, H.A.R. Thompson; **Music:** Ron Goodwin; **Cast:** Richard Burton, Clint Eastwood, Mary Ure, Ingrid Pitt, Patrick Wymark, Michael Hordern, Peter Barkworth, Donald Houston, Robert Beatty.

The Wild Geese

GB 1978 134 mins

Richard Burton leads a squad of retired mercenaries back into action in this spirited boys' own adventure, an all-star tribute to middle age which aims to prove that no matter how old, grey or out of shape a man might be, he never forgets how to kill, maim and destroy. God bless the fighting spirit.

Gruff, poker-faced and stiff as a board, Burton plays it straight as Colonel Faulkner, a veteran of the war game hired by callous industrialist Sir Edward Matherson (Stewart Granger) to rescue deposed African President Limbani (Winston Ntshona) from the clutches of an evil general. Joined by single father and master tactician Rafer (Richard Harris), cigar-smoking scoundrel-about-town Shawn (Roger Moore), and down-on-his-luck South African bigot Peter (Hardy Kruger), Faulkner dedicates the first hour of the movie to hiring and training the remainder of his 'Wild Geese' before parachuting with them into central Africa, land of adventure. Then comes the double cross...

Familiar faces drift across the screen in droves, from Sergeant Major Jack Watson and *Van Der Valk*'s Barry Foster, to Ronald Fraser, Patrick Allen and heterosexually challenged doctor Kenneth Griffith. It's a boys' club, alright, and they seem to be enjoying themselves, playing soldiers with a variety of lethal weaponry.

This is a silly, almost cheeky actioner, too long for its own good but lots of fun nonetheless. Laugh with it, laugh at it, cheer the slaughter, boo the bad guys and shrink in horror from some truly terrifying 1970s fashion gear. *Soldier of Fortune* magazine never prepared us for this.

Three years before directing his first James Bond picture, *For Your Eyes Only*, 007 veteran John Glen doubled here as both editor and second unit director.

Sequel: *Wild Geese II*.

Director: Andrew V. McLaglen; **Producer:** Euan Lloyd; **Screenplay:** Reginald Rose, based on the novel *The Wild Geese* by Daniel Carney; **Production Design:** Syd Cain; **Editor:** John Glen; **Photography:** Jack Hildyard; **Music:** Roy Budd; **Cast:** Richard Burton, Roger Moore, Richard Harris, Hardy Kruger, Stewart Granger, Frank Finlay, Barry Foster.

Death Becomes Them 26

Bruce Willis plays the hero game in the awesome *Die Hard*.

Name: WILLIS, Bruce

Real name: Walter Willison

Born: Germany, 1955

Characteristics: One of the guys, a streetwise star, from the trademark smirk to designer stubble.

Previous professions: Security guard at a nuclear generating station on an artificial island on the Delaware, bartender.

Debut feature: *The First Deadly Sin* (1980)

Life and times: Born in Germany, where his father was stationed in the army, but raised, from the age of two, in New Jersey, Bruce Willis sampled a variety of careers, learned to play the harmonica and jammed with a band called Loose Goose before finally turning to acting. Following years of stage work, Willis auditioned for a

part in a new ABC TV series called *Moonlighting*, beating thousands of hopefuls to the star-making role of cocky private eye David Addison. The show was an instant success, running for four years from 1985, and it made Willis very famous indeed. In 1987, Bruce took advantage of his popularity by realizing what must have been a boyhood dream: recording an album for Motown records (*Bruce Willis: The Return of Bruno*). The very same year he set his sights on big-screen success. Joining forces with director Blake Edwards, Bruce cranked out a couple of cheesy comedies before striking the mother lode as hard-boiled detective John McClane in the greatest action movie of all time, *Die Hard*. Since then, Willis has made a lot of turkeys, from Brian De Palma's ill-conceived *Bonfire of the Vanities* to superflop *Hudson Hawk*, but as John McClane he's always been on safe ground, cleaning up at the box office in a pair of successful sequels, *Die Hard 2* and *Die Hard With A Vengeance*. In 1995, Willis earned the best reviews of his career with a small (only 22 minutes of screen time) but significant role as a boxer in Quentin Tarantino's ultra-hip *Pulp Fiction*. Married to actress Demi Moore, Willis owns a pair of gorgeous Harley-Davidson hogs and a healthy share of the Planet Hollywood restaurant chain.

Greatest contribution to action movies: Heroic underdog John McClane.

Speech, speech: 'Action films serve the same function as Westerns - they present morality plays, albeit with cursing, a lot more blood, and violence, and tits.'

'In my mind, a big, exciting, thrilling, scary, violent film is no different from the newest ride at Disney World. You're sitting in a darkened room with 100 or 200 people, and these little flashing points of light on the screen are able to scare you, thrill you, make you jump. That's the trick. That's the art form.'

Selected filmography: *Blind Date* (1987), *Sunset* (+ co-exec prod; 1988), ***Die Hard*** (1988), *Look Who's Talking* (voice only; 1989), *In Country* (1989), ***Die Hard 2*** (1990), *The Bonfire of the Vanities* (1990), *Mortal Thoughts* (1991), ***Hudson Hawk*** (+ co-story; 1991), *Billy Bathgate* (1991), ***The Last Boy Scout*** (1991), *Death Becomes Her* (1992), ***Striking Distance*** (1993), *North* (1994), *Color of Night* (1994), *Pulp Fiction* (1994), *Nobody's Fool*

(1994), ***Die Hard With A Vengeance*** (1995), *Twelve Monkeys* (1996), *Last Man Standing* (1996), *The Fifth Element* (1997).

Willow

USA 1988 126 mins

Good versus evil in this harmless Lucasfilm fantasy from director Ron Howard, a lightweight sword-and-sorcery adventure with a plot borrowed from Moses, a David and Goliath message, a setting straight out of Tolkien and some fairly special effects, courtesy of Industrial Light and Magic.

An evil, all-powerful sorceress of panto proportions, Queen Bavmorda (Jean Marsh) has a problem. A child has been born, an infant destined to cause her downfall, and she wants it dead. Boo. Hiss. Meanwhile, over where the little people, the Nelwyn, live, good-hearted farmer, family man and aspiring sorcerer Willow Ufgood (aka *Return of the Jedi*'s Wicket, the Ewok) discovers the baby and, sure enough, embarks on a long and dangerous quest to deliver the child safely to some kindly folk in a distant castle, far from Bavmorda's grasp.

Joining our pint-sized hero's crusade, we have sword-fighting scoundrel Madmartigan (a little Errol Flynn, a dash of Han Solo, water the mixture down, and serve as Val Kilmer), friendly sorceress Fin Raziel (Patricia Hayes, shape-shifting like crazy in the first example of movie 'morphing', a technique perfected in *Terminator 2*), helpful military type Airk (Gavan O'Herlihy) and a pair of nine-inch high 'brownies' (Kevin Pollak and Rick Overton, comic relief). Assisting the forces of wickedness, meanwhile, man-mountain Pat Roach menaces from behind a skull mask as General Kael, while Joanne Whalley (shortly before she became Whalley-Kilmer) tries her best to look mean as the Queen's hard-hearted daughter Sorsha, a swashbuckling babe with a soft-spot for Madmartigan.

With trolls to flatten, troops to fight and snowy mountains begging for a sled sequence, there's no shortage of rough-and-tumble action in *Willow*, with a particularly showy battle scene in a cursed castle, home to a butt-ugly, buck-toothed, two-headed, fire-breathing (and really rather cheesy) monster.

Kids should get the most out of this one, but the feeble ones should prepare themselves for the odd intense moment. As for the rest of us, this is a textbook example of average, watchable enough, and reasonably entertaining, but predictable with it, and entirely forgettable.

Director: Ron Howard; **Producer:** Nigel Wooll; **Screenplay:** Bob Dolman, story by George Lucas; **Production Design:** Allan Cameron; **Editors:** Daniel Hanley, Michael Hill; **Photography:** Adrian Biddle; **Music:** James Horner; **Cast:** Val Kilmer, Joanne Whalley, Warwick Davis, Jean Marsh, Patricia Hayes, Billy Barty, Pat Roach, Gavan O'Herlihy, David Steinberg, Phil Fondacaro.

You Only Live Twice

GB 1967 116 mins

'High above an extinct Japanese volcano, four heavily-armoured black helicopters spin through the sky in a dance - of death! Their target: one man in a flying arsenal that fits in two alligator suitcases. The odds: four to one. They haven't got a chance!'

It's clear from radio promos like this that Sean Connery's fifth Bond adventure was intended as a blockbuster first, and a spy thriller second. The movie was now the star, with 007 taking third billing after Q's increasingly fantastic gadgets and the general big-budget grandeur of the production.

The series had changed, and Connery's enthusiasm was fading fast, a lack of commitment seized upon by the critics, who accused the Scottish star of sleepwalking through his role.

Elsewhere, a last-minute decision to cast character actor Donald Pleasence as Bond's arch-enemy, Ernst Stavro Blofeld, left a lot to be desired. This was, after all, the first time audiences ever came face-to-face with Blofeld, and you can't blame them for feeling cheated when the supremely evil and all-powerful head of SPECTRE turned out to be nothing more than a short, bald, scarred and sneering stereotype.

Preaching a big-budget, all-action, comicbook message that bigger is not only better, but best, *You Only Live Twice* overdoes everything from the plot to the sets to the action and beyond, yet by today's standards, it doesn't seem anywhere near as flawed and overblown as it must have to shell-shocked audiences back in 1967. As for Connery's performance, although it might seem a little blunt at times, he's still the main man, the best Bond, and no amount of special effects or personal disenchantment could ever serve to obscure Sean's inherent charm and overpowering star quality. And that's that. On with the story.

Russian and American spaceships are disappearing left, right and centre, snatched out of orbit by a mysterious rocket of unknown origin. Naturally enough, the superpowers are blaming each other, eager to heat up the cold war with a little nuclear action. Fortunately for the whole world, British Intelligence is on the case, tracking the interceptor rocket to Japan, where they believe a third party is pulling all the strings. You know what? This sounds like a mission for James Bond...

Making the most of his stay in Japan, James enjoys himself with a pair of Oriental babes (Akiko Makabayashi, Mie Hama) and, in the interests of national security, a Russian assassin (Karin Dor) too. After playtime, 007 tries a little spying, digging around for clues with the help of his latest best buddy, 'Tiger' Tanaka (Tetsuro Tamba), head of the Japanese Secret Service and a terrific guy, too, with a cool subterranean office and an underground train system of his very own. And if you think Tiger's office is hot stuff, just wait until you cop a load of Blofeld's, a picture in piranha nestled deep within a colossal volcano hideout, a classic piece of production design courtesy of Ken Adam.

As for the action, there's a rather tasty, hands-on slug-fest between Bond and a Sumo bruiser to keep us going until we're blown away by Bond's 'four to one' battle in 'Little Nellie', a miniature autogiro equipped with machine guns, flame throwers and even heat-seeking missile launchers. Later on, following a crash course in 'the art of concealment and surprise' at Tiger's Ninja Training Academy, Bond is joined by an army of martial arts heroes, a lively bunch of guys available for weddings, bar mitzvahs and high-concept, big-budget finales.

You Only Live Twice might be a big, noisy kid with a *Man From U.N.C.L.E.* mentality, but, for all its faults, it never fails to entertain, a slick 1960s adventure polished off with a classic John Barry soundtrack.

⊕ **Four years before he played the best of the Blofelds in *Diamonds are Forever*, Charles Gray turned up in this earlier Bond flick as Dikko Henderson, a man who, for some unknown reason, offers Bond a Martini, 'Stirred, not shaken'. Weird, huh?**

The end of *You Only Live Twice*. But James Bond will return in *On Her Majesty's Secret Service*.

Director: Lewis Gilbert; **Producers:** Albert R. Broccoli, Harry Saltzman; **Screenplay:** Roald Dahl, based on the novel *You Only Live Twice* by Ian Fleming; **Production Design:**

Ken Adam; **Editor:** Thelma Connell; **Photography:** Freddie Young; **Music:** John Barry, title song performed by Nancy Sinatra; **Cast:** Sean Connery, Akiko Makabayashi, Tetsuro Tamba, Donald Pleasence, Mie Hama, Teru Shimada, Karin Dor, Lois Maxwell, Bernard Lee, Desmond Llewelyn.

Zulu

GB 1964 135 mins

Had the events portrayed in this spectacular boys' own adventure not taken place, the battle at the heart of *Zulu* would be difficult to

Stanley Baker surrounds himself with death and destruction in *Zulu,*

swallow, exciting but implausible, a movie contrivance of epic proportions. Just think about it for a second: how could 100 men possibly hold their own against an army 40 times their size? It seems impossible, the stuff that Rambo movies are made of, but the history books confirm that writer/director Cy Endfield is telling the truth, the whole truth, and nothing but the truth, and this classic British film is all the more powerful because of it.

These, then, are the facts, and this is the story: in 1879, 100 men of the South Wales Borderers stood firm against a mighty army of 4000 Zulu warriors. Defending the tiny mission station of Rorke's Drift, which stood alone in the immense South African wilderness, these brave soldiers fought for King and Country against a horde of natives determined to drive them from their land. You might not agree with the politics, but you have to admire the guts, determination and military know-how of this relatively tiny band of men, 11 of whom were awarded the coveted Victoria Cross for 'valour and extreme courage beyond that normally expected of a British soldier in face of the enemy'.

There's no double act on Earth better suited than warfare and motion pictures, and Endfield brings the two together perfectly, taking his time as he slowly works his way towards the climactic struggle, carefully establishing the characters and developing their relationships before knocking us out with some of the most finely detailed and exciting battle sequences ever filmed.

Endfield draws us into the story and leaves us in the thick of things, spurred on by John Barry's thunderous soundtrack and Stephen Dade's breathtaking photography (widescreen videos only, please), but you'll be glad you're fighting this particular battle from your sofa when the Zulus finally close in on our heroes, lining the horizon surrounding Rorke's Drift, the earth trembling beneath the weight of their marching feet.

The cast provide the icing on the cake, the cream of a British crop which includes Stanley Baker as stalwart Lieutenant John Chard, Michael Caine, here making his screen debut as aristocratic Lieutenant Conville Bromhead, Jack Hawkins as frantic preacher Otto Witt, Nigel Green as oh-so British Colour Sergeant Bourne, and James Booth as cowardly Private Henry Hook.

So stand to attention, strap on your bayonet, your moustache and your stiff upper lip, build up those sandbags and prepare for one of the most awesome adventures ever filmed.

Prequel: *Zulu Dawn*.

Director: Cy Endfield; **Producers:** Stanley Baker, Cy Endfield; **Screenplay:** John Prebble, Cy Endfield; **Production Design:** Ernest Archer; **Editor:** John Jympson; **Photography:** Stephen Dade; **Music:** John Barry; **Cast:** Stanley Baker, Jack Hawkins, Michael Caine, Nigel Green, Ulla Jacobssen, James Booth, Paul Danemann, Ivor Emmanuel.

BRAINSTORMS: The Answers

PEOPLE ARE STRANGE

1. *Death Wish 3*; 2. *Diamonds are Forever*; 3. *National Lampoon's Loaded Weapon 1*; 4. *Romancing the Stone*; 5. *The Dead Pool*; 6. *Hot Shots! Part Deux*; 7. *Lethal Weapon 3*; 8. *The Octagon*; 9. *Tank Girl*; 10. *China O'Brien*; 11. *Conan the Barbarian*; 12. *Under Siege*; 13. *Terminal Velocity*; 14. *The Beastmaster*; 15. *Demolition Man*; 16. *Gun Men*; 17. *Road House*; 18. *Ricochet*; 19. *Kickboxer*; 20. *Die Hard*

WHO KILLED WHO?

Connor MacLeod & The Kurgan, *Highlander*; Harry Callahan & Scorpio, *Dirty Harry*; Jack Burton & Lo Pan, *Big Trouble in Little China*; Roger Murtaugh & Arjen Rudd, *Lethal Weapon 2*; Trash & Hammer, *Bronx Warriors*; Eric Draven & Top Dollar, *The Crow*; Matt Hunter & Rostov, *Invasion USA*; Paul Kersey & Fraker, *Death Wish 3*; John Hatcher & Screwface, *Marked For Death*; Ben Richards & Damon Killian, *The Running Man*.

TWENTY QUESTIONS

1. Rats; 2. SPecial Executive for Counter intelligence, Terrorism, Revenge, Extortion; 3. 36 years; 4. Serve the public trust, protect the innocent, uphold the law; 5. They can both dodge bullets; 6. A guitar case; 7. The Three Stooges; 8. 2525; 9. King Willy; 10. Wellington; 11. Mars (where else?); 12. Nuke; 13. Scarface ('Say hello to my little friend!'); 14. His hands; 15. Aramis, Athos, Porthos and D'Artagnan; 16. The one-armed man; 17. Puréed on the blades of a helicopter; 18. 900, give or take a week or two; 19. *The Running Man*; 20. Domination.

TAG LINES

1. *Hard Target*; 2. *Cobra*; 3. *Universal Soldier*; 4. *Trancers*; 5. *Passenger 57*; 6. *Death Wish*; 7. *Army of Darkness: The Medieval Dead*; 8. *Toy Soldiers*; 9. *Predator 2*; 10. *Blind Fury*.

Picture Credits

All the photographs were originally used for publicity or promotion by
Buena Vista International (UK) Limited (p208, p213),
Cannon (p103, p123, p142, p225),
Castle Premier Releasing (p157),
CIC video (p237),
Columbia Pictures (p181, p197),
Columbia Tristar Film Distributors (p87),
Danjaq S.A./United Artists Pictures Inc. (p121, p135),
EMI (p227),
Entertainment Film Distributors (p189),
First Independent Films Ltd (p169),
Fox Video (p46),
Guild Film Distribution Ltd (p42, p50, p211),
Lorimar Film Entertainment (p7),
Made in Hong Kong (p111),
Metro Tartan (p40),
Miramax Dimension Films (p115),
Polygram Video (p177),
Rank Film Distributors (p153, p172, p182),
Thorn EMI (p194),
Tri-Star Pictures (p99),
Twentieth Century Fox (p73, p155, p175, p185, p192, p196, p233),
United Artists Corporation (p95),
United International Pictures (UK) (p34, p66, p85, p88, p97, p170,
    p184, p217, p220),
Universal City Studios Inc. (p81),
Warner Bros Distributors (p18, p77, p117, p162, p167, p171, p183,
    p190, p205, p222),
Warner Home Video (p20, p83, p91, 92, 148).

The publisher will be happy to correct any unintentional omissions or oversights in future editions of this book.

Cover image: *RoboCop*